Poetry's Catbird Seat

THE CONSULTANTSHIP IN POETRY

IN THE ENGLISH LANGUAGE AT THE

LIBRARY OF CONGRESS, 1937–1987

William McGuire

LIBRARY OF CONGRESS · WASHINGTON

1988

This book was prepared under the auspices and with the support
of the Library of Congress's Gertrude Clarke Whittall Poetry and Literature Fund.
Its publication is supported by a generous grant from the
Morris and Gwendolyn Cafritz Foundation.

Cataloging in Publication Data

McGuire, William, 1917–
Poetry's catbird seat.

Bibliography: p.
Includes index.
1. Library of Congress. Poetry Office—History.
2. Poetry consultants—United States—History—20th
century. 3. Literature and state—United States—
History—20th century. 4. Poetry—Appreciation—
United States—History—20th century. 5. American
poetry—20th century—History and criticism.
I. Title.
Z733.U6M38   1988   811'.5'09   87-33876
ISBN 0-8444-0586-8

Available from the Superintendent of Documents,
U.S. Government Printing Office,
Washington, D.C. 20402

*The job is such a rare and special one in
the library world and the federal bureaucracy,
as well as within the world of poetry,
that it is a job of opportunity, a catbird seat.*

REED WHITTEMORE

Contents

Illustrations

Photographs are from the collections of the Library of Congress
unless otherwise noted.

[9]

ILLUSTRATIONS

The Consultants in Poetry

1937–1941
JOSEPH AUSLANDER (1898–1965)

1941–1943
VACANT; *Auslander served as Gift Officer*

1943–1944
ALLEN TATE (1899–1979)

1944–1945
ROBERT PENN WARREN (1905–   )

1945–1946
LOUISE BOGAN (1897–1970)

1946–1947
KARL SHAPIRO (1913–   )

1947–1948
ROBERT LOWELL (1917–1977)

1948–1949
LÉONIE ADAMS (1899–   )

1949–1950
ELIZABETH BISHOP (1911–1979)

1950–1952
CONRAD AIKEN (1889–1973)

1952–1956
VACANT; *William Carlos Williams (1883–1963)*
was appointed in 1952 but did not serve

1956–1958
RANDALL JARRELL (1914–1965)

1958–1959
ROBERT FROST (1874–1963)

1959–1961
RICHARD EBERHART (1904–   )

[12]

1961–1963
LOUIS UNTERMEYER (1885–1977)

1963–1964
HOWARD NEMEROV (1920–   )

1965–1966
STEPHEN SPENDER (1909–   )

1966–1968
JAMES DICKEY (1923–   )

1968–1970
WILLIAM JAY SMITH (1918–   )

1970–71
WILLIAM STAFFORD (1914–   )

1971–1973
JOSEPHINE JACOBSEN (1908–   )

1973–1974
DANIEL HOFFMAN (1923–   )

1974–1976
STANLEY KUNITZ (1905–   )

1976–1978
ROBERT HAYDEN (1913–1980)

1978–1980
WILLIAM MEREDITH (1919–   )

1981–1982
MAXINE KUMIN (1925–   )

1982–1984
ANTHONY HECHT (1923–   )

1984–1985
ROBERT FITZGERALD (1910–1985);
*appointed but unable to serve because
of illness, and Reed Whittemore was interim Consultant*

1985–1986
GWENDOLYN BROOKS (1917–   )

1986–1987
ROBERT PENN WARREN (1905–   ),
*with the title
Poet Laureate Consultant in Poetry*

Prologue

Thirteen poets assembled in Washington on Monday, March 6, 1978. What they had in common, besides their practice of the poetic art, their middle-to-elderly ages, and for most of them an academic connection, was their service for one year or two as Consultant in Poetry in the Chair of Poetry in the English Language at the Library of Congress: twelve Americans, one Englishman; eleven men, two women; thirteen poets, the remnant of twenty-three Consultants who had served since 1937, when the Chair came into being, supported by the gift of a philanthropist who took pleasure in poetry and on occasion wrote it. Of the ten absent poets, seven had died, two within the year—Robert Lowell and Louis Untermeyer; two—Allen Tate and Léonie Adams—were kept away by age and illness; and for another, Robert Penn Warren, the pressures of a busy if retired life precluded this opportunity, as he wrote, to "renew old pleasures and find new ones in those halls." There was a shadowy twenty-fourth poet, who was of the company and yet not of it, appointed to the Chair but kept by mischance from taking it. That was the late William Carlos Williams.

The Consultants convened that morning around a table in the Woodrow Wilson Room, a paneled and book-lined place of assembly on the second floor of the great Library. Before them was an agenda of questions for discussion, suggested by the Library's administration. "How do you see the role of the Consultant? Should it be redefined or changed in any way? What do you consider the chief problems facing the Consultant? What are the strengths and the weaknesses of the poetry and literature program? Most of the poets in the Washington area feel they are unjustly excluded from participation in this program, since they are rarely invited to read at the Library. What are your opinions and suggestions regarding this matter? As former Consultants, do you think it possible or desirable for the Consultant to try to 'educate the public' through workshops, seminars, etc.?" The Librarian of Congress, Daniel J. Boorstin, greeted them. He had become the twelfth Librarian in the fall of 1975 and was a new face to most of the Consultants. His greeting was echoed by John C. Broderick, the chief of the Manuscript Division and the supervisor of the Library's poetry and literature program. Broderick had planned the reunion, and he reminded the poets that his division would welcome the deposit of their manuscripts and private papers, even though a 1969 law denied authors the right to claim an income tax deduction for such gifts.

The round table discussion took up the morning. The tape recorder was whirling away. Here are salient moments from those hours of conversation.

Stanley Kunitz (Consultant in 1974–76): "Robert Lowell called the Consultantship a sinecure, with nothing to do, back in 1947–1948. There's been a sudden shift in the demands on a Consultant's time. Now it's equivalent to a full-time teaching job. It wants a reevaluation."

Spirited agreement from Daniel Hoffman (1973–74). He recalled the terms of the donor Archer Huntington's gift and the view of Archibald MacLeish when he was the Librarian of Congress. "They expected the Consultant to have free time. Now so much detailed work has accumulated—"

"But," said Roy P. Basler, who had managed the poetry programs for more than twenty years before he retired in 1974, "remember that MacLeish put on Tate and Warren the burden of editing the *Quarterly Journal*. In my time I observed how much the poets brought on themselves, agglutinating everything around them, running off in different directions."

William Jay Smith (1968–70) remarked that Nemerov had put together his book *Poets on Poetry* during his tenure. And Smith himself had found the traveling he himself did, to lecture and read, notably valuable. "How important that was in getting poetry before the people!"

James Dickey (1966–68) concurred. But what had most interested Dickey during his term was the idea of filming poets on video as they read. "How little of the great poets has been recorded, by either sound or video."

Basler: "Well, I tried to get Leger—St.-John Perse—to record on video and he wouldn't. Nor would Eliot."

Stephen Spender (1965–66) propounded a serious topic. He urged meetings of writers on the crisis in literacy. He talked about the importance of students' learning to express themselves in writing, learning to communicate. (Spender, the solitary Englishman, was teaching that year at the University of Houston.)

Reed Whittemore (1964–65), eagerly: "Getting the whole humanities problem out into the world—that's what it is!"

Howard Nemerov (1963–64): "I had no problems. I always did what Phyllis [Armstrong, the Assistant in Poetry] told me to do."

Kunitz: "Why doesn't the Library of Congress have a poetry reading room? That would have great meaning for the people of this city."

Robert Hayden (1976–78): "The Poetry Office has been doing that every Thursday afternoon."

Basler: "Yes, in my time every Consultant was expected to formulate his own program. Some of the richness of the job results from this freewheeling. I get the impression from this discussion that the Consultant's role lacks focus."

Boorstin: "How can we provide a channel without imposing a job description?"

Broderick, noting that Elizabeth Bishop (1949–50) hadn't spoken, asked her if she'd like to say anything. "Oh—I'm rather out of it," she replied. "I don't like video tapes and I don't like recordings. I think it's more important for a student to sit home and read a book or write a poem than hear or see any of these things in the classroom. A poetry reading room seems a good idea, though the atmosphere would be so hush-

[17]

hush I wouldn't enjoy it. Well, I can't stop progress, whatever that is."

Broderick: "What about a longer term for the Consultant?"

William Stafford (1970–71): "A longer term is a kind of scary thing in a person's life. Revolving it often, as now, seems a better idea."

Spender: "To give more than one or two years bars other poets from the appointment, which is a great honor."

Basler: "Stephen Spender was invited for only the one year—the only Consultant so. It was International Cooperation Year. The Chair is for poetry in *English,* as defined by the donor, so it was appropriate. Should other non-Americans be appointed?"

Smith: "In my term A. D. Hope was invited from Australia for one month. Then I proposed a Canadian, and was told that was no longer possible."

Hoffman: "It's the only office in the United States Government that gives recognition to poets. I'd favor residencies for *shorter* periods for younger poets, or grants that could be used anywhere."

Broderick: "The Library was forbidden in the late 1940s to *award* grants. What the Library needs is another Archer Huntington or Gertrude Clarke Whittall."

Basler: "I tried to get a little cooperation out of the National Endowment for the Arts. I couldn't get one dime. —Well now, *should* the Consultantship be limited to American poets?"

Dickey: "I'm for it. This is an American institution; it's *our* country. American poets should be the ones to fill the incumbency."

Hoffman seconded him. There was a murmur of dismay.

Dickey: "I defer to no man in my admiration for Stephen Spender, a great god to me when I was young, and no less esteemed in my personal pantheon now."

Stafford: "Just get the right person wherever he or she is from. I wouldn't like to see the Consultantship saddled with a rule to keep the Library of Congress from getting the best person."

Smith: "We Americans aren't the only users of the English language."

Richard Eberhart (1959–61): "Well, I favor having a visiting poet in residence, from wherever he may be, for a *brief* time."

Broderick: "Yes, I'd suggest the Consultantship be a unique position, with poets in residence for shorter times."

Whittemore: "I don't see why the Consultant in Poetry couldn't be another Stephen Spender."

Spender: "Surely you'd have made an exception for W. B. Yeats, the greatest poet writing in the English language."

Bishop: "There are other institutions in this country that honor foreign poets. We needn't. Yeats would have been too busy, for one thing. For him it would have been a minor honor."

Kunitz: "The phenomenon we are witnessing is the democratization of culture, the dispersal of genius. There are no towering figures in poetry today."

On that note the discussion adjourned. A convivial luncheon followed—in the Whittall Pavilion, another gift to the Library—and after a restorative hiatus the Consultants received the press.

Dickey, the extravert in the party, got the dialogue going. "Here we are on this Olympian altitude! I'd rather talk back and forth with the newsmen." And, responding to a question, he launched into the difficulty of adapting a novel like his *Deliverance* to film: "the problem of objectifying on screen what was in the writer's words."

Spender: "It was the same difficulty for Pinter and Shaffer, getting their plays from theater to screen. The language."

Kunitz: "High language *was* the voice of the theater. It's been displaced by visual display; basically we have a nonverbal medium now."

Eberhart: "At Harvard's Poets Theater, in the late 1940s, we were trying to write and produce high verse theater; it wasn't a success. We did MacLeish's *Trojan Horse,* Bill Alfred's *Hogan's Goat,* Dylan Thomas's *Under Milk Wood.* I had to conclude that verse drama is inimical to the American theater."

Smith: "As for radio plays, nobody really listens. The ear isn't trained to hear radio drama."

Kunitz: "Poetry has become a vessel of the vernacular idiom."

Hoffman, impatiently: "Who's afraid of poetry? We all go around the country reading our poems! People don't quail at poetry."

Hayden: "There's a lack of transcendence in our lives, a suspicion of the heroic, a decline of the possibility of the heroic. Those who believe in God use language in a different way than those who don't."

Josephine Jacobsen (1971–73): "And there are too many how-to books trying to pull people out of their sense of inferiority."

Nemerov: "It's a prose world. We're here to provide the poetry. The conversation of poets among themselves is a matter of utter charm. Writing poetry is a great privilege, an exalted pleasure—when you have it. Nobody drafted you, you volunteered."

Dickey: "Imaginative language is life-giving, and not only in poetry—you can get it in the sports page, in the work of comedians— they can have the essential poetic afflatus, the flash of poetic insight, the very stuff of wit, of poetry. People hunger for the word, the thing well said, and will find it by chance or design. We're privileged to give it in poetry. And that's the end of that sermon!"

Hoffman: "Imagination . . . Lowell's verse play *Benito Cereno* engaged our imagination."

Jacobsen: "We get too much of the 'guess what happened to me last night' school of poetry—so often with amateurs."

Kunitz: "Ours is an age of very little optimism about the future. Yes, there's a yearning for some kind of transcendence—thus these cults and half-cults, these spurious forms of 'transcendence.' Poetry by its *nature* is the language of transcendence; it comes from the intensity of the spiritual life. It requires a lot of effort and immersion in the language. There's no easy way of finding it. Most people want cheaper forms, and it's all around them. [Someone mentioned science fiction.] Yes, I'm a sci-fi buff. It's an easier form, a glib form of poetry."

Hayden: "Poetry is the coming to grips with reality. Sci-fi—I'm a buff too—doesn't come to grips with fundamental questions. Clichés like death and falling in love, that's what poetry is concerned with. It says about our existence what can't be said in any other way, or can't be said at all."

❊

In the evening, more than a thousand people lined up in the corridors of the Library, hoping to hear the poets read from their work. The crowd filled the Coolidge Auditorium and the neighboring Whittall Pavilion, where chairs had been set up for seeing and hearing the poets on closed-circuit television. Two hundred had to be turned away for want of seats. Boorstin, in his opening words, called the gathering "the most spectacular display of poetic talent in our generation." (The National Poetry Festival, which had brought thirty-five poets to the Library in 1962, belonged to the previous generation, or at any rate to the previous decade.) The program went on for two and a half hours, though the poets had been asked to read for not more than ten minutes each. The audience listened raptly, they followed with their books, they applauded (and occasionally whistled), and afterward they sought a handshake, an autograph, a word. The Chair of Poetry, over its twenty-one years, had seen a poetry public grow up in Washington.

One

1800 TO 1943

The Library of Congress's Consultantship in Poetry in the English Language—or the Chair of Poetry, as it was called originally—was created by the gift of a fund in 1936 and filled by its first appointment in 1937. Throughout the fifty years that have followed, it has been occupied by a succession of thirty poets. All of them have been American citizens, and American-born, except for one, a British subject. Six have been women. Two have been black. Five may be called Southerners, by birth or upbringing; four, Midwesterners; two, New Englanders; two settled in the Far West in their later careers; all the rest are Easterners, or some cosmopolitan product best so described.

The incumbent's stipend derives not from taxpayers' money but from funds donated to the Library of Congress by private citizens; the Consultant is not appointed by Congress—though precedent and courtesy prompt him or her to respond, ordinarily, to congressional requests for information and advice. The Consultant is appointed by the Librarian of Congress, who may, at his option, consider recommendations from above (the President and his staff or members of Congress), below (the staff of the Library), present and former Consultants, and the general public. The Consultant, however, unlike a government employee, is not expected (nowadays, at least) to take an oath of allegiance, keep specified office hours, or otherwise assume the mantle of a bureaucrat.

Certainly the Consultant was not meant to be the Poet Laureate of the United States of America, though in 1986 this title was added to that of Consultant of Poetry. Over the half-century, journalists in particular have liked the flourish of calling the Consultant the Poet Laureate, and one or two Consultants would possibly have welcomed the designation. The British laureate, appointed by the monarch for life as a member of the Royal Household, is expected to do little more than write Court odes and such occasional verse. He receives a pittance as stipend. Several of the American states have laureateships, whose incumbents have not always been distinguished poets.

The Chair of Poetry owes its origin to two men, Herbert Putnam, who conceived the idea, and Archer Milton Huntington, who gave the funds to realize it. By way of introduction, let us consider each of these men and their friendship and the history of that remarkable institution, the Library of Congress.

Putnam (1861–1955), the eighth Librarian of Congress and the first experienced librarian to hold the post, was appointed by President McKinley on March 13, 1899. Upon taking the oath of office on April 5, he assumed charge of a collection of some 900,000 volumes, a staff of 134, a budget (for the fiscal year 1898) of $280,000, and a palatial new building in Italian Renaissance style, which had been completed and opened to the public less than two years earlier—on November 1, 1897. "It is the largest, most ornate and most costly building in the world yet erected for library purposes," the next edition of the *Encyclopaedia Britannica* stated. Today it has been outstripped in size and in cost, though not in architectural and ornamental splendor, by a third Library of Congress building, the James Madison Memorial Building, southward across Independence Avenue, which is believed to be the largest library structure anywhere. (The new National Library of China, now under construction in the suburbs of Peking, is destined to be the largest library building of all.) The Library of Congress, altogether, is today the largest library in the world. And it is remarkable for its dual nature as both a legislative library for the Congress and a national library for the country as a whole.

The Library of Congress wasn't quite a century old when Putnam took charge. Beginning as early as 1774 with the Continental Congress, informal arrangements were made to supply necessary books for "the gentlemen, who are to meet in Congress." The Library of Congress as an official body was established, in a quite modest way, by a Congressional act in April 1800, with the approval of President John Adams; its initial appropriation was $5,000. The collection (which included the poems of Robert Burns) was housed in a room in the uncompleted Capitol building, and the first two librarians—John J. Beckley and Patrick Magruder, both appointed successively by President Jefferson—also held the job of Clerk of the House of Representatives. A catalog prepared in 1812 had a subject classification for poetry and drama. Thomas Jefferson, before, during, and after his presidency, was the most prominent advocate of the Library, and after the British burned the books along with the Capitol in 1814, Jefferson sold the government his personal library—6,487 volumes, for $23,950—described in the *Annals of Congress* as "a most admirable substratum for a National Library." The poets represented included Homer and Virgil, Tasso and Dante, Chaucer, Spenser, and Milton, and, among Jefferson's contemporaries, Philip Freneau and Phillis Wheatley.

The third Librarian, a novelist and journalist named George Watterston, wasn't obliged to double as Clerk of the House, and in 1824 he moved the Library into a spacious new room designed by Charles Bulfinch, the architect who oversaw the completion of the Capitol. Five years later, President Andrew Jackson replaced Watterston with a local printer who had been a political partisan of his, John Silva Meehan, who built the collection to fifty-five thousand volumes by 1851, when fire destroyed thirty-five thousand, including nearly two-thirds of Jefferson's collection. Within two years the Library area was restored in an elegant style, fireproof, enlarged ("the largest room made of iron in the world," it was said), in the west front of the Capitol. The fifth Librarian, appointed in 1861 by President Lincoln (again, to reward political support), was a physician, John G. Stephenson, who on occasion absented himself to take part in Civil War battles. He appointed as Assistant Librarian a Cincinnati newspaperman, Ainsworth Rand Spofford, who succeeded to the Librarianship in 1864. More than any other person, Spofford was responsible for transforming the Library of

Congress from a legislative library to a truly national institution. He was the Librarian until 1897, and then Chief Assistant Librarian until his death, in 1908, at the age of 83.

During Spofford's regime, the passage of the Copyright Act of 1870 brought into the collection everything deposited for copyright; the Smithsonian Institution's library of forty-four thousand volumes was acquired (obviating the continuation of what threatened to be a rival national library); important private collections were purchased or acquired by gift, such as the Peter Force Collection of Americana, sixty thousand volumes, and the J. M. Toner American and Medical Library, twenty-four thousand volumes; and a new building was discussed, argued over, planned and replanned, and finally approved by an act of Congress in 1886. (Spofford had reported to Congress as early as 1876 that all shelf space was exhausted and "books are now, from sheer force of necessity, being piled upon the floor in all directions." This chaotic state of affairs may have been one reason why, in 1872, when the Joint Library Committee considered a petition from a Kentucky citizen asking Congress to establish a "bureau of poets and poesy," no action was taken. Poets and poesy didn't come officially into the Library's ken until 1936.)

Construction of the building by the U.S. Army Corps of Engineers— in Italian Renaissance style and bearing a resemblance to the Paris Opera House—progressed at a stately pace over more than a decade. The cornerstone was laid in 1890, and the Library was officially opened to the public on November 1, 1897, after Spofford had stepped down from the Librarianship.

The year 1897 saw, on July 1, the appointment of the seventh Librarian of Congress, John Russell Young, by President McKinley; he was a journalist of some renown and had been minister to China. Young at once appointed Spofford as Chief Assistant Librarian. A skillful and innovative administrator, Young succeeded in keeping the Library out of politics. He confided to his diary, "I am trying to build the library far into the future, to make it a true library of research." The opening of the new building was the signal event of Young's tenure. Over the Thanksgiving holidays thousands of visitors toured the public rooms and galleries to admire the sculpture, mural paintings, and other lavish decoration. (The first poetry reading in the Library's history occurred in Young's time. Paul Laurence Dunbar, who served books from the stacks—which he likened to a prison in one of his poems—read from his work in a program for the blind. Another black poet did not give a public reading at the Library until 1962.) After a year of serious illness, however, Young's promising librarianship ended with his death in January 1899. Upon the insistence of the American Library Association that the next Librarian of Congress be an experienced library administrator, McKinley appointed Herbert Putnam—who retained Spofford as Chief Assistant Librarian and Librarian Emeritus for the remaining nine years of his life.

Putnam, a New Yorker born in 1861, was a son of George Palmer Putnam, the publisher. After a Harvard A.B. and a Columbia law degree, young Putnam planned to open a law practice in Minneapolis, but temporarily became librarian of the Minneapolis Athenaeum. He found the work appealing, remained at it for three years, and in 1887 became the librarian of the Minneapolis Public Library. In 1891 he resigned and returned to the law, in Boston. His reputation as a library administrator caught up with him, however, and in 1895 he became librarian of the Boston Public Library. Putnam rapidly achieved a national eminence, so that in 1896 he testified on behalf of the American Library Association before the Joint Congressional Committee on the Library of Congress, making recommendations to improve its systems and services. Before accepting the appointment as Librarian of Congress—with some misgivings, as the annual stipend of $5,000 seemed barely adequate for a family in expensive Washington—Putnam had served a year as president of the American Library Association. In his forty years as Librarian of Congress, from 1899 to 1939, Putnam introduced numerous new procedures, established a new system of classification, and transformed the collection into one of the world's most splendid.

According to a contemporary observer, Putnam possessed an impersonal attitude that gave him the reputation of being "austerely cold, aloof and reticent; but he must have unusual persuasive qualities to be able to induce Congress to grant the large appropriations for the Library . . . since he has been its head." His physical appearance, the same

witness went on, is "delicately molded and aristocratic," and his man-
ner "courteous, sympathetic, precise and energetic." Putnam was in-
deed slight of stature. An article about him by a member of his staff,
Edward N. Waters, was entitled, "The Tallest Little Man in the World."
Another of his colleagues, David C. Mearns, told an interviewer, "To
the staff, Herbert Putnam bore relationship not unlike that of the Great
White Father to the aborigines of North America. He was venerated.
He was endowed with extraordinary gifts. He was changeless and time-
less. He was a spirit cast in the image of other men but too carefully
socked and booted ever to suggest affliction with ceramic feet." In sum,
Putnam "had a mandate from Congress and used it well: he is the man
most responsible for the basic services and structure of the Library of
Congress as we know it today."

✻

A friendship between Putnam and Archer M. Huntington existed as
early as 1903. Writing from his estate, "Pleasance," at Baychester, in
the Bronx, on March 12, Huntington invited Putnam to the opening of
a library at the Hampton Institute, a college for blacks near Newport
News. Huntington's mother had given the library as a memorial to his
father, the railroad builder Collis P. Huntington, "whose interest in ne-
gro education was very great," Archer Huntington wrote. (His father
bequeathed a half million dollars to the Institute.) The speakers, he
said, would include Booker T. Washington, as well as the governor of
Virginia and the president of Yale. Whether Putnam attended the occa-
sion we don't know, but the cordial tenor of Huntington's letter suggests
a warm acquaintance. Huntington was then thirty-three, nine years Put-
nam's junior, and was undoubtedly known to the Librarian not only as
an amateur of Hispanic studies but also as the scion of one of the
wealthiest families in the country.

Archer Milton Huntington should be better known today. He was a
generous philanthropist of remarkably varied interests, and he was also
a person of an extraordinary stamp. By temperament, and perhaps also
because of the particular circumstances of his childhood, he was self-
effacing to an almost reclusive degree. His nephew by marriage, the art
historian A. Hyatt Mayor, has written the story of Huntington's origin

and upbringing in his introduction to a liberally illustrated book about the sculptures at Brookgreen Gardens, a notable creation of Archer and Anna Hyatt Huntington, on the South Carolina seacoast. The book appeared in 1980, twenty-five years after Huntington died. Previously, the personal details of his life were scarcely known outside his family.

Collis Potter Huntington, his father, was born on a Connecticut farm in 1821, one of a large family, and started out as an itinerant hardware salesman in New England. In 1849 he trekked across the Rockies to join the California Gold Rush, but instead of prospecting he and Mark Hopkins started a hardware business that catered to the new railroads. By 1861 he was a principal organizer of the Central Pacific Railroad, and he moved to New York to push the transcontinental tracks westward. As Mayor tells the story, "While acquiring railroads in the South in 1868–70 he seems to have stayed in a Richmond boarding house run by Mrs. Richard Milton Yarrington, whose remarkable daughter Arabella joined the Huntington household in New York to take care of Collis's invalid wife Elizabeth, whom he had married in 1844, and who died of cancer in 1883. Collis discovered in Arabella a woman who matched him in intelligence, in ambition, and in the capacity to develop. They could not help falling in love. When Arabella was twenty she bore him a son on March 10, 1870. To gloss over the situation she took the name of a Richmond gambling-house proprietor, John Archer Worsham, who was already married and who lived until 1878. She combined Worsham's name with her father's to christen her son Archer Milton Worsham." In 1877, as the widow "Mrs. Worsham," with her mother and small son, Arabella moved to a town house at 4 West 54th Street in New York. She gave Archer "his heroic thirst for knowledge by sharing with him the histories and biographies she was studying for her own self-education [and] took him to European museums while she scrutinized them to guide her in collecting works of art. . . . When Archer was fourteen, his father was freed by the death of his first wife to marry Arabella Yarrington and to adopt their son."

Young Archer was first attracted to Hispanic culture during a visit to Mexico with his father, on railroad planning negotiations. Collis Huntington wanted his son to take over the management of a shipbuilding enterprise of his at Newport News. (A story persists in the Tidewater that, on April 24, 1889, when Collis Huntington arrived in his private railroad car from New York for the official opening of his Chesapeake Dry Dock and Construction Company, the poets Walt Whitman and Joaquin Miller were in his party. In fact, Whitman was sick at home in Camden that day, but Miller may have come along, for he wrote a poem, "Newport News." Archer Huntington, aged nineteen, would surely have come along too.) After a year or so of shipyard experience, young Archer told his father that his one driving interest was to pursue studies in Spanish and Portuguese culture; his father agreed. Archer, having a distaste for formal schooling, was tutored in Spanish and Arabic. He spent several years in the Iberian peninsula, traveling like Don Quixote with one servant, sometimes on donkeyback, mastering the dialects as well as Castilian, which he learned to speak "not just correctly, but with wit, with eloquence." Mayor speaks of "the ringing silver of his voice, in Spanish as in English." Among Huntington's many poems on Spanish themes there is one dedicated to "Spanish Words," which includes these lines:

> With what soft tread across the centuries,
> Came this ancestral progeny of fire
> Decked in the scented silences of time?
> Swift children of the valleys of desire
> Legions of pain and passion vaguely heard
> Moving to their high places and wide powers
> With what soft tread across the centuries?

Huntington was a fine figure of a man. A friend of later years described him with considerable zest: "Tall, dignified, and massive of build, he dominates without domineering over whatever group he may join. Friendly, democratic, and buoyant, his mind and imagination work at high speed, often enigmatically, and he is at times a bit baffling, especially when, with tongue in cheek, he comes forth with a truly 'outrageous' question or comment to see how it will be taken. He knows men in and out and sees through pose, pretence, and insincerity with a probing eye." A Spanish scholar who met Huntington in his late sixties observed, "I shall never forget that striking figure, some six feet high, immaculately attired and of aristocratic bearing; he seemed to me a gentleman such as those Velázquez painted back in the seventeenth century."

"Not that his early life was especially happy," Mayor goes on. "The reticence imposed by his illegitimacy scarred him with a compulsion for secrecy that kept him from confiding the whole of any major project to any one person." In his late twenties he produced a critical translation of the Spanish epic *Poema del Cid,* which he cast in 3,735 lines of blank verse. Though he published it under his own auspices, the work commanded scholarly respect and brought him an honorary degree from Yale. He collected Spanish books and paintings, and when these outgrew his home, he established in 1904 the Hispanic Society of America, endowed it generously, and erected a handsome building for it, on Audubon Terrace at Broadway and 155th Street. Among the paintings he gave the Society there are three Velázquezes, nine El Grecos, five Goyas, and a spacious gallery of Sorolla murals. Besides many ancient maps and illuminated manuscripts, there are over a hundred thousand books, including ten thousand printed before 1700 and more than eight thousand early editions of great Hispanic classics such as *Don Quixote*—all given by Huntington. Neighboring is the church of Nuestra Señora de la Esperanza, for which Huntington, a Protestant and a skeptic at that, gave the land and a substantial building fund. (According to another nephew, Hyatt Mayor's brother Brantz, Uncle Archer lamented the power of the Church in Spain. He was furious that the Inquisition had destroyed the records of the Romans and the Moors.) Inevitably, Hispanic scholars referred to him as "the Maecenas of Spanish studies in the United States."

Huntington had been married in 1895 to his cousin, Helen Manchester Gates, like him a writer of verse, and like him an amateur of translation from the Spanish. They traveled widely in Europe, the Near East, and South America, and she shared his enthusiasm for an archaeological dig he led, at the site of a Roman town near Seville. Finds from the dig are in the Hispanic Society's collection. From boyhood Huntington had been fascinated by maps. In 1911, while president of the American Geographical Society, he gave funds for its building, also on Audubon Terrace. Three years later, he and his wife were traveling in Germany when the first World War broke out. Huntington's briefcase full of maps aroused suspicion that he might be a spy. He and his wife were arrested, searched, and confined to their hotel rooms, from whose windows they watched German troops mobilizing in the square below. Huntington felt more concern about his chauffeur, who was a Frenchman. He advised the man to take the car and make a run for the border, and he gave him all his cash. The chauffeur made it to Switzerland and notified the American Ambassador, who effected the Huntingtons' release and departure, with other Americans, on a special train to Amsterdam. A few years later, as Hyatt Mayor tells it, Helen Huntington "pinned a note on [her husband's] dressing table to say that she had gone away with the British theatrical producer Harley Granville Barker. In a torment of mortified rejection, he threw himself into gluttony and kept awake for work around the clock with black coffee and cigars. One of his frantic throng of projects was to have a medal struck for William Dean Howells." He asked the sculptor Anna Hyatt, Mayor's aunt, to design it. The consequence, beyond the medal, was that Huntington asked her to marry him. She realized that she loved him, but "should she, in her mid-forties, give up a way of life that supported her as water does a fish? . . . Divided by doubts and loyalties, she went as usual for the summer of 1922 to Annisquam, Massachusetts. There, one night at three or four in the morning, she woke my mother and said, 'Harriet, Archer is dying. I know it. I must go to him.' She was gone before breakfast. She found him in a hospital, bloated to some 400 pounds." (We should note that Huntington was six feet five and broad of shoulder to match.) "He simply said, 'I want to die. Overeating is more gentlemanly than shooting myself or jumping out of a window.'" Anna Hyatt said yes, Huntington lost some one hundred pounds, and they were married in her studio on March 10, 1923, their common birthday. They spent their honeymoon in the Caribbean on a yacht Huntington had called Rocinante, after Don Quixote's horse. After returning to New York, the Huntingtons sat for photoportraits by Laura Gilpin, whom they had met through Herbert Putnam's daughter Brenda. (It was Gilpin who persuaded Putnam to change the photograph-collecting focus of the Library of Congress, orienting it toward fine contemporary work.)

Up to this point in his life, Archer Huntington's benefactions, though by his wish usually made anonymously, had been undeniably grand. Besides funding the Spanish church, the quarters of the Hispanic Society of America, and in large part those of the American Geographical Society on the land he owned at Audubon Terrace, he contributed substantial amounts of money for the neighboring buildings housing the American Numismatic Society, the Museum of the American Indian, and—jointly with his mother, Arabella Huntington—the American Academy and Institute of Arts and Letters. In 1923, when New York City observed its silver jubilee, Huntington was awarded the flag of the city as one of the men who had done the most for New York and its people. He was equally generous in Spain. For his efforts to preserve historical monuments (in particular, the house of Cervantes at Valladolid and that of El Greco at Toledo) King Alfonso XIII bestowed on Huntington the Order of Isabel the Catholic. When Nicholas Murray Butler consulted Huntington about bringing a professor from Spain to head a new department at Columbia University, Huntington nominated a friend, the Unamuno scholar Federico de Onís, who arrived from Salamanca in 1916.

Upon the death of his mother, in 1924, Archer Huntington's wealth increased splendidly. Arabella Huntington had been remarried, in 1913, to her late husband's nephew Henry E. Huntington, who was of comparable means (having inherited a third of Collis P.'s estate) and just her age. While she had concentrated on collecting paintings and antique furniture under the guidance of Joseph Duveen, Henry Huntington had formed an exceptional collection of rare books and manuscripts, tutored by Dr. A. S. W. Rosenbach. Arabella and Henry Huntington transformed their ranch at San Marino, California, into the Henry E. Huntington Library and Art Gallery, with its extensive and magnificent gardens. While the greater part of Mrs. Huntington's art collection had gone to San Marino before her death, she left several paintings to her son, who gave some of the Rembrandts to the Metropolitan Museum of Art but retained *Aristotle Contemplating the Bust of Homer*. Later, he sold it to Joseph Duveen and donated the proceeds to the American Academy of Arts and Letters. The painting is today in the Metropolitan Museum of Art.

The Academy of Arts and Letters had become a compelling concern of Huntington's. Founded in 1904, the institution lacked its own quarters for some years. In 1915, Huntington gave it an endowment of $100,000 in Central Pacific gold bonds and land on Audubon Terrace (which he declined to have renamed after him). While construction proceeded, Huntington lent the Academy office space in his house at 15 West 81st Street, facing the American Museum of Natural History. In 1919, on the nomination of William Dean Howells and others, he was elected to the Academy, and accordingly he composed a sonnet, "Genius: to the American Academy of Arts and Letters":

High mystery prophetic that men cry!
The splendid diadem of hearts supreme
Who shape reality from hope's vast dream
And gild with flame new pantheons in the sky!
Thus are we led to nobly raise on high
An edifice of deeds that may redeem
The lowliness of being, 'neath the gleam
Of mists all colorless where life must lie.

When strength and joy and youth's propitious day
Unveil perception, that uprisen souls
May walk in paths undreamed, a fairer world,
And learn the cherished but uncharted way,
There 'gainst the light of new uplifted goals
This oriflamme of glory is unfurled.

When the new building was formally opened in February 1923 (Huntington missed the event; he was at the ranch in San Marino, visiting his mother) it completed the Beaux-Arts complex on Audubon Terrace, which was widely admired at the time, if less so today. The *AIA Guide to New York* calls it "a vacuous and pallid exercise," and in another guidebook Paul Goldberger finds the grouping "a sad and rather silly dream . . . not especially distinguished and not a little awkward." The museums and libraries within, however, are of an untarnished magnificence, as Huntington would have hoped. (The surrounding neighborhood has become a Hispanic *barrio* and the Church of Our Lady of

Esperanza, with its stained-glass windows presented by the King of Spain, is an indispensable center of welfare work. The American Geographical Society building is now the home of Boricua College, whose students are chiefly from the Hispanic community.)

During the 1920s, Huntington gave the Academy a large share of his attention, besides an annual check to cover its budgetary deficit. He appeared more or less regularly at the offices of both the Academy and the Hispanic Society, quiet but all-observing. It was said that a light bulb couldn't be changed without his approval. The Academy's librarian went at Huntington's behest to Washington to study the systems of the Library of Congress, when it was planned to place all the books by the Academicians in the Academy library. (His expense account was OK'd by Huntington. "Hotel, 4 days, $12.51 . . .") Huntington personally interviewed young women applying for research assistantships in the Society. According to an associate, he believed that women should receive full credit for their achievements and not be "buried in a department." It is said, however, that he preferred to employ deaf women. He insisted on a noiseless library, and signs demanding "Silencio!" were in view. He decreed that it was unnecessary for the contents of the Hispanic Museum to be insured. Huntington's affinity with Audubon Terrace, however, lessened with the years. Two letters, during the 1930s, to the executive secretary of the Academy, Mrs. William Vanamee, give us a glimpse of his attitude as well as his epistolary style. In 1931, when Nicholas Murray Butler proposed placing upon one of the Academy buildings "the friendly burden of my [Huntington's] name," Huntington declined gracefully, adding, "I am filled by no ambition to be celebrated, and it has been a life-long practice to attach my name to no monument. I am stirred to no sense of pleasure with the thought of self-contemplation in a mirroring pool filled by the silver drippings of a cheque book!" Seven years later, Huntington had suggested that the Academy hang in its museum oil paintings of the members. "In my own case," he wrote to Mrs. Vanamee, "I regret that I cannot at this time give you a portrait, because I have never felt that I was a member of the Academy, but only an outsider who has been permitted to devote some time to the development of its work. If, after my death, the Trustees . . . still consider what I have done of any value, a post-mortem request might possibly elicit from my executors a portrait." No portrait of Huntington hangs in the Academy today, though several are displayed in the Hispanic Museum nearby.

There surely were contacts between Huntington and Herbert Putnam since the prewar years, at board meetings and official ceremonies. Certainly Huntington continued to send the Library of Congress, in Putnam's care, the successive reprints of his *El Cid* and the numerous publications of the Hispanic Society. With his second marriage, Huntington acquired a more personal link with Putnam, whose daughter Brenda was also a sculptor and shared Anna Hyatt's studio in Greenwich Village. In 1925, Brenda Putnam, at the commission of Huntington, made a basrelief of the Academy's first president—that not-quite socialist the late W. D. Howells, whom Huntington had revered—and in the same year Putnam was elected a member of the American Institute of Arts and Letters. (Sculpture had naturally become one of Huntington's preoccupations. In 1928 he made an unsolicited gift of $100,000 to the National Sculpture Society for what was then to be the largest exhibition of sculpture in this country, in San Francisco.)

✴

In February 1924 the Library of Congress sponsored three chamber music recitals at the Freer Gallery of Art, supported by Elizabeth Sprague Coolidge, who also at that time gave the Library her outstanding collection of original orchestral scores. (The first concert was a memorial to Woodrow Wilson, who had died four days earlier.) As Putnam noted in his annual report, this was "the first notable recognition by our Government . . . of music as one of the finer arts—entitled to its concern and encouragement." Less than a year later, another gift of Mrs. Coolidge's was announced: $94,000 to construct and equip an auditorium for the performance of chamber music and for assemblies and meetings. And shortly afterward, in January 1925, Mrs. Coolidge established an endowment, sufficient to yield income of about $28,000 a year, to enable the Library's Music Division to hold music festivals, give concerts, award prizes for compositions, and provide an honorarium for the chief of the division in recognition of the "special labor, responsibility, and personal expense imposed upon him."

Born in Chicago in 1864, Mrs. Coolidge was heiress to the Sprague Warner wholesale grocery fortune. She studied the piano as a child and, in her youth, performed as soloist with the Theodore Thomas Orchestra, the forerunner of the Chicago Symphony. After being married and then widowed, her interest turned to the philanthropic support of music, and particularly of chamber music. She established the Berkshire Chamber Music Festival, at Pittsfield, in 1916, and later the Berkshire Prize for composition. Concerned to find an institution to carry on her prizes and festivals, she turned to Herbert Putnam, who was more concerned that the Library acquire her collection of musical autographs but agreed to a trial series of concerts under Mrs. Coolidge's patronage. The other gifts followed. The Coolidge Auditorium, constructed in the northwest courtyard of the Library, with a seating capacity of more than five hundred, was inaugurated with a three-day chamber music festival on October 28, 1925, two days before Elizabeth Coolidge's sixty-first birthday. The Library's Coolidge Foundation, besides supporting a program of chamber performance ever since, has commissioned works by Bartok, Schoenberg, Copland, Stravinsky, Barber, Ravel, and other contemporary composers. In the opinion of the critic Olin Downes, Mrs. Coolidge's support of music was "without parallel in the modern period on either side of the Atlantic."

These Coolidge benefactions (and another endowment in 1924 by James B. Wilbur for acquiring American historical materials) initiated, in Putnam's words, a "new era" for the Library. There were two almost immediate consequences. President Calvin Coolidge (not related to the benefactress) approved an act of Congress creating the Library of Congress Trust Fund Board to accept and administer gifts or bequests for the benefit of the Library. The Board consisted—and consists—of three ex officio members, the Secretary of the Treasury, the Chairman of the Joint Committee on the Library (representing both houses of Congress), and the Librarian of Congress, and two public members appointed by the President. The other consequence was Herbert Putnam's chairs.

In Putnam's report for 1926, he outlined his idea of "endowments for service and superservice," citing the precedent of Mrs. Coolidge's provision for an annual honorarium to the division chief as part of her gift. "It is therefore," he wrote, "analogous to the endowment—or part endowment—of a Chair of Music. Similar endowments for other departments would lift the staff of the Library to the position of a faculty, and the Library to the plane of an institution of learning: an actual university of the people." The "chairs" for which endowments were most pressing Putnam listed as the following: the fine arts, American history, cartography, Semitic, Slavic, and Oriental literature, political science and economics, and applied science. The following April he was able to announce the endowment of two chairs, each with a gift of $75,000, one in American history, funded by William Evarts Benjamin, one in the fine arts, funded by the Carnegie Corporation. As a "stop press" coda to his report, Putnam could not resist announcing that Archer M. Huntington had offered the Library "an endowment not merely generous in amount ($105,000) but so unusual in its provisions that though the formal procedure of acceptance is not yet completed, I can not omit mention of it here." Huntington's endowment, offered in a letter to Putnam on November 14, 1927, would provide for the purchase of books relating to "Spanish, Portuguese, and South American arts, crafts, literature, and history." The Hispanic Society of America, Huntington stipulated, could borrow any of the books for a period of three months. And the entire income had to be spent annually. The endowment, in Central Pacific gold bonds, was duly accepted by the Trust Fund Board. Meanwhile, in December, Putnam visited the Hispanic Society and was shown around by Huntington, its perennial president; and Huntington, on his way to Biltmore Forest, near Asheville, North Carolina, for a winter vacation, stopped off for a tour of the Library of Congress— "your endless and magnificent library," he wrote Putnam, on New Year's Eve. He went on, "You and those you have brought together have made the great library out of the mere mass of books which existed before, and all our little infant collections (Hispanic etc.) are your eternal debtors."

A few months later, in April 1928, Huntington donated still another fund, of $50,000, to establish a chair of Spanish and Portuguese literature—or rather, a consultantship, which Putnam preferred to call this one, as the income would provide an honorarium of merely $2,500 per annum, more or less. Its first recipient was the recently retired Spanish ambassador to Washington, Juan Riaño y Gayangos, who wanted to stay on in the capital. (The same spring, with funds donated by "public-spirited citizens," Putnam established an American folk song project, to collect and preserve the songs and ballads "endangered by the spread of the radio and phonograph, which are diverting the attention of the people from their old heritage.") The idea of consultants as well as chairs had arrived, and in 1929 Putnam could announce a grant from the General Education Board that provided consultantships also in English and classical literature, European history, economics, science, and philosophy. In October 1929, the Daniel Guggenheim Fund for the Promotion of Aeronautics gave the Library $140,000 to establish a chair of aeronautics and to provide for a complete aeronautical library for research purposes. And, in February 1933, the Trust Fund Board approved the use of an endowment from James B. Wilbur (originally provided in 1928 but sequestered in litigation after Wilbur's death in 1929) to establish a chair of geography.

As early as November 1930, Huntington suggested a special "Hispanic Society room" in the Library. Putnam was interested, but he demurred at the designation as implying "a permanent surrender . . . to the uses of a private organization," and the subject was dropped, it seems, for six years.

❋

During the 1930s, Archer Huntington gave much of his time, energy, and money to the establishment and development of the Mariners' Museum in Newport News and of Brookgreen Gardens. The museum, a memorial to his father, grew from Huntington's collection of artifacts to do with seafaring. The gardens were the consequence of a chance visit of Archer and Anna Huntington to the South Carolina seacoast, which charmed them with its forests and wetlands, animals and birds. Huntington was inspired to write:

> Come to the silver gardens of the South,
> Where whisper hath her monarchy, and winds
> Deftly devise live tapestries of shade,

In glades of stillness patterned,
And where the red-bird like a sanguine stain,
Brings tragedy to beauty.

In 1930 the Huntingtons bought four abandoned rice plantations, constituting a tract of ten thousand acres on the Waccamaw River. They planned an outdoor museum for native plants and trees, surrounded by a preserve for wild life. The plan of Brookgreen Gardens, designed by Anna Huntington, is in the form of a butterfly with outstretched wings. A first thought was to place some of her sculpture in this setting. The concept enlarged as, during the Depression years, Huntington wanted to give commissions to artists who were in straits and to create local employment. The collection is today extensive; Brookgreen Gardens, under the administration of a board of trustees, now belongs to the state of South Carolina and is enjoyed by throngs of visitors. Interspersed among the sculpture, engraved on stone slabs, are poems and fragments of poems, some by Huntington and others that he selected from his favorites. (During the decade of the thirties, Huntington published, privately for the most part, eighteen volumes of his poetry in English and Spanish.) Not only at Brookgreen but around the Mariners' Museum, on the Hudson near Haverstraw, in the Adirondacks, and in western Connecticut, Huntington created wildlife refuges that he gave to the public. Both Huntingtons loved animals. Anna Huntington's sculptures, often monumental, were notable for her figures of horses, lions, and dogs. She bred Scottish deerhounds, and Archer Huntington wrote:

I saw her walk in silver mist of morning,
Under the yellow trees, October lighted.
I heard her call her great gray dogs to her,
Caressing each in turn, that none be slighted.

Before Christmas 1935, Huntington paid another visit to Putnam at the Library of Congress and met the occupants of some of the chairs, including an Augustine friar, David Rubio, the consultant in Spanish and Portuguese literature. Through Rubio's efforts the Hispanic collection had grown from fifteen thousand to one hundred thousand volumes, shelved in overcrowded stacks, which he pointedly showed to the visitor. Afterward Huntington wrote to Putnam from Atalaya, the fortress-like beach house the Huntingtons had built near Brookgreen, "I have never seen a finer group of men. It has quite cleared my mind on various points for the future." He and Putnam were now on first-name terms. The following autumn, Putnam and his daughter Brenda visited Atalaya, possibly to talk over a sculpture of hers, a sundial, later to be acquired by Brookgreen Gardens, but also, one can surmise, to talk over Huntington's proposed new benefaction to the Library of Congress—which, indeed, had been incubating for six years.

On November 18, 1936, Huntington executed a deed of trust, consisting of five thousand shares of Newport News Shipbuilding and Dry Dock Company stock—face value $500,000, market value $874,000—one half of the income to go to the Library of Congress Trust Fund Board for two purposes: the equipment and maintenance of a "Hispanic Society Room," in which would be assembled the Library's holdings and later accessions in the Hispanic fields; and the maintenance of "a Chair of Poetry in the English Language." The other half of the Huntington Trust's income was designated for the American Academy of Arts and Letters (and still is). Huntington served as trustee, along with the Bank of New York. Two months later he added a personal check for $40,000 to be disbursed immediately for equipment in the Hispanic Room. When some of the Library's stacks and offices moved to the new annex that opened in 1939 across Second Street to the east, space became available for a vaulted reading room some 130 feet in length, decorated to reflect the taste of the Spanish and Portuguese Renaissance. The room, with its frieze displaying the names of celebrated men of letters of the Hispanic world, has an atmosphere of cloistered quiet and serenity. A marble tablet bears an inscription stating that "The Hispanic Foundation," as it was first called, had been established with "the generous cooperation of the Hispanic Society of America." As he preferred, Huntington is not mentioned.

Putnam announced the endowment in his annual report for the fiscal year closing in 1937, giving emphasis to the provision for a Consultantship in Poetry: "It has been promptly taken advantage of by the engagement for the present year of Mr. Joseph Auslander, well known in the field of poetry, lecturer on poetry at Columbia University during the past 8 years and poetry editor of the North American Review. As in the case of other consultants, the service to us will not preclude those other interests, nor in his case necessitate continuous residence at Washington, as his service to the public will be largely by correspondence or in the field."

(The creation of the Consultantship and Auslander's appointment to it was nearly anticipated on March 27, 1936, by Joint Resolution 549, introduced in the House of Representatives on that day by Joseph P. Monaghan, of Montana, proposing to make his colleague John Steven McGroarty, of California, the "honorary poet laureate of the United States of America." McGroarty, a seventy-four-year-old Democrat, had been elected poet laureate of California by his state's legislature in 1933. One of his poems, "The Lady Eleanor," a gracious tribute to Mrs. Roosevelt, had been published in the *Congressional Record*. Monaghan's resolution was referred to the Committee on the Library, where it dropped out of sight. Had it led to the official designation of a poet laureate, might Putnam and Huntington have decided a Chair of Poetry was superfluous?)

Putnam's annual report for 1936–37 called attention to another benefactor of the arts, Gertrude Clarke Whittall, who during the previous year had given the Library a set of Stradivari stringed instruments and Tourte bows, followed shortly by a donation of $100,000 to maintain them and to support concerts in the Coolidge Auditorium at which they would be played upon. On a desk pad Putnam jotted the following note for September 17, 1937:

> Constitution Day: Leading Events at the L.C. . . . Mrs. Whittall drops in with a check for $50,000 as an addition to her Endowment. God save the Constitution!

And, in April 1938, Mrs. Whittall mailed the Librarian still another check, for $30,000, to pay for the construction of a room she described as "the future beautiful sanctuary of the precious Stradivari." The Whittall Pavilion, furnished and decorated under the eye and at the further expense of Mrs. Whittall, adjoining the Coolidge Auditorium and giving onto a courtyard garden, was opened in March 1939 with a concert of violin and piano sonatas by Adolf Busch and Rudolf Serkin. Like Elizabeth Coolidge, Gertrude Whittall was a woman of formidable determination and rather unpredictable generosity; unlike her, she had no musical training, though she was as deeply devoted to chamber music; and, as we shall see, she loved the art of poetry as well. Born in 1867 in a well-to-do family of Bellevue, Nebraska, Gertrude Clarke was educated by tutors and at the Sorbonne. In 1906 she was married to Matthew John Whittall, an English-born carpet manufacturer in Worcester, Massachusetts. When the Flonzaley String Quartet came to Whittall Manor to perform, Gertrude Whittall was first "exposed," as she said, to chamber music, and became an ardent devotee. Some time after her husband's death, in 1922, she began to form a collection of Stradivari instruments and engaged musicians to play them at her soirees. After moving to Washington in the mid 1930s and taking up residence in the Shoreham Hotel, she intended that recitals on her "Strads" be the feature of a salon in her apartment. But soon afterward she wrote Herbert Putnam offering the instruments to the Library, with the wish "that under proper protection they be played on from time to time in your Auditorium." They were not to be treated as relics; they were to be enjoyed.

Still another benefaction in 1938 was designed to serve the various chairs. One of the most valuable pieces of real estate in downtown Washington was conveyed to the Trust Fund Board—upon its sale one-half of the proceeds would go to the Smithsonian Institution as an addition to its endowment and one-half to the Library of Congress for the maintenance of consultantships. Miss Annie-May Hegeman, of Pittsburgh, was the donor; on the property, assessed at $372,000, at the corner of 16th and Eye Streets N.W., was a mansion which she and her late parents had occupied seasonally. The Library's fund was to be called, in honor of her stepfather, "The Henry Kirke Porter Memorial Fund." Porter (1840–1921), a New Englander, had been a founder of the YMCA, a church worker, a manufacturer of locomotives, a Congressman, and, it appears, a humanitarian. For six years the property was leased to the Public Buildings Administration for use by the Executive Office of the President, Defense Housing Administration, for

$10,000 per annum. It was sold in 1946 to the Motion Picture Association of America for $600,000, and in due course an office building replaced the Porter mansion. The income from the Porter Fund has sometimes provided supplementary resources for the Chair of Poetry.

✼

No documentation has turned up in the Library of Congress to explain by what official procedures Joseph Auslander was selected as the first occupant of the Chair of Poetry, or whether other candidates were considered, or precisely what his responsibilities were to be. There is no doubt, however, that he was Archer Huntington's candidate and that Putnam congenially agreed. Witness a handwritten note of Huntington's dated February 22, 1937, from Atalaya:

> Dear Herbert,
> I fear Auslander has taken on work with the N. American Rev. which may tie him. However I wrote Miss Perkins to get in touch with him with a view to an appointment when you are in town. If you will let her know when you come she will get in touch with him.
> All pleasant messages from us both. When are you voyaging this way?
> Faithfully   Archer

Putnam evidently offered the Chair thereupon to Auslander, who responded in verse on May 31, on the *North American Review* letterhead:

> The simple phrase of gratitude
> Is something rather felt than heard:
> Your quiet graces render rude
> The overstrident thought or word.
>
> Wherefore this letter I indite
> Returns in but a meagre measure
> The courtesy that gave delight,
> The fellowship that furnished pleasure.

And, on June 16, a letter went to Auslander from the Personnel Office, at Putnam's direction, offering him the appointment as Consultant in Poetry for the coming academic year, at an honorarium of $3,000, the date of his actual entrance being subject only to his convenience. "In the case of the Consultants, who are not upon the Government roll . . . it is understood that the relation with the Library does not preclude other activities not inconsistent with a reasonable service to it." Putnam subsequently designated July 1, 1937, as the beginning of Auslander's term. On the 21st, Auslander wrote Huntington: "I have tried a hundred times to write you a letter that might, in some faint measure, acknowledge the splendour of your deed. Alas, a hundred times I have found the vocabulary of gratitude a lame and shrill business at best. Perhaps one day we shall meet again and hand speak for tongue."

Auslander's acquaintance with Huntington had begun before January 1932, when he wrote the older man to tell him of the death of his wife in childbirth—"the bitterest occasion I have ever known. . . . Forgive my pressing this upon you. It had been my hope to tell you of happier tidings." Possibly they had met at the Hispanic Society of America, of which Auslander was a corresponding member. He contributed to the society's publications and in the fall of 1936 was working on a translation for the society of *Martin Fierro,* the Argentinian classic by José Hernández. Huntington had agreed to pay him $1,000 upon completion, but apparently that never came to pass. Auslander was born in Philadelphia in 1897—in the slums, he once wrote to Marie Bullock, and in his boyhood he worked three years in a sweatshop. Nevertheless, he went to a Brooklyn high school and then to Harvard for an A.B., graduate study, and an instructorship; spent a year at the Sorbonne; tried the freelance life in New York; and, in 1929, accepted an appointment as lecturer in poetry in the extension division at Columbia University. He edited little magazines and published a great deal of poetry, which was disparaged by at least two of his young contemporaries, Louise Bogan and Archibald MacLeish. Bogan, in her letters during the early 1920s when she and Auslander were editors of *The Measure,* took unkind digs at him. And MacLeish, writing to Pound in 1926, while in Paris, pronounced on him cruelly: ". . . of him I know nothing good. He is a word fellow. With the labial not to say digital dexterity of a masturbating monkey and as little fecundity." Untermeyer was kinder, including Auslander in his influential anthology, *Modern American Poetry*, though commenting on his verse: "Verbal felicity becomes a coddled facility, and the simplest of objects is described with excess; . . . inclined to overdecorate; . . . an ineradicable impulse to rely on the frayed trappings of the poetic stock-room. . . ." Yet "there is a genuine lyricist here. He can turn from light songs to the darkness of a deep human experience." And Untermeyer commended Auslander's sound taste in his history of poetry, *The Winged Horse,* and his *Winged Horse Anthology* (both with F. E. Hill, 1927 and 1929). Auslander gave one of his Harvard pupils, Ogden Nash, credit for proposing both works. Another pupil who attended his lectures, Marie Bullock, remembered Auslander's teaching with appreciation and said that he inspired her to found the Academy of American Poets in 1934, of which she was president until her death in 1986. "He rather resembled Poe, and he fancied he did," she told a visitor. "He liked to strike poses when he read, which he could do beautifully. He was notably kind about helping untalented poets, chiefly ladies, with their verse." A winged horse is, still today, the emblem of the Academy of American Poets.

A year after his first wife's death, which left him with an infant daughter, Auslander married the poet Audrey Wurdemann, then twenty-two—she claimed descent from Percy Bysshe Shelley, she had published her first poems at sixteen, and she won the Pulitzer Prize for poetry in 1935. With the Consultantship the Auslanders established a pied-à-terre at the Willard Hotel in Washington, and Putnam approved a post for Audrey Auslander as her husband's secretary and an assistantship, which was filled by Kenton Kilmer, Joyce Kilmer's son. The Auslanders' appointments were automatically renewed each year, evidently with no consideration of a terminus ad quem—until the arrival of Archibald MacLeish. Auslander had no reason not to assume he had the Chair for life.

One must regard with a certain awe the enthusiastic vigor with which Auslander and his wife (they worked as a team) went about their duties, in particular their notably effective campaign for donations of literary gifts. Appropriately, the first acquisition was the manuscript of Shelley's *The Mask of Anarchy,* in Mary Shelley's hand—thus a memento

of Audrey Auslander's great-great-grandparent. By happy coincidence
it was presented on the Librarian's seventy-sixth birthday and inspired
these verses:

> For Herbert Putnam Esquire
>
> That day I put into your proper hands
> The Shelley Manuscript, I could not know
> It was your birthday, but the heart will glow
> With truths the mind too seldom understands.
>
> I watched your fine and eager face light up
> With pleasure as you held those glowing pages;
> Your hands were filled with light as 'twere a cup
> Holy with humanity's noblest rages.
>
> And thus Apollo in his providence
> With the occasion now and then conspires,
> And in his wisdom orders such events
> To shed a glory on mundane desires.

Two women of Long Island had purchased and donated the manu-
script to the Poetry Archives, an entity apparently conceived by the
Consultant. Two others, of New York City, gave several Edwin Mark-
ham manuscripts. And Mrs. Whittall gave the holograph of *Lancelot,* a
narrative poem by her favorite poet, Edwin Arlington Robinson, and,
a year later, a collection of Dante Gabriel Rossetti manuscripts. (It is
said that Auslander wrote poetic tributes also to Mrs. Whittall, but none
of them have come to light.) Other gifts in the fiscal year were, from
William Rose Benét, a collection of papers of his late wife Elinor Wylie
and, from Lincoln's granddaughter, Mrs. Charles Isham, a poem Lin-
coln had written in his youth and other family relics. In his other per-
sona, as poetry editor of the *North American Review,* Auslander
devoted a special issue to a selection of Archer Huntington's poems.
His report to the Librarian for fiscal 1939 listed nearly fifty persons
who made gifts through Auslander's enterprise. A characteristic letter

of solicitation went as follows (this one to the Anglo-Irish dramatist St. John Ervine):

> Having been appointed to the task of building in our National Library for the People of the United States a permanent sanctuary for the manuscripts and memorabilia of the poets of our tongue, I take the liberty of inviting your cooperation.
>
> Such a room, dedicated to the best and noblest utterances of the best and noblest minds, is intended not only as a storehouse of treasures to inspire and instruct the multitude that daily throng our doors; it is to serve also as one more heartening sign, in a confused and darkened world, of the power of the poets and dramatists, the glory of our common heritage and common tongue, and the unity of our ideals and aspirations.
>
> I write to acquaint you with these tidings, and to express the earnest hope that . . . [etc.]

Among the names reported in 1939, as donors or subjects, are Hilaire Belloc, Lord Alfred Douglas, Vachel Lindsay, Amy Lowell, Joyce Kilmer, V. Sackville-West, George Santayana, Siegfried Sassoon, and Walt Whitman; also (Auslander having begun to style himself Consultant in Poetry and Drama) Maxwell Anderson and Lennox Robinson. Auslander made an expedition to Princeton to solicit papers of Einstein and Thomas Mann, apparently without success. He was involved with a Poetry Pavilion at the New York World's Fair. Both Auslanders joined in persuading Eugene Meyer, the publisher of the *Washington Post,* to give the Library a commonplace book of Thoreau's (containing notes and extracts on English poetry, Greek philosophy, and Hindu scripture), and they obtained from his wife, Agnes E. Meyer, a gift of one thousand dollars toward the purchase of Vachel Lindsay's literary estate from his widow, a project never realized. In May 1939, the Library opened an exhibition of the Walt Whitman collection of Mrs. Frank Julian Sprague, organized by Auslander. A popular success, it remained on show for three years, though the hope that Mrs. Sprague would give her collection to the Library was disappointed; it ended up in the Library of the University of Pennsylvania.

[48]

In early May 1939 Ezra Pound visited the Library of Congress, dur-
ing a two-month sojourn in the United States, his first visit since 1911.
Pound came to Washington chiefly to talk to congressmen and officials
about his economic and political ideas, which, along with music, were
his main concerns while at the Library. He lunched with Putnam and
presented a scheme for the Library's exchanging five thousand dollars
worth of photocopying equipment for fifteen thousand dollars worth of
microfilms of musical and other manuscripts in Italy. Nothing came of
that worthy idea; Putnam said the Library didn't have the means. Pound
may have looked at the Whitman exhibition (he couldn't have missed it
as he came in) but, according to Kenton Kilmer, he didn't visit the
poetry office. There was surely no rapport between Pound and Aus-
lander, who some years later wrote to Marie Bullock: "I knew him in
Paris as a foul-mouthed lecher." Among those whom Pound saw while
in the States was William Carlos Williams, a friend since college days,
who wrote his (and Pound's) publisher, James Laughlin, about the en-
counter: "He does have some worthwhile thoughts and projects in
hand. . . . [But] the man is sunk, in my opinion, unless he can shake
the fog of fascism out of his brain. . . . You can't argue away wanton
slaughter of innocent women and children by the neoscholasticism of a
controlled economy program. To hell with a Hitler who lauds the work
of his airmen in Spain and so to hell with Pound too if he can't stand
up and face his questioners on the point." After returning to Italy in
June, and learning of MacLeish's appointment as Librarian of Con-
gress, Pound wrote sending "hearty if delayed congrats" and importun-
ing him about his notion of swapping copying machines for microfilms
of manuscripts—"to put the thing thru the dept of State. . . . Hang it,
Putnam did such a MAGnificent job that anyone who succeeds him has
got to show a leg."

Auslander's report for fiscal 1940 (the year, of course, began in mid-
1939) included as subjects or donors Langston Hughes, Douglas Hyde
(the President of Eire), Joaquin Miller, Muriel Rukeyser, Bliss Carman,
and again Whitman. The most celebrated gift he engineered came
through Mrs. Whittall's largesse: "A comprehensive collection of the
manuscript poems of A. E. Housman [comprising] all that has been
preserved of the four notebooks described by Laurence Housman in his

[49]

Memoir . . . and [including] almost all the original Housman manuscripts and rough drafts on record." According to David A. Randall, in *his* memoirs, the poet's brother had sold the notebooks in 1938, two years after Housman's death, to the London branch of Scribner's rare book department for two thousand pounds (then about $10,000). They were sent to Scribner's New York office, then managed by Randall, who was approached by the dealer Barnet J. Beyer with an offer on behalf of a buyer who would donate the collection to a national institution. The Scribner's price was $15,000, which Beyer paid; but some months later he asked Randall for a 10 percent discount, explaining that his client had understood $15,000 to be the price Beyer was charging. Randall granted the discount. He discovered several years later, from MacLeish, that Mrs. Whittall, the client, had actually paid Beyer $40,000. Furthermore, Beyer had delivered the manuscripts directly to the Consultant in Poetry rather than to Mrs. Whittall, who was able to inspect her purchase only after it came to the Library of Congress. At exactly what point Auslander had entered these transactions is unknown. As for the Housman manuscripts themselves, they will turn up again in this chronicle.

Putnam had informed President Roosevelt, in June 1938, of his wish to retire, but a year elapsed before the President got round to considering a successor and wrote to Felix Frankfurter asking his opinion of MacLeish for the appointment. "He is not a professional Librarian nor is he a special student of incunabula or ancient manuscripts," Roosevelt wrote. "Nevertheless he has lots of qualifications that said specialists have not." Justice Frankfurter wrote back endorsing such a nomination and sent MacLeish a copy of his letter to the President. In his reply to his old law professor, on May 15, 1939, MacLeish almost unequivocally rejected the idea. ". . . the one thing I have ever wanted to do with all my heart was to write poetry and the one thing I have ever wanted to be was a poet. As it is, I have never wanted to write as much as I do at the moment and have never had so many things which demanded to be written. I am afraid they would never be written . . . with the Library of Congress as the principal interest in my life." He went to

Washington to lunch with the President, however, and less than a fort-night later he declined. Then, four days later—after F. D. R.'s assurances that time could be found in which to continue his own writing—he accepted the nomination, which the President announced on June 6. Despite the opposition of the American Library Association because MacLeish was not an experienced library administrator, Congress confirmed the nomination, and he assumed his duties as the ninth Librarian of Congress on October 2. His first ceremonial occasion, on Columbus Day, was the opening of the Hispanic Room, Huntington's gift to the Library.

During that first week MacLeish, replying to a pressing memorandum from Auslander, declared: "In principle, I am against the idea of putting stained glass windows in the Poetry Room." The establishment of such a room—"warm and rich and inviting," as Auslander wrote Marie Bullock—was a pet idea that he had been hoping to take up with Huntington during the summer. MacLeish, too, had tried unsuccessfully to meet with Huntington, who was often away from New York. The new Librarian's dissatisfaction with Auslander, harking back to the 1920s in Paris, was exacerbated by an episode that autumn.

Earlier in the year, Auslander had been approached by Ted Malone, who was the compère of a radio program called "Between the Book-ends," which he proposed to devote to a series of Pilgrimages in Poetry—broadcasts originating in such historical and poetic settings as Poe's cottage in the Bronx and Emerson's house at Concord. He invited and received Auslander's collaboration. The opening program, apparently with Putnam's approval, would be broadcast from the Poetry Room, at that time a small inner room still unfurnished. MacLeish was asked to speak during the program (to "the masses of America in the cause of poetry," as Malone put it). Not wanting to give the impression that the program was sponsored by the Library, MacLeish said no. When the broadcast went on the air (from "a beautiful white-walled room in the new Poetry and Drama Wing . . . a new sanctuary of poetry in America") the impression was nevertheless created that it was indeed sponsored by the Library of Congress and had been planned, if not actually written, by MacLeish. To confuse matters further, Malone had circularized colleges and other institutions, describing the Library as "honorary sponsor." MacLeish insisted that the president of the National Broadcasting Company recircularize the institutions with a rectifying statement. No more of Malone's Pilgrimages involved the Library of Congress.

For the Librarian of Congress to be a poet, and particularly a poet like MacLeish, created some unusual eventualities. In mid-October, W. H. Auden asked MacLeish to support his application for inclusion in the British immigration quota, with the object of becoming an American citizen. Auden had come over from England the previous January, on a visitor's visa, which precluded employment. When Richard Eberhart, on the staff of a boys' school in Massachusetts, offered Auden a month's teaching appointment he took it, and subsequently he took a job teaching at the left-wing League of American Writers. The immigration authorities, learning of the jobs, had ordered Auden out of the country. MacLeish wrote him: "Dear Wystan, I should be not only happy but very proud indeed to learn that you had become a citizen of this republic. I can think of no other man of letters I should rather see received in this democracy. . . . I admire both your poetry and your long and courageous fight for human liberty in our time." Thanks to the interest of MacLeish, Walter and Katie Louchheim, and other influential people, the immigration bureau allowed Auden to reenter the country from Canada, on November 24, 1939, under the regular quota of British immigrants. He became an American citizen, however, only on May 20, 1946.

The Librarian's exasperation with the Consultant in Poetry came to the point on October 31, when he wrote to Stephen Vincent Benét offering him the Chair the following year, with the idea that he "use it as a means to getting together the material you are working on in connection with *Western Star.*" MacLeish had formulated his conception of the post: "first, it should bring to the Library of Congress a practising poet able and willing to answer the inquiries about American and English poetry which occasional readers may bring in, and to have general supervision of the collection in a non-technical way; and, secondly, to offer to practising poets a place where for a period of a year or two a man may have time and access to the Library for the purposes of his work." So lucid a statement of the purpose of the Consultantship had not previously been framed. For whatever reason, however, Benét was unable to accept the Chair, and MacLeish next, on November 29, offered it to Allen Tate. Tate was interested, but he had suddenly to undergo an operation and the offer was postponed indefinitely.

During early 1940, Auslander continued to submit memoranda to MacLeish, outlining his ambitious plans for the Poetry Room, ideally in the new Annex, and for a reorganization that would place in the room all materials to do with poetry. He made far-ranging trips around the country, speaking to poetry societies, Rotary clubs, teachers' conventions, and colleges on the subject of the Library of Congress and the place of poetry within its structure and encouraging verse-speaking choirs, a special interest of his. MacLeish, meanwhile, finally met Archer Huntington in late May, at luncheon in New York, and heard Huntington express admiration for *his* poetry. He already knew that Huntington, entering his seventies, was beginning to yield some of his responsibilities. Shortly before, Huntington had directed that the Newport News shipyard stock be sold and the proceeds invested in other securities (the Library's half of the fund, at a price of $180.25 per share, was now worth $450,625), and he had resigned as trustee of his Huntington Trust and was replaced on MacLeish's motion by Agnes Meyer.

MacLeish's concern about the Consultantship was undoubtedly on the luncheon agenda. In early June, he offered the Chair to Carl Sandburg—"to bring you to the Library of Congress as frequently as possible . . . [and] to make the Consultantship in Poetry in the Library of Congress a position of the greatest possible distinction and prestige. . . . I have already told Joe that I am going to replace him at the end of this next fiscal year, i.e., on July 1, 1941. I won't go into the details of all that: you can certainly supply them for yourself." Sandburg also declined the appointment. Auslander was in Seattle, where his wife had fallen ill, when he heard from MacLeish: "As I told you when we discussed it a little while ago, I feel that a rotation of this chair among American poets would be a grand thing for American poetry. I know you feel the same way about it as your long and devoted interest in the cause of American poetry proves. . . . I'd like to talk to you about the date which would be most convenient from your point of view." Upon returning to Washington in late August, Auslander replied: "My answer to your suggestion about rotating the chair of poetry is what it was when you first popped the question: by all means; it's a healthy idea; go ahead, and more power to your elbow." He went on to say that he was anxious to go on building up the poetry collection, there were a number of gifts and more exhibitions in the wind, and he was planning a series of readings by poets under the heading "The Poet in a Democracy." MacLeish answered: "Do you mean that you would like to work full time on a regular Library of Congress job? I had assumed that you wanted only a part time job. . . . Would you let me know a little more about it?" He thought the series of readings sounded most interesting, "since it goes along with an idea I have had for recordings of readings here."

MacLeish treated Huntington—as both donor of the Consultantship and Auslander's friend—with consummate delicacy. On September 13, 1940, he wrote him: "As I told you when we discussed the Chair . . . I feel that your wishes should be controlling—and by your wishes I mean your every inclination of mind." He repeated his conception of the post with more eloquence: "My feeling has been that the Chair . . . could be made a source of great strength to American poetry by making it available to a succession of poets who would use it not as a Library position for Library purposes, but as a means of carrying on their own work for a period. Over the course of many years, the Library would be enriched by the presence from time to time of such men. The occupants of the Chair would be enriched by the experiences of the Library and the world which immediately surrounds it and the award would become, I should suppose, one of the greatest distinctions in American letters." With a show of fairness, MacLeish continued: "Auslander has used the Chair most effectively in the increase of the Library's collections and has done work which no one else in the Library is doing and which needs doing very badly. I am now struggling with the possibility of establishing a position specifically devoted to the work with which he is now concerned, leaving the Chair of Poetry free. . . ."

The new post MacLeish proposed for Auslander was that of Gift Officer, at a better salary, drawn chiefly from the Library appropriation and only partially from the Huntington Fund, allowing a larger balance for the purchase of books in the Hispanic Room. He wrote Huntington on October 18, describing the proposal; it met with the latter's approval. But another proposal of MacLeish's did not: to dissolve the Huntington Trust and divide the principal between the beneficiaries as a permanent loan to the United States Treasury, thus almost doubling the Library's income, "since the Treasury is obliged by law, as I believe you are aware, to pay four percent upon the funds invested in our Permanent Loan Account." Huntington replied at once: "I am practically always willing to meet you more than half way, but in this case I have doubts. . . . I would prefer to let the matter stand for the present and see what a few years bring forth." MacLeish acceded, observing that "my letter was far too long and far too prosaic to pass between you and me." Because of the terms of the trust Huntington had created, it never was dealt with in the way that MacLeish had proposed.

Almost simultaneously another prescient idea arose. On October 22 Harold Spivacke, the chief of the Division of Music, where a recording laboratory had been established through a grant of some $40,000 from the Carnegie Corporation, suggested the equipment be used to make a series of recordings of poetry by living authors. At MacLeish's direction he wrote up a project for submission to one of the foundations, but because of the pressure of defense work (and, soon, of war work) the scheme was tabled for nearly two years. And, after Auslander vacated the Chair of Poetry for his new post (on December 8, 1941), a year and a half would pass before the Chair was filled again.

Some other appointments came more readily. MacLeish was able to bring in as special consultants a half-dozen European intellectuals, among whom were Thomas Mann, as consultant in Germanic literature, and Alexis St.-Leger Leger, as consultant in French literature. The honorariums of both men were funded by private contributions. Agnes Meyer played the leading part in financing the post for Mann, who delivered several lectures at the Library and gave advice from his home in California. Leger—whose nom de plume as a poet was St.-John Perse—kept regular office hours at the Library, compiling bibliographies and dispensing advice but declining public appearances. As early as 1927, MacLeish, living in Paris, had written to Tate, "By the way, do you know St. J. Perse's *Anabase?* Somebody ought to get out a procession for that book." Leger's chief literary sponsors in Washington, besides MacLeish, were Francis Biddle, the Attorney General, and his wife, the poet Katherine Garrison Chapin. As the Secretary-General of the French Ministry of Foreign Affairs, a post he held during most of the 1930s, Leger had been forced into exile when the Germans occupied Paris and the Vichy Government abrogated his French citizenship. After leaving France he had renounced the writing of poetry, and in wartime Washington he was in continual touch with the American Government and the French Resistance. But his situation at the Library and his association with MacLeish, who became one of his closest friends, revived his muse, and in late 1941 Leger handed MacLeish the manuscript of his first work in his adopted country, the long poem *Exil,* whose publication (in French) in *Poetry* magazine followed soon after. T. S. Eliot's translation of St.-John Perse's epic poem *Anabase,* in 1930, had made the French poet known in England and the United States. MacLeish hoped to produce a translation of *Exil,* and Kurt Wolff, the publisher of Pantheon Books, hoped to publish it, but the Librarian's insistent responsibilities interfered. The appearance of *Exil* in the translation of Denis Devlin, First Secretary of the Irish Embassy, poet, and friend of Allen Tate, in 1949, confirmed St.-John Perse's reputation in the United States.

※

In his last phase as Consultant, Auslander was in a veritable whirlwind of activity. During the fall of 1940 he concentrated on organizing what MacLeish described as a long-time dream of both of theirs, the first readings of poetry in the Coolidge Auditorium, funded by a contribution of $2,200 that Auslander had solicited from Eugene and Agnes Meyer. (Those efforts were interrupted by a winter trip that both Auslanders made to Honolulu in the interest of the Library. Auslander mentioned to Marie Bullock his "fervent hope that Doris Duke Cromwell, on the rebound from domestic infelicity, may be susceptible to the noble uses of poetry." Apparently nothing came of that, but, according to the *Annual Report of the Librarian of Congress* for 1941, Auslander acquired for the Library a collection of ancient Hawaiian poetry "in recordings made by the last of the native chanters"—whaling songs, battle chants, missionary hymns, a song of creation, etc., with written commentaries by the donor, Charles W. Kenn.)

Both Eugene Meyer and Auslander hoped that MacLeish would open the series, "The Poet in a Democracy," with a reading from his poetry. He declined—"I don't want to seem in any way to use the Library of Congress as a platform myself," he wrote Meyer—but he agreed to introduce the poets. The first to read, on February 27, 1941, was Robinson Jeffers (and it was the first public appearance he had ever agreed to make). MacLeish in his introduction thanked the Meyers and "Dr. and Mrs. Auslander, tactful and enthusiastic emissaries and arrangers of all this," and took the occasion to remind the audience that there "never has been and perhaps never should be a Poet Laureate." The audience, "hundreds of Washingtonians, Supreme Court justices, Government workers, Cabinet officers," the *Washington Post* reported, overflowed into the Whittall Pavilion. Jeffers, undaunted, not only read his poems but made a ringing speech: "It may be the destiny of America to carry culture and freedom across the twilight of another dark age. . . . Our business is to . . . keep alive, through everything, our ideal values, freedom, courage, mercy and tolerance." Thanks to a recording laboratory that had been set up in 1940, Jeffers's readings were recorded, another "first," as were the subsequent readings, over the spring, by Robert Frost, Carl Sandburg (who sang ballads as well), and Stephen Vincent Benét, which also drew crowds. The Library announced that, because of the overwhelming popular interest, the series would continue during the 1941-42 season, with younger poets, and a program was drafted that included E. E. Cummings, Edna St. Vincent Millay, Conrad Aiken, and Mark Van Doren. (MacLeish again declined to be one of the readers, and Auslander wrote him: "I am downright sorry. It's just too goddam bad that a poet with so much fire and truth in his belly and so much music in his mouth should be shut off from the people whose hearts would be lifted by his voice and his words.") Understandably, given the outbreak of the war and MacLeish's numerous distractions, another series of readings was not presented in 1942. The idea was by no means dead. Spivacke was in touch with Eugene Meyer, who seemed willing to make another grant.

In December 1942, however, MacLeish wrote Meyer, "Although the readings . . . have been enormously successful, and there is undoubtedly a large audience for more . . . I cannot help feeling that it would not be appropriate to continue giving this type of poetry readings, for the present at least. My feeling is probably as much the result of conditions in the world of poetry as the war situation itself." He put a different suggestion to Meyer. Using the Library's "extremely well-equipped recording laboratory," MacLeish proposed to record informal readings by new young poets in the Whittall Pavilion as well as by poets of established reputation, presumably in the Coolidge Auditorium, and "to make albums from time to time which we could sell to the many schools, colleges, and interested individuals who are continually hounding us. . . . It would do something really effective for young poets . . . who should have some recognition and who are usually ignored. Nothing, quite frankly, is as close to my heart as that." He suggested a subsidy of $1,500 per year.

Meyer agreed that it would not be appropriate to continue the poetry readings. "As to the other suggestion, I think I will pass that up for the present."

❊

Auslander's years in the Library's service were impaired by conflicts with the stringencies of a bureaucracy. He was gently rebuked by MacLeish for negotiating directly with the Meyers on the "Poet in a Democracy" series rather than going through channels and for setting out to program the second series before discussion with the Library administration. When he asked MacLeish to exempt his office from a rule against smoking, the Librarian replied, "Sorry, no." When he committed the Library to the cost of shipping the Hawaiian poetry collection by air freight on the Pan American Clipper, the Chief Assistant Librarian, Luther H. Evans, reprimanded him for not getting proper approval. (In fact, the Kenn collection never did reach Washington. It is still in Honolulu, at the Kamehameha Schools.) On more than one occasion Auslander was stopped by a guard when leaving the Library after hours with books that had not been checked out. He and his wife were criticized for not keeping regular office hours and for taking trips on Library business without prior authorization. Obviously, temperament was the issue. Certainly some of Auslander's unorthodox brain-children were creditable, such as his acquisition in 1941 from RKO of the shooting script and stills of the film of Stephen Vincent Benét's *The Devil and Daniel Webster*. For such materials, including radio scripts, he reported, "a very real place exists in our archives." And, in March 1941, he proposed in a memorandum to MacLeish "the possibility of building up an archive of important motion picture films," seemingly the first recorded instance of such an idea. More than a year later, on May 18, 1942, MacLeish announced a program of "selecting motion pictures for preservation," in collaboration with the Museum of Modern Art, under a Rockefeller Foundation grant.

❉

When Auslander assumed his new post as Gift Officer, which MacLeish described as an "experimental attack upon the problem of the solicitation of gifts to the Library," his salary rose from $3,000 to $4,000, and an unambiguous description of his duties was recorded, including the stipulation that he was "to adopt the Library practices and procedures appropriate to regular Library employment." He retained the secretarial services of his wife but lost Kenton Kilmer to the Reading Room, where Kilmer was assigned to deal with questions about poetry. Auslander now, before each of his trips, submitted to his superior, Luther Evans, an agenda of the prospective donors he intended to call on. On a junket over Christmas 1941 he and Audrey had appointments in New York, as he reported, with Otis Skinner, Irving Berlin, George Arents (the collector of tobacciana), Jean Hersholt, Walter Pforzheimer, Owen D. Young, Bernard Baruch, Sir Thomas Beecham, and a good many other prospects.

Misadventure persisted. Auslander had become the target of criticism, when not merely a figure of fun, for the professional librarians on the staff. Evans, as Acting Librarian of Congress in the absence of MacLeish (whom, in October 1941, the President had appointed to an additional post, as director of the Office of Facts and Figures), discovered that Auslander had solicited gifts from members of the Librarian's Council who were important officials of other libraries, and he instructed David C. Mearns, the Reference Librarian, to examine all of the Gift Officer's correspondence to prevent such a contretemps. Then came the "Chambered Nautilus" case. An autograph manuscript of Oliver Wendell Holmes's poem, in the author's hand, was sold at an auction at the Parke-Bernet Galleries, in early 1941, for $75. In May 1942, Mrs. W. S. Farish and Miss Rowena L. Teagle gave checks totaling $500 to the Library of Congress, via the Auslanders, to pay for that manuscript, as set forth in a bill for that amount from Barnet J. Beyer, Inc., to the Library in Auslander's care. Mearns took an interest in the matter. He discovered that Beyer (the dealer who had figured in an earlier transaction, that of the Housman manuscripts) had bought the autograph at the Parke-Bernet auction; that Holmes had written out numerous copies of the poem, none of which had ever brought more than $75 in the autograph market; and that Auslander had contracted for the purchase from Beyer at an "exorbitant and unwarranted price" without authority. Auslander rose to his own defense: "There is no blinking the fact that I have been indeed at fault, but it is a zealous fault. . . . I have committed a foolish and unfortunate error of judgment, but I reject any imputation of dishonorable dealing." He proposed going to the parties concerned, canceling the acquisition, and offering to return the money, and he was prepared then to resign. MacLeish, for a while back at his office in the Library, was satisfied there was no imputation of dishonorable dealing, considered there was no reason for Auslander to resign, and counseled him in future to discuss any prospective gift, in particular of money, with the Reference Librarian or higher authority. He approved Auslander's proposal for dealing with the "Chambered Nautilus" manuscript, and that evidently ended the affair.

Mearns, however, in February 1943, submitted to Evans a detailed case against Auslander, whom he considered at best an appreciative and responsive amateur, not a bookman. "Among the collectors to whom he has written his letters of solicitation have been some corpses, some beneficiaries of the professional papers of distinguished physicians, and some second, third, and fourth rate literary figures. . . . It is my impression, based upon first hand reports, that he has alienated the respect for the Library of Congress of some of the leaders of the antiquarian book-trade. He is considered by them too small a cartridge for so large a gun. He does not understand the language of their tribe." He recommended that the post of Gift Officer be abolished or drastically narrowed.

While Auslander rather desperately continued to submit his everlengthier agendas for prospecting trips to New York and elsewhere, MacLeish on April 19, 1943, reported to Huntington that "it has finally been possible to arrange for the use of the Chair of Poetry in the manner you and I talked [of] in New York some time ago. As you will recall, it has been my feeling that the importance of the Chair . . . is so great that it should be filled from year to year by distinguished men of letters who will bring to the Library a contact with the living world of creative writing. The income from the fund is now increased by a small reserve we have been able to build up over the last two years, and it will be possible for us to begin in the fiscal year 1944 with a full-time appointment. I have had the great good fortune to secure for this appointment Mr. Allen Tate . . . [who] will serve for one year only, at the end of which time he will be succeeded, I hope, by another writer and literary scholar of comparable achievements." To which Huntington replied: "This is real news! I rejoice with you in the permanent warming of the Poetry Chair. It will help to stave off the hour when the poets will be found in the coolers of the black market, with muskrats and horses! And who can select the enthroned better than a king."

The Poetry Archive that Auslander had collected was transferred to the Division of Manuscripts that April, and in June MacLeish wrote him: "Dear Joe, I have just now finished the last of a long series of conferences on the new Acquisitions Department. . . . It was with this development in view that your appointment as Gift Officer was continued on a month to month basis following the end of the year's term." The new department, directed by Verner W. Clapp, would be responsible for all the acquisition activities of the Library, including the gift program. Auslander's duties would be of a rather more mechanical character; the salary might be decreased. But his present stipend would go on for up to six months "to give you plenty of time for action. I am deeply grateful to you for your pioneer work in opening up this field. There have been . . . some snarls and some difficulties, but your enthusiasm has never flagged." Auslander declared that he and his wife could not undertake duties less responsible than those they were now performing; and after first proposing, with no success, that they represent the Library as field agents in New York, they decided in agreement with MacLeish to carry on their work for six months and then discuss the situation. They embarked July 21 on a cross-country trip, at their own expense, to wind up unfinished business with prospective donors—some seven hundred, Auslander said—and promised to keep in contact. They left town a week before Allen Tate arrived to take up his duties and were out of touch until November, when Auslander wired that they had been selling war bonds in the Midwest. He also had been publishing "The Unconquerables," poems that "saluted the undying spirit of the Nazi-occupied countries," in the *Saturday Evening Post* and other magazines, and he and his wife were collaborating on a novel. Inquiries of them from Capitol Hill went unanswered.

The *Annual Report of the Librarian of Congress* for 1944 mentioned the resignation of the Auslanders at the end of March and their "return to literary work." In June, Verner Clapp reported to MacLeish on the state of the office of the late Gift Officer and his assistant: "there are, jumbled together, to the number of several thousand, books belonging to the Library, books belonging to the Auslanders, at least one book belonging to Harvard, and books whose ownership it is impossible to determine, although it seems that many of them must have been intended for the collections of the Library. The files, which comprise at a guess 10,000 pieces, are in such a state that it is not possible to ascertain anything with accuracy. The place is a jumble of personal and official property—unopened express packages, lemonade sets, loose papers, and accumulated files of all sorts. . . . My people will now have to review the entire work of the Auslanders since 1937—a truly Augean task."

Archer Milton Huntington (1870–1955)

Huntington, spring 1923, shortly after his marriage to Anna Hyatt

Huntington, with Scottish deerhounds, at his estate, "Rocas," near Haverstraw, New York, in the 1930s

Archer Huntington and Anna Hyatt Huntington at the New York World's Fair of 1940

Herbert Putnam: the bronze bust by his daughter Brenda (ca. 1924), presented to the Library of Congress by his colleagues upon his retirement, April 1939

Herbert Putnam in the early 1930s, with the Gutenberg Bible in the Otto H. F. Vollbehr collection of incunabula. Congress had authorized the purchase of the collection in summer 1930, the first instance since Jefferson's time of the federal government's "aiding the arts from the Public Treasury" (as a Congressman observed).

Gertrude Clarke Whittall, probably in the early 1930s

Joseph Auslander, around 1940

AUDREY WURDEMANN and JOSEPH AUSLANDER

are both endowed with charming personalities, with rich and pleasing voices; both are a delight on the platform, with the ability to lift folks out of themselves to a richer and fuller appreciation of life and poetry. For their delightful Poets' Symposium, they suggest the following subjects:

"POETRY COMES OF AGE IN AMERICA"

Let the Auslanders tell you the fascinating story of the Poetry Treasure House they are building in the Library of the nation.

"POETRY AND THE MORE ABUNDANT LIFE"

This uniquely stirring program could be called a case of Applied Poetry.

"POETRY IN A DEMOCRACY"

You will be moved to the depths and lifted to the heights when you hear this tremendous defense of Poetry in a Democratic Society.

"GREAT POETS AND GREAT POETRY"

Wherein these two gallant poet-adventurers stress the inspirational power of great poetry. This is more than a lecture, it is a rare and vital experience for the listener.

LET THIS BE THE LITERARY NUMBER IN YOUR NEXT SERIES

FOR TERMS, DATES, WRITE, PHONE or WIRE

EXCLUSIVE MANAGEMENT

ALKAHEST CELEBRITY BUREAU

RUSSELL BRIDGES, President

Mortgage Guarantee Bldg.   Atlanta, Georgia

Audrey Wurdemann and Joseph Auslander, in the early 1940s: a circular from a lecture bureau, issued while they were still at the Library of Congress

Allen Tate, Marcella Comès Winslow, and Robert Lowell, at Monteagle, Tennessee, 1943

David C. Mearns, Archibald MacLeish, and Verner W. Clapp, September 1944. The Declaration of Independence and other muniments had just been returned to the Library from safekeeping at Fort Knox.

Allen Tate, 1944

Robert Penn Warren, 1945

Two

1943 TO 1950

Their acquaintance began with a fan letter. MacLeish, living in France, wrote to Allen Tate on July 26, 1926, describing himself as "someone of whom you have never heard, [who is] lost in admiration of your New Republic review of Eliot's Poems. I understand you are a poet—which explains." Within a few weeks, they were planning to collaborate on an anthology of modern poetry, and their letters continued in a cordial and gossipy vein. "Don't expect anything of Pound. He's cucku. A foin pote but no critic."—MacLeish, in the manner of Pound, February 1927. The anthology project finally came to nothing. The correspondence became more reserved and, after MacLeish returned to the United States in spring 1927, it petered out. During the 1930s, when MacLeish was an editor of *Fortune*, he wrote several long, ruminative letters on poetic theory to Tate, who for his part sent felicitations on the awarding of the 1932 Pulitzer Prize to MacLeish's long poem *Conquistador*. "Up to you the list of winners has been depressing, but if your getting the prize means that the judgment of the givers has been reformed, you are to be congratulated." (MacLeish's immediate predecessors had been Benét, Aiken, Frost, and George Dillon; his successors were Hillyer,

Audrey Wurdemann, Coffin, and again Frost.) The letters revived, then died out again. The objective severity of Tate's criticism, and what MacLeish considered his academic tone, may have been the cause.

When MacLeish, as Librarian of Congress, wrote Tate in November 1939 inviting him to come and discuss the Consultantship after Benét had declined it, he began, "You may recall that you and I had some correspondence 15 years ago when I was in Paris." Had their subsequent exchanges slipped his memory? Tate came down from Princeton, where he was teaching in the Creative Arts Program, on January 12, 1940: it was their first meeting. Tate's news a week later that he had to undergo an appendectomy obliged MacLeish to withdraw his proposal, though he assured Tate that "I'm deeply committed to the purpose to get you and your wife here at the Library of Congress in some capacity." For two years the Chair was vacant. After Roosevelt, in October 1941, appointed MacLeish to an additional post as director of the Office of Facts and Figures, a newly established clearinghouse for defense information, Tate inquired about a job on its staff, but MacLeish's quota of writers was full. Nine months later the OFF was merged into the Office of War Information, of which MacLeish became assistant director. He resigned from the OWI in February 1943 and resumed the Librarianship full-time. Finally, in April, MacLeish again offered the Consultantship to Tate, who wired from Tennessee, "Caroline consents so I shall consider it final." Tate and his wife, the novelist Caroline Gordon, arrived in Washington in July. They rented a house in the Anacostia section, called "The Bird Cage," allegedly after a whorehouse in a novel by their friend Brainard Cheney. The house was shared at various times by Cheney and his wife, Frances, Katherine Anne Porter, and John Peale Bishop. Tate's term was explicitly set at one year; the stipend was $3,500 for the part-time appointment. Tate took the oath of office and signed a personal affidavit before a notary. He was assigned a two-room office on the main floor of the Library (Joseph Frank, then working in Washington, recalls that Tate had a crossed pair of Confederate flags on the wall) and an air-conditioned cubicle in the Annex, where he could write and do research.

The Consultant's duties were outlined in a memorandum from the Reference Librarian, David C. Mearns. Taking all English and American literature as his province, the Consultant was to survey the existing collections, initiate recommendations for purchase, engage in correspondence with a view to securing important gifts of books and manuscripts (*pace* Auslander), respond to reference questions, compile occasional bibliographies, confer with scholars, and make suggestions. "He should be warned that some of the questions . . . will emanate from school girls as well as from scholars, from poetry groups, and women's clubs, and program makers, and catch-penny anthologists, and talent testers, and moon-struck (perhaps moon-stricken) novices too ponderous to be raised by Pegasus. Such work is a part of the job; but it can be rather instructive and amusing."

At Tate's suggestion, MacLeish had appointed John Peale Bishop as Resident Fellow in Comparative Literature. Bishop had served only two weeks, in November, when he had a heart attack, and Tate put him on the train for home. He died in April 1944. Beginning in February, also on Tate's recommendation, Katherine Anne Porter served through August as Resident Fellow in Regional American Literature. Such Resident Fellowships in literature, however, didn't survive the MacLeish era, though fellows and consultants, often honorary, in a surprising variety of disciplines were appointed by the next Librarian, Luther Evans.

As his assistant Tate was able to employ Frances Cheney, who was on a leave of absence from Vanderbilt University, where she was the Reference Librarian. Her husband was on the staff of a Tennessee senator. Tate and Mrs. Cheney undertook a survey of the collections in American and English poetry, a byproduct of which was *Sixty American Poets 1896–1944: A Preliminary Check List,* published by the Library in 1945. Tate chose the sixty poets, beginning with Edwin Arlington Robinson in 1896, and for each of them he supplied a critical note—"the judgment of a distinguished poet and critic, whose own appraisal of his contemporaries is at once the justification and the purpose of its publication," Mearns noted in a preface. Frances Cheney was responsible for the bibliographical data, which comprised poetry and prose works; translations, if in the Union Catalog; and information about phonographic recordings. Twenty-five years later, Tate said, addressing an audience of librarians, "The only work I performed was to approve Mrs. Cheney's work . . . an impressive check-list, for which I received the official credit and Mrs. Cheney did all the work." (A revised edition, retaining Tate's original sixty poets but with additional data prepared by Kenton Kilmer, was issued by the Library in 1954 and republished elsewhere in 1969.)

In his own preface Tate observed: "What use this check list will have I cannot foresee, beyond the pious and even ritualistic justification, frequently asserted by scholars, that bibliographies make it easier to 'study' the works of a poet or the poetry of an age. . . . It is my impression that poets in the past, before the era of Teutonic efficiency in letters, had to make their own way, and they did it without benefit of library science. . . . I think that no one should suppose that [library science] can 'do something for literature' unless the society sustaining the literature has already done it or is doing it, and the 'science' is a mere instrument of that deeper will."

Thus, Tate on MacLeish, 1944: "MacLeish's public career as Librarian of Congress and head of the short-lived Office of Facts and Figures has obscured with politics the essential features of his achievement as a poet. This achievement is very considerable, for there is no doubt that he is one of the best American poets. In him more than in almost any other poet of his generation we see the problem of finding the poetic subject, and he is thus the epitome of modernism, for the engrossing subject is the chief problem for the modern poet. He has written, first and last, a dozen or more very fine lyrics."

Tate's most demanding assignment had not been foreseen in his job description and had little if anything to do with poetry: the editorship of *The Library of Congress Quarterly Journal of Current Acquisitions,* which was MacLeish's solution to the problem of giving "its principal clients a more appetizing account of its newest holdings than a pile of catalog cards in printer's proof." Its contributors would be the Library's fellows, consultants, reference specialists, chiefs of divisions, and the occupants of Chairs, writing "*as* scholars but not necessarily *for* scholars." The anticipated reader was "the educated man of general information to whom books are not tools alone but objects of human and humane interest and concern."

The *Quarterly Journal* editorship made Tate's part-time job full time, and his stipend was increased to $5,000. The first issue, July-

September 1943, contained articles on Americana, serial publications in India, Ethiopian publishing, a rare-book policy for the Library, a George Washington holograph, and the first Protestant hymn book. A quarterly accounting of significant acquisitions was a feature. Tate wrote only one article, in the second issue, reporting that the literary remains of "one of the best novelists the South has produced," Elizabeth Madox Roberts, who had died in 1941, had been given by her family. "That I should have been the recipient, on behalf of the Library, of the Roberts Collection," Tate wrote, "has given me greater satisfaction than any other incident of my tenure of this office." The editorship of the journal passed to Tate's successor as Consultant in Poetry, Robert Penn Warren, and thereafter was in the care of a regular staff member who was permanently appointed. The *Quarterly Journal* continued publication until 1983—eventually as an organ of general interest.

In the fall of 1943, after MacLeish has assumed still another hat, as editor of the Yale Series of Younger Poets (succeeding Stephen Vincent Benét, who had died the previous March), Muriel Rukeyser recommended William Meredith to him; and Tate, who had admired the young poet's work at Princeton in 1940, had Meredith send a set of poems from Alaska, where he was based as a Navy flier. MacLeish, when he accepted Meredith's volume *Love Letter from an Impossible Land* for the series, observed that "it interests me to see how you have shaken off the sterilizing and numbing influence of Auden and the Audenists."

The figure of Ezra Pound, in Italy, loomed early in Tate's term. On July 26, 1943, a Federal Grand Jury in the United States District Court (District of Columbia) indicted Pound for treason on the basis of his broadcasts over the Rome radio to the English-speaking world—one hundred and twenty-five, between December 7, 1941, and July 25, 1943, monitored and transcribed by the Federal Communications Commission. MacLeish obtained the transcripts and sent photostats to Ernest Hemingway, who responded that the man who emitted them "is plainly crazy. . . . He deserves punishment and disgrace but what he really deserves most is ridicule. He should not be hanged and he should not be made a martyr of. He has a long history of generosity and unselfish aid to other artists and he is one of the greatest of living poets. . . . His friends who knew him and who watched the warping and twisting and decay of his mind and his judgment should defend him and explain him on that basis." MacLeish wrote to Tate on August 20: "I don't know what precisely an honest man can do, but I'd be interested to have your views. . . . I have never had anything from Pound but vituperation and obscenity. Nevertheless, I agree with Ernest's estimate of his work, and I emphatically agree that he should be dealt with in some other way than by martyrdom." Next day, Tate to MacLeish: "I agree with Ernest about Pound's value and also about his imbecility. I am convinced that any line of defense should stress his plain insanity. . . . You are a lawyer. What possible procedure is there?" Tate had suggested presenting sworn statements to the Attorney General, but MacLeish decided to approach a close friend, Harvey Hollister Bundy, the Assistant Secretary of War. Pound's broadcasts, he wrote, "are the product of a completely distracted mind . . . obscene, rambling, spiteful, and altogether foolish. . . . I am not asking you, however, to think of the problem in terms of Pound. . . . The real question seems to me to be a question of the way in which this government should treat as tragicomic a figure." MacLeish wondered if Bundy might suggest to the Secretary of War that "orders be given to prevent any summary disposition of the case by the military authorities in Italy" and that Pound be brought to civil trial. In due course, Pound was taken into custody by the American military only in May 1945.

Tate's view of Pound in 1944, recorded in *Sixty American Poets,* disregards the foregoing context. "Pound is a great poet *in petto,* and an even greater instigator of literary enthusiasms and schools. . . . He brought to American poets for the first time a consciousness of the late nineteenth century French poets, who subsequently had a profound influence on us. His own poetry is mixed and eclectic, a collection of magnificent fragments, which younger men have used in their own work. For Pound, even as a poet, has been a great teacher of other poets in the principles of the craft. . . . He has never been able to construct a long poem: his *Cantos* have neither form nor progression, and remain a chaotic museum of beautiful fragments. He is a poet of profound 'literary sense' but of not much intellectual power, as his critical books, in spite of their seminal value, very sadly prove."

Among other tasks and distractions during Tate's year in the Chair of Poetry: Following through on the project that was so close to Mac-Leish's heart, he developed a plan for a collection of poetry recordings, with a view to an eventual series of albums. With Harold Spivacke, the chief of the Music Division, Tate drew up a budget for fees to poets coming to record, at $200 per, which MacLeish found too steep; funds for such things were scarce. That figure would have to cover travel expenses and permissions as well as the poet's fee. Tate during his year got only two poets to the Recording Laboratory, in the basement, and both were locals: Katherine Garrison Chapin and himself. (At that stage of history, the recordings were made on 16-inch cellulose acetate discs. After around 1950, when tape came in, the readings on disc were transferred to tape.) He negotiated with Maxwell Perkins, of Charles Scribner's Sons, for permission to make an abridged Recording for the Blind of Thomas Wolfe's *Look Homeward, Angel.* Perkins said the novel shouldn't be cut; Tate agreed. Again with Spivacke, he spent a lot of time planning a series of poets' readings with music commissioned by the Coolidge Foundation, another pet idea of MacLeish's: Roy Harris for Carl Sandburg, Nicholas Nabokov for Tate, William Schumann or Walter Piston for Marianne Moore. (Leger had opted out.) Nothing came of it. He wrote a statement for the OWI to broadcast, about writers exiled from Nazi Germany and in particular the Austrian novelist Stefan Zweig, who had committed suicide. He lectured in the Coolidge Auditorium to the Library of Congress Writers Club on "Some Techniques of Fiction." He questioned H. L. Mencken about Edgar Lee Masters, said to be ill and in straits. The Library might be able to help by buying some of Masters's manuscripts. Mencken replied that Masters was indignant about the rumor but he *would* welcome an offer. When Private John Welsh, the editor of the Puptent Poets Section of *Stars and Stripes,* offered to send the Library the manuscripts submitted by soldier poets, Tate replied that the Library would be delighted. "From the vast numbers of soldier poets, one among them will surely rise to prominence after the war." Whether this transpired for any of the Puptent Poets is not recorded. But Tate, responding to a request from the State Department to see some work by young poets, apparently for a cultural program, sent two poems each by Meredith, Shapiro, and

Jarrell. "I believe these three are the best young poets in the country today, and they are all in the service."

Most notably, Tate proposed and was largely instrumental in establishing the Fellows of the Library of Congress in American Letters—"whose activities," the Librarian stated in his 1944 report, "may eventually have a profound effect upon the collections of the Library." The first panel of Fellows—Katherine Garrison Chapin, Katherine Anne Porter, Willard Thorp (professor of English at Princeton, friend of Tate and Eliot), Mark Van Doren, Van Wyck Brooks, Paul Green, Carl Sandburg (who didn't turn up), and Tate himself—held their organizational meeting on May 26 and 27, 1944. No minutes have survived.

During spring 1944, both Tate and Caroline Gordon sat for their portraits by Marcella Comès, an artist friend from Tennessee days who had settled in Washington and made a specialty of painting writers, particularly the Consultants in Poetry. Katherine Anne Porter and Mark Van Doren sat for her the same year, and Robert Penn Warren the next. Comès went on to do portraits of Eudora Welty, Denis Devlin, Karl Shapiro, Ezra Pound (at St. Elizabeths in 1948), Léonie Adams, Katherine Garrison Chapin, Elizabeth Bishop, Robert Frost, Richard Eberhart, and, not until 1974, Robert Lowell.

"I have been very much tempted by your desire to keep me here," Tate informed MacLeish in November 1943. "But even if a full-time job were open here, I could not, for obvious reasons, take it permanently. . . . I have decided that I had better go down to Tennessee and edit The Sewanee Review. . . . I think it may be my duty to take that job." So he did, and as early as the following spring Tate was working at both the Washington and the Sewanee desks. In May 1944 he invited MacLeish to submit to the *Review* his hoped-for translation of St.-John Perse's *Exil*. MacLeish would be willing, he replied, "if I could see any opportunity of getting it done in a form which I would be willing to submit to you and willing to have Alexis read." He passed the torch soon afterward to Denis Devlin. No traces of MacLeish's version have come to light.

Robert Penn Warren was Tate's candidate to succeed him in the

Chair. (Consider Tate's appraisal in *Sixty American Poets* just at that time: "This poet's recent *Selected Poems* (1944) has done much to create for him the reputation which has been overdue for about ten years. Warren has a richness and inventiveness of language unusual in contemporary poetry, and a technical virtuosity which transmutes the most heterogeneous materials into a single order of feeling. From first to last there has been a steady growth in complexity and depth of approach.") MacLeish made him an offer in February 1944; Warren wanted more money and/or a permanent arrangement. MacLeish tried a double play. He had Warren come from Minneapolis (in an upper berth, such was the congestion on the trains) for an interview on March 11, and while the question hung fire, he phoned Marianne Moore and offered the Chair to her. She declined, partly because she had the care of her mother and partly because "my knowledge—I should say information—in the field of poetry is criminally eclectic, and although the Library is both source and resource, I was not a good reference worker when assistant in one of the branches of the New York Public Library. If I may say so, however, your letter has not been *to me* in vain, for I am lastingly benefitted by your even having considered me." MacLeish then offered Warren the same arrangement as Tate's—the Chair plus the *Journal* editorship, for $5,000. Bargaining continued. On May 2, Warren wired his acceptance at $5,628, somewhat closer to his University of Minnesota salary.

Later in March, MacLeish flew to London for several weeks as a delegate to the Conference of Allied Ministers of Education (a precursor of UNESCO), and while there he opened a campaign to enlist T. S. Eliot for the 1945–46 appointment. On May 9, he wrote describing the "practical details" of the Consultantship, then going on:

> What I have principally in mind is this: that everything depends now upon a true common understanding between the British and ourselves; that a true common understanding must rest not upon emotional unity, but upon a defined and quite explicit single-mindedness . . . which should go far deeper than problems of trade and transportation, and the like; that that single-mindedness involves a meeting of minds between those capable

of intellectual and moral leadership on the two sides of the water; that there are only a handful of people capable of bringing about any such meeting of minds; that you are one, and, I think, the chief, of these; that if you would and could spend a year in America now as the war ends and the "peace" begins, you could do more toward accomplishing this end than you could do in London, since the principal difficulties to be overcome are here.

Eliot, replying on May 29, said he was interested. He wanted a clearer picture, however, of the function which he should perform. "With the end which you have in view I am of course in warm sympathy: there remain the questions, whether anything can be accomplished by these means, and whether I am not too obscure in some quarters, and too unpopular in others, to be the right man. (I am not thinking of obscurity and unpopularity only in America—I may be too obscure or alternatively too unpopular here: and you want someone who enjoys the right status in both countries)." He asked specifically about travel, lecturing, talking freely, how far his conduct would have to be regulated as a Library employee and as a representative of Britain. "In what guise would the press, both friendly and unfriendly, put me over?"

After consulting Tate, MacLeish wrote to Eliot on July 4. As he saw it, beyond Eliot's formal duties at the Library he would speak at colleges and universities about "some aspect of the general problem of the community of ideas which seemed to you most important. . . . The real purpose would be to reach those who shape intellectual opinion in this country." Eliot didn't reply until September 9. "I must assure you that the delay was intentional, to let my views mature and become more articulate," Eliot began a rather long letter, which wound up, "I have come to the conclusion that I should not accept the invitation. I am extremely sorry, for I share your purpose and I appreciate warmly your personal kindness."

The decision, Eliot said candidly, was based partly on the problem of personal sacrifice of two kinds—forgoing his salary and his income from other work, and losing a year from work he was planning to pursue. But there were deeper considerations. "It would be natural for many people to presume that I had come primarily in the British interest, or even for some clandestine purpose undisclosed. . . . If I was suspected in this way (as I certainly should be by those who would be glad to think so) then the fact that I was on the payroll of the American Government . . . might inflame the suspicion into a grievance. Ordinary people, besides, can attach no meaning to such terms as 'cultural relations', and will be therefore all the more inclined to imagine them to be a cover for sinister political, financial or industrial machinations. All this might easily be stimulated to such a point that my activities might do more harm than good. I am not aware of having any enemies, but there is a great deal of malice in the world, as well as mischievousness, which is far short of enmity but can do as much harm; there are also plenty of people with ignorant prejudices against me (e.g. Carl Sandburg, who called me a 'fascist' a few years ago!) and others with defensible dislike of my views." He would be constrained, he feared, by the feeling that "I couldn't speak my mind freely about either American or British men and opinions, words and actions." He might, however, be of some use if he could come for a short visit, "with the true purpose quite overt and manifest," or could spend a year at some university, "really earning my keep by lecturing and tutoring, and, *au surcroît,* in a private capacity and on my own sole responsibility trying to exert the sort of influence you have in mind for me." That Eliot did come to the Library eventually, though not as the Consultant, was, in the main, Allen Tate's doing.

As early as the summer of 1943, MacLeish had told Roosevelt that he wanted to leave the Library of Congress, and that fall he suggested as his successor Julian Boyd, the librarian of Princeton University, where he was also editor of the voluminous Jefferson Papers. Roosevelt was unwilling to lose MacLeish, but more than a year later, in December 1944, he nominated him for a new post at the State Department as assistant secretary of state for public and cultural relations. An acrimonious battle over his confirmation by the Congress ensued, led by Senator Bennett Champ Clark, in the Senate Foreign Relations Committee. At the height of it, Tate wrote MacLeish, "I was surprised to learn in the pages of the Chattanooga Daily Times that Sen. Clark (D.,

Mo.) questions your standing as a poet. You are not in *any* (his word) of the anthologies. I suppose he means the Home Book of Verse. As Librarian of Congress you have failed to educate the Senate. Now it is too late." Several years later MacLeish recalled the Committee hearings: "The word *poet* was pronounced with a particular intonation . . . the implication being that this man regards himself as a poet and this obviously disqualifies him not only for public life, but for those sensible conversations . . . by which ordinary men communicate." One hears an echo in MacLeish's poem "A Poet Speaks from the Visitors' Gallery":

> Have Gentlemen perhaps forgotten this?–
> We write the histories.
>
> Do Gentlemen who snigger at the poets,
> Who speak the word professor with guffaws—
> Do Gentlemen expect their fame to flourish
> When we, not they, distribute the applause?
> . . .
> Gentlemen have power now and know it,
> But even the greatest and most famous kings
> Feared and with reason to offend the poets
> Whose songs are marble
>
> > and whose marble sings.

The Senate confirmed the appointment on December 19, and MacLeish resigned from the Librarianship. Luther H. Evans, the Chief Assistant Librarian, immediately became the Acting Librarian—a title he had often borne during MacLeish's absences for governmental wartime assignments—and on June 30, 1945, he was sworn in as the tenth Librarian of Congress. Boyd, whom Roosevelt had favored, had been unwilling to leave the Jefferson Papers. Evans, born in 1902 on a Texas farm, was a political scientist by profession, though the most notable part of his career had been as organizer and director of the Historical Records Survey, one of the principal cultural programs of the New Deal under the designation "Federal Project Number One."

MacLeish's accomplishment as Librarian of Congress was summed up years later by a scholar librarian of the tradition he had fostered: "[He] initiated a full-scale reorganization of the Library. He devised Canons of Selection and Canons of Service. He expanded cultural programs and interrelations with the world of learning. Primarily, he sought to inspire the staff to a new dedication. He charged the cataloging staff with laboring in an 'enchanted lethargy.' Not everyone responded to his witty goading, but for those who did . . . the Library became an exciting place and MacLeish's tenure 'the brush of a comet.' " The last phrase was Luther Evans's, who also observed that MacLeish "possessed unusual personal qualities, a first-rate mind, which absorbed and penetrated and understood; energies that could be at once exhausting, graceful and yet dynamic; marked powers of concentration and a concern for rationalization; an insistence on definition; and a gift of expression beyond any similar gift [the staff] had ever known. . . . But he was (and is) a poet, and it was not always possible to know at once in which capacity he confronted his subordinates. His drive was tremendous, and the fresh air that he brought with him was invigorating. Working with Archibald MacLeish was almost never easy, but it was almost always fun."

※

Warren took up his duties as Consultant in July 1944. Washington and the Library were scarcely new to him—he had spent considerable time on Capitol Hill, on research for his novels and literary scholarship. During his year in the Chair he was working on *All the King's Men* (which received the Pulitzer Prize for Fiction in 1947) and a study of Coleridge's *The Ancient Mariner,* which was published with illustrations by Alexander Calder. His chief official responsibility was to the editing of the *Quarterly Journal.* For the first issue of volume two he wrote a paper on "The War and the National Muniments," an account of how the great national documents—the Declaration of Independence, the Articles of Confederation, and the Constitution—as well as a copy of the Gutenberg Bible, Lincoln's Second Inaugural and Gettysburg addresses, and the Magna Carta (which the British Government had entrusted to the Library for safekeeping) had been transported by train, on December 26, 1941, to Fort Knox, in Kentucky. (The Stradivarius instruments given by Mrs. Whittall were sent at the same time to a secret site in Ohio.) In September 1944, with the approval of the War Department and the Joint Chiefs of Staff, MacLeish had the muniments returned and placed on public display at the Library. In the first draft of his article on the muniments, Warren wrote that the deteriorated parchment of the Declaration of Independence had to be repaired with "Japanese tissue." His phone nearly jumped off his desk when MacLeish, reading the draft, saw that phrase. Warren changed it to "paper fibres moistened with rice paste."

Among the applicants for the job as Warren's assistant was Kenton Kilmer. Mindful of Cleanth Brooks's and his treatment of "Trees" in their *Understanding Poetry*, Warren opted instead for Sheila Corley, whom he had taught when she was a graduate student. MacLeish assigned Warren to an office high on the top floor at the northwest corner of the Library, with a view of the Capitol and the city. The room had been used since early in Herbert Putnam's day for the Librarian's "Round Table" luncheons, attended by the division chiefs and sometimes guests. Katherine Garrison Chapin, whom Warren remembers as thoughtful in anything to do with the Chair of Poetry, supplemented the government-issue office furniture with several more graceful pieces and a few touches of decor. The room was the scene of the second meeting of the Fellows in American Letters, on November 16 and 17. The group lunched there; they dined with the Biddles one night and the MacLeishes the other. That room continued as the preserve of the Consultant for several years more, until in 1950 it was transformed into the Poetry Room, with finer appointments, and the Consultant moved into an adjacent office.

A leading item on the Consultant's agenda was the recording project, for which Tate had laid plans during his term. Warren, spurred by advice from the Fellows and the Librarian, began to bring in the performers. During the year he arranged recordings by thirteen poets: in sequence, Selden Rodman, Jesse Stuart, Louise Bogan, Richard Eberhart, himself, John Crowe Ransom, William Carlos Williams, Alfred Kreymborg, Oscar Williams, Robert P. Tristram Coffin, Gene Derwood, Willard Maas, Karl Shapiro, and again himself. He also recruited novelists to read from their writings. Joseph Hergesheimer and Henry Miller were both recommended to Warren by his friend Huntington Cairns, the polymathic counsel to the National Gallery of Art. Recently, Warren recalled with gusto the visit Miller paid to the Library in December 1944. "I had some misgivings, but Cairns thought a recording by Miller would be a great asset. Miller asked for all of his books to be brought to him—though some of them weren't publishable in this country, they were in the collection. 'Can I read anything I want?' he asked me. 'It's pretty strong.' All right, I said. At that time, a group of soldiers and Marines were assigned to the Recording Lab, to listen to tapes made in battle and say whether they sounded authentic. They took a dim view of the poets I'd been bringing to the Lab. 'Boys,' I told them, 'this morning I brought you something different— Henry Miller.' They knew who he was and were real set up. 'Can we listen?' Miller had been marking places in his books, a lot of them. I remember this mousey little man going into the booth and those brawny soldiers waiting with their mouths open. Well, Miller read and read— nothing 'strong' at all, just philosophical passages. I thought I was going to be lynched."

Warren, among his chores, compiled a bibliography of American poetry in the period 1860–1910, entitled *Poets of the Golden Age,* as a basis for filling in gaps in the holdings. Ranging through the stacks, he spotted many first editions which were transferred to the Rare Books Division. Out of poetic curiosity he examined the A. E. Housman notebooks that Mrs. Whittall had bought for the Library in 1940. When the four notebooks were received, they had been radically changed both in content and in form. Laurence Housman, before he sold them, had cut up their 731 pages and mounted the pieces on unbound sheets of folio size. As a Library official observed, the state of the material "must be understood to represent the fulfillment of the poet's wish that all of his manuscripts below a certain standard should be destroyed." Warren, after poring over the sheets, suggested that the adhesive used in fastening the pieces to the sheets might, in time, have deleterious effects. Furthermore, he observed that there appeared to be writing on the glued-down side of many of the pieces. During spring 1945, the technicians in the manuscript repair shop removed the 266 pieces from the sheets, cleaned them of adhesive, and hinged and remounted them on the original sheets, without disturbing the order. It was found that 136 of the slips contained legible writing on the verso side—that is, many more of Housman's drafts than had met the eye. The discovery arising from Warren's curiosity was an important one for Housman scholarship; it also provoked a controversy in the *Times Literary Supplement* and elsewhere over the propriety of meddling with the poet's brother's intentions.

In the choice of the next Consultant in Poetry, Evans had Warren poll the Fellows. The process was laborious. Tate favored R. P. Blackmur, whom he had come to know at Princeton; Thorp agreed, and so did Van Doren and Porter; Theodore Spencer, of Harvard (he had replaced Brooks, who had resigned), was for Winfield Townley Scott, a New Englander; Chapin favored Spencer; Green favored Paul Engle; Warren added Louise Bogan (recently appointed a Fellow) and Delmore Schwartz to the list. MacLeish, whom Evans consulted, also favored Engle "ahead of Spencer and Schwartz, because he comes from Iowa, and I think we ought to get back into the heart of the country, and because he is an able lad and a good worker as well as a first-rate poet." But he thought Spencer, Schwartz, or Bogan would be excellent too. Bogan had been a second choice of some of the Fellows. Warren ran the poll again, listing Blackmur, Spencer, Engle, Scott, Bogan, and Schwartz. Tate, by now the gray eminence, opted this time for Blackmur and Bogan equally, then, in order of his preference, Schwartz ("with Miss Bogan the best poet on the list"), Spencer ("a scholar and teacher first"), Engle ("I cannot feel that he is anything more than the geographical 'heart of the country,' like . . . all of his fellow citizens in that section"), and Scott ("has no claim to consideration for this job"). Evans offered the Chair to Louise Bogan.

✳

May 16, 1945. Upon learning that Pound had been taken into custody by the American Army in Genoa, Eliot cabled MacLeish, at the State Department, urging his help on Pound's behalf. MacLeish replied at once: "There is nothing I can think of now which can be done . . . at least at the moment." He explained Pound's indictment for treason by a

Washington court and speculated on his probable transfer there for trial. "I should be very happy to keep you informed . . ." The tone was stately.

August 7, 1945. Eliot cabled MacLeish again, asking when it would be possible to communicate with Pound about the choice of American counsel to defend him. MacLeish replied on the thirteenth that the Department of Justice had indeed informed him that Pound was in Italy, in the hands of the Army. "For your private and personal information, I should add that I am further informed that Pound's conduct since his arrest has suggested the desirability of psychiatric examination. . . . Pound has written the Attorney General admitting in effect the substance of the charges against him and contending that the Constitutional guarantee of freedom of speech justifies his actions. . . . If I can be of any further assistance to you, I hope you won't hesitate to call upon me." He gave Pound's address as the Disciplinary Training Center at Caserta, near Naples, though in fact since May 24 Pound had been in the D. T. C. at Pisa, where he was confined until his transfer to Washington on November 18. Thus the *Pisan Cantos*.

December 18, 1945. Tate, at Sewanee, to Eliot: "Ten days ago I was in Washington and had a talk with Luther Evans, who very much wants to work out an arrangement which will bring you to the Library of Congress. He discussed the question with the . . . Fellows in American Letters, of whom I am one; and I need not say that the Fellows are very keen on your coming. . . . You could expect the utmost consideration and understanding of your needs and purposes, and the full cooperation of the Fellows, most of whom are friends of yours—Willard Thorp, Ted Spencer, and myself, among them. . . . I for one would like nothing better than your excellent conversation."

❋

Louise Bogan, in 1939, scorned Auslander as Consultant in Poetry; since the 1920s she had regarded him as a square. She scoffed at Audrey Wurdemann's Pulitzer Prize. (She scorned and scoffed at much and many.) In the late 1930s, furthermore, Bogan found herself in opposition to poets who took a political stance. "Time-servers," she considered them; and she singled out Archibald MacLeish in particular, not so much for his poetry as for his oratory. In July 1938 she wrote to Rolfe Humphries, "Have just finished reading A. MacLeish's great speech ["In Challenge, Not Defense"], all about poets being challengers. It's the most awful tripe I ever read in my life . . .; of all the tub-thumping performances I ever read, it is the worst. . . . It's exactly the kind of sophomoric oration that brings the house down at college reunions." Bogan, with her pals Edmund Wilson and Morton Dawen Zabel, privately called him "MacSlush"; she also tagged him a stuffed owl. Wilson's verse parody "The Omelet of A. MacLeish" in *The New Yorker* in 1939 was entirely to her taste (though she might have got as much pleasure out of MacLeish's equally funny and far more indecent riposte in a letter to Hemingway). She severely reviewed *America Was Promises:* ". . . he is writing political poetry . . . and therefore the strict checks and disciplines of poetry written for itself . . . do not hold." But she went on, "Bury his gifts though he may, Mr. MacLeish is a private, a lyric poet through and through; it is somewhat of a loss that he did not allow himself to remain one." Zabel, spurred by Bogan, published a two-part attack on MacLeish in the *Partisan Review* in 1941, charging him with literary pretension, persistent imitation of Eliot and Pound, egotism, sanctimoniousness, and other failings.

In November 1944, MacLeish wrote Bogan inviting her to become a Fellow in American Letters and attend the fall meeting; Warren followed up with a friendly phone call. She replied to the Librarian, "For many years I have thought that my value as a writer consisted, in some part, in my separation from most of the activities of 'the literary scene.' This separation I never wanted to become rigid; and during the last year I have found a more flexible attitude a natural thing: part of a process of growth.—I was touched, therefore, to receive your invitation at this particular time. I'll be happy to see you all, and to give your projects any help I am able to give." The following July she wrote Zabel: "The great and overwhelming surprise occurred last November. . . . So I went. And there was Allen and T. Spencer and Willard Thorp (the Princeton one) and Mrs. Biddle and others. *And* A. MacL! And we had meetings and listened to experts, and had a drink or so, and a dinner or so. . . . It was v. good for me, because I had for so long indulged in tail-lashings about the good seed being passed by, etc., etc. . . . It did

me good to face reality that was somewhat rosier in hue than usual.—
So there you have it; and there has been a sequel to all this which you
will perhaps hear about before this letter reaches you.—Remember . . .
that the sequel requires a good deal of courage on my part. . . . It really
is the damndest development." The sequel was her appointment as Con-
sultant, and she wrote Tate (a friend since the 1920s) that she had de-
cided to take the job "with both eyes wide open to the difficulties
involved." (Fortunately *The New Yorker* was willing to hold her job as
its poetry reviewer.) Tate's opinion of Bogan's poetry had been sounded
in *Sixty American Poets:* "Miss Bogan and Miss Adams are . . . the
best women poets in America in the traditional lyric mode: I make that
qualification, looking towards Marianne Moore. . . . Miss Bogan has
a sustained power and a sense of form that nobody else can quite equal,
and with very little of the violence of language typical of her contem-
poraries she achieves a fine originality."

Bogan subleased Selden Rodman's Georgetown apartment, "a com-
bination of something out of Conrad's earlier period . . . and those
Josef von Sternberg chicken coops in which Marlene Dietrich used to
find herself," she wrote to her editor. In her Georgetown neighborhood
she found a new and lasting friendship with Katie Louchheim, an as-
piring poet and patron of poets, who later wrote of Bogan: "She
laughed a lot, her laughter was deep in her throat and mocking. There
was something diabolic about her; this was a woman one could both
admire and fear." Bogan's principal assignments, in the Chair, were to
compile a bibliography, issued as *Works in the Humanities Published in
Great Britain 1939–1946,* with 978 entries—a record of achievement
during the impossibly difficult period of the war; to make a study of the
"little magazines" devoted to poetry; and to pursue the recording proj-
ect. In spite of Warren's and her energetic recruitment of readers, funds
were unavailable to take the next step foreseen by MacLeish, albums.
Tate came to the fore. As *amicus curiae,* through Huntington Cairns,
he put the Librarian, Luther Evans, in touch with the new Bollingen
Foundation, of which Cairns was a trustee. (Tate, Cairns, and Mark
Van Doren had been colleagues on an intellectual radio program, "In-
vitation to Learning.") The consequence, in January 1946, was a grant
of $10,500 for a year's work preparing five albums of twenty-five 78

r.p.m. records of twentieth-century poetry in English. This was the first benefaction awarded by the Foundation, which had been formally established the previous month by Mary and Paul Mellon, of Virginia, though its programs had been set in motion several years earlier. (Mellon to Cairns from Hobe Sound: "Mary and I have decided that the Library of Congress record project will be excellent for Bollingen Foundation. We wonder if we may add two names to their proposed list . . . George Dillon and Paul Engle.")

Bogan spent February listening to the poetry recordings already in the collection, in order to check on the vocal quality of each reader and to discover the poems most effectively read by the poets themselves. The work of auditing, consulting, listmaking, technical preparation, and text compiling continued through the tenures of the next two Consultants before the albums were published, in 1949. (Later, the Bollingen Foundation gave a second grant of $10,500, which made possible a second series of albums.) Bogan got Auden to the Library to make additional recordings, and she and Tate persuaded Eliot to record at a studio of the National Broadcasting Company in New York.

On February 13, 1946, in Federal District Court, District of Columbia, a formal hearing was held to determine Pound's mental condition. Lunacy inquisition, the record called it. The jury, sworn on voir dire, returned its verdict: the respondent is of unsound mind. Pound was committed to St. Elizabeths Hospital. A different sentence was proposed at the time by Louis Untermeyer: life imprisonment in a cell lined with the poetry of Edgar A. Guest.

Bogan's own recordings were considered models. One of her successors in the Chair, William Jay Smith, in a tribute after her death in 1970, said, "With her rich contralto voice, she has the most perfect enunciation that you will encounter among poets today: every consonant, every vowel, every syllable is given its proper value, and then there are the pauses around which the poems are constructed, all carefully observed."

The versifying public had become aware that the Library of Congress had an Official Poet on its premises. Consultant meant consultable. In September, Bogan stated her policy to an applicant who wanted a sheaf of poems criticized. "Unfortunately my duties as Consultant in Poetry are fairly concentrated and do not allow me much time for analysis and criticism of individual manuscripts. I am sure that you derive much personal pleasure from writing verse—the kind of satisfaction which any artist feels." But she grew more charitable. A week later, when a man in Florida wanted to know what came after "The boy stood on the burning deck," she had the entire text of Felicia Hemans's "Casabianca" copied out for him. To a young aspirant, she wrote: "It is commendably ambitious for a young person of your age to wish to have her creative writing published. On the other hand, you should never pay to get your work into print; and you should view with suspicion any advertised offers concerned with printing poetry at your own expense. . . . The only feasible way to get your work printed is to send it out to magazines and newspapers, always with a stamped, self-addressed envelope for return."

The Division of Manuscripts consulted Bogan about an offer to sell more A. E. Housman material, from the poet's brother Laurence: a commonplace book and a collection of letters, written from 1922 through 1935, well after Housman had written *The Shropshire Lad.* "As I have gone over the matter in my mind," Bogan advised, "the figure of Laurence Housman appears. This brother of A. E.'s is, I think, a rather grasping character; and he is playing the Housman 'market,' as it were, for all it is worth. In the last analysis, I am convinced that it is better for the Library to spread its money over as large a field as possible, and not go in for merely showy items." Laurence Housman's offer wasn't taken up, ostensibly for lack of the funds.

On March 18, 1946, Bogan participated in a group reading in the Coolidge Auditorium by members of the Writers Club of the Library, under the title "This Is My America." All of the poems read had been published in the *Washington Post,* whose poetry editor was Kenton Kilmer. He and his wife Frances were the readers for most of the program. Among the three dozen poets whose work was included, only one name is readily recognizable—that of Oliver St. John Gogarty, no American.

Bogan read his "The Apple Tree." Had she sneaked that number in? Another event, on April 20, she may have found more diverting, even in a contrary sense: the appearance of W. Somerset Maugham at the Library to present the original manuscript of *Of Human Bondage* as a way of thanking America for its wartime hospitality, since 1940, and perhaps also a way of thanking the Library for making him a Fellow in Modern English Letters. Luther Evans, Maugham, and Howard Mumford Jones made speeches in the Coolidge Auditorium. Altogether, as Maugham remarked, the observance was "a great beano."

As Bogan's term drew near an end, the choice of the next Consultant became moot. Léonie Adams was the preference of most of the Fellows. In late June, Bogan wrote Tate: "A good deal of shilly-shallying seems to be going on . . . a certain weighing of various names . . . not only of names suggested by the Fellows, but of names suggested by 'others.' Does this mean that pressure-grouping has started; and that the Fellows' votes are no longer an absolute recommendation? Good God! I sincerely hope not; and I trust that my now-enemy, 'Creepy' Kilmer, is not agitating for one of *his* pets. . . . Tell Léonie of the intrigues. . . . She needs someone, for the first few months, with L of C background and knowledge." She observed soon afterward that the Library officials wanted a strong hand in the Consultantship the next year, because of the recording project. "After all, Allen Tate got the money!" In late July Tate told her he had written Evans suggesting "he add to our list the name of Karl Shapiro. . . . I am sure that Léonie would do this job, but alas, I suspect that Luther would like to have a man to consider. . . . Malcolm [Cowley], for the reasons that you know, is out of the question." Shapiro was the preference. Before leaving Washington, Bogan wrote Tate, "I'll recommend him, certainly."

In a valedictory letter to her friend William Maxwell: "Now that the time draws near that I shall leave (a bad translation from the Sanskrit, that last!) I am feeling rather warmly toward Washington, Georgetown, the L. of C. . . . The Library machinery still baffles me; but I have leaned over backwards to be cool and detached and cheerful and obliging. As a matter of fact, it has all been v., v. pleasant, and I have learned a lot; and the Library has learned a few things, too. Such as the fact that R. M. Rilke is a man, not a woman, and writes in German, not Italian." She remembered the shady side, too, writing her friend Morton Zabel: "It was a true exile, in many ways, in spite of the frequent week-ends. I could not move about freely at night, for example, because of my situation on the edge of a Depressed Area (no one will ever know how brave I was . . . lying in bed listening to the drunks of all shades cursing up and down the street and breaking bottles on the front piazza)."

July 1946. Eliot was in the United States on business. He came to Washington to see Pound, who was now confined at St. Elizabeths Hospital, and wrote Tate: "His conversation (or monologue) was so concentrated and slipped so quickly from one subject to another . . . that I can't remember most of it; but he wants me to try to meet William Carlos Williams in New York, which I should be glad to do. I am sure that Ezra ought to be removed to a private sanatorium as quickly as possible." The Library of Congress was not on his itinerary.

> Karl Shapiro has, at this writing (April, 1944), published a single book in the United States; but a second is due very soon; and we shall be better able to take his measure. *Person, Place and Thing* seems to me to be the most impressive first volume of verse to be published in the 1940's. It is full of "influences," but it has enough of Shapiro's own voice to place him among the best poets of his generation. If any other young poet has written better poems than "Necropolis" and "The Banjo" and half a dozen others, I have not seen them.—Tate, in *Sixty American Poets*.

Tate had virtually eulogized Shapiro when he cast a review of that "impressive first volume" as a "Letter to a Poet." "Your poetry moves me," he wrote, "because it has, for the first time since T. S. Eliot's arrival more than twenty-five years ago, that final honesty which is rare, unpleasant, and indispensable in a poet of our time." (Louise Bogan also reviewed *Person, Place and Thing* with distinct favor in *The New Yorker*—her article was "a lifesaver for us," Evalyn Shapiro recalled

long after.) The correspondence that sprang up was conducted on Sha-
piro's end through V-Mail letters: he was a company clerk in the Army
Medical Corps, stationed in Australia and New Guinea. His fiancée,
Evalyn Katz, who was working in New York City as a literary agent,
looked after his interests. In October 1943, she wrote Shapiro that Tate
and MacLeish were using their influence to have him placed in a more
congenial Army assignment. He hoped for the Office of Strategic Ser-
vices but to his disappointment went to duty at an Army hospital in
Missouri, in spring 1945. That year he received the Pulitzer Prize for
poetry and married. In summer 1946, he and his wife were living on
his Army mustering-out pay and a Guggenheim fellowship in a house
borrowed from Robert Coates, with a Model A Ford borrowed from
Conrad Aiken, at Gaylordsville, Connecticut, in what Shapiro called
"the *New Republic* magazine belt." He wrote Tate, "The fact is I am
looking for a job and have only the most elementary idea how to go
about it. If you come upon anyone in your travels who can put an
unemployed poet to work, I hope you will mention me. I want the kind
of job that has some connection with poetry and will allow me time to
write." Tate put in a word, and so did Warren: "He is a sensible, modest,
energetic person, and I am sure would most ably fulfill all the obliga-
tions of the position." Evans's offer of the Chair soon followed. The
stipend struck the Shapiros as munificent. They moved into an apart-
ment in Arlington, and on October 2 Shapiro wrote Tate, "The job is
just perfect; it is the only job I have ever been happy about or could
tolerate cheerfully for a year. . . . I noticed in the files that Léonie
Adams was practically appointed before I put my oar in. I hope she was
let down quietly. I feel rather sheepish about it."

Tate replied, "As to Léonie Adams, we all felt she had prior claim
because of age and distinction, but that a man might do this particular
job this year better than any woman that could be selected, and when
that consideration became decisive, you were obviously the right per-
son." It is difficult to understand what aspect of the Consultant's job that
year demanded masculine stamina, which the Librarian evidently stip-
ulated. Adams as Consultant demonstrated stamina beyond the most
macho expectations.

Years later, Shapiro recalled (in the third person) his impressions of the early days. "The poet's office was on the top floor in a great room that had been a lounge of some kind, and it faced the massive Capitol across the park, which made the poet's heart swell when he went out on the little balcony. . . . The big room was furnished with authentic 16th-century Italian Renaissance furniture and museum-quality rugs . . . loaned by the wife of the Attorney General of the United States . . . except for a common American anti-artistic desk with its six steel drawers and a typewriter sitting anachronistically on top." For his first meeting with the Librarian of Congress he dressed carefully-carelessly. "He imagined that the Librarian was a gentleman . . . in crumpled tailor-made clothes and a pongee shirt with a black stringy tie, black for the recently dead President." The door was open and he walked right in. "A stocky man in a blue suit got up in a kind of crouching position and held out his hand. 'Shapiro,' the Librarian of Congress said, 'we don't want any Communists or cocksuckers in this Library.' " (That brand of humor was vintage Evans, according to one who knew him.)

After interviewing about twenty applicants for the job of secretary, Shapiro picked the only one who knew literature—a Canadian who had served in the Women's Royal Naval Service, tall, military in bearing, a chain smoker. (She reminded Randall Jarrell of T. S. Eliot.) This was Phyllis Armstrong, a poet herself, who continued to manage the Poetry Consultant's office for twenty-four years: "one difficult poet after another, for which she deserved the Congressional Medal of Honor," Shapiro said, in retrospect.

To Shapiro's disappointment, he had to edit the *Quarterly Journal* for the first quarter, in the absence of its editor. "My own papers usually need heavy editing, and I am not the man for the work," he complained to Tate. But then he settled down to his main task, the albums. "He met the Living Anthology, poets he had never dreamed of being with." More hours of listening, more poets brought in to record, rights obtained for Harvard recordings, negotiations with publishers. Tate felt that Jarrell and Lowell should be included "but I should certainly not insist upon it." Jarrell replaced Wallace Stevens, who could not be persuaded to record. Robert P. Tristram Coffin was dropped in favor of Katherine Garrison Chapin ("Mrs. Biddle had been hurt, I think, when I showed her the list without her name"). MacLeish, who had not had time to make recordings, gave way to E. E. Cummings. The Librarian suggested to Shapiro that he go out to St. Elizabeths and get Pound to record some of the Cantos, but he felt uncomfortable about doing that. The Library never did record Ezra Pound.

Shapiro found time also to compile a bibliography of modern English and American prosody, a subject he was then absorbed in; the Library's resources encouraged him to be exhaustive. What he chiefly read that year, however, were esoteric and mystical books—the Kabala, the *Zohar,* theosophy, Jung, Ouspensky, Plotinus, and such. As he observed recently, "Not only was I going through a quasi-religious crisis; that literature was a gold mine of imagery. As for Jung, he was the only reputable psychologist who was a scholar of the mystical."

And there was the social facet of Washington literary life. "What he liked best was the brushing of elbows, the slight looks and exchanges of the poets who were great, who were held in awe by the world, even by the stuffy diplomats he had begun to meet . . . , who prided themselves on having one of these lions at their house. . . . He glanced from time to time into another room where sitting beside the fire T. S. Eliot was in close converse with St.-John Perse, actually talking about Eliot's translation of *Anabasis,* which the French poet had reservations about, Perse told the poet [Shapiro] the next day at the Library. But what he really cherished . . . was a moment when he was talking to the French poet and a woman appeared in the doorway . . . and the Frenchman's face lit up like a sunrise and he excused himself and went to her." That was, most likely, Dorothy Milburn Russell, whom Leger married in 1958.

Shapiro, already an admirer of Leger's *Anabasis* and *Eloges* (via the translators, Eliot and Louise Varèse), got to know him at the Library of Congress. "Perse had read some of my stuff, and he immediately remarked on the few prose poems I had published. For someone who was as marvelous a poet as he was to point me in the direction of this more complicated form that he had developed—that did it."

In March 1947, Evans asked Shapiro to stay on for another year. "If I were inventing a position for myself," Shapiro replied, "I could not improve on the job of Poetry Consultant . . . the duties, the freedom of policy, the zeal and intelligence of the staff, the facilities for work, and the surroundings all seem to me perfect." He declined, however, because he and his wife planned to make their home in England for a year or so and travel on the Continent. "I think a foreign atmosphere will give me the added clarity of perspective I need." But ordinary reality intervened. Shapiro cast about for an academic job. Paul Engle wanted him to teach creative writing at the University of Iowa but that didn't work out. "We were getting along very well until I started to quote Helena Blavatsky." Just as the term opened, he accepted a post in the Writing Department at the Johns Hopkins University.

Robert Lowell was the Librarian's choice to succeed Shapiro, over Adams, Eberhart, and Blackmur. On behalf of the Fellows, Tate broke the news to Lowell. The last Library event that may have engaged Shapiro during his term was, at midnight on July 25, the unsealing of Robert Todd Lincoln's collection of Abraham Lincoln's papers. Sandburg, orating and singing, was the star of the occasion.

May 23, 1947. Eliot gave a poetry reading (recorded, with his comments) at the National Gallery of Art, in Washington, to an audience that included Alexis Leger. He probably went to see Pound at St. Elizabeths, as he customarily did on his Washington visits.

August 19, 1947. Luther Evans invited Eliot, along with Auden and Conrad Aiken, to be Fellows in American Letters. Eliot accepted on October 31.

For Lowell the year 1947, his 30th, was a zenith of achievement, or at any rate of celebrity. He received the Pulitzer Prize in American Poetry, for *Lord Weary's Castle,* an award of $1,000 from the American Academy of Arts and Letters, and a Guggenheim fellowship of $2,500. He was invited to spend most of the summer at Yaddo, the writers' colony near Saratoga Springs. He was approached with offers to teach at the University of Iowa (in Paul Engle's courses) and the University of North Carolina. The magazine *Life* devoted a feature article to the phenomenal young poet, with illustrations that dwelt on his photogenic quality. (The latter provoked an eager inquiry from a film producer in Holly-

wood, wanting to know if Lowell could act.) He had accepted the Iowa
offer ($3,000 a year) when, in June, Tate sounded him out for the Chair
of Poetry ($5,000). Lowell withdrew his Iowa acceptance; Jean Stafford
was suing him for divorce and demanding alimony. He wired Tate, his
friend and mentor for ten years (though Tate had not included him in
Sixty American Poets): "Would you give the Library my official accept-
ance. Thanks for everything."

After Yaddo, Lowell arrived in Washington. Shapiro had drafted Lu-
ther Evans's letters describing the appointment, and the terms offered
Lowell were somewhat more explicit than those that had been offered
him. "It is understood that the more technical aspects of library science
do not fall in your sphere. We earnestly hope that you will find time to
continue with your own work. . . . The allocation of time will be up to
you." The incumbent's duties were to survey the existing poetry collec-
tions and determine their strengths and weaknesses, initiate recommen-
dations for additions, correspond with authors and collectors with a
view to gifts, answer reference questions, compile occasional bibliog-
raphies, and confer with scholars and poets. Also: the specific respon-
sibility, with the Fellows' advice, of the recording of poets and the
publishing of their recordings. He would have an excellent assistant, "a
trained reference librarian and secretary . . . familiar with the Library
as a whole and with the problems of the Poetry Chair in particular."
And, for this particular year, good news: his salary would be subject to
a 14 percent increase voted by Congress for government employees,
i.e., $700.

Fortunately, Shapiro was still near enough at hand for consultation.
As one of his first acts Lowell sent through a memorandum: "Mr. Sha-
piro and I are convinced that the list of poets to be recorded in the first
series of albums should be amended. As it stands, it represents neither
the best poetry in quality or popularity. It would be considered odd by
any critic. The inclusion of all six of the Fellows, in particular, will be
regarded . . . as favoritism." He continued to argue: "The selection of
poets is idiosyncratic. Four or five of the inclusions are absurd." He
would drop Chapin, Brinnin, Spencer, Engle, and Meredith ("a prom-
ising poet, but, as recorded, a poor reader") and substitute Frost ("I
would like to see a whole album . . . to match the Eliot album"),

Pound, Aiken, Sandburg, and Elizabeth Bishop. The preparation of the first series of recordings had gone too far, however, and as he wrote Tate, in his block-letter script, "The albums went through unchanged—arguing with Dr. Spivacke is enough to melt the Capitol." He went out to St. Elizabeths to see Pound and reported to Evans, "He doesn't want to be recorded while he is shut up, and wasn't sure that he was up to the strain, in any case. The talk went well, and he wants me to come back. He may change his mind about the recordings and he may not. I don't think he should be pressed." Lowell visited Pound often, sometimes taking poet friends with him—at various times Bishop, Jarrell, Berryman. (According to a member of the St. Elizabeths psychiatric staff, during Pound's confinement his other literary callers—relevant to the present discussion—included MacLeish, W. C. Williams, Cummings, Aiken, Tate, Spender, Wilder, Marianne Moore, Katherine Anne Porter, and James Dickey, who was surprised at Pound's "big hearty laugh, which reminded me of Santa Claus.")

Though Lowell had cousins in Washington, he preferred to live at the staid and prestigious Cosmos Club, whose members were only men. He got Evans and Tate to sponsor him for membership and was finally admitted "after mistaking one of the members for a waiter," he wrote Tate. "I think most of the waiters are Marshal Petain's uncles. . . . My quarters here remind me of Wormwood—no cats, . . . no 3-handed bridge, not much company in the evenings." The allusion to Oscar Wilde's confinement at Wormwood Scrubs echoed his own prison term, as a conscientious objector, at a federal detention center in Danbury, Connecticut, during the winter of 1943–44. A few weeks after Lowell became Consultant, Austine Cassini picked him up in her column, "These Charming People," in the local Hearst paper. "Lowell looks the part of a poet. . . . Dark-eyed, soulful-looking, esthetic and stuff. . . . He was sentenced to six months in a federal prison when he refused to go in the Army." A personnel official at the Library clipped the column and sent it to Evans with a note, "I'm concerned that normal personnel procedure didn't bring this out. This is the first time I've heard of this." Lowell's C.O. episode had, of course, been well publicized at the time. And the Library then had no formal procedure for "security clearance," though both Tate and Shapiro have spoken of taking a loyalty oath. In any event, Evans took no action. Some time later, an American Legion post in East St. Louis spotted a *Time* magazine item in a similar vein and, voicing disapproval of the appointment of any C.O. to a government position paid by taxpayers' money, urged its congressman "to cause the discharge immediately of Robert Lowell." When the matter reached Evans's desk, he replied to the congressman, "Although Mr. Lowell's position is not supported from appropriated funds, I know of no statute relating to employment of any character in the Federal Government which denies employment to American citizens because of their religious convictions."

Lowell got out numerous letters inviting poets to record or rerecord, though relatively few actually came to perform during the year—only Tate, Jarrell, Spender, Auden, Ransom, Berryman, Howard Baker. On Lowell's invitation, Williams came a second (and last) time, but as he could get away only on a Saturday (October 18), the recording was made in the NBC Studio in Washington. In November, aiming to wind up details of permissions and fees for the first series of albums, Lowell wrote to Eliot, as he did to each of the other poets, confirming the arrangement: a standard fee of $50 for each record, but a flat fee of $250 for the Eliot album, containing "The Waste Land" (three records), "Ash-Wednesday" (two and a half records), and some short poems (another half record). Concerned over the offer of a flat fee rather than a royalty, Eliot wrote to Tate, who explained that the recordings had been made primarily for the Library archives, with a view to inclusion later on in an album for sale to the general public on a nonprofit basis. Replying to Lowell, Eliot agreed to allow the Library to produce the recordings, but he was still unhappy about payment. "The only point on which I cannot see eye to eye with the Library . . . is the matter of a flat fee. On my recordings of the *Four Quartets* I receive the usual gramophone royalty from the H.M.V. Gramophone Company. I cannot see why I should accept any other kind of contract. . . . An outright payment of $250 is a very minor advantage. I do not really need this money now and my purpose in making contracts . . . on a royalty basis is to benefit eventually the heirs of my small estate. . . . It is not as if I had written a great many poems and better ones, in which case I could afford to release such a small number and would gladly do so." The negotiations had become tricky, and Evans took over. His solution, which Eliot accepted, was to limit the first issue to 500 copies of the album, for a first payment of $250, and to pay a further $250 for each additional 500 albums. Evans affirmed, furthermore, that "no part of the edition will be released for sale through the ordinary trade channels." As of 1986, 10,600 copies of the Eliot readings (now on LP and cassette) had been issued, earning for the poet and his estate nearly $2,500. The Eliot recording has sold more than any other in the Library's "Twentieth-Century Poetry in English" series, which now comprises more than thirty long-playing records.

Lowell spent Christmas with the Randall Jarrells and the Peter Taylors in Greensboro, then gave some poetry readings at Harvard and at Wellesley. Back at the Library, he worked sporadically on a bibliography, *British Poets of the Twentieth Century,* planned as a companion piece to Tate's *Sixty American Poets.* He never finished it, and it seems to have perished. He participated in arrangements to bring two senior poets to read their poems in the Coolidge Auditorium, Frost on March 17 and Ransom on April 12. Both events were recorded, and Lowell had the poets also read at considerable length in the laboratory, for the continued enrichment of the archives. It was the Bollingen Prize in Poetry, however, that began to crowd the Consultant's time during spring of 1948.

Tate, according to literary legend, had conceived the idea of an award for American poetry. Phyllis Armstrong's notes of the Fellows' meeting on January 23, 1948, however, record that Willard Thorp introduced the proposal of an annual award, and the Fellows designated Auden and Tate as a committee to approach the Bollingen Foundation. It was Tate who, with the blessing of the Fellows and the Librarian, spoke to Huntington Cairns, who was willing to propose to the Bollingen Foundation a donation of funds for a prize. The Bollingen people, encouraged by Cairns, had already demonstrated a cordiality toward poetry, not only by the grants for the Library's recordings, but later in 1946 by a contribution to the Modern Poetry Association, of Chicago, to support the publication of the journal *Poetry.* (The latter subsidy continued for eight years and provided $82,500 for the journal.) The Foundation's trustees voted an allocation of $10,000 for ten years of awards. When the creation of the prize was first in view, Tate proposed naming it the Mary Conover Mellon Prize, in memory of Paul Mellon's wife, who had died suddenly on October 11, 1946, less than a year after she and her husband had established the Foundation. Mellon demurred (his wife, though she had approved a Bollingen fellowship for Alexis Leger, had been interested less in poetry than in Jungian psychology), and somewhat reluctantly, as his Foundation had nothing to do with the bestowing of the award, he consented to Evans's request that the prize be named in honor of the Foundation itself. (The Foundation's name had been Mary Mellon's oblique way of honoring C. G. Jung, who had a country retreat near a Swiss village called Bollingen.) That same spring, once again via Cairns, the Foundation supported an international symposium on literary criticism at Johns Hopkins University; the lecturers included Ransom, Tate, and Blackmur.

On March 4, 1948, a Library of Congress press release announced the Bollingen Prize in Poetry. Carrying a purse of $1,000, the prize would be awarded each February for the best book of verse by an American author published during the preceding calendar year. The jury of selection would be composed of the Fellows in American Letters of the Library of Congress. The prize poet had to be a United States citizen or, if a citizen of another country, had to be born in the United States, and couldn't have been a Fellow in American Letters during the preceding two years.

It fell to the Consultant in Poetry to deal with the inquiries that followed on the news of the prize. Lowell, in consultation with Tate and the Library hierarchy, ran a form letter of response through several drafts, and during the rest of his tenure he was busy signing and dispatching copies of the approved version. During the spring the Fellows met and, with a minimum of contention, agreed on nominees for the Chair during the following two one-year terms. The Librarian was content to invite Léonie Adams for the 1948–49 term and William Carlos Williams for 1949–50. Williams, who had been stricken with the first of a series of heart attacks, had to postpone serving, but Adams was happy to have her appointment. In August, Lowell went to Maine to escape the Washington weather, and he visited Elizabeth Bishop for part of the month. He returned to Washington in time to welcome Adams, who wrote Tate, "Robert Lowell took a lot of trouble about me on my arrival. I like him very much." Lowell went on to Yaddo, where he wrote to the Tates, "I liked Washington, but what a delight to be done with it; and back to work. With what I've saved from the Library and Yaddo and my Guggenheim, I can easily last two years before I have to think of teaching."

❀

On June 15, 1948, James Laughlin's publishing house, New Directions, brought out William Carlos Williams's *Paterson II*. (Lowell, in *The Nation:* "It is a book in which the best readers, as well as the simple reader, are likely to find everything.") On July 30, New Directions brought out Pound's *The Pisan Cantos*. (Bogan, in *The New Yorker:* "I cannot think of any other record by an artist or a man of letters, in or out of prison, so filled with a combination of sharp day-to-day observation, erudition, and humorous insight." The publisher's press release quoted appreciations by Aiken, Eberhart, Eliot, Lowell, Ransom, Schwartz, Spender, and Tate.) The British edition, published by Faber and Faber, Eliot's firm, didn't appear until a year later, with a number of omissions and expurgations.

❀

While MacLeish, in March 1944, was negotiating with both Robert Penn Warren and Marianne Moore for the Consultantship, Tate had also sounded out Léonie Adams, who was indeed interested. The nod went to Warren, of course; he did invite Adams to record, but she declined because she couldn't afford the trip to Washington. Tate's regard for her work is notable: "Miss Adams' last volume was published in 1929, but even if she never issues another book her reputation is secure as one of the best American poets. More than any one else today she continues at the highest level the great lyrical tradition of the English romantics, with whom, in their own time, she would have held her own" (*Sixty American Poets*).

In the deliberations during the spring of 1946, both Tate and Bogan felt that Adams was a sure bet. Bogan had valued her work and her friendship since the 1920s, even through Adams's turn to radical politics in the 1930s. But David Mearns, who was Acting Librarian while Evans was attending the Pan American Copyright Convention in July, cast his usual sardonic eye on the proceedings. Reporting to Evans on the snag in selecting "an incumbent (or recumbent) of the Chair," he observed that "Miss Bogan was under the impression that the selection was a prerogative of the Fellows, with the Librarian acting as ratifier only. I corrected that assumption . . . and she perfectly understands now that the Fellows are not an independent establishment." Observing that the principal duty of the next Consultant would be the production of the albums, he thought that "we should exchange the over-stuffed Morris chair for a straight-back, on the assumption that its occupant should not relax. . . . I am troubled by the allusions of the Fellows to Miss Adams—'poor Léonie,' they call her, and they agree 'that a year in the Library may be just the thing' to make her psychologically adjusted once again." As we have seen, the appointment went to Shapiro.

Two years later, when Adams was appointed for the 1948–49 term, the record shows no concern about her stability. After her grueling year was over, Evans thanked her for serving "under difficult and sometimes painful surroundings"; he called her work for the recording project "a great achievement," and her "conduct of the trying business connected with the Bollingen award magnificent and altogether admirable." Indeed, the demands of the recordings would have made up a full agenda for the Consultant even without the exertions and anxieties brought on by the Bollingen Prize. For the first series, Adams had to oversee the preparation of the leaflet accompanying each poet's work, and here a curious problem arose. Occasionally a reader departed from the published text of a poem. The decision: to follow the recorded words, though this obliged the Consultant to monitor the sound vis-à-vis the text in the most diligent manner. Settling questions of copyright with over-finicky publishers was another vexation that Adams coped with. The albums were ready for the public in January 1949. Each one, containing five unbreakable vinylite records, was priced at $8.25; single records, $1.50; available only at the Library of Congress. Each poet was given a copy of his or her own record. (Besides Eliot, the poets, album by album, were Chapin, Van Doren, Auden, Eberhart, and Bo-

gan; Engle, Moore, Tate, Fletcher, and Brinnin; W. C. Williams, War-
ren, Cummings, Jeffers, and Spencer; Ransom, Meredith, Winters,
Jarrell, and Shapiro.)

The press that gradually ensued was in the main gratifying. For ex-
ample, William Slocum in *Furioso:* "The historical and critical value of
these recordings is alone considerable. Critics of the future will not
have to conjecture . . . how the author of our time's 'world-weary mas-
terpiece' meant 'The Fire Sermon' to be read. And the pleasure to be
derived from an acquaintance with a poet's personality, and from the
skill of his reading, is scarcely incidental. . . . Mr. Eliot's serious crit-
ics and admirers . . . will welcome the opportunity of reviewing *The
Waste Land* in the light of the interpretation he offers here. Interpreta-
tion apart, it is a brilliant performance, very much to be prized for its
own sake." Obviously, Eliot's recordings got the spotlight.

During January of 1949, Léonie Adams participated in negotiations
with Gertrude Clarke Whittall that led to the Library's acquiring, by
means of funds given by Mrs. Whittall, the Louis Ledoux Collection
of Edwin Arlington Robinson manuscripts, comprising some twenty
autograph items, "perhaps the finest collection of original Robinson
materials in any American library," as Evans observed when he thanked
Mrs. Whittall. The poet was her favorite, and coincident with her ben-
efaction she suggested that the Library arrange a public reading of Rob-
inson's work, possibly by Joseph Auslander (who, she told Evans, was
one of the best readers of poetry she had ever heard). Mrs. Whittall was
known to prefer hearing poetry read by an actor or a master of elocution
rather than by the poet himself. Nonetheless, when Adams gave a read-
ing from her poems in the Coolidge Auditorium on January 31, Mrs.
Whittall was in the audience despite a snowstorm so remarkable that
Verner Clapp, the Acting Librarian at the time, mentioned it when he
introduced the poet. Clapp observed that "this evening belongs to the
tradition, established eight years ago," when Jeffers, Frost, Sandburg,
and Benét appeared on the same platform. Adams was in fact inaugu-
rating a new tradition: Evans had made it a stipulation that "a reading
early in his tenure will be expected of each consultant." Mrs. Whittall
could have been only gratified by the essay that Adams subsequently

wrote for the *Quarterly Journal,* subjecting the Ledoux Collection to critical analysis and citing Yvor Winters's and Allen Tate's ranking of Robinson with the greatest English poets of the nineteenth century.

✳

The award of the Bollingen Prize in Poetry to Pound gave sudden and uninvited celebrity to the Bollingen Foundation, the Library of Congress, and its Fellows in American Letters, and intensive employment to the Consultant in Poetry. Early in her term Adams, on Lowell's advice, compiled lists of eligible publications. According to her "statement of procedure of the jury," before the Fellows' meeting she received nine letters of nomination, which named, in all, fifteen books of verse. There is no record of all of these, but Adams stated that the nominations "foreshadowed the final vote, both as to first and second place choices."

The crucial meetings, over two days, preceded a lecture, on November 19 in the Coolidge Auditorium, by T. S. Eliot, entitled "From Poe to Valéry." Eliot had come to Princeton in October to fill an appointment at the Institute for Advanced Study, where he spent his time chiefly working on a new verse play, *The Cocktail Party.* Early in November he had been chosen as recipient of the Nobel Prize in Literature. A sense of the excitement attending Eliot's presence at the Library of Congress, for his first meeting of the Fellows, is conveyed in a letter of Louise Bogan's to Morton Zabel: "I sat beside the Great Man at lunch; and I looked into his Golden Eye! How beautiful is the combination of physical beauty (even in slight decay), high qualities of mind and heart, and *perfect humility.* . . . That evening, the lecture on E. A. Poe scandalized quite a few Southern diehards. . . . Eliot had sat in on all our Fellows' Meetings: v. quiet, shy, reserved. He smokes incessantly, and at one point took time off to *sharpen a pencil* (with a pen-knife, in his lap). He looks quite frail, really. . . ." Bogan went on, "Léonie, by the way, conducted the meeting with great charm and acumen and poise. She is being visibly benefited by Washington. What a good idea to send her!"

(William Carlos Williams had come to Washington just then, possibly to talk with Evans about the Consultantship, having notified the Librarian, in late October, that he had to decline because his health would not permit it. Evans replied that he hoped Williams's decision might be construed as a postponement rather than a renunciation. In December, Adams wrote Williams, "It is their [the Fellows'] unanimous hope that you will feel able to accept the [Consultant's] post for 1950–51 as it is their unanimous wish that you be invited to do so at the appropriate time. Everyone was delighted that you could be present for the Eliot lecture and some of the get-to-gethers of the group." Robert Penn Warren recalled, in a recent conversation, the encounter of Williams and Eliot at such a gathering, when Eliot, ignoring or unaware of Williams's animosity toward him, greeted him warmly and shook his hand. Afterwards, Williams murmured to Warren, with evident emotion, "Did you see that? He took my hand! Yes sir, he took my hand!")

At their first meeting, the Fellows were addressed in Evans's absence by the Acting Librarian of Congress, Verner Clapp, to the following effect: They were not, in awarding the prize, "to be deflected by political considerations or other questions of expediency from a decision rendered strictly in terms of literary merit." They set up a committee— Lowell and Shapiro, with the Consultant—to take care of the procedure of the vote, inasmuch as there would not be another meeting before February 1949, when the prize had to be announced; furthermore, other eligible books might be published before the end of the year. The recording project was discussed at exhausting length. Eliot hoped the records could be distributed in England. And it was resolved that records of Pound be purchased for the Library. The day wound up with cocktails at the Institute for Contemporary Arts.

The second day: the nominations for the prize were reduced by agreement to four: Pound, for the *Pisan Cantos;* Williams, for *Paterson II;* Jarrell, for *Losses;* and Muriel Rukeyser, for *The Green Wave.* The ballot: eight votes for Pound, two for Williams, two abstentions, two absences. Eliot questioned whether the award would bring Pound into an undesirable publicity which might be exploited by the wrong elements. It was decided that the special committee should go into the whole question. After nominating a slate of possibilities for the next year's Chair (Moore, Bishop, Jarrell, Delmore Schwartz, and Richard Eberhart) and recommending new Fellows (MacLeish and Williams), the Fellows adjourned to prepare themselves for "From Poe to Valéry," followed by supper at Dumbarton Oaks with Mrs. Robert Woods Bliss.

Soon afterward, Lowell reported to Adams a conversation he had had with Pound's lawyer, Julien Cornell, "who believed that the prize would not, on the whole, endanger Pound's situation and would be psychologically helpful." Asking for more information, Adams wrote Cornell (in Paris), who replied that he had deduced from discussion with Dr. Winfred Overholser, the superintendent of St. Elizabeths, that the award of the prize and the public interest it would prompt would have no positive effect on Pound's situation at the hospital; and "there appears to be no prospect for his release." As for Pound's welfare, Cornell went on, he believed the prize would not jeopardize his legal or personal position, "and might serve to support his wavering ego. . . . Those who are imprisoned always feel forgotten and isolated."

✳

In the midst of the Pound embroglio, the imperatives of succession had still to be satisfied. In late December, Evans offered appointments as Fellows in American Letters to MacLeish and Williams. They accepted but did not participate in the Bollingen Prize ballot. The 1949–50 Consultantship had still to be filled, and in January Evans offered it to Marianne Moore. She declined by return mail: "I cannot, Mr. Evans, in conscience, digress from the translation of La Fontaine's fables which I am under obligation to complete by 1950–1951. . . . I dare not be tempted to digress even partially." Then Evans asked Léonie Adams to stay for a second year. It was after she said no, because of other commitments, that he offered the Chair to Elizabeth Bishop.

✳

In late January, after "wrestling with his soul," Shapiro switched his vote from Pound to Williams. He informed the Librarian that he believed that Pound's "moral and political philosophy ultimately vitiated the *Cantos* and lowered the literary quality of the work." At one point, he recommended that the first award be made for 1949 rather than 1948, and the "highly compromising business of Pound be forgotten." During the weeks preceding the final ballot and public announcement, strongly charged letters passed between Shapiro and Tate, the one defending his change of vote and analyzing the climate of the Fellows' meeting, the other first seeking to turn Shapiro's vote back to Pound and then, after seeing a letter Shapiro was sending to the *Partisan Review*, taking a more severe tone. "I fear it is very difficult for us to communicate on this question. . . . I am not pro-Pound: I think that Pound is an old fool. I simply don't think that your point of view is sufficiently searching. I voted for the *Pisan Cantos* because it was the best book available, and I deeply regret that it was the work of Ezra Pound. If my vote had any political implications it was a vote against Fascism, or any form of Statism, and anti-Semitism—the very things that congenitally immature old man thought he was for. . . . These public statements of yours are inconsistent with the views expressed in [an earlier letter]. Shall I accuse you of dishonesty? No, I simply observe that you are in great distress, and the result is confusion." The friendship was put at serious risk. It survived, though never again as warm.

The profuse and often confusing convolutum of letters among the Fellows during the Bollingen Prize crisis, centering principally on Tate, is deserving of literary scrutiny even forty years later. The documentation to be found in the Library archives is not altogether clear. An undated memorandum, on yellow lined paper, apparently in the hand of a Library official who followed the case, Robert Gooch, lists a tally of votes: seven for Pound (Adams, Lowell, Bogan, Tate, Eliot, Spencer, and Auden), four for Williams (Shapiro, Aiken, Chapin, and Thorp), and three not voting or absent (Warren, Green, and Porter). Both Warren and Thorp, when consulted recently, could recall voting only for Pound.

Katherine Garrison Chapin, in any case, voted consistently for Williams. Her husband, Francis Biddle, the Attorney General, was opposed to the award, Adams wrote Tate; he believed that "its effects would be most unfortunate." Mrs. Biddle had told her that "the Justice Department was bothered by Pound's becoming Exhibit A, visited by fashionable people." (Francis Biddle, in a memoir some years later: "She felt that it was unwise for the Library . . . to single out a traitor for recognition; and that the traitor could not be separated from the poet—his anti-democratic, anti-Semitic fulminations ran through his whole work. She believed, too, that such a choice would do incalculable harm to the Fellows.")

In January, Adams reported as chairman of the committee, "no new titles had been nominated for the prize, nor had the two Fellows abstaining from the ballot, the two not present at the meeting, nor any Fellow wishing to revise his vote, signified a desire to cast or revise a ballot." She reported also that Evans, in a conference with the committee, said he believed the Fellows "would be correct in exercising the competence in literary judgment for which they had been appointed. He supposed from the nature of the reviews . . . that the award on the whole would have critical support and the support of the intelligentsia. . . . He himself felt no alarm concerning adverse reaction although some was to be foreseen." While Francis Biddle's strong recommendation (to his wife) against the award was not mentioned in Adams's report, other documentation shows that another poll of the Fellows was decided upon "in the light of Biddle's statement."

A final ballot was cast by mail in February (as the 1948 prize would lapse on February 28): ten first places for Pound, two for Williams, one abstention (Paul Green's)—and the vote of Theodore Spencer, who had died a few weeks before, was taken to stand as a first place for Pound, as it was he who had placed the *Pisan Cantos* in nomination back in November.

In announcing the decision, the special committee asked Tate to cooperate with them in drafting a statement that was attached to the Library's press release, on February 20: "The Fellows are aware that objections may be made to awarding a prize to a man situated as is Mr. Pound. In their view, however, the possibility of such objection did not alter the responsibility assumed by the Jury of Selection. This was to make a choice for the award among the eligible books, provided any one merited such recognition, according to the stated terms of the Bollingen Prize. To permit other considerations than that of poetic achievement to sway the decision would destroy the significance of the award and would in principle deny the validity of that objective perception of value on which any civilized society must rest."

The story was broken on Saturday night, the nineteenth, by Charles Collingwood in his radio news broadcast. The Sunday *New York Times* headline was characteristic of the press reaction: "Pound, in Mental Clinic, Wins Prize for Poetry Penned in Treason Cell." As Evans later observed, "The award possessed that bizarre quality that makes news. Along with excited reports, indignant editorials appeared in the press." An editorial in the *New York Herald Tribune,* however, stated: "This emphasis on an objective criterion of beauty and excellence, akin to belief in an objective truth, is fundamental to a free and rational society. In maintaining it the judges acted in the only way that is open to men who are sensitive to a later verdict of history." In the same paper, Louis Untermeyer called the *Pisan Cantos* "a ragbag and tail end of Pound at his worst. It shows a very disordered mind, one affected by the seeds of Fascism," and Robert Hillyer thought the award "regrettable" for aesthetic rather than political reasons. "I never saw anything to admire, not one line, in Pound." William Barrett, in the *Partisan Review,* declared that the content was Fascist and anti-Semitic. A columnist in the *Daily Worker* discovered a cabal of the United States Government, "the anti-Semites Eliot and Pound," the "giant Mellon industrial and financial interests," and the Liberty League. Dwight Macdonald, in *Politics,* praised the award for its freedom from prejudice and called it "the brightest political act in a dark period." Hillyer was heard from again in a letter to the *Herald Tribune:* "The protests must not be allowed to die away. The Committee has defied the decencies of the American tradition. Let us find out more about these people."

Robert Frost, in a memorandum to his secretary Kay Morrison soon after the award was announced, called it "an unendurable outrage" and Pound "possibly crazy but more likely criminal." He went on, "In the list of names I saw at once the Chapin lady at the head . . . as Mrs. Francis Biddle the wife of the former Attorney General and the explanation of why Ezra had been protected by the New Deal from being tried for treason like poor friendless Axis Sally. . . . I suppose Louise Bogan wrote the manifesto of the wild party. Well if her logic carries through it will say that we should admire Ezra for being a great poet in spite of his being a great traitor, so we must condemn him for [being] a great traitor in spite of his being a great poet."

Samples from the Library's mail: "Your action is the same as the freeing of Ilsa Koch . . ."; "I view with nothing short of horror . . .";

"vile, antisocial, anti-human . . . permeated with a gutter ideology
. . ."; "Why do we continue to have such people as Whittier [sic]
Chambers and the present Librarian of Congress in tax-paid Govern-
ment positions?" (from a Georgia superintendent of schools); "We
strongly urge you to rescind . . . the most serious disgrace to American
poetry" (from the Contemporary Writers League).

Huntington Cairns, in his journal, described one of his visits to St.
Elizabeths. "I saw Pound for an hour on Saturday, Feb. 19th. The di-
rector of the hospital had informed him that he had won the Bollingen
Prize, and he was obviously excited by the news. He had prepared a
statement for the Press: 'No comment from the Bug House,' but he had
decided not to give it out. He referred to the Prize as 'Bollingen's bid
for immortality.' " Pound refused to see reporters. The *Washington Post*
sent in a list of questions, and Pound merely wrote in the margin, "I
have not betrayed anyone. Inaccurate statements in press very tiring."
Walter Winchell quoted Pound's comment on the same occasion: "De-
mocracy is more stupid than ever I said it was." Tate, incensed, asked
Pound's wife to check on that. "Total lie" was Pound's answer. He
called Winchell a "Jewish bedbug."

Only on March 20, the Soviet Overseas Service, in English, got
around to broadcasting the news of the prize. After remarking on
"[Pound's] senseless, decadent verses which tickle the ears of an insig-
nificant clique of aesthetes and literary snobs in Boston and Philadel-
phia [and] set the style in the salons of the bored and fat U.S.
millionaires and of the admirers of modernism and symbolism," the
S.O.S. stated that "the court found him guilty of betraying his country.
But at this point something happened which is very much part and
parcel of U.S. court practice. . . . Instead of prison, the traitor, with
the help of his friends, landed in a comfortable hospital for nervous
disorders. . . . One is prompted to ask how low and miserable the de-
pravity of modern bourgeois poetry in the U.S. is, if even the insane
versified ravings of a confessed madman could win a literary prize."

Shortly after that, Shapiro had a mysterious visitor at his office at the
Johns Hopkins University. (He reported the episode to Adams, for the
file on the prize.) A man had telephoned him from New York, asking
to see him and discuss his reasons for voting against Pound. Shapiro

was curious and gave him an appointment; he asked his chairman, El-
liott Coleman, to be present during the interview. Shapiro recalled the
visit some thirty years later. "His name was A. D. Parelhoff, and he
looked like a caricature of a Red—slouch hat pulled down over one eye
and chewing a cigar, and he kept his hat on. He asked me in a low voice
if Coleman was 'all right,' which put me on my guard. He showed me
papers purporting to prove that Jung was a Nazi, explaining the name
Bollingen, and suggesting that the donors of the prize were political
sympathizers of Jung. He wanted to enlist me to attack them and the
'political principles' which he believed lay behind the Foundation."
Shapiro wrote Adams, "The resemblance between [Parelhoff's] conver-
sation and Hillyer's first article leaves no doubt in my mind that Hillyer
accepted his facts from Parelhoff without making any attempt to verify
or judge them."

✳

For a time, controversy over the prize subsided. It was suddenly revived
when the *Saturday Review of Literature,* in its issues of June 11 and
18, published two long articles by Robert Hillyer—"Treason's Strange
Fruit" and "Poetry's New Priesthood." Hillyer, earlier a professor at
Harvard (his students Howard Nemerov and Robert Fitzgerald remem-
bered him as a gifted teacher), won the Pulitzer Prize for poetry in
1934, and in 1939 was president of the Poetry Society of America.
Untermeyer had described his verse as traditional, "uncompromisingly
classical," "delicate to the point of elegance," possessing "a high seri-
ousness." Tate had not included him in his *Sixty American Poets.* Hill-
yer was regarded by many of his literary peers as an isolated figure who
had carried on a long critical campaign against Eliot and Auden, whom
he regarded as his poetic rivals.

During the late spring, Evans and Adams had had letters from Hillyer
and from Harrison Smith, the editor of the *Review,* putting questions
about the award. Hillyer's were marked by a threatening tone, with
insulting references to conspiracy and negligence. The F.B.I. had been
alerted, he said; and an article would be published. Replies from the
Library were courteous. In May, Smith sent proofs of the articles to
several writers, including MacLeish, for comment. MacLeish's re-

sponse, though invited, was not published by the *Review*. His perora-
tion: "I cannot understand how a responsible publisher can offer his
pages to personal aspersions as little supported by evidence as those
Mr. Hillyer has committed to paper. In sending me the proof, you wrote
me, Mr. Hillyer's articles might at least 'clear the air.' The air, particu-
larly the high air of poetry, is not cleared by personal affront." Norman
Cousins, the publisher, told MacLeish that as the result of his criticisms
the articles had been much modified, but MacLeish felt that his criti-
cism applied as pertinently to the second version as to the first. Evi-
dence is available of at least one emendation that was made in the
proofs: Hillyer's reference to the late Theodore Spencer as Eliot's
"agent and operative" was deleted. MacLeish sent the proofs on to
Evans, with a covering letter that contained the following paragraph:

"My attitude on the whole thing is that the choice of that particular
book . . . under the conditions was not only misguided but damn close
to irresponsible and that it put you as Librarian in a position the Fellows
had no right to put you in unless the book in question was clearly *The*
book for the award—that they had no choice. And it wan't [sic]. On
that point my mouth is closed by the fact that ACTFIVE was published
in the year in question. I will content myself by saying that it is pretty
obvious that there were other books available which have a good chance
of surviving when the current critical fashions are forgotten. There was,
in other words, no necessity for doing anything as foolish and footling.
But beyond that—when it comes to accusing Eliot and Ted Spencer and
a dozen of the best writers in America of fraud or worse I get up on my
hind legs and protest. . . ."

In his two articles, Hillyer declared that the *Cantos* are "the vehicle
of contempt for America, [of] Fascism, anti-Semitism, and . . . ruth-
less mockery of our Christian war dead." He implied that the award was
part of a conspiracy against American ways of life and literature, and
that the conspirators included T. S. Eliot, Paul Mellon, Jung, the Bol-
lingen Foundation, Pantheon Books, most of the Fellows in American
Letters, admirers of Eliot and Pound, the New Criticism, and various
literary quarterlies. Their common aim, he argued, was to seize power
in the literary world and undertake "the mystical and cultural prepara-
tion for a new authoritarianism. . . . In a spiritual morass where lan-

guage, ethics, literature, and personal courage melt into something obscure and formless, a guided impulse has stirred the amorphous haze into something approaching form, something shaped out of stagnant art by groping Fascism." The editorial board of the *Saturday Review* associated itself with Hillyer's charges, though shortly after the *Review* published the first of several corrections: the Bollingen Foundation had influenced neither the composition of the Fellows nor the determination of the award.

Luther Evans stated the Library's position in a letter of June 14 to the editor of the *Saturday Review,* which was published in the issue for July 2. The charge against the Fellows "of being politically motivated members of a clique or a particular esthetic group, or of being under the domination of any individual . . . is very damaging to the Fellows and to the Library of Congress, since it amounts to a charge that the Fellows have not acted . . . as public servants, but rather that they have abused the authority entrusted to them for evil ends. I think evidence should be produced, rather than pure supposition, to sustain such an insinuation. You and Mr. Hillyer are under a public duty to produce the evidence.

"I personally regard the choice of 'The Pisan Cantos' for the Bollingen prize as an unfortunate choice. . . . I would be engaging in an improper interference with free scholarship if I were to substitute my own decision . . . for the decision of the Fellows. . . . I would have been striking a blow against the cause of liberty by overriding scholarly judgment, and I do not feel that the blow for unrighteousness which the award may represent, is nearly as grave. . . .

"I am deeply disturbed by one point of view which you and Mr. Hillyer seem to share, and that is that poetic quality must somehow pass a political test. In my many years of study and teaching in the field of political science I came to regard a political test for art and poetry as a sign of a dictatorial, illiberal, undemocratic approach to matters of the mind."

Tate wrote Evans, "It is a statesmanlike document, and I am personally proud that one of our Government officials, in this disorderly time, was capable of the calm appeal to principle which animates the letter.

"We have got to face the fact that much of Hillyer's smear cannot be dealt with. We cannot in detail show the low quality of his critical judgments, and we cannot *prove* publicly that he is motivated by personal spite. It is a plain fact that not one member of the group of Fellows or a single one of the 'new critics' has ever noticed Hillyer's work, even to denigrate it. He has hated Eliot for thirty years. . . . To combat this sort of thing is to combat a fog."

Adams sent Eliot, in London, the Hillyer articles and the Evans letter. Eliot found the latter admirable. With regard to the former: "I think that I am the last person who ought to throw himself into the fray at this moment, inasmuch as I am almost the principal object of attack. I should like to point out that, far from being a 'disciple of Jung', I do not think I have ever read anything by that author. . . . This is not an important enough point to raise by itself; though it does cast some doubt on Mr. Hillyer's conscientiousness in verifying his assertions. . . . The idea of proposing Pound for the prize did not originate with me; there was no question of my trying to influence other Fellows, nor did I do so. In fact, as the one non-resident and non-citizen Fellow, I do not consider that it is my place to take such initiative or to exert such pressure." Apparently Adams had suggested that Eliot make a public statement. His reply continued:

> All I have to say in justification of my casting my own vote in favour of "The Pisan Cantos", is that I was convinced that this was the best volume under consideration. . . . I am convinced also that this was the conviction of the other Fellows; I have no reason to believe that any one of the Fellows has the least sympathy with fascism; I am sure that not one of us does not deplore Pound's way of referring to Jews. There are, I have become aware, people who *wish* to believe that I am myself an antisemite; and I am afraid that it is hopeless to try to convince such people that I am not. I have sometimes wanted to point out that I myself am a Christian and an Englishman, and that some of Pound's remarks about Christianity and about England have been very offensive to me. But this is not the occasion for pointing out in public how antithetical to Pound's philosophy my own is.

TWO: 1943 TO 1950

On June 24, Congressman Jacob K. Javits, of the 21st District, New York, wrote Evans: "After having read the editorial 'Treason's Strange Fruit' . . . I am particularly concerned about the awarding of the Bollingen–Library of Congress Award of $1,000 to Ezra Pound. I would very much appreciate your advising me how the Fellows who make this award were chosen, who they are and the basis of their selection." The information was duly supplied. (Cousins had put Javits in touch with the situation.) On July 19, another congressman, James T. Patterson, of Connecticut, addressed the House regarding the award ("Should we encourage the activities in literature of moral lepers?") and inserted into the *Congressional Record* the Hillyer articles, Evans's letter, and the *Saturday Review*'s reply. On the twenty-first, Javits called for an investigation ("Must we not be equally diligent to investigate the infiltration of Fascist ideas especially in so august an institution as the Library of Congress?"), and the matter came before the Congressional Joint Committee on the Library of Congress, whose chairman was Senator Theodore F. Green, of Rhode Island. What transpired was not an investigation but a resolution, on August 19, to the effect that the Library should abstain from giving prizes or making awards. ("I think it is a bad policy for the government to give prizes and awards, especially in matters of taste," the Senator told the press.) Evans immediately announced compliance. The awards that the Library discontinued, besides the Bollingen Prize, were the Elizabeth Sprague Coolidge Medal for "eminent services to chamber music" and three prizes endowed by Lessing Rosenwald in connection with an annual national exhibition of prints.

When Evans had learned that the Joint Committee was taking up the matter of the Bollingen Prize, he suggested the framing of a statement from the Fellows' point of view, for the committee's use. The task was taken in hand by the special committee that had dealt with the ballot: Adams as chairman (and the chief author), with Shapiro, Bogan, and Thorp—the last two in place of Lowell, who since the spring had been a patient in a mental hospital near Boston. On August 11, the Library issued as a press release the "Statement of the Committee of the Fellows of the Library of Congress in American Letters in Reply to Published

Criticisms of the Bollingen Prize in Poetry." Evans described it in his *Annual Report, 1949:* ". . . long and detailed, occupying nearly fifteen single-spaced pages of text. It was intended 'to examine and expose the means of insinuation' by which 'Mr. Javits and others may have been misled.' It specifically and categorically denied the allegations which had been lodged against them. It adduced facts to support their denials. But, perhaps because of its length, the press contented itself with reporting little more than the fact of disavowal. The statement was not reprinted in the *Saturday Review of Literature* to which copies were sent by special delivery as soon as they were issued." It was indeed a notably comprehensive and eloquent refutation. One critic called it a latter-day *Areopagitica*. It knocked down the Hillyer case under three rubrics: "Attempt to Link the Bollingen Foundation with Jung's Alleged Nazism," "Eliot's Alleged Fascism and His Supposed Influence on the Jury," and "The Award Itself as an Alleged Fascist Action." The Library mailed a thousand copies of the statement but, as Evans observed, only brief quotations were picked up. A group of the Fellows urged that it be reissued; the librarians declined; enough had been done. In October, the statement was published as the chief content of a 72-page pamphlet, *The Case Against the "Saturday Review of Literature,"* by *Poetry* magazine, with the addition of articles, editorials, and letters by various writers—Tate, MacLeish, Malcolm Cowley (a long article reprinted from the New Republic, dissecting the case), Meredith, Mark Van Doren, Hayden Carruth, and others. (See Appendix 1.)

Several Fellows were discountenanced because Evans had not communicated with them directly regarding the summary end of the Bollingen Prize. Without that responsibility, would the Fellows be continued? With what functions? Could they continue with dignity? (Eliot wrote Adams, "I do feel that this oversight on the part of Evans, if it was an oversight, is somewhat less than civil to the Fellows." MacLeish wrote Tate, "I can't defend Luther against the charge of bad manners. But I don't think it's intentional or that it conceals a plot. His manners are just naturally bad. And they are made worse by the fact that he is sluggish. He works hard but it takes him days to do what most people do in an hour. When I was Librarian I was more than once on the point of setting off fireworks under his seat. I wish I had.") There was talk among the Fellows of resigning, but none did.

※

In July, Hillyer's *The Death of Captain Nemo,* a lengthy narrative poem inspired by a novel of Jules Verne's, was published by Knopf. Bogan wrote to her editor at the *New Yorker,* William Shawn: "The number of books I have found myself kept from reviewing, over the years, have been few, as you know.—I cannot bring myself to deal with Robert Hillyer's book . . . because of the attack by Mr. Hillyer upon a group of which I am a member. After the workout he gave to our characters and aims, I feel that I should be fighting *prejudice* in *myself*—and that would never do!"

※

In that same feverish summer of 1949, William Carlos Williams was also the object of a small cloud of protest, raised by his review of the *Pisan Cantos* in the spring issue of *Imagi,* a very small poetry quarterly published in Baltimore. During July, Evans received a few letters, all alike in content, protesting Williams's appointment as Consultant in Poetry—evidently the result of confusion with his appointment as a Fellow earlier in the year. Some of the letters came from the editors of other small verse magazines (in Arkansas, California, etc.), saying for example, "That [Williams] should defend such a work places him in the same category with Pound, that of utter contempt and treachery to all the ideals for which America stands. . . ." One letter came from Harrison Smith, of the *Saturday Review of Literature,* who asked Evans to examine thoughtfully a quotation he cited from Williams's article: "Heeded, Pound's loyalty, humanity (conspicuously revealed by the devotion he inspires in other men who devote themselves to him), kindness and good sense, would strike like lightning into us. So we proceed to legally slaughter him (in the face of the lice and swine that we let live) that we may escape the implications of his genius. We might better acquire stronger stomachs against his pecadillos [sic]." Williams's review ran on with rather murky literary comment, other than such pungent statements as "Give him the prize and hang him if you like, but give him the prize" and "They might (Pound's fiduciary conceptions) if paid attention to even save us from Russia!" Evans responded with appropriate statements of correction, including the fact that Williams had not participated in the Bollingen award. "His appointment as Fellow was based solely upon his attainments as a poet and the distinguished place he occupies in contemporary literature." He quoted a statement about Pound that Williams had published earlier: "I am not trying to minimize his crime, it was a crime and he committed it wilfully." The cloud—that particular cloud—drifted away.

After the prize was barred (and $9,000 returned to the donor) the Bollingen Foundation received a number of requests from universities to carry it on. In early 1950, the Yale University Library was granted the funds to continue making the awards. The winner of the 1949 Prize, selected by a committee whose members—Adams, Aiken, Shapiro, Chapin, Warren—had all been Fellows in American Letters, was Wallace Stevens. MacLeish had also been invited by Yale to act as one of the judges and had declined. "I have been critical of the actions which led up to the loss or rather 'surrender' by the Library of Congress of its right to give prizes . . . ," he wrote Tate. "Yale University proposes to take over the Fellows in American Letters as a body to serve as judges of the new award. The implications of that action could be taken as critical of the administration at the Library. . . . I should not like to put myself in such a position, not only because of my previous connection with the Library, but also because I don't think the Library administration alone is to blame for the unhappy outcome. . . . It would have been wiser all around to start out with new judges."

The Bollingen Foundation had asked Tate to find out Evans's attitude before they would consider transferring the prize to Yale. Tate wrote MacLeish: "Luther not only applauded the idea, . . . he thought it highly desirable that the Fellows be taken over as the jury this first year at Yale, so that our enemies could not say that either the Foundation or Yale had repudiated us, and thus congratulate themselves upon another victory." In 1963 the amount of the award was increased to $5,000, and thereafter it was given every other year. After 1968, when the Bollingen Foundation ended its programs (except for the Bollingen Series, which it gave to Princeton University Press to carry through its publication), the Andrew W. Mellon Foundation took over, and in 1973 made an outright endowment of $100,000 to enable the Yale Library to continue awarding the prize in perpetuity. By now more than thirty poets, including many of the Consultants, have received the Bollingen Prize. They keep coming on.

Cowley to Tate, October 21, 1949: "I went to a literary tea for Nehru. Present were the editors of the *Saturday Review*. . . . Harrison Smith saw me and advanced beaming. 'I was going to write and congratulate you,' he said, 'on the article about Hillyer. I think you had the right dope. Of course, we just printed the Hillyer articles and the editorial to start a controversy. It was a great success. We thought it would give us three exciting issues but it went on for six.' "

❋

Léonie Adams stayed on at the Library of Congress well into September, seeing to details of the second series of poets' recordings. Among her last acts were letters to MacLeish and Frost asking to include their readings in the series. Elizabeth Bishop arrived from Key West to succeed her on the 19th. Then Adams left to join her husband, William Troy, at their telephoneless house on Candlewood Mountain, near New Milford, Connecticut, with imaginable relief.

❋

Elizabeth Bishop's report on her term in the Chair of Poetry pictures a calm, uncomplicated, somewhat tedious year, during which—as she reported apologetically—because of ill health she didn't accomplish as much work as she "would like to have done or probably should have done." Poetry she did write. Her disturbing "Visits to St. Elizabeths," a work seemingly colored by Ravel's *Bolero* and "The House That Jack Built," gathers force incrementally from its first stanza,

This is the house of Bedlam.

This is the man
that lies in the house of Bedlam.

This is the time
of the tragic man
that lies in the house of Bedlam.

to its climactic twelfth stanza:

This is the soldier home from the war.
These are the years and the walls and the door
that shut on a boy that pats the floor
to see if the world is round or flat.
This is a Jew in a newspaper hat
that dances carefully down the ward,
walking the plank of a coffin board
with the crazy sailor
that shows his watch
that tells the time
of the wretched man
that lies in the house of Bedlam.

She worked agreeably with Phyllis Armstrong, whose diligence she mentioned in her annual report; she recommended a promotion. They labored at getting the file on the Pound Affair in order. Where was Katherine Anne Porter's eight-page letter to the *S.R.L.*, she asked Tate, which the magazine refused to print and she had mimeographed and distributed on the West Coast? Her recording targets included Kenneth Fearing (didn't record—a pity), Muriel Rukeyser (did), the New Zealand poet Allen Curnow (did), and Dylan Thomas (did). She finally captured the voice of MacLeish, at a Boston studio, as he had become Boylston Professor of Rhetoric and Oratory at Harvard. "I have admired 'You, Andrew Marvell' now for almost twenty years and should very much like to hear a recording of it, and also of 'The End of the World.' " She had her wish. The recordings Frost had made two years before, which were sent him to hear, he found to be full of mistakes, and he came in December to remake them to his satisfaction. She gave a tea for Frost in the Poetry Room, the first function of this sort to take place there, though its refurbishment was not completed. The thirty-five guests included Karl Shapiro and Carl Sandburg. On another occasion she had forty members of the Library staff up there and gave them a talk about what she did. "It was interesting to learn how little they knew of the actual work of the Consultant." She gave the customary reading of her poems in the Coolidge Auditorium. She went through manuscripts sent in by some twenty-five amateur poets. "I regret to say, however, that I have made no discoveries of new poetic talent whatever." She dealt with a swarm of reference inquiries. Armstrong's meticulous statistics: 1,946 general and 1,070 administrative phone calls, 772 letters answered, 445 visitors seen and talked to, 120 readers assisted. A large proportion of that, Bishop reported, "is a serious waste of the time of the Consultant and the Assistant and should probably be handled elsewhere."

Bishop's view of the recording project, too, was vaguely jaundiced. She found the critical response to the first series disappointing and also disappointed. Technical quality was below par, and the "poet-readers themselves vary greatly and are not usually subject to improvement. However, as poetry recordings become more popular and widespread . . . it is possible that more poets may learn how to read their poetry effectively." In later years Bishop said she would rather read a poem in peace than listen to a recording.

A meeting of the Fellows, postponed from the autumn, was held on January 20. This was the first meeting that W. C. Williams attended. He had been doubtful about becoming a Fellow, anyway. The previous summer he had written Tate: "To me the only disturbing element of any serious moment brought out by this controversy was Eliot's presence among the Fellows. . . . As I shall be called upon to take part in your next meeting . . . I must know just what Eliot's part is to be. Is he a Fellow? If so, I cannot consent to remain one." A month later: "I've changed my mind. I stick. For there are worse sons of bitches than T. S. E. tho' its hard to find them. One apparently is in Congress and took my name in vain. So I'll transfer the fight to him & take on E. later." (The troublesome Congressman hasn't been identified.)

Eliot, off on a six-week cruise to Cape Town, was absent from the Fellows' January meeting. It was suggested that an *older* well-known poet be appointed. Williams was nominated once again for the Chair in Poetry, and declined on the spot, though he said he might consider it in a few years when he would have given up his medical practice; John Crowe Ransom likewise declined; Conrad Aiken was invited and accepted.

The Pound controversy had not entirely been dissipated. In December 1949, the *Nation* had published still another statement of protest, signed by eighty-four intellectuals, from Agee to Zabel (including several future Consultants and Fellows but no current ones). John Berryman wrote the statement and Tate helped him circulate it. They sent it to the *Saturday Review,* which stalled about printing it, and the *Nation* came through. It was timely, then, that the feature of the January meeting was a talk by Luther Evans summarizing the issues and the recent reverberations of the Bollingen award. The Fellows voted a resolution commending him for his steadfastness during the tumult: "his directness and courage, and his upholding of their freedom of judgment." There was a cocktail party afterward, in honor of Léonie Adams for *her* steadfastness, followed by dinner at the Biddles'.

The Librarian's *Annual Report* for 1949 appeared in March 1950, with a detailed account of the controversy. Fat was again in the fire, on account of Evans's statement that the Fellows had been warned of the probable consequence of giving the award to Pound: "Reaction would be, for the most part, emotional rather than intellectual; Public conscience would be outraged; The progress of poetry would be arrested for a generation; International relations, particularly with Italy, would be embarrassed; Confidence in the Library of Congress, which had given them corporate entity, would be seriously impaired; Their faculties would be suspected, their motives would be rejected, their principles would be deplored; Congress, inevitably, would intervene." (It was likely that Clapp and Mearns had drafted that part of the Librarian's report.)

"The Fellows are planning to resign in a body," an officer of the Bollingen Foundation wrote, in a memorandum reporting a phone call from Tate on March 30. "They consider they have been repudiated by

Evans in his annual report. . . . Tate says that Evans did not warn the Fellows of the undesirable consequences of their action or urge them not to choose Pound. . . . On the contrary, when the Fellows discussed their selection of Pound with Evans before announcing it, Evans said that they would be 'suckers' if they backed down on their choice because of fear of the public reaction. . . ." Again, it all blew over; nobody resigned.

❊

Riding a different poetic wave, on March 24, the Senate of the United States passed a resolution, submitted by Senator Taft, in honor of Robert Frost's seventy-fifth birthday on March 26—"Whereas [his] poems have helped to guide American thought with humor and wisdom, setting forth to our minds a reliable representation of ourselves and of all men, and . . . his work through the past half century has enhanced for many their understanding of the United States and their love of country"—and extending him "felicitations of the Nation he has served so well." (March 26, 1950, was actually Frost's seventy-*sixth* birthday.)

❊

Toward the end of her term Bishop was asked for advice by the Department of State magazine *Amerika*, published for foreign readers, those in the Soviet Union especially. The editors planned a story on American poetry and in particular the younger poets. The questions were detailed and so were Bishop's answers. One paragraph stands out: "I think it is undoubtedly true that there has been an enormous increase in interest in poetry in the United States since the war. Whether some of the present enthusiasm is well-directed or not remains to be seen. Of course it is still true that no poet can earn a living by poetry, that magazines pay very small sums for it, and that the various awards and fellowships are drops in the bucket; I do not believe you can paint a really glowing picture of poets and poetry in the United States at present."

❊

The seven-year period 1943–50 was vital for the Chair of Poetry. The pattern of rotating appointments introduced by MacLeish was firmly established, and the roster—Tate, Warren, Bogan, Shapiro, Lowell, Adams, and Bishop—was arguably the strongest in the Chair's history. The recording program was effectively launched, and occupants of the Consultantship became presences on the Washington social and cultural scene. The period ended with the most famous crisis in the Library's literary career, the award of the Bollingen Prize to Ezra Pound, an episode whose repercussions still echo. The prize, the Fellows, the Consultant, and the Library administration were the ingredients in a complex recipe that yielded tension, friction, muddle, and embittered feelings, besides the positive accomplishments envisioned in 1936 by Putnam and Huntington.

In retrospect, Allen Tate emerges as the most influential figure in the early years of the Consultantship, more so than MacLeish, despite the latter's imagination and resolve about the direction the post should take, and certainly more so than Evans, though the Consultants and Fellows had reason to be grateful for his rough-hewn courage and conviction. It was Tate who gave the Consultantship credibility with his peers, made the telling recommendations for appointments, and drew other poets to the Library's cause by the force of his reputation and stature. And it was Tate to whom the Fellows turned as a leader and a spokesman.

Indeed, Tate was a mentor and friend of poets in the Chair over the following three decades, and he himself participated in the literary programs into the 1970s. Through his impress, the poetic style and taste exemplified by Auslander and even by MacLeish were now fading.

The Consultants were far from idle, but their role remained largely undefined. The Fellows, clustered around the Consultant, were what might today be called a "support group." But they sometimes seemed to be wild cards strewn upon the Library's table. It should have become evident that the Librarian of Congress could not devote the time and attention to the Consultant and Fellows that MacLeish had done through choice and Evans through necessity. Increasingly, a cadre of Library officials, some of them among the most able in Library of Congress history and some as quixotic as any poet, became involved in the Consultantship. This led to confusion and misunderstanding on both sides. What seemed wanted were a clearly defined program, a single Library official to manage it, and an improvement in funding. Within the next few years these needs were met, but not before additional crises were overcome or, at least, endured.

Three

1950 TO 1956

Conrad Aiken, senior among the Consultants up to his appointment (he was sixty-one in August 1950), was surely the feistiest. Some years later, when asked if he had enjoyed his stay at the Library of Congress, he replied, "Well, yes and no. I found myself in a battle royal with the bureaucracy from the moment I got there. They were critical of everything I did—even objected to the way I signed letters, because I had a habit of putting my signature way out to the right, you see, not under the 'yours sincerely,' and they said would I please center my signature, so I took pains to put it still further out to the right." Did his duties keep him busy? "As a matter of fact, there was quite a lot to do but it didn't take much time and so I started writing. I had a great standard typewriter right in the office and I went to work on my autobiography, *Ushant,* and wrote half of it while I was there."

He had felt ambivalent about the job from the outset, as he did about some of his poet friends. He and Eliot had been friends since Harvard undergraduate days, before the First World War, and they remained so, though it was a friendship, as Peter Ackroyd has noted, "marked by a jocular uneasiness" and interrupted by occasional lacunae. Aiken was uncomfortable with Eliot's late work: in April 1950, regarding *The Cocktail Party,* he observed that "I haven't had the heart to write Tom about it, for it seems to me to be a real declaration of intellectual, if not moral, bankruptcy. . . . It makes one look back to the quartets with a renewed suspicion that perhaps all was not too healthy there too." In 1941 he was deploring modern poets—such poets as Auden, Spender, Warren, Tate—who followed the tradition of Pound and Eliot. The poetry of "the Tate-to-Blackmur-to-Winters-to-Brooks (Cleanth)-to Ransom roundelay" was a menace, he observed. Aiken cast his vote for Pound, however, in the Bollingen Prize ballot. His association with Tate in the meetings of the Fellows in American Letters apparently fostered a warm friendship, so their letters persuade us. Tate's appraisal of Aiken's poetry in *Sixty American Poets* is discreet, given its timing: "Aiken is a very mixed poet; at his best he is unsurpassed in our time, as in 'Tetelastai' and *Preludes for Memnon;* at his worst, as in the sonnets *And in the Human Heart,* he is virtually unreadable. His influence has been very wide, and his occasional critical articles are among the best of his generation."

After Aiken had accepted Evans's invitation to the Chair, he wrote Tate, in April 1950, that he had done so "with the understanding that he [Evans] meant what he said when he claimed that the Library hoped the incumbents could continue with their own work while at Washington. . . . I made this point not merely for selfish reasons, . . . but because it seems to me that the original intent was such, and has become a shade obscured. I get the impression anyway that Léonie and Elizabeth were worked pretty damned hard, and I don't feel that this squares with the idea." He had heard about the statement in the Librarian's report that the Fellows had been warned of the consequences of the Pound award. "Of course the statement is mendacious, I don't recall any such warning whatever. . . . It seems to me we have not only been morally repudiated, but treated dishonestly into the bargain, and I am still by no means sure we oughtn't to resign." But Adams, Shapiro, and Chapin agreed with Aiken that he should nevertheless accept the Chair—"an outpost in enemy country!" He continued to fulminate in his letters to Tate. "It is a sort of masterpiece of equivocation and tergiversation. . . . The Library of Congress, in whatever persons [sic], has treated us publically as if we were naughty children. . . . I think we *must* resign, if we are to regain self-respect." He liked Malcolm Cowley's suggestion that "Harvard/Yale/Princeton" take over the Fellows and the prize. Only a probe of all the Fellows' papers would reveal whether they were as exercised as Aiken. None of them resigned, Aiken took the Chair ("only once in my life—a year of tutoring at Harvard—have I had a desk job"), and he and his wife settled into a house in the southeast section on Capitol Hill, a few blocks from the Library.

In October he could write his daughter: "This Lib Cong job is thus far pretty much what St John Perse told me it was, 'not exactly fictitious, but shall we say slightly imaginary': so little to do that I am bored except when I can do work of my own. . . . It's largely a matter of receiving visitors and answering peculiar questions and turning down invitations to speak or read. And . . . the wretched business of being introduced facetiously as the Lib.'s 'short-haired poet' to the Staff of the Library assembled in the Library theatre, standing up and making a bow to the multitude. Painful. But I survived. The best thing is my office, generally reputed to be the handsomest in the city, top floor, overlooking Capitol on one side and Supreme Court on tother, with view out to river and country too—all Washington. A fine stone balcony on which to perch, too. And a nice english gal as permanent assistant, who is of course really the Chair of Poetry and does the real drudgery. . . . I disregard office hours, drifting in at 9–15 in the morning, out for nigh two hours for lunch, then vamoose at 5 to the awaiting orange blossoms. Washington is dull, I think, like something abandoned by a World's Fair . . . and the traffic terrifying; and the people reputedly dull, too. But against this are the quite fascinating slum negro quarters, on the fringe of one of which we live,—these are good, various, rich, human, everything." He rejoiced in the "fine miniature Covent Garden within walking distance"—Eastern Market—and its provender, "everything from brains and chicken gizzards to hard and soft shell crabs and the largest oysters you ever saw." And a "very superior tom cat" had firmly adopted the Aikens.

Conrad Aiken had a phobia of speaking publicly. His first official letter as Consultant declined an invitation to address a librarians' association: "Unhappily, I am one of those wretches who simply cannot

[135]

speak—three attempts at it in as many decades have at last taught me that the net result is to inflict great and needless suffering on others as well as myself." His affliction was no bar to reading his poetry for recording. Nor was conviviality a problem. He relished a luncheon with Charles Laughton, who was at the Library for a reading of Shaw's *Don Juan in Hell* (with Charles Boyer, Cedric Hardwicke, and Agnes Moorehead). "It was all very gemütlich, but dry; they never serve drinks in ye Librarie, it's a pity; I always rush three blocks home for a couple of quick ones . . . then back to the Library with a brightened eye and sharpened tongue, nobody knows why! Heh heh." The meetings of the Fellows were fun. "Wilder and John Crowe Ransom and Wm Carlos Williams and so on all came to drinks, myself receiving in bathrobe with a fever of 101 and drinking five double martinis, then collapsing. Wilder very amusing. So's Red Warren. . . ." Another source of delectation during Aiken's time in Washington: productions of his play *Mr. Arcularis* on national radio and television, both, and also by a local theater group, the Arena Stage, for three weeks in spring 1951.

With a view to "restoring a shade of function to the poor castrated Felons," deprived of bestowing the Bollingen Prize, Aiken conceived the idea of the Library's awarding annual fellowships of $2,500 in creative writing, which Evans declared would pass the congressional test as not constituting a "prize," and he thought it a good scheme. "Tom Eliot, who was here for drinks last night," Aiken wrote Tate in November, "was all for it, feeling as strongly as I do that without *some* such we lead an existence so exiguous as to be meaningless." Eliot (whom Aiken nicknamed "the Tse-Tse") suggested applying to the Bollingen Foundation. Aiken's idea was aired at the Fellows' meetings in 1951 and 1952. It won administrative approval, and a fund-raising committee was appointed—Thornton Wilder and MacLeish (now Fellows) with Aiken—but despite approaches to both the Bollingen and the Rockefeller Foundations the scheme never got over the funding hurdle.

Meanwhile, the second series of recordings underwritten by the Bollingen Foundation was published during the Aiken regime; the five albums included the voices of Adams, Aiken, Bishop, Fitzgerald, Lowell, MacLeish, Roethke, Rukeyser, Schwartz, Spender, and others. Another application to the Foundation got a response only in 1957, with a grant of $2,500, chiefly for the technical aspects of further recordings. Two additional Bollingen donations of that figure came through in subsequent years. The project was helped along during the lean times by the poet Lee Anderson, who traveled about taping poets' readings for the Library, for a modest honorarium or none.

Though he boasted of his idleness in the Chair, Aiken did keep the recording project moving—his prizes included a "little band of visiting English poets," David Gascoyne, Kathleen Raine, and W. S. Graham, and the "psychiatrist psonneteer" Merrill Moore. Besides, he inaugurated the broadcasting of readings over a local radio station under the Library's sponsorship. He felt constrained to avoid one poet who hoped to record. Robert Hillyer wrote wanting to take up Warren's invitation extended in 1945. Aiken replied, "After the Saturday Review ruckus, I don't really feel that any useful purpose would be served by our meeting." He suggested Hillyer arrange with Phyllis Armstrong to record during the summer, in Aiken's absence. Hillyer did indeed record and give a public reading in the Coolidge Auditorium in 1955, and he lectured there on Robert Burns in 1959.

At the Fellows' meeting in February 1951, the succession to the Consultantship was to be decided by offering it to one of the panel of "elder" poets, Ransom, Marianne Moore, and Williams—an approach that originated the year before, on Bishop's recommendation. None of the three was available, even after Evans decided to increase the stipend from $5,000 to $7,500 by drawing upon the Porter Fund. Though Kenneth Rexroth, Theodore Roethke, and R. P. Blackmur were mooted, Evans reappointed the fractious incumbent, the first of the Consultants to serve a second year. (He might rather have wanted to be rid of that meddling poet.) At the Fellows' meeting the next year, on February 29, the "Permanent Panel of Older Poets" was enlarged by adding Winters, Cummings, Schwartz (aet. 39!), and Roethke (44), and a "Panel of Younger Poets" was nominated: Jarrell, Richard Wilbur, Berryman, Anthony Hecht, and W. S. Merwin. Evans opted for W. C. Williams, whose acceptance of the Chair obviated the Librarian's consideration of the rest of that panoply.

❋

Gertrude Clarke Whittall, not long after her first musical benefactions to the Library of Congress, affirmed beyond any doubt what her preferences were in programming. "As you know," she wrote to the chief of the Music Division in 1940, "I do not believe in reaching out my hand beyond the grave, but it will give me much satisfaction to know—'when my name is called,' that the concert programs, given by The Gertrude Clarke Whittall Foundation, will continue to be made up of time-honored compositions. Mrs. Coolidge has done such a grand and noble work for the moderns that it would seem almost like a duplication of her established sponsorship of living composers to plan otherwise." Mrs. Whittall's choice of literary gifts to the Library corroborated her regard for the time-honored. In 1941, during the Auslander time, she hoped that MacLeish would set up a "Poets' Corner." "Strange as it may seem," she remarked to him, "I was interested in poetry long before I became acquainted with music." That MacLeish not only did not follow her express wish but did away with Auslander's stained-glass vision and with Auslander left her with a scunner against him for years. And MacLeish regarded her as a nuisance. Thanking her for her gifts—such as the statue of Pan, by F. W. MacMonnies, that she gave in 1940 for the garden entered from the Whittall Pavilion—he wrote her the fulsome acknowledgments he thought she expected. She wrote him pointedly, in 1941, that "a chief incentive to the initiation of those gifts was the prospect, then presented, of a distinct unit, or Division of the Library, devoted to Poetry. Will you kindly let me know whether such a division now is still a part of your program." MacLeish replied, in a rather chilly letter, that the earlier proposal for a poetry room had been abandoned in favor of a unit devoted to "reference tools and bibliographical apparatus . . . and quiet and agreeable alcoves for reading."

The discord crested in November 1943, when MacLeish wrote Mrs. Whittall suggesting that, since the cafeteria was temporarily closed and outside catering in his office was awkward, the Whittall Pavilion, "the most charming room we have in the Library," be used for occasional luncheons to distinguished guests and a table be purchased, in keeping with the furniture already there. Replying to the Librarian's "strangely surprising" letter, Mrs. Whittall requested an appointment in order to tell him personally "the purpose for which [the Pavilion] was built—and forever after to be used—and the agreement on conditions relating to the furnishings. . . . You were not the Librarian of Congress at the time the Whittall Pavilion was constructed or when the agreements were reached. Perhaps therefore you are not fully cognizant of the facts. . . ." Apparently no appointment was made, and a few days later the lady sent a note on her Shoreham stationery—unsigned, absent-mindedly one must assume—which so annoyed MacLeish that he tore it up. (It was pasted together, however, for the file.) Mrs. Whittall wanted to "acquaint you with my plans for the still unfinished furnishing of the Whittall Pavilion." She intended there to be "special glass, china, and other equipment . . . for the kitchenette." MacLeish sent the note to Harold Spivacke: "[It] is so unusual, and its implications as to the making of administrative decisions in the Library by persons other than its authorized officials are so unexpected, that I hesitate to accept it without some further indication as to its author."

Roy P. Basler, who came to know Gertrude Clarke Whittall well, wrote that "for one whose love of poetry was first stimulated, as she once confided, by an early girlhood gift of a copy of Bulwer-Lytton's [novel in verse] *Lucile,* her taste in poetry was by no means as atrocious as it was purported by Conrad Aiken. She preferred Shakespeare above all and admitted to liking E. A. Robinson and A. E. Housman best among her contemporaries, although Robert Frost held for her a personal charm as well as poetic stature." She was by no means a Puritan. She had a penchant for Manhattan cocktails and cigarettes.

After Auslander left, Mrs. Whittall said no more of her hope for the "Poets' Corner," though she continued to give the Library manuscripts of music and poetry (such as the Ledoux Collection of E. A. Robinson) and additional funds for her Whittall Foundation in support of chamber music. Luther Evans's Special Assistant in the Whittall heyday, Marlene Morrisey, recently recalled Mrs. Whittall's way of doing things. "I remember a day when she lunched at the Methodist Building cafeteria and walked around Capitol Hill, carrying a hatbox, which she handled rather carelessly. After lunch she called on the Librarian, still with her hatbox, and casually remarked that she had a few more items for him.

She reached in her hatbox and pulled out $100,000 worth of bonds, which she handed to him."

In 1950, by Mrs. Whittall's testimony, during a friendly chat with Librarian of Congress Emeritus Putnam (who long after retiring retained an office in the Main Building), "the subject of Poetry was resumed, and I expressed regret that the Muse had been so abruptly deserted. 'Perhaps it is not too late—I will see Dr. Evans tomorrow,' said Dr. Putnam; and he did as promised." She wrote to Evans on November 27, offering him the gift of a $100,000 U.S. Treasury Bond to establish a poetry fund in the Library, "the income from which is to be expended by the Librarian of Congress for the development of the appreciation of poetry in this country. Among the activities for which these funds may be used are expenses connected with lectures on poetry; public poetry readings; the service and upkeep of the Poets' Corner; the publication of bibliographies and other scholarly works designed to encourage the creation and appreciation of poetry, etc. These are to be regarded as suggestions but not limitations, and although I desire during my lifetime to be consulted on the choice of activities resulting from these gifts, I do not wish to impose any special conditions. . . ." The Library's Trust Fund Board unanimously accepted the offer, and when the Fellows in American Letters next met, on February 9 and 10, 1951, the gift was announced by the director of the Reference Department, Burton W. Adkinson, who suggested that the program be inaugurated formally with a reading of Edwin Arlington Robinson's poems "by an outstanding reader with commentary by a noted critic." Conrad Aiken, already alerted, had approached Cleanth Brooks, then a professor at Yale, who had made a selection of poems and was prepared to appear with a reader if the proposal was approved.

The Fellows' reaction was not spontaneously enthusiastic. There was discussion: poets should read their own poems; first attention should be given to American poetry of the present day; "the long-range program should be under the direction of the Consultant in Poetry but . . . administrative detail should be delegated elsewhere"; the Fellows should "outline a program which successive Consultants could follow"; and perhaps some of the income from the Whittall benefaction could be used for fellowships. Still, Adkinson's suggestion was approved, and the Fellows adjourned for a reception and luncheon tendered (and attended) by Mrs. Whittall in the Poetry Room—a harmonious occasion, apparently, though the preceding meeting had been dampened by Tate's and Thorp's news that they would resign, not out of any pique but because they felt they had served for a long enough time.

The Poetry Room was going through a transformation. Mrs. Whittall had begun to take a hand in its decor and furnishings. As Marlene Morrisey remembers, "Mrs. Whittall was forced (because of physical and aging problems [she was then 83]) to vacate her long-held apartment at the Shoreham Hotel for a less commodious environment, and she was anxious to put some of her best-loved belongings elsewhere where she could still enjoy them." She gave the Poetry Room a collection of furniture, pieces that are there still. Some are reproductions in several English and French styles, in particular the graceful French Régence, caned, painted, gilded, decorated with pastoral scenes. (Aiken's opinion that it resembled a French brothel may have been the result of the orange blossoms.) There are two loveseats, a wicker settee with painted medallions, a Chinese printed-silk screen, a mirror with a gold frame embossed with fighting cocks, a teak stand holding a figure of the Buddha, five prints (Fragonard?) elegantly framed, an escritoire (where visitors may sign a guest book), and a glazed breakfront where, at Mrs. Whittall's wish, some of her gifts to the Library, both books and manuscripts, were originally placed on permanent display. A few of the pieces given earlier by Mrs. Biddle may still be among the medley of furniture. (Kenton Kilmer, though assigned elsewhere on the Library staff, had a look at the newly furnished room and turned in a memorandum criticizing much of what he saw as impractical and unattractive and suggesting that poets who came to the Library to read should have their autographs reproduced in gold on the walls.) The Fellows, sitting there during their February meeting, discussed what the room should be called. Thorp proposed "The Whittall Poetry Room," but someone observed that Mrs. Whittall thought her name was "too much in the Library" already. "The Robinson Room" was pondered and discarded; "Poets' Corner" was abandoned to prevent association with the one in Westminster Abbey. "Poetry Room" suited best, and suits to this day. It was no longer to be the private office of the

Consultant, who moved down the corridor to a less sumptuous room with a vista of rooftops. Mrs. Whittall's treasures were later transferred to the Rare Book and the Manuscript divisions, except for her girlhood Bible, in French, and some of her volumes of Robinson. An original portrait of her, in oils, rather idealized, stands on an easel. (Another portrait of her, in watercolor, similarly idealized, with a dog, hangs in another Library office. She is by no means forgotten.) The Poetry Room is, as all who visit it would agree, an entirely pleasant place, suitable for "persons seeking an appropriate atmosphere for enjoyment in reading," the intention in 1951. And it has its magnificent view of the Capitol.

The Poetry Room was officially opened with an informal reception on the evening of April 23—Shakespeare's birthday. The guests, some sixty, including members of the press, were met at the elevators by Library staff and escorted along the gallery overlooking the Great Hall far below. Mrs. Whittall attended, and the Fellows in American Letters were represented by Mrs. Biddle and Conrad Aiken. On the occasion, some of the poetry recordings in the second series of albums of "Twentieth Century Poetry in English," soon to be issued, were played for the party.

The inaugural program under the sponsorship of the Gertrude Clarke Whittall Poetry Fund took place a week later, on May 1, in the Coolidge Auditorium. The actor Burgess Meredith (who at MacLeish's request, in 1943, had read Stephen Vincent Benét's poems from the same stage) was the choice to read poems of Edwin Arlington Robinson selected by Cleanth Brooks, who interposed a lecture on the poet. The audience that filled the auditorium was, as Aiken was not too disaffected to observe, "lively, young, and relatively distinguished." Meredith, though ill, delighted the audience with his performance, in particular with a favorite of both the convivial and the temperate, "Mr. Flood's Party." Mrs. Whittall was in a seat always reserved for her, No. 101 in row S, which had been especially equipped with a jack for her earphones, in order to amplify either music or poetry. The evening was memorable, but the audience—except for some of the Library officials and the Consultant in Poetry—couldn't have anticipated the storm that was brewing.

Mrs. Whittall had not been consulted about the poems to be read, as her deed of gift had stipulated she should be. In view of the many Robinson first editions and manuscripts she had given the Library (a list was printed in the evening's program, and some were on display at the entrance to the auditorium), she hoped that something from her gift would be included. Her favorite, Robinson's Arthurian narrative poem "Lancelot" (1920), was not represented even by a fragment, as she learned before the event, and she let her disappointment be known. A Library official inquired of Brooks whether he couldn't include in the program at least a brief selection from "Lancelot." According to the Consultant's later account of the episode, Brooks declined on the grounds that "it didn't fit in with what he had prepared to say, and wasn't anyway a very good poem. And that was that." In fact, however, it was not altogether that. Two weeks before, Aiken had wired from New York, where he was on a visit, to Robert F. Gooch, of the staff: "Feel most strongly about this interference with Cleanth Brooks which is really in effect telling him what to say moreover I am convinced Mrs Whittall if she understood situation would fully endorse my disapproval." Gooch jotted a note on the telegram: "I talked with Prof. Brooks. . . . He had no objection to changing the readings and said he would gladly go along with our decision. I decided, however, that we would not make any substitutions for the poems already selected."

Mrs. Whittall's disappointment at the omission of "Lancelot," nevertheless, was transformed into annoyance, and she let that, too, be known. Something near to an impasse now existed. The Consultant insisted that he alone should be responsible for deciding what the Whittall funds should be used for. He hoped especially for lectures about contemporary poets by distinguished critics rather than readings by actors, and even before the Robinson evening he had proposed to the head of the Reference Department a series of three or four lectures by R. P. Blackmur on American poetry by decades—the 1910s, the 1920s, the 1930s, and perhaps the 1940s—each to be followed by a reading of a poet typical of that decade, such as Frost or Sandburg for the first, Stevens or Marianne Moore for the second, Cummings or Tate for the third, and Lowell or Eberhart or Wilbur or all three for the fourth. "I further wondered whether . . . we might not institute the first of the

Library's spring festivals for poets, inviting twenty-five or so from all over the country to participate, and letting them run their own show." A file notation on the memorandum indicated that the Fund's resources that year would not be adequate. Aiken's proposal was unrealistic, if not mischievous under the circumstances. Instead, in the fall there was an evening of readings of selections from Shakespeare's sonnets and plays by the actress Margaret Webster, upon which Aiken commented: "a glazed, skilful, but essentially theatrical performance, and a very dull audience, all old toads. . . . it will not send a single person to a single book. Alas, alas, alas." In January 1952, in a program entitled "The Paradox of Poe," Burgess Meredith again read, and the psychiatrist Fredric Wertham gave a psychoanalytic interpretation of Poe's life and work. And in March, the actor Basil Rathbone, famous for his movie impersonation of Sherlock Holmes, gave a program of literary readings—twelve poets, including Shakespeare, Keats, Shelley, Elizabeth Barrett Browning, Housman, and Benét. Rathbone also intended to read the Resurrection chapter from the Gospel of St. John, but Mrs. Whittall vetoed that number because, she explained, she had received an unpleasant impression when she visited the Holy Land. Aiken, in his annual report, called the program "nothing less than deplorable. The very type of audience drawn by these 'literary readings' (and how Victorian that very phrase sounds!) was in itself a painful criticism of the level that one fears must almost inescapably be reached if the literary judgments of Mrs. Whittall and such actors as Basil Rathbone must be deferred to. . . . While this Consultant does not in the least wish to exalt his own judgment in such matters, he does feel that the Library should consider whether it is worth paying $7500 a year to an expert in his field whose expertise is then ignored."

As a Library official put it, "What was at variance was [Aiken's] unwillingness, or inability, to consult with Mrs. Whittall effectively, or to consider her wishes in any case." Consequently the librarians ceased to consult the Consultant. The poetry programs would be conducted by the Reference Department, in collaboration with Edward Waters of the Music Division, who had had long and amiable experience of working with Mrs. Whittall on programs under her fund for music. Aiken unburdened himself of his resentments in a communication to the Fellows

in American Letters, anticipating their February 29th meeting. It con-
cluded:

> It is obviously an anomalous position that future Consultants
> will inherit; one in which they will be *thought* to be responsible
> for programs in which, in reality, they have no hand. It is cer-
> tainly not a prerogative of the Consultant to criticize the overall
> policies of the Library. Yet this incumbent of the Chair would be
> less than candid if he concealed his misgivings at seeing the Li-
> brary, and in the field of public relations, as this is, permitting its
> policy to be shaped, at least partially, by one whose judgment in
> poetry is all too lamentably betrayed by the books which she has
> provided for the Poetry Room. (They are in my opinion a dis-
> grace!)

The Fellows also received a letter from the director of the Reference
Department, Burton Adkinson, giving the administration's point of
view. At its heart was this passage:

> The Library is obligated to consult Mrs. Whittall in the formu-
> lation of plans for the poetry readings which her generosity has
> made possible. In accepting Mrs. Whittall's gift the Library
> acceded to her stated wish that she be brought into the discus-
> sions relative to the selection of readers and of poems to be read.
> As for the character of the programs Mrs. Whittall has expressed
> a strong wish to have readings by well-known persons who are
> competent interpreters and who will attract public attention to
> this activity. She has stated a further wish that the readings be
> based, for the time being, on the works of famous poets of long-
> established reputation, which, in effect, rules out the contempo-
> rary period. Within this limitation there is, of course, a wide field
> for choice. Mrs. Whittall particularly wished not to pattern the
> program around a series of lectures on poetry. As Dr. Evans has
> stated in his letter to you, the Library has agreed to follow Mrs.
> Whittall's wishes.

Evans's letter, also anticipating the agenda, had proposed that the Fellows discuss what activities the Consultant should engage in, the advantages of a two-year appointment, an active role in acquiring the manuscripts and personal papers of important American literary figures (he felt strongly that the Consultants after Auslander had neglected this aspect), and fund-raising to subsidize fellowships for creative and critical work in the field of letters.

The annual meeting of the Fellows, on February 29 and March 1, drew considerably less than a quorum. Present: Adams, Aiken, Auden, Blackmur, Brooks, Chapin, and Warren. Absent: Bishop, Eliot, Green, Lowell, MacLeish, Samuel Eliot Morison (appointed to represent the field of history; he never attended a meeting), Porter, Ransom, Shapiro, Wilder, and Williams. (Bogan had resigned the previous December. She wrote a friend, "I really couldn't feel happy going back without Allen Tate and Willard Thorp and some of the original group present. So that phase of things is over.") Evans made a speech that aimed to be soothing, even disarming: the Consultant's functions should be more clearly defined, he shouldn't be unnecessarily overburdened, his office hours should not be obligatory, it might be proper for him to have two months off in the summer, he could accept pay for lectures elsewhere, his tenure should be flexible; and, regarding the Whittall Fund, the Library was adhering to Mrs. Whittall's expressed wishes, etc., people can have different opinions about the program, the general reaction of the public has been fairly good.

The Fellows focused on the topic of the fund. "Finding themselves in unanimous agreement that a matter of principle was here at stake, while sympathizing with the Library in the predicament in which it found itself, passed the following resolution . . .":

The present confusion between the Reference Department and the Consultant in Poetry in the administration of the funds for the poetry program seems to the Fellows deplorable. It seems to them that the Consultant should have a decisive voice in all such matters, especially when, in the public view, he is held responsible. If he can not have a decisive voice in any particular program, it should be clearly announced that the program is being given under other auspices. In any case, there should be consultation between the Library and a committee of the Fellows with the principle in mind that, if there is to be a Consultant in Poetry, he should be concerned with the administration of any permanent poetry funds.

Evans, upon receiving the resolution, proposed a committee, appointed on the Fellows' recommendation, to advise the Consultant on the Library's program and act as liaison with Mrs. Whittall. The advisory committee, not restricted to Fellows, comprised Adams, Chapin, Thorp, and Marianne Moore. There is no evidence that it ever met.

All this acrimony and contention must have begun to be wearisome. Yet there is more. Imagine the Librarian's surprise, about a month later, to receive a severe letter from Katherine Garrison Chapin, surely the gentlest among the Fellows. "We were under the impression," she wrote, "that you concurred in the purpose of [our] resolution—that the 'consultant should have a decisive voice' in the administration of the poetry program, 'especially when, in the public view, he is held responsible'; and that where this was not possible . . . it should be clearly announced that the program was being given under other auspices." And yet, she pointed out, scarcely a week later the Library presented the Basil Rathbone readings, which "had not been mentioned at the meeting of the Fellows, and was not submitted to the Consultant." There was no indication that the program was not being given under the Consultant's auspices. "This action apparently puts the whole matter back where it was before the meeting of the Fellows, and makes their relationship to the Library ambiguous and untenable." She had written, with Aiken's approval, to the other Fellows who had been at the meeting, and they all shared her concern. Witness Cleanth Brooks: "I do not think we can nominate future consultants without telling them that as consultants they will not have a decisive voice in making the programs." Before taking any drastic action they had asked Mrs. Biddle to write to Evans. And she told him: "I feel certain that the matter can be clarified . . . if you would confirm in a letter your understanding and acceptance of the resolution, if it meets with your approval." She thought he would like to take the matter up with Dr. Williams, the

Consultant-to-be, and with Aiken and her, when Williams came to Washington the next week. Evans replied that Aiken and Phyllis Armstrong *had* been informed of the Rathbone event well before the meeting, and it didn't occur to any of the staff to mention it. The program stated that the performance was offered by the Reference Department (though it didn't state that it was *not* the responsibility of the Consultant). And Evans said that he *had* approved the Fellows' resolution.

In September 1952, Evans recruited a non-librarian of literary and academic background, Roy P. Basler, as chief of the General Reference and Bibliography Division. As a part of that job, Basler was to be responsible for administering the Chair and its incumbent, the poetry programs under the Whittall Fund, and relations with Mrs. Whittall in the literary sphere, which Edward Waters gladly ceded to him, retaining whatever there was in the musical sphere. While Basler had taught English at a half-dozen institutions, his renown was as a Lincoln scholar; for some years he had been the executive secretary of the Abraham Lincoln Association, in Springfield, editor in chief of *The Collected Works of Abraham Lincoln,* and author of a distinguished roster of articles and books about Lincoln, as well as about kindred aspects of American history and a variety of topics in American and English literature. (He was also a poet of genuine gift.) "As a tryout," Basler said later, "I spent a week going through the files hoping to see how things had gone wrong, how the Bollingen affair had blown up in Evans's face, how the Consultant and the Reference Department had come to be at loggerheads." He handed Evans his report. "Evans didn't know what poetry was. He wanted somebody to run it all for him. When he asked me if I'd do it, quick as a duck after a June bug I answered, 'I was scared you wouldn't ask me.'"

✳

Dr. Williams . . . has conducted for many years a one-man campaign against "tradition" and academicism, in favor of a native American tradition both in style and in materials. Much of his poetry is casual and half-finished; more of it is solid and brilliant. He is, perhaps, the only writer of free-verse who has found a formal technique for it. —Tate, in *Sixty American Poets.*

When William Carlos Williams accepted, in the first instance, Luther
Evans's invitation to take the 1949–50 Consultantship, he seemed en-
tirely pleased and willing. "Aware of the honor that has been bestowed
upon me," he wrote, "I will do my best to live up to it." That was on
March 3, 1948, shortly after he had been stricken "with the first of the
steady series of heart attacks that darkened his last fifteen years." The
words are Reed Whittemore's, in his sympathetic biography of Wil-
liams. Williams expected to recover quickly, but the attack laid him up
for three months; and when he was well he went to Seattle for a term
of teaching at the University of Washington (and some carousing with
Ted Roethke). It was poor health he gave as the reason for withdrawing
from the appointment the following October; he recommended Roethke
as his replacement. To Tate he wrote, "It will be quite impossible for
me to go to Washington as adviser to the Custodian of Poetry . . . or
whatever the official title may be, my health won't permit it. . . . I
believe you to be one of the committee which selects incumbents for
the honor, therefore I am coming to you for advice as a friend. Whom
shall I officially notify of my decision? It seems to me that the proper
person would be the Librarian himself, if so what is his name, official
title, and his address?" After Tate refreshed his memory, Williams
wrote the Librarian with due propriety; but he also wrote Tate, "Taken
all together a solitary life in Washington in a hotel room or a room at a
club . . . would not be wise or attractive for me. It wouldn't be possible
. . . to work profitably, turn out additional work as a writer in short.
But if Floss [his wife] went with me and we set up housekeeping we
couldn't afford it." And, writing Léonie Adams, after her friendly letter
hoping he could take the Chair in 1950–51: "If I knew how I could live
in Washington with my little wife close beside me I'd be most happy to
consider accepting. . . . But it doesn't seem possible for me to make
such an arrangement and survive. For I should have to go back to my
practice of Medicine afterward and there might not . . . be any practice
to go back to. In addition to which I'd be busted. No kidding."

By spring 1952 Williams had had the experience of two, perhaps
three, meetings of the Fellows. He liked being a Fellow, Whittemore
tells us; he thought they were a "good gang" who wanted to do some-
thing for literature. And Evans's conduct in the Pound affair had im-

pressed him, so much that he wrote Aiken, "Had Evans not stood like a rock for the Fellows they would have been wiped out." Furthermore, in 1951 the Consultant's stipend had risen from $5,000 to $7,500, as Aiken informed him by way of a feeler. On March 12, 1952, he wrote Aiken, "This is rather sudden but I am inclined to react favorably toward it. . . . At $7500, I could do it. . . . I am not as young as I was, [and] it rather frightens me. But perhaps I'd get used to it and even like it in the end." The appointing letter, from Verner W. Clapp, the Acting Librarian of Congress in Evans's absence, came back in ten days, inviting Williams to assume his post when Aiken's term would expire, in mid-September, "for 1952–53, and, if you wished, for the year 1953–54 as well." (Williams's view of Eliot had continued to mellow, too. On March 11, he had written Lowell thanking him for a "discerning and friendly letter . . . that has changed my attitude toward Eliot more than anything I have ever read of him. I accept him now for what he is, . . . a 'strong man' of letters, unrelated to the scene. Surely he knocked us higher than a kite in the early days.")

Let Whittemore take up the story at this point: "Williams arranged with Aiken to rent Aiken's apartment near the Library on Capitol Hill, and he began to wind up his medical affairs; but then once more his health betrayed him. First he became inordinately depressed, writing Charles Abbott, 'Something's come over me that has knocked me off my feet, something personal, you might properly call it an illness—of a nervous sort. It's been going on for the past two weeks. . . . My illness, my nervous instability has me seriously disturbed. . . . I know I'm a coward, many have greater burdens to bear than I, in fact I have none, but I am nevertheless in trouble.' What had come over him bothered him so much that he traveled to Boston to see his poet-doctor acquaintance Merrill Moore, a psychoanalyst, about it. The episode passed, [and] he and Flossie went off on vacation to [Abbott's] estate near Buffalo."

The attack precluded a May meeting at the Library with Aiken and Adkinson to discuss the next year's work, and instead Adkinson wrote Williams describing the possibilities, including Mrs. Whittall's ideas. Since her initial $100,000 establishing her Poetry Fund, in March 1952 she had given $50,000 more to establish a Poetry *and Literature* Fund, with the aim of broadening the program to include prose and drama. She was prepared to pay over and above that for another engagement by the *Don Juan in Hell* company, and the Welsh actor Elwyn (i.e., Emlyn) Williams, the Fredric Marches, and Charles Laughton were prospects. Williams responded enthusiastically from upstate New York, where he had evidently regained his health. He liked all of Mrs. Whittall's ideas and had some as well—readings from Yeats's poems and from his own book *In the American Grain*. "If Elwyn Williams would give us an evening of *Martin Chuzzlewit* it would bring down the house. . . . Laughton could do *The Song of Myself* (Whitman) to perfection."

While Williams was at the Abbott estate, however, Whittemore goes on, "he had what Flossie later described as a severe stroke and suffered temporary loss of speech. Flossie, writing immediately to Merrill Moore, was told that the speech loss definitely indicated another 'vascular accident,' that WCW was going to have a series of them and that they would be followed by 'one great big one' after which he wouldn't get out of bed. Moore recommended, however, that he take on the Library job anyway—'he could take it easy there'—and it was arranged with the Library that WCW arrive in Washington for his sinecure three months late, in December."

A press release announcing Williams's appointment had been issued by the Library on August 8. Only a week later, a weekly newsletter entitled *Counterattack: Facts to Combat Communism* published a list of accusations against Williams: between 1937 and 1941 he had signed seven petitions and letters calling for closer cooperation with Russia, clemency for Earl Browder, and the elimination of the House Committee on Un-American Activities; he had contributed to the *Partisan Review* before it became anti-Communist; he had been billed to speak at a rally in April 1951 for three of the "Hollywood Ten." The first letter parroting the *Counterattack* charges arrived in the Librarian's office within a few days. Verner Clapp immediately had the records of HUAC checked. Only one reference to Williams turned up: in mid 1939 he had cosigned an open letter calling for unity of antifascist forces and cooperation with the Soviet Union. The Library's replies to the *Counterattack*-inspired letters were inescapably cagey: "Dr. Williams is, of course, an outstanding American poet, and wholly qualified in this respect to serve as our Consultant in Poetry. The information in . . . *Counterattack* was unknown to us at the time of his appointment. . . . We have not as yet questioned him for the reason that he is seriously ill. . . ." Epidemically the denunciations followed, from the citizenry directly and from Congressmen, transmitting letters and newspaper articles from their constituencies: including Senators Smathers and Holland of Florida, Wiley of Wisconsin, and Lyndon B. Johnson of Texas, and Congressman Franklin D. Roosevelt, Jr. The Hearst columnist Fulton Lewis, Jr., replayed the charges with embellishments: "One of the Truman administration patronage job-holders who probably will be given a careful going-over by the Republicans is the Librarian of Congress, Luther H. Evans. He seems to be running a sort of employment service for indigent Left-wingers."

It was actually September 2 when Florence Williams notified the Librarian of her husband's state of health and requested the three-month delay, which the Library granted at once. "It did him a world of good . . . and will hasten his recovery," Mrs. Williams wrote. Perhaps the political attacks hadn't got to Williams yet.

According to Basler's account of Williams's experience with the Consultantship, appointments to federal posts had been subject to "loyalty investigation" since an executive order in March 1947. On October 15 Clapp questioned Evans, "Should we not ask Dr. Williams to fill out Standard Form 85 now?" Williams filled out his part—the application for federal employment—on October 21, certifying among other details that he was not now and never had been a member of the Communist Party, U.S.A., or of any Communist organization, or of a Fascist organization, and so on. As to physical handicap, he stated: "Residual effects of a cerebral thrombosis." The paperwork was sent on to the Civil Service Commission. An investigation, if warranted, would be carried out by the FBI. (One may recall that the spirit of Joseph McCarthy had been abroad in the land since February 1950, when the Senator first got public attention by charging, in a speech in Wheeling, West Virginia, that the State Department had been infiltrated by Communists.)

One particular attack on Williams had poetic implications: it took the form of a circular distributed countrywide in mid-October by the Lyric Foundation, publishers of a poetry magazine, *The Lyric,* edited by Virginia Kent Cummins. She was also head of the foundation, whose vice president was Audrey Wurdemann—Mrs. Joseph Auslander. Cummins repeated the *Counterattack* charges and added a fresh note, a sample of Williams's poetry which she called "the very voice of Communism": "O Russia, Russia, come with me into my dream and let us be lovers . . . I lay my spirit at your feet . . . ," and more, from a poem he had published in *The New Republic* in 1946. Whittemore comments, "She managed to miss the main point of the poem, which was that Russia had long been a dream to Americans and WCW wished that Russia would now live up to the dream."

Williams was now aware of the attacks. In late November, when his wife wrote to Phyllis Armstrong confirming that they would be in Washington on December 6 for a week, "just to let Bill get the feel of it," she went on to say, "The sudden publicity about Bill being a Commie is of course another irritant to him. He who has fought all his life against that sort of thing! . . . He will have to rely on you to stave off the angry mob, for he is in no condition to waste his energy on that sort of thing. A group of local men are up in arms and want to beat up the bastards . . ." Indeed, the American Legion post in Rutherford was incensed at the charges against the doctor who had delivered most of the town's babies. As for staving off angry mobs of anti-Communists, Phyllis Armstrong consulted Basler, who advised her: "Make plain [to Mrs. Williams] that any idea of shielding Dr. Williams is not in your power, and that any federal employee must stand the gaff. If Mrs. Williams feels that her husband's health requires a sheltered life, she would be well advised to keep him away from Washington, for I am certain he is going to be more and more in the public press for his past activities, in view of what I have ascertained."

Before the Williamses got to Washington, a letter reached Florence Williams from Verner Clapp, acting in Evans's absence. "I very much regret to have to tell you that we have received from the Federal Bureau of Investigation a preliminary report resulting from our request for a loyalty investigation, on the basis of which we have felt it necessary to ask for a further and full investigation. It will not be possible for Dr.

Williams to enter upon the duties of his appointment pending adjudication of the allegations contained in this preliminary report and in the report of the pending investigation. I am sending this message to Dr. Williams through you rather than directly to him out of regard for his condition." The Williamses did meet with Clapp and other staff members on Monday, December 8. Basler, in his version of this episode, states that "the loyalty processes, which had become increasingly exacerbating with the onset of the 'McCarthy Era,' were explained to them, and they were told that a hearing before the Library's Loyalty Board would be afforded if necessary after the full report had been received and evaluated. The visit terminated on a friendly note, but Dr. Williams, obviously still in delicate health, seemed to be understandably annoyed and non-plussed." As Florence Williams wrote Phyllis Armstrong afterward, "Bill stood it very well, but today has cracked quite a bit. It's all so bewildering to him. He's rather bitter about *not* being informed as to what was going on,—as I am too. . . . Thank you so much for all you did for us. . . ."

In still another account of the affair, in the Washington *Star*, Mary McGrory, whose beat included the Library of Congress and its cultural events, wrote, "Several days later, Dr. Williams himself received a letter from the director of personnel at the Library of Congress. This one told him that as soon as the Loyalty Board . . . received the full FBI report, he would have the right . . . to be represented by counsel." Williams accordingly retained as attorney James F. Murray, Jr., of Jersey City (who was also a Democratic member of the New Jersey legislature), and on December 22 Murray wrote Clapp and other Library officials to the effect that Williams had been ready to take up his duties since December 15 and "in no way waives his right to assume this position . . . nor his right to any salary or other payment due him." Relying, furthermore, on assurances given him, Williams had rented a residence in Washington. (Clapp's office sought advice from the Comptroller General of the United States as to whether the Library was liable for salary and expenses in a case like Williams's. The advice is not on record, but it may be inferred that it was negative.)

After Evans's sufferance of Pound, the *Saturday Review*, Aiken, the tetchy Fellows, the earlier allegations of Fascist leanings laid against

Williams, and the fulminations of *The Lyric* and Fulton Lewis, Jr., Murray's letter must have been a last straw. In a notably austere, even harsh, letter dated January 13, 1953—two days after the Bollingen Prize for Poetry had been awarded by a Yale jury jointly to Williams and MacLeish—Evans canceled the appointment to the Chair of Poetry and the loyalty investigation. "I have determined that the conditions no longer exist which at an earlier date made your appointment . . . appear desirable and profitable to the Library. This change in the situation results not only from our view of the present state of your health, but also from the new elements introduced into the relationship between yourself and the Library in letters recently addressed by your attorney to various members of my staff. I accordingly hereby revoke the offer of appointment . . . and terminate the negotiations which have been in progress. . . . I wish to make it very clear that the above action has nothing to do with any allegations regarding your loyalty which may have been published in various places. . . . All further investigation is being stopped, and the case removed from the Board's docket. . . . Perhaps I can put the loyalty aspect of your case in proper perspective by saying that if the aforesaid allegations were completely disposed of as of now in a manner completely favorable to you, I would nevertheless revoke the aforesaid offer of appointment."

Whittemore found Evans's action "uncivil and dictatorial," and Williams's attorney Murray, who responded immediately, regarded it with "a mixture of disgust and incredulity." Williams, he wrote, took exception to Evans's "self-appointment as an expert" on his health, and he would not permit the investigation by the FBI to lapse; "he strongly resents your inference that you are doing him a favor by suggesting that such investigation be not completed." Murray advised that "steps are now underway not only to clear Dr. Williams' status at the highest possible level but also fully to investigate within Washington and elsewhere the sources of the attacks against him." "I propose not to reply," noted Evans on Murray's letter, "I agree," noted Clapp, and four other Library officials added their initials.

(In the midst of these unhappy proceedings, some of the Whittall Fund programs offered moments of calm and possibly of delight and edification: on December 15, the Irish poet Oliver St. John Gogarty read from Housman and other poets in the Coolidge Auditorium; on February 2, Merrill Moore read a program of his sonnets; on February 23, Fredric March and Florence Eldridge—who also had had their innings with HUAC—gave their interpretations of poems of Robinson, Frost, and Whitman.)

Friends of Williams rallied round. His editor at Random House, David McDowell, came to Washington to mobilize support. According to Whittemore, he appealed to the FBI through Vice-President Nixon and urged that they investigate Williams "relentlessly"; the FBI responded that since Williams was "no longer on Civil Service rolls [which he never had been] they could not investigate him further." Aiken continued to take a busy interest in the case, undoubtedly buoyed up by the recent good critical reception of his autobiographical *Ushant*. Some of the Fellows had a protest meeting in New York and deputed Léonie Adams, W. H. Auden, and Cleanth Brooks to intermediate with Evans. He received Adams and Brooks (Auden was tied up with rehearsals of *The Rake's Progress*) in his office on February 8, a Sunday, for several hours of discussion, in the course of which a compromise was worked out. (Brooks told McGrory, a year and a half later, "I think it was a question of hurt feelings. I don't think any one ever took seriously the Communist charges. I went in thinking that the charges were the basic issue, but after two or three hours of heated talk I was convinced that Dr. Evans felt very badly that Dr. Williams had had his lawyer write to him instead of contacting him on a personal basis.")

Evans conveyed his decision in a letter, oddly, not to Williams or even Murray but to Léonie Adams. (A carbon copy went to Williams.) Adams had become the go-between that all parties seemed to accept, and Williams was eager to clear up the affair, though he never again wrote to Evans. Matters were settled as follows, in Whittemore's account: "Evans agreed to be less of an expert on WCW's health if a statement by a 'qualified physician' vouching for his health was put into play, and to revive the loyalty investigation if WCW undertook to 'disavow' his claim of a right to the disputed appointment. It was like Gilbert and Sullivan, but not funny, with Evans in effect making no concessions at all. WCW gave in, obtained a physician's certificate [fortunately, before he had another heart attack, later in March, and

then was hospitalized for mental depression] and wrote the Library to
say that he had no intention of suing anyone. And on April 24, 1953—
two months before the period of the Consultantship would be for prac-
tical purposes over anyway (the office was vacant in the summer) and
four months before it would be officially over—Evans wrote to say that
WCW had been appointed to the job again, the appointment to become
effective May 15 'or as soon thereafter as loyalty and security proce-
dures are successfully completed.' " Among the procedures, Williams
had to be fingerprinted at his local police station, an experience he
considered an indignity. The Library received the full report of the loy-
alty investigation from the Civil Service Commission on June 26, 1953.
Library records state that it was never "evaluated"; its receipt was not
reported to Williams for a long time, and by then the report had been
returned, apparently, to the FBI.

In the interim, however, on June 15, 1953, the Executive Board of
the United Nations Educational, Scientific, and Cultural Organization
(UNESCO) meeting at its Paris headquarters, had nominated Luther Ev-
ans to be its Director General, succeeding the British scientist Julian
Huxley, and on July 1 the General Conference confirmed the nomina-
tion. On that date Evans resigned as Librarian of Congress, effective
four days later. The President of the United States didn't nominate a
successor to the post of Librarian of Congress until April 1954. Evans
served as the head of UNESCO until 1958.

There is a rather unhappy and unsatisfactory epilogue to the Williams
case, but before going into that, a brief intermezzo may be welcome.
Over the troubled time, Evans had several cordial letters from the "psy-
chiatric psonneteer" Merrill Moore, commenting on his friend Wil-
liams's health problems, saying "please feel free to call on me" if he
could be useful in any way, and reminding him that both his parents
had served as state librarian of Tennessee. In April he volunteered to
assume the Poetry Chair on a part-time basis; he could take a night train
down from Boston and back. "I am a Colonel in the Reserves of the
U.S. Army and have never had any contact with any Communist or
subversive group, not even 'neo-fascists.' You may recall that I was a
member of the famous Fugitive group in Nashville . . . but when it
became the Agrarian group, I resigned because I felt it had too much

of a neo-fascist tinge. . . . I am writing out of basic public spiritedness and my great concern for The Library of Congress and its wonderful work." Evans replied, "Dr. Williams and I are in the clear again . . . and we are trying to finish up the loyalty investigation as soon as possible." Then Moore offered his help with that. "Bill Williams is basically sound even though at times he may have erred slightly (and who hasn't) towards what used to be called liberalism. . . . He is a kindly soul, but sometimes he stands in his own light and then wonders why it is dark." Moore continued to practice as a psychoanalyst and write sonnets (more than a hundred thousand, it is said) until his death four years later.

❊

Williams's appointment, conditionally reinstated by Evans in April, expired in September 1953. After Evans had left Washington for Paris in early July, Acting Librarian of Congress Clapp didn't offer Williams at least a pro forma appointment for the few remaining weeks nor, certainly, did he suggest the second year in the Consultantship that he had offered him in March 1952—assuming, of course, that the unevaluated investigative report had not proved to be damaging. Williams heard nothing from the Library for more than a year. He told a reporter that he did not feel well enough to press the matter and, besides, he kept hoping that an amicable agreement would be reached. After his attack in spring 1952 he never again regained full use of his right arm and had to learn to write with his left hand.

In April 1954, President Eisenhower nominated L. Quincy Mumford, the director of the Cleveland Public Library and president-elect of the American Library Association, to be Librarian of Congress. Even more than Evans's, this was an appointment the library profession viewed only with favor, for Mumford was the first professionally trained librarian in the post. The appointment was duly approved by the Senate, and on September 1 Mumford was sworn in as the eleventh Librarian of Congress. Soon after, he received detailed memoranda from Basler and Clapp, briefing him on the Consultantship in Poetry and the Fellows in American Letters and in effect forewarning him of shoals ahead. Within the month, the Williams case was again in the headlines, now with a different emphasis.

On September 17, an article in the *Times Literary Supplement* of London, in an issue devoted to American writing today, stated that "the last poet nominated for the position [of Consultant in Poetry] had failed to receive a security clearance." It appears to have been Mary McGrory, the Washington *Star*'s Library of Congress watcher, who first spotted the statement, and it keynoted a long article on the Williams case in the *Star*'s issue of Sunday, September 26. She quoted former Acting Librarian Clapp: "I think . . . the word 'failure' does a possible injustice to Dr. Williams by implying that he was unable to meet security requirements. By the time the security investigation had been completed, the appointment of a new librarian was impending, and I felt the new librarian should not be committed to an appointment about which he might have other views. The report therefore has been marked 'nonaction.' " McGrory, a thorough reporter indeed, phoned Archer M. Huntington, who in his eighties was living in retirement at his estate in Connecticut. "He did not seem to be too aware of the fact that his endowment was being used to finance any chair of poetry in Washington," McGrory wrote. "He took the news that the chair was vacant very calmly. 'There is nothing disagreeable to me in that thought,' he said. 'I assume the money is being used for some other purpose.' " (At that time, Huntington had something of an obsession with communism. When he was approached for a donation to the Academy of American Poets, he hoped that the Academy "works along lines contrary to those influences such as communism." Reassured, he came through generously.) McGrory rang up Williams, too. "He would still like to come to Washington as consultant. . . . Failing that, he would like to have his record cleared. . . . He added, 'I have never had the courtesy of an explanation.' "

The press response, especially in New Jersey, was profuse and almost altogether sympathetic to Williams. (The McCarthy sensibility was fading. Two months later, the Senate voted to condemn the Senator's actions.) The *Washington Post* editorial called the whole affair "surprising, shocking, and distressing" and quoted the critic John Barkham,

"Williams is the concentrated essence of Americanism in everything he says and does," and the poet himself, "For heaven's sake, what kind of country is this?" Attorney Murray announced that he would go to Washington "to learn why the [security] report was pigeon-holed." MacLeish wrote Mumford from Harvard, on October 21, a long and eloquent "confidential" letter. "I am troubled for your sake and for the Library's sake about the . . . Williams matter. . . . I feel, and I know you will feel with me, that the Librarian of Congress must be the foremost champion of intellectual and spiritual freedom in the country. . . . I would rather see all the Fulton Lewises and Joe McCarthys in Washington howling for your blood than see the writers and the artists of the republic suspicious of your concern for the freedom by which they live. . . . I would hope very much that the Library might go out of its way to make a clear and forthright public statement to the effect that [it] has no reason to doubt Williams' integrity or loyalty to the United States." (MacLeish had remarked the previous year that "McCarthy has already attacked me as belonging to more Communist front organizations than any man he has ever mentioned.")

Mumford, however, after the McGrory article appeared, had moved quickly. He asked Clapp for a summary of the Williams case, which was duly prepared by Lucile M. Morsch, the Deputy Chief Assistant Librarian. Clapp also drafted a letter to Williams for Mumford "which you might care to use. I do not recommend that you communicate with him." Mumford did choose to communicate with him, by letter of October 7—Clapp's draft, evidently. "Because the [September 1953] date has now long passed, I have presumed the matter to be a dead issue. However, it has recently been brought to life by an article in the [*TLS*, etc.]. . . . As we have pointed out to the newspapers . . . , this wording is capable of misinterpretation as implying that you were refused security clearance, which is not the case. The fact was that the period contemplated by the appointment expired before the reports were evaluated. They have been returned to the investigative agency and remain unevaluated until this day." Mumford went on to say that in his inquiries he had found many outstanding questions regarding the role and manner of financing of the Consultantship as well as the Fellows, "which seem to me to require resolution before any further appointment is made to the Consultantship. None of these questions has anything to do with your security status, and I shall take pains to make this clear. . . ." Williams replied by return, signing in a left-handed scrawl: "Thank you. . . . You have been very kind, as soon as you learned of the situation as it concerned me, to write as you did that my record with the Library of Congress has not been questioned as far as my being a 'security risk' is concerned. That at least is something. . . . For your private information I am not a 'red' and never have been." And he asked permission to use the letter. Mumford phoned (and wired) Williams giving him permission to release the letter, but asking if the Library could release it first, to which Williams agreed.

The case would appear to have been closed on a reconciling note, and so the other accounts wind up the story. But Williams scarcely saw it that way. He told the *New York Post* that "the letter does not satisfactorily explain why I was barred from the post. It doesn't explain anything at all. I'm as much in a cloud as ever." Murray reiterated his determination to clear his client's name in Washington. He didn't persist at that, but Williams's bitterness never entirely dwindled away. A year later, when Mumford invited Williams to a meeting of the Fellows he added a courteous word of "regret to me personally that you should have been the victim of circumstances" (drafted by Basler), Williams answered, "In view [of] the discourtesy I have suffered at the hands of your predecessor, which cannot be overlooked, I cannot meet you on even terms. Much as I might like to see you personally at another time I cannot officially meet you until the insults to my name have been retracted."

As for MacLeish's "confidential" letter, Mumford's reply (drafted by Clapp) went out a fortnight later, with a copy of his October 7 letter to Williams. "It may be that Dr. Williams feels that the Library should provide him with a forum for reply. Unfortunately, this is not possible under . . . President Eisenhower's Loyalty-Security Order [of] May 1953. In the procedure there is no provision for hearings in preappointment cases. Consequently, even if I should now once more tender an offer of appointment to Dr. Williams, I could not assure him of a hearing unless I should first appoint him, despite any 'derogatory information' which may lie against him, and then suspend him on account of that very same 'derogatory information.'"

A double bind, indeed. The fact was, Mumford didn't want to make *any* appointment to the Consultantship at that time, and he cited "the very concrete fact that the fund for the support of the Consultantship falls short of the honorarium which we have been paying in recent years, and the gap has had to be made up from other sources."

The Fellows in American Letters were never to meet again—at the Library of Congress, that is, in official convocation. Aiken, however, whose attachment to (or cathexis on) the Library outlasted his term as Consultant, had convoked what he called a rump meeting at his apartment in New York on April 11, 1953: Warren, Adams, Bogan, Brooks (also speaking for Auden), himself (also speaking for Eliot, whom he had recently seen in London), and, as proxy, Florence Williams. Concerning her husband, they noted that Evans had set the clearance process in action, "a happy termination of an unfortunate business." They agreed that a meeting of the Fellows should be called as soon as possible, by the fall in any case, to reconsider and redefine the function of the Fellows. "In some sense the Library, while perhaps not abusing us, was at any rate not properly *using* us." The party expressed eagerness to get on with the endowed fellowships, manuscript collecting, and the poetry programs in the spirit of their resolution of the previous year. A few days later, Aiken came down to Washington hoping to see Evans; in the Librarian's absence he saw Basler and told him the Fellows felt they were being "allowed to die on the vine" and were thinking of resigning. When the conversation turned to recordings, Basler told him he was reluctant to approach Huntington Cairns about another Bollingen Foundation grant without the backing of a Consultant. Aiken volunteered to serve in that capacity for a few days, provided he got his expenses. Next day he repaired to the Poetry Room and, with Phyllis Armstrong as amanuensis, wrote a long letter to Evans reporting all the foregoing and suggesting he come to New York for a dinner meeting with some of the Fellows, "a more personal pow-wow." Evans temporized. He preferred to let the questions they raised wait until the Williams case was settled and a Consultant was in the Chair, available to participate.

Not until August 1955 did Mumford and his advisers decide that a Consultant *should* be appointed, with the advice of the Fellows in American Letters—whose ranks had lost eight members through the expiration of their seven-year terms or through resignation. The survivors: Adams, Bishop, Blackmur, Brooks, Lowell, MacLeish, Morison, Ransom, Wilder, and Williams. In seeking their advice, the Librarian included Aiken and several other literary figures. Under new legislation, the Library had no funds for travel expenses; public monies could no longer be used for the compensation or expenses of any body whose creation had not been authorized by law, and no gift fund could be "reasonably construed" as being available. Rather than ask the Fellows to meet in Washington at their own expense, the Librarian was seeking their advice in writing. The letter (drafted by Basler) went also to ex-Fellows and some other literary personages—including Mark Van Doren, Lionel Trilling, and James Laughlin. It reviewed what the Fellows and Consultants had done in the past and now asked for recommendations for the Consultantship. The thought was also aired that, when the Chair of Poetry was again filled, the Fellows' appointments could lapse and "the Library . . . seek suggestions and advice from the literary profession on an ad hoc basis."

Among those who replied, Willard Thorp observed that, with the Chair of Poetry being discontinued and the *Quarterly Book Review* folding up, the Librarian must feel like Winston Churchill saying that he didn't intend to preside over the disintegration of the British Empire. Thorp and other Fellows had contributed to the *USQBR*, as it was usually called, which since 1944 had been circulated chiefly abroad; the Department of State considered it a useful instrument of foreign policy. But both funds and interest had waned, and with the June 1956 issue publication ceased.

And from Robert Lowell: "It seems to me that the Fellows have nothing really to be ashamed of: they have kept up standards in choosing Consultants, giving prizes and having poets recorded. As awards and academies go, I think our group has been a model, that we have been neither idiosyncratic nor foolishly popular in our choices. . . . I feel that the failure of the relationship between Fellow and Library to work out is a disaster. . . . The position of Consultant in Poetry will have little meaning or prestige unless he is chosen by other writers."

And, from MacLeish, there was another articulate communication, rehearsing the formerly ill-lettered state of the Library of Congress and subsequently the "benefit of the presence from time to time, as well as the counsel, of the country's foremost living writers. . . . If the Library can't pay the expenses of necessary consultants . . . you ought in some way to hold the gains made in the brief years in which the Fellows flourished. It would be tragic if the country's national library and the country's writers drifted back into the condition of mutual disinterest which obtained fifteen years ago. . . . If you are going to liquidate the Fellows, as you imply, do by all means call a meeting of the present and immediately past members and give them a chance to be heard. . . . Making nominations [for the Chair] without a chance to discuss is a pretty unsatisfactory proceeding. . . ." Mumford's reaction to all this avuncular advice is not on record.

He did, however, propose a New York meeting in December. Only two Fellows—Blackmur and Brooks—replied that they could attend, and plans for the meeting were abandoned. Numerous nominations for the Consultantship had come in nevertheless. Richard Wilbur, Randall Jarrell, and Richard Eberhart led the list. After lengthy meditation, the Librarian appointed Jarrell for a term beginning in September 1956.

❈

During the hiatus between Aiken and Jarrell, the responsibility for the Library's poetry establishment (and many other duties) rested in the hands of Roy Basler, with the assistance of Phyllis Armstrong. The programs under the Whittall Fund became their concern, and they worked in close liaison with Mrs. Whittall. As Basler observed, from his privileged vantage point, "Of the 'younger' poets, whom the Fellows . . . for the most part had represented, she admitted no liking, but she agreed readily enough that 'her programs' should not ignore them. In the course of the ensuing decade, as the 'younger' poets appeared more and more frequently under her auspices, as it were, she studied their works beforehand and in every instance made perceptive observations, not merely on their qualities as poets, but on their frequent deficiencies as readers of their own best pieces." She continued, though, to prefer Shakespeare and other classics, when read by theatrical professionals; and she preferred male readers, "giving good argument that their voices were simply better instruments for poetry."

On December 17, 1954, Mrs. Whittall had made still another benefaction to the Library: $100,000 in bonds (out of the hatbox, no doubt) for a Fund for the Development of Appreciation and Understanding of Good Literature. A year later, she added $50,000. The income was meant to enhance further the programs under the first two Whittall literary endowments. (It should be said that, evenhandedly, Mrs. Whittall had continued to make additional gifts to the foundation for music that carried her name.) Mrs. Whittall's literary gifts to the Library, however, were placed in jeopardy through a near contretemps. The story calls for a flashback. In November 1952, Mrs. Whittall had belatedly received a copy of the minutes of the Fellows' meeting the previous March, including the resolution deploring the Consultant's exclusion from planning the programs under her Poetry Fund. When Basler visited her soon afterward, as he reported two years later to Mumford, "she was tearful and indignant. . . . I assured her that the Fellows had no authority to change the terms of her gift in any way, that my directive . . . was to discuss everything with her, and that I could assure her that everything was going to be all right. She seemed satisfied, and we parted in very friendly fashion. Since then, she has never referred to the matter again until—" (It appears that, after Basler departed, Mrs. Whittall sat down and wrote Evans to express her amazement at the Fellows' resolution and her "personal and vital" concern. "Strange misunderstandings and discord threaten the very life and usefulness of the project—and I suggest that no Readings be given—and that the Gertrude Clarke Whittall Fund lie fallow until such a time as it can function as intended, now and forever, as a distinct independent entity—and amicably." She never sent the letter; at any rate, Evans never received it, and Mrs. Whittall never mentioned the matter again until—) "yesterday, when she presented the copy of the letter and said she thought she should have an answer. She said that she is well pleased with how things are going, as evidenced by a new gift, but that she is worried about the future." Hurriedly, a letter to her was prepared for the Librarian's signature, concluding that the 1952 letter must have been lost and assuring her that her Funds will function "as a distinct independent entity now and forever as intended by you." All the Library officers who were involved in the meeting in 1952 "felt only deep regret that the remarks of the Fellows were such as to hurt your feelings." The Fellows had never been empowered, the Librarian stated, to direct the affairs of the Whittall Funds. Amity prevailed.

We may note some highlights, under those Funds, during the years of hiatus. Most of the programs were broadcast from the Coolidge Auditorium over a Washington radio station, and many were recorded for the archive. *Season of 1953–54:* Claude Rains, with piano accompaniment, reading poems from Chaucer to Eliot. (On Rains's performance of Tennyson's "Enoch Arden" with music of Richard Strauss, Mrs. Whittall remarked, "Good reading of second-rate Tennyson set to second-rate Strauss.") Katherine Garrison Chapin, reading selections from Emily Dickinson and other poets. The actor Arnold Moss, readings on the theme "The Seven Ages of Man," beginning a long run of his appearances on the Whittall programs. *Season of 1954–55:* Carl Sandburg, readings and commentary. Merrill Moore, a lecture on the "Fugitive" poets. Jessica Tandy and Hume Cronyn, dramatic readings. As part of a celebration of the centennial of Whitman's *Leaves of Grass,* lectures by Charles Feinberg, Mark Van Doren, Gay Wilson Allen, and David Daiches, and a reading by Arnold Moss. Lord Dunsany, "observation and banter on poets old and new." Thornton Wilder, reading the first two acts of his new play, "The Alcestiad." *Season of 1955–56:* Robert Frost, readings (and an exhibition of Frostiana). Readings (on separate occasions) by Robert Hillyer, Robert Penn Warren, and Richard Eberhart. R. P. Blackmur, four lectures entitled "*Anni Mirabiles,* 1921–1925: Reason in the Madness of Letters." (When the Library brought out the Blackmur lectures in pamphlet form, Phyllis Armstrong sent Aiken a copy. He read them, he wrote Basler, "with great admiration and satisfaction—satisfaction in a personal sense, for it was I who first made the suggestion. . . . This series is far and away the finest thing ever offered by the Library, and . . . the *sort* of thing now to be aimed at. . . . More power to you." He suggested that Bertrand Russell on poetry and science might be a lot of fun.)

During the summer before the Frost reading and exhibit, the poet's daughter, Lesley Frost Ballantine, visited the Poetry Room ostensibly to ask about plans. Phyllis Armstrong wrote up a minute of their conversation, for the record. Mrs. Ballantine inquired pointedly why the Chair of Poetry was still vacant. "The best incumbent they ever had was Joe Auslander," she said; "since then it's been nothing but a fiasco . . . what they really need is not a poet, but someone interested in poetry! I wish they'd give me the job." Armstrong reported that her visitor "brought up the subject of MacLeish's term in office, venting her wrath over how he had 'destroyed' poetry along with Joe A., as far as the Library was concerned." Lesley Ballantine informed Armstrong that the Assistant to President Eisenhower, Sherman Adams, "is a very, very good friend of mine and Robert's, and would do *anything, just anything,* to exploit New Hampshire *or* Frost . . . just let me know if you need my help."

The Whittall programs heaped responsibility and labor on the Poetry Office—invitations, tickets, telephone calls, press arrangements—and the poetic traffic that had been visited on the Consultant was heavy still. In an administrative report Basler pointedly remarked that many persons turned up with "the usual routine questions, 'How to go about writing poetry?' or, having already written some, 'Where might one find a publisher?' . . . Poets, critics, professors and students, a number of them from abroad, came to inquire about some phase of poetry." Phyllis Armstrong also completed a bibliographical project: listing authors whose first editions should be considered for deposit in the Rare Book Division. As the Bollingen Foundation's grants for recording poets reading their poems had long since been used up, in 1954 Basler and Armstrong prepared an elaborate presentation seeking a renewal of Bollingen help. That nothing ensued pro or con was attributed to the foundation's wariness because of the absence of a Consultant in Poetry. The Library administration, in any event, recognized the Poetry Office's exertions and approved for both Basler and Armstrong honoraria drawn from Whittall money.

✴

On September 10, 1954, Harvard University Press published Pound's translation into rhymed verse of the three hundred "Odes" of ancient China, under the title *The Classic Anthology Defined by Confucius*. Pound had been working on it throughout the years at St. Elizabeths.

March 1955. For the first time Eliot read the transcripts of Ezra Pound's wartime broadcasts from Italy. He wrote Tate: "My first reactions to the broadcasts (which are unpleasant enough, God knows), . . . is that nobody could read these outpourings and regard the writer as sane. It seems to me that if Ezra was off his head after Pisa, he was off it a good long time before. That is perhaps where I differ from most people who seem to think Ezra saner than I think him. This makes it still more difficult for me to be clear in my mind as to what should be done for him, as I feel that if he is released, he will simply get into more trouble than ever, sooner or later. I confess I look forward with no pleasant anticipations to visiting him in Washington."

Eliot did come to Washington for two days in May primarily to call on Pound. Basler, learning he would be in town, drafted a letter for Mumford inviting him to visit the Library and record anew for the archive. Eliot replied courteously. "My time has been pretty fully engaged in advance of my arrival"; a visit was impossible. As for recording hitherto unrecorded poems, "I have become increasingly severe with my own recordings. . . . I don't want to make any more . . . until I can do it at leisure, hearing every recording and re-recording the records with which I am not satisfied. My experience is that . . . I should never record for more than twenty minutes at a time [because] after a period of about twenty minutes the strain and fatigue of the voice becomes evident." The Library's archive contains no recording by Eliot later than 1948.

✴

In 1955: the deaths of the two founders of the Chair of Poetry. The Librarian Emeritus of Congress, Herbert Putnam, died on August 14,

THREE: 1950 TO 1956

at the age of 94. He had brought the Library into the twentieth century, in any sense. He regarded as his greatest achievement the passage by Congress in 1925 of the act creating the Library of Congress Trust Fund Board, marked by the establishment of the Coolidge Foundation. Thus his program of Chairs followed. In Putnam's years the Library's collections grew from less than a million volumes to over five million.

Archer M. Huntington died on December 11, at his estate, Stanerigg Farm, near Redding, Connecticut. He was 85. During his lifetime and at his death, Huntington gave away his entire fortune, except for a provision for his widow, the sculptor Anna Hyatt Huntington. (*She* died in 1973, at the age of 97, a few years after finishing her last monumental sculpture, of General Isaac Putnam.) In his will, Huntington left bequests ranging from approximately $100,000 to $300,000 to most of the cultural institutions he had favored in his earlier philanthropies. The Library of Congress Trust Fund received $99,902, "to be used as it may deem wise." The income is shared equally by the Chair of Poetry and the fund for the maintenance of the Hispanic Society Room.

Joseph Auslander, though not remembered in Huntington's will, had ample experience of his patron's generosity in the late years. During the 1940s, Auslander's poetry, often on patriotic themes, appeared in popular magazines, and he and Audrey Wurdemann collaborated on two novels that had a fair success. In the early 1950s, their luck began to run out. They were living at the Royalton, a New York residence hotel favored by literary and theater people. Huntington now and then invited them to the Farm and sent checks to help them along. Auslander sent him tributes in rhyme and gallant bread-and-butter notes, such as "Whenever we come away from seeing you two wonderful people it is always with a sense of a rainbow around our shoulders and the great warm glow of beauty in our hearts." In April 1952, Joseph and Audrey Auslander became the parents of a son, Louis, and two years later a daughter, Anna. They were evidently in difficult straits; Auslander was writing radio scripts, and for a while he worked in a Long Island factory. He appealed to Mrs. Whittall for help, but she declined. When the Academy of American Poets, in 1953, devoted its *Poetry Pilot* newsletter to Huntington as a poet, Auslander wrote an appreciative tribute to his patron, "a reincarnated troubadour in a pedestrian and sordid

[169]

age." Subsequently, Huntington agreed to compensate Auslander, at the rate of $500 per month and expenses, including a car, for writing a book about Brookgreen Gardens. The Auslander family visited the Gardens several times, in the interests of the project. But the book, if ever finished, was never published. And after Huntington's death, the Auslanders—with their two "autumn crocuses," as their father called them—moved south to Coral Gables, a suburb of Miami.

Louise Bogan, late 1940s

Léonie Adams, December 1948

Karl Shapiro in the Poetry Room, 1946

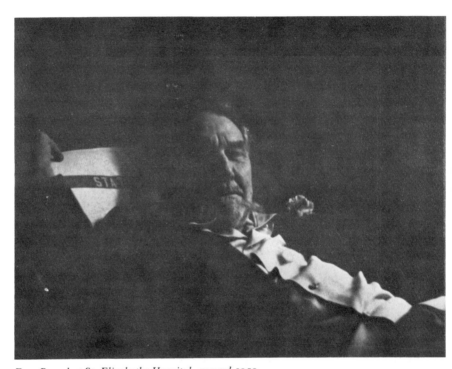

Ezra Pound at St. Elizabeths Hospital, around 1950

Allen Tate, Léonie Adams, T. S. Eliot, Theodore Spencer, and Robert Penn Warren, in the Whittall Pavilion, November 19, 1948

Elizabeth Bishop and Robert Frost, December 1949

Conrad Aiken, with the cast of his play Mr. Arcularis, *produced at the Arena Stage Theatre in Washington, May 1951*

William Carlos Williams, February 1951, during a visit to Aiken's office

Luncheon meeting of the Fellows in American Letters, February 9, 1951, in the Whittall Pavilion. Gertrude Clarke Whittall is speaking; at her left, Luther H. Evans, Robert Penn Warren, and Dan M. Lacy (the Deputy Chief Assistant Librarian).

Cleanth Brooks, Mrs. Whittall, Luther Evans, and Burgess Meredith, in the Librarian's office, May 1, 1951, before the Edward Arlington Robinson program

Pre-luncheon drinks at the Fellows' meeting, February 29, 1952, in the Whittall Pavilion. Standing: Conrad Aiken, Cleanth Brooks, R. P. Warren; seated: W. H. Auden, Katherine Garrison Chapin, Luther Evans, Léonie Adams, and R. P. Blackmur

Warren and Mrs. Whittall, on the evening he read his poetry in the Coolidge Auditorium, December 5, 1955

Randall Jarrell, fall 1956

Quincy Mumford, Randall Jarrell, and Archibald MacLeish, in the Poetry Room, fall 1956

[183]

The first meeting of the Honorary Consultants in American Letters, April 18, 1958, in the Poetry Room. Seated, left to right: Cleanth Brooks, Eudora Welty, John Crowe Ransom, and Randall Jarrell; standing: Quincy Mumford, Roy P. Basler, Phyllis Armstrong, and R. P. Blackmur

Robert Frost making a recording for the blind, in the Recording Laboratory, 1959

Richard Eberhart, at the Library to read his poetry, 1956, three years be-fore he became the Consultant

Carl Sandburg, Quincy Mumford, and Robert Frost, May 2, 1960

Frost and Sandburg in the Whittall Pavilion, May 2, 1960

Robert Lowell, at the Library to read his poetry, October 1, 1960

Louis Untermeyer and his wife, Bryna, entering the Coolidge Auditorium for the first evening's program of the National Poetry Festival, October 22, 1962

Louise Bogan

Langston Hughes

Registering for the National Poetry Festival on the first day, October 22, 1962

Delmore Schwartz

Mark Van Doren

Herbert Read

Frost's lecture, the second evening of the National Poetry Festival. In the audience, bottom row: Stanley Kunitz, Louis Untermeyer, Gwendolyn Brooks, Allen Tate, W. D. Snodgrass, Henry Rago; middle row: (unidentified), Muriel Rukeyser, Vaun Gillmor (vice-president of the Bollingen Foundation), Sophie Read, Herbert Read; at top: Randall Jarrell

Four

1956 TO 1963

Randall Jarrell was a celestial navigation tower operator in the United States Air Force, stationed at an airfield near Tucson, Arizona, when Tate wrote, in *Sixty American Poets:* "What the war will do to Jarrell's talent . . . no one can predict, but much may be expected of him if he has any luck at all. He has marvellous fluency and richness of invention. I put him with Shapiro and Schwartz as among the best poets of his generation." Jarrell had begun flight training and would have become a pilot, but he washed out and was assigned to the specialized duty that, as it happened, kept him out of combat and in the States until his discharge in early 1946.

Nashville and the New Critics were Jarrell's home ground. As a Vanderbilt University freshman he discovered (or was discovered by) the Fugitive writers Warren, Tate, and Ransom. Warren admitted him to his sophomore "survey of literature" course "because he had read everything." Jarrell's friendship with Tate was of first importance to him for years, until a literary difference caused a coolness shortly before Tate came to the Library of Congress. Warren remained one of Jarrell's masters, together with Ransom, who had brought him to Kenyon College to teach freshman English and coach the tennis team during 1937–39. At Kenyon, Jarrell came to know Lowell; they shared a room in the Ransom family's attic and, in Mary Jarrell's words, "forged a friendship that withstood marriages, divorces, honors, and breakdowns." "Upsettingly brilliant" was how Lowell described Jarrell at Kenyon; "knowing everything—Marx, Empson, Auden, Kafka and the ideologies and current events of the day" (in a letter to his prep-school teacher Richard Eberhart, quoted by Mary Jarrell). Jarrell saw Lowell's promise early and, in his critical writing, fostered his recognition as one of the leading poets of their generation.

All the Consultants who had preceded him (except, it would appear, Auslander) were known to Jarrell in some degree. With Bogan his relations were not quite cordial, owing to a critical disagreement. With Aiken, also, there was far less warmth, because of Jarrell's unfriendly reviews of Aiken's poetry in 1941 and again in 1948. About the latter case, John Berryman wrote, "He [Jarrell] was a terror as a reviewer. . . . He was immensely cruel, and the extraordinary thing about it is that he didn't know he was cruel. . . . That rather sweet-souled man, Conrad Aiken, wrote a letter to . . . the *New Republic* saying that Jarrell's reviews went beyond decency—that he was a sadist. I was very fond of both Conrad and Randall. Jarrell's reviews did go beyond the limit. . . . Conrad was quite right. . . . Jarrell then wrote a letter in a rather aggrieved tone . . ."—after all, Aiken had let fly with references to "malicious preciosity," "highbrow intoxication," "insecurity," and so on. MacLeish also experienced Jarrell's critical ferocity in 1942 and would have again in 1949 if Jarrell had not decided to withdraw the review, because "it would be too hard on the poor dope . . . nobody thinks anything of him any more." Williams fared far better. Jarrell was enthusiastic about Williams's work and wrote an introduction to his *Selected Poems,* published in 1949. In March of that year, hearing news of the Bollingen Prize from Lowell, he wrote him, "They had plenty of courage to give it to Pound—and if they lose their nerve and give it to Williams, that's good too." Though not a wholehearted admirer of Pound, he had gone with Lowell to visit him at St. Elizabeths in spring 1948.

And Frost: Jarrell's essay "The Other Frost," the same year, was "all about 'my' Frost; maybe it'll get a few people to change their minds, at least it would if they'd read the poems." The critic Christopher Benfey recently suggested that with that essay Jarrell "really discovered Frost for serious readers of poetry, and showed them how to read him." And also Bishop: Jarrell wrote her, from Washington in early 1957, "I like your poetry better than anybody's since the Frost-Stevens-Eliot-Moore generation."

During the years when Warren, Shapiro, and Lowell were in the Consultantship and Jarrell came to Washington to read in the Recording Lab, he had become well acquainted with the Chair. Thus, in March 1952, when he was teaching at Princeton, it interested him to learn from Blackmur, then a Fellow, that the salary had been raised, regular office hours no longer existed, the job might run for two years—"*And,*" Jarrell wrote his fiancée, "they have a sort of permanent list to pick from (I'm on it); so inside the next six or eight years that's something we're almost certain to get." In fall 1955, among literary lights Mumford asked to make suggestions, Lionel Trilling named Jarrell and Babette Deutsch. After trying Wilbur and then Eberhart, Mumford settled on the North Carolinian and, in March 1956, invited him for a two-year appointment. For Jarrell the offer was opportune. He had become embroiled in a ruckus at the Woman's College of the University of North Carolina, where he had been teaching since 1953. A woman graduate student, who was also a social personage in Greensboro, accused him of "a violent and unprovoked attack on my conduct and my work." He allegedly told her, "You older women are a nuisance, constantly taking up the time of the class." Around the same time, Jarrell was playing a leading role in a faculty-administration quarrel over curriculum. He arranged a welcome leave of absence, filled out the Library's obligatory security questionnaire, got fingerprinted, and was interviewed for the *Star,* over the telephone, by Mary McGrory. Shortly after his appointment was announced, in late March, a perturbed Roy Basler phoned Jarrell. A report had reached the Library that Jarrell was a Communist, on the grounds that he had published in such radical publications as the *Nation* and the *New Republic* and had associated with Marxists while teaching at the University of Texas before he enlisted in the Air Force. His appointment was in jeopardy. Basler had to ask for his sworn oath that he had not been a Communist Party member and for a character testimonial from the Chancellor of the College, both of which Jarrell readily supplied. His politics had, in fact, shown traces earlier of Marxist interest, but a Party member he scarcely had been. In any case, this ghost was laid.

※

It has been a common misconception from the beginning that the Consultant in Poetry is the Poet Laureate of the United States. High school English teachers, teaching "Sea Fever" in the years from 1930 to 1967, inculcated in all of us an awareness of John Masefield and *his* famous appointment as Great Britain's poet laureate over those years. Newspaper reporters writing about the Consultant are notably prone to the error. Furthermore, poets laureate, so called, are appointed in many of the states. The honor is comparable more often than not to a Kentucky colonelcy—though not always, as witness Robert Frost (Vermont), Gwendolyn Brooks (Illinois), and Richard Eberhart (New Hampshire). Not surprisingly, Congressmen and government officials from time to time feel that what this country needs is indeed a national poet laureate. In the summer of 1956, before Jarrell arrived in Washington, a member of the House of Representatives from New York, W. Sterling Cole, proposed legislation that would authorize the President to designate a poet laureate and wrote the Librarian of Congress about it. Mumford's reply, which required the drafting genius of Basler, Adkinson, and Clapp, ran in the main as follows: "I am thoroughly in accord with your objective of providing an incentive for creative effort in the field of poetry. I must confess, however, that I have doubts as to whether the arts, in a country such as ours, can successfully or indeed should be promoted by the Government through the creation of prizes and other similar distinctions.

"In our cosmopolitan and democratic civilization the arts survive by their ability to establish themselves with relatively large groups[,] and few artistic styles or movements fail to secure some adherents. For the Government to make a choice from among the practitioners of one or another school would, I believe, tend to discourage rather than encourage experimentation and artistic development by putting the Government's imprimatur on one style as opposed to another.

"Here at the Library of Congress we have had an unfortunate experience in the making of awards. . . ."

On that occasion, the proposal never got out of committee.

From the new Consultant's first letter in office, dated September 25, 1956, to his predecessor a decade earlier, who was in Nebraska editing *Prairie Schooner:*

> Dear Karl:
>
> I was, honest and truly, just about to write you when your letter came. The first thing I found in my desk was a little memorandum or list in your handwriting; it says, Auden, Day Lewis, Sitwell, Mer . . .[sic]
>
> I'll send you a Rilke translation for your magazine—I have eight or nine done and mean to do many more. . . . I have—oh joy!—a week-old poem that I send you not for your magazine but just for yourself.
>
> I like the Library and Washington very much—Mary and I are delighted that we're here for the two years. How do you like your new university and new job? I wish your mother didn't live here, so that you could stay with us when you come to Washington to read your poems. Do plan to have dinner with us or do something with us.
>
> How'd you happen not to write a poem about the Library? Walking through the Tunnel listening to the turbines and looking at the different tribes walking along, I marvelled that you hadn't. But don't now, I will.

(A subterranean passage linked, and links, the main building, where the Consultant's and Basler's offices were, and the Annex, where the Manuscript Division was in those days. Off the passage was the employees' cafeteria, and the traffic was heavy. Nowadays still another passage, warrenlike, leads to the James Madison Memorial Building, which was completed in 1981.)

The poem Jarrell sent Shapiro was "The Woman at the Washington Zoo." The Jarrells had soon discovered the zoo along with the tribes of civil servicedom. During the two Washington years, Jarrell wrote only three other poems but translated a fair parcel of the poetry of Rilke and Goethe. And wrote many letters. Another to Shapiro, October 18:

> I'm just back from two and a half weeks on the West Coast, otherwise I'd have sent the poems long before. . . . I just had a long letter from Elizabeth Bishop [living in Brazil], in reply to a long one of mine. She sounds wonderfully happy and well settled.
>
> I fairly often, on the Coast, read Rilke, Yeats, Hardy, Hopkins, Stevens, Bishop, Auden, and so forth to audiences; I read your "The Leg." It certainly is a wonderful poem.
>
> I met a really good (and wholly delightful) new young poet named Gregory Corso. He's all that the tea-party or grey-flannel or World-of-Richard-Wilbur poets aren't. Not that I don't like Wilbur, but one is enough.
>
> I hope you like Nebraska a lot. We flew over it yesterday, but whether or not we saw you I don't know.

Jarrell also met Allen Ginsberg and Kenneth Rexroth, neither of whom he took to. Later, Corso turned up in Washington, broke. Mary Jarrell recalls that, "remembering his own hard times as a beginning poet, . . .[Randall] obligingly took on Tate's role as mentor [and] invited Corso to stay indefinitely and work on his poetry. He stayed six weeks, writing a poem a day. . . ." Corso wore out his welcome and went on his way to New York. Jarrell later observed, "Failure to select, exclude, compress, or aim toward a work of art makes it impossible for even a talented beatnik to write a good poem except by accident."

As a first assignment in the Consultantship, Jarrell undertook to study the entire course of the Fellows in American Letters and make recommendations concerning their future. He sent a lengthy memorandum to the Librarian on November 20: impressive, considering everything else he had been doing. (His legibly scribbled working notes survive in the Library's files. One of his *topoi* that didn't make it to the final draft may be worth saving: "With so few duties, the Devil finds work for idle Fellows to do.") Jarrell agreed with Luther Evans's point of view, in 1952, that the Fellows' functions needed to be more clearly defined. Since they hadn't met since that fateful year, and only a few survived (on paper at that, one could say), the Library might consider the advantages or disadvantages of their continued existence. A summary by Basler helps here:

> [Jarrell] thought the main disadvantage to be obvious: since the Fellows were an autonomous or semi-autonomous group with standards that were not, necessarily, the Library's, it had been possible for them to take actions that had been either publicly (as in the case of Pound) or privately (as in the case of the administration of the Whittall Poetry Fund) embarrassing to the Library. He believed, however, that if the Fellows were a more varied and more widely representative group, this disadvantage would be minimized. It was because the Fellows had been a specialized, homogeneous body of poets and critics that they had tended to act, sometimes, in a specialized way, and if the Fellows could be made more truly representative of the variety of American literature and art and thought, they might reflect more exactly what seemed to be the original motives for the appointing of fellows and honorary consultants.

Jarrell suggested a variety of new Fellows in a variety of fields, several of which reflected his own interests. The list included Edmund Wilson, Lionel Trilling, Eudora Welty, Eric Bentley, Saul Bellow, J. D. Salinger, Wolfgang Köhler, James Gould Cozzens, Paul Tillich, Reinhold Niebuhr, Erwin Panofsky, Meyer Schapiro, C. L. Lewis, A. L. Kroeber . . . and Hemingway, Faulkner, and Frost. Jarrell believed that the Library would derive the most benefit from the Fellows' help in the acquisition of the manuscripts and personal papers of authors, in the acquisition also of European books in the realm of belles-lettres, in obtaining endowments from foundations, in establishing a lecture series (and publishing the fruits), in setting up fellowships, and in selecting readers of poetry, lecturers, and the Consultant in Poetry. There's little very new in that platform, but it was surely salutary for those points to be codified, and by a distinguished poet and critic of a constructive disposition. Jarrell's concluding and most original observation, as noted by Basler, was that "the Fellows were the Government's only official connection with literature, and . . . their existence made apparent to everyone the Library's interest in, and concern for, American literature."

Quincy Mumford took no action on Jarrell's recommendations until August 16, 1957, when he wrote to the surviving Fellows—Bishop, Blackmur, Brooks, Ransom, and Wilder—explaining that there were still no funds for financing a meeting, but Consultant Jarrell felt that his work would benefit if there were a panel of American men and women of letters whom he might call upon for advice and help. Furthermore, the Library now intended "to convert the titles and terms of all those who serve it in an unsalaried, advisory capacity to a uniform basis": the Fellows in American Letters would become Honorary Consultants in American Letters, with a term of three years. The five survivors consented to the new dispensation, and Mumford also invited Maxwell Anderson and Eudora Welty, who accepted, and William Faulkner and James Gould Cozzens, who declined. (Cozzens to Mumford: "I am, and I always have been, out of touch with current literary trends. With the exception of Mr. Thornton Wilder, I would be most unlikely to agree with any of the Fellows who are consultants-to-be that you list.") Actually, funds proved to be available the following spring, and a meeting took place on April 18 and 19, 1958, attended by Brooks, Blackmur, Ransom, and Welty, as well as Jarrell and a contingent of Library staff led by Mumford. The "carefully organized" discussion, as Jarrell later reported, turned on all the points that he had proposed, and also on the recording program, the desirability of preparing bibliographies, and "the real function of the Consultant in Poetry." Jarrell commented, "Both the Consultants and the Administration seemed to consider the meeting a notable success."

Subsequently, nearly forty Honorary Consultants have been appointed. In the 1970s, however, the Honorary Consultantships in American Letters were gradually phased out as it became apparent they no longer served any significant purpose.

❉

While the Honorary Consultants in American Letters were meeting on April 18, the United States District Court for the District of Columbia was in session, hearing a motion to dismiss the indictment of Ezra Pound on charges of treason. The motion was heard by the same judge, Bolitha J. Laws, who had presided at Pound's commitment to St. Elizabeths in 1946. Pound's counsel was the distinguished jurist Thurman W. Arnold. In the account of one of Pound's biographers, David Heymann: "It was a brief and perfunctory proceeding. Mr. Arnold told the court that he represented not only Mrs. Pound (as Committee for Ezra Pound) but 'the world community of poets and writers.' The mainstay of his argument, as outlined in his motion and accompanying documents, was that unless the indictment against him were dismissed, the defendant would spend the rest of his life at St. Elizabeths, a virtual prisoner condemned for 'alleged acts and events which could never be proved.' A new element in Mr. Arnold's motion 'was the probability that Pound had been insane at the time he made the broadcasts'; another was 'the difficulty the government would face in producing witnesses for any future prosecution of the case.' " A representative of the Department of Justice told the court that the motion was in the interest of justice and should be granted. "When the order freeing Pound was handed down, Mrs. Pound rose from her seat, walked to the rear of the courtroom, and embraced her husband."

It was MacLeish who had taken the lead in working for Pound's release, after visiting him at St. Elizabeths for the first time in December 1955. He wrote Quincy Mumford: "I should have done it years ago but just plain lacked the stomach. . . . I'd only met Pound once in my life in any case and so I let my conscience sleep. Well, it was as bad as I had feared but far more poignant. . . . What disturbed me most was that he had few books within which to make a life in that place. When he was first incarcerated the Library made books available to him but somehow that petered out. Do you suppose it could be arranged again on a moderate basis? He very much wants Joseph F. Rock's *The Ancient Na-Khi Kingdom*."

MacLeish's efforts were seconded closely by Eliot and Hemingway. Robert Frost's apparent influence was, in the ultimate effect, the most telling, through his reputation as a popular poet and his friendliness with officials in the Eisenhower administration, in particular Sherman Adams, the Assistant to the President. Arnold's motion to dismiss carried with it an affidavit (that Pound was "permanently and incurably insane") by the psychiatrist Winfred Overholser, superintendent of St. Elizabeths Hospital, and statements by Frost (read to the Court), MacLeish, Eliot, Hemingway, Tate, Sandburg, Marianne Moore, Auden, Robert Fitzgerald, and several comparable others.

Frost had had no sympathy for Pound "the traitor," but in 1954 his attitude had begun to soften. The publication that year of Pound's literary essays, edited by Eliot, was a reminder to Frost that Pound had reviewed his work appreciatively in 1914. In early 1957, MacLeish, who recognized that his New Deal background was no recommendation to a Republican administration, asked Frost to join his efforts in Pound's behalf, and Frost agreed reluctantly. A crucial letter to the Attorney General, written by MacLeish, was signed by Hemingway, Eliot, and Frost, on the letterhead of the American Academy of Arts and Letters. In late spring, when Frost was in London, he discussed Pound's case with both MacLeish, returning from a visit to Pound's daughter in Italy, and Eliot (who recalled that he had first heard of Frost from Pound), and his concern livened. MacLeish was "the most self-effacingly active and successful," Lawrance Thompson wrote. "He conducted his backstage manipulations of Frost with exceptional tact. Eventually and mistakenly, Frost assumed he had played a truly decisive part in securing Pound's freedom. . . . Arnold secured the dismissal of the indictment . . . without difficulty, and refused to take a fee for his part in the fight. By contrast, Frost seemed to feel he had done more than any other toward the liberation of Ezra Pound. 'I did it,' he kept saying to reporters."

Pound lingered in Washington for some weeks after he had been freed. A research analyst in the Legislative Reference Service of the Library of Congress, Herman A. Seiber, had in early 1958 prepared a report on "The Medical, Legal, Literary, and Political Status" of Pound, at the request of members of Congress who were interested in the case. Seiber, interviewing Pound, learned that he retained only friendly feelings toward the Library of Congress and was willing to read from his poetry in the Recording Laboratory. But, as Basler put it, "The epidemic of McCarthyitis which had ravaged all government agencies was ebbing but by no means past, and the Library administration declined to permit an invitation to be extended to Pound."

Before he sailed for Italy on June 30, Pound paid a brief visit to William Carlos Williams at his house in Rutherford. "The two old men, each sick in his own way, had little to say to each other," Reed Whittemore wrote. "[Williams's wife] Flossie reported that 'Bill couldn't talk to him but sat around looking unhappy' while Ezra was 'definitely a mental case' and 'jittery as an eel.' "

✳

There would have been the means to fund a recording by Ezra Pound, too. In December 1956, on a tip from Huntington Cairns, Basler wrote the president of the Bollingen Foundation, John D. Barrett, "With Randall Jarrell our new Consultant in Poetry, . . . the activities of the Poetry Office are beginning to pick up again. We should like very much to reactivate the program in recording modern poets . . . [and] hope that the Bollingen Foundation may give serious thought to the proposal submitted by the Library in 1954." The Bollingen mills usually ground slowly, but within only a year another grant had been approved: the Foundation gave $2,500 for each of three years. The idea now was to focus on recording poets who couldn't come to Washington for the purpose, but also to "take advantage of the fortuitous presence of these personages in Washington . . . to record them on the premises." The former aspect developed on two fronts: first, Jarrell (also Phyllis Armstrong, and later Eberhart when he was Consultant in Poetry) wrote to selected poets, inviting them to record at the Library's expense, on their home ground, not only their poetry but also "their reflections about their work, the associations and inspirations that brought it about, etc."; second, Lee Anderson in the course of his travels made recordings at the Consultant's behest, on a piecework basis. A tremendous enrichment of the archive was the result—the work of some fifty poets, both British and American, nearly half of whom had been recorded by Anderson. In 1958, however, Anderson broke off from the Library and took up with the recording program at Yale University, which offered him better recompense.

The Bollingen Foundation wasn't the only benefactor of the Library's recording program. In April 1959, a grant of $15,000 was received from the Ambrook Foundation, established by the businessman/poet Hy Sobiloff. The money was designated expressly to fund eight more records continuing the series "Twentieth-Century Poetry in English."

Jarrell also helped get the effort to acquire literary papers into gear. He prepared a leaflet outlining the Library's interest in such acquisition, which was sent around to prospects, and he wrote, often chattily, to a goodly number, including particular friends such as Jean Stafford: "It's really astonishing that *The New Yorker* hasn't told you, Peter [Taylor], or A. J. Liebling about the tax provisions for literary manuscripts: maybe its Unconscious (I can't make up my mind whether or not it has one) wants to keep you slaves of a benevolent overseer." He explained the intricacies that, at that time, governed such deposits or donations. One of his catches was Vladimir Nabokov, who began to consign installments of his papers to the Library and claim the permissible tax deduction—until a change in the tax law occurred in 1969, disallowing deductions for giving one's own papers to an educational or governmental institution. Nabokov thereafter let his papers pile up in Montreux.

An unusual service that Jarrell performed—or aimed to perform—for poetry was his reply to an inquiry from the director of Princeton University Press, Herbert S. Bailey, Jr., in spring 1957, asking advice on the idea of starting a program of poetry publication. Jarrell gave strong encouragement in a long, constructive letter that wound up: "The most important thing about publishing poets is, simply: which poets do you publish? If you have a kind of jury system, or academic or conservative or Poetry Society judges, you end up printing exactly the sort of mediocre, mildly talented poetry that would certainly get printed anyway. I think that publishing books of poetry can be a very good but risky thing; if it isn't risky it can't be good." Perhaps for budgetary reasons, Princeton had to wait nearly twenty years—after the Press had the assistance of Bollingen funds—to launch its Princeton Series of Contemporary Poets.

The readings and lectures under the Whittall Fund continued on their separate course, supervised in the main by Basler, in diplomatic consultation with Mrs. Whittall. (Documentary evidence that she and Jarrell ever met has not come to light, nor has evidence of discord.) During the 1956–57 season, among various programs there were readings by Katherine Anne Porter, MacLeish, Robert Graves, and Shapiro; a series of lectures on the novel, by Irving Stone, John O'Hara, and MacKinlay Kantor; and concert readings of drama. The following season included readings by Wilbur, Berryman, and Oscar Williams; lectures on "American Poetry at Mid-Century" by Ransom, Delmore Schwartz, and John Hall Wheelock and a lecture by Lionel Trilling; and more drama. Mrs. Whittall's ninetieth birthday was observed, under the auspices of the Music Division, on October 7, 1957, by a recital of chamber music, performed by the Budapest String Quartet with the pianist Rudolf Serkin and the violist Walter Trampler.

Quite beyond the Whittall programs, Jarrell put on each fall the appearances in the Coolidge Auditorium that Luther Evans had made a feature of the Consultantship. His lecture on December 17, 1957, "The Taste of the Age"—a slashing, funny, and deeply serious consideration of American mass culture—can only be described as a smash hit, and it was even more of a hit when it was broadcast shortly afterward and extensively reported in the newspapers and newsmagazines. A deluge of letters followed; Jarrell replied personally to each one. To requests from magazines to publish the lecture he said (as he did to *Harper's Bazaar*), "I'm saving it so as to have a lecture to give when places ask me." He did give it as the Phi Beta Kappa lecture at Vanderbilt, Howard University, and elsewhere, and finally let the *Saturday Evening Post* publish it, as "The Appalling Taste of the Age." Another lecture in the same vein, "About Popular Culture," which Jarrell delivered at the National Book Awards event in 1958, was a forerunner of his essay "A Sad Heart at the Supermarket." One of his official assignments, which he put his own heart into, was to speak to a convocation at the Pan-American Union marking the recent death of the Chilean poet Gabriela Mistral. In his annual reports Jarrell enumerated more than fifty occasions when he lectured, read, and broadcast around the country. In the spring of 1958 he absented himself for nearly a month to give the George Elliston Lectures at the University of Cincinnati. Among the many people who came or wrote for advice about poetry, he was especially pleased with being "able to persuade one old gentleman, a retired clerk, not to pay a vanity publisher $2,500 to bring out a book of his poems. He has been publishing them, instead, in country newspapers."

Jarrell closed his final report: "[The Consultant's] second year at the Library had a particularly happy ending when his favorite living poet, Robert Frost, was appointed the new Consultant."

❊

Deliberations about a new Consultant began in late 1957, when the Fellows were asked to send in recommendations. Only Maxwell Anderson, R. P. Blackmur, and Cleanth Brooks chose to reply; nothing was heard from Bishop, Ransom, and Welty. (Ransom at that time was hoping that Jarrell would succeed him as editor of the *Kenyon Review* and may have wanted to avoid a conflict of interest.) The nominations, including Jarrell's, presented the Library with sixteen names. A study of how these were boiled down, and what Jarrell's recorded opinions of several of them were, would be entertaining but painful to certain of the subjects. Samples, anonymously: (a) "Pretty wild. Might have quarrels. Not any more dangerous than Aiken. Might need the money." (b) "Lightweight. Very frivolous. Cheap jokes." (c) "Not very good. Easy, patriotic success. Lady's club lecturer. On the make." (d) "Just a pleasant, slightly younger poet . . . a personal friend and protege of ———." (e) "One of the best younger poets. Somewhat like —— but less tame and decorous." Of his preference, Marianne Moore, Jarrell said, "One of the two or three best poets in the country, best known, mild, eccentric in loveable manner. Age 71 this coming November. Retired librarian. Lives on small independent means." (Since 1949 she had held a lifetime fellowship, paying $100 a month, from the Bollingen Foundation.) Basler also favored Moore. Katherine Biddle, he reported, believed she would make a real contribution and lend distinction. Again, Marianne Moore was unavailable.

When the Honorary Consultants (four-sevenths of them) met on March 17 and 18, 1958, they may have talked about the appointment—no full minutes have turned up—but the problem was solved almost at once when Sherman Adams, who a couple of months before had suggested that Frost might one day serve as a White House adviser on cultural activities, now proposed that he be appointed to a comparable post, the Chair of Poetry. Mumford promptly agreed, and on May 2 he sent Frost a letter of invitation, with a contract, which Frost accepted as promptly. He had turned 84 a few weeks before. The arrangement with Frost was unique: he was to be at the Library for only four visits, October 13–18, December 8–12, March 30–April 3, and May 18–22, and during two of those spells he would give a talk in the Coolidge Auditorium to an *invited* audience. The stipend was set at $8,000. Kathleen Morrison (Mrs. Theodore Morrison), who had been Frost's secretary and assistant since 1938, shortly after his wife's death, was his "staff," through whom, for the most part, the Library kept in touch with the poet. Most of the replies to the deluge of mail were written by Phyllis Armstrong, sometimes in consultation with Frost, more often not. The burden was much lightened by the notation Frost jotted on a great many letters: "NR"—"no reply."

Aside from Jarrell and possibly Auslander, Frost had been rather little involved with the preceding Consultants. Certainly Tate paid him a full measure of respect in *Sixty American Poets:* "No commentary on Frost is necessary in this check list. From his first volume to his last he has known precisely what he was doing, and sticking close to his own field he has produced a body of poetry which is as impressive as any of our time, in English, with the possible exception of Yeats and Eliot, with whom it is both difficult and unfair to compare him."

During Frost's year as Consultant, no member of the Library of Congress staff was closer to him than Roy Basler, both as administrator and as friend, and his recollections, for their immediacy and candor, have a unique value. What follows is in considerable debt to Basler's essay "Yankee Vergil—Robert Frost in Washington," which he published some years after Frost's death.

❊

In the spring of 1958, Robert Frost became the Consultant with a purpose. For many years his poetry had received wide acclaim indeed, but it became increasingly evident that he wanted more, and meant to get it. The role he conceived for his remaining years—prophet and wiseman to the nation—he developed craftily as the stage widened, and with some luck, good timing, and a fair portion of ham acting, he was able to play out his part, perhaps farther downstage than he had ever suspected possible. He was avid for the appointment, unlike Sandburg, who wanted no part of it. As Basler saw him, Frost was "a shrewd old cuss, as sly as Adam's old fox."

He came to discuss terms with Quincy Mumford on May 1, and on May 12 the appointment was announced. The interest that was provoked in the press exceeded expectations, and a press conference was set up on May 21, to be followed by a reception. At the press conference, Frost was in grand form. After he referred briefly to his pleasure in being appointed to follow Randall Jarrell, whom he described felicitously and tartly as "one of the most *pronounced* literary figures in America," the reporters began to ply him with questions.

What did his position consist of? "Making the politicians and statesmen more aware of their responsibility to the arts. . . . And I wouldn't have much confidence in myself that way if I hadn't been so successful in Washington lately in a law case. But, I surprised myself." Frost remained certain he had obtained Pound's release from St. Elizabeths.

How did he intend to make politicians and statesmen aware of the arts? "I guess we'll have to ask them to dinner once in a while. And then, you know, you can keep giving them your books. . . . I've got one with me for somebody very high up right now—very, very high up—about as high as you can get." What would he inscribe in it? "I hadn't got as far as that, but it'll be as farmer to farmer."

Did he discuss the Pound case with the President? "No. With the Attorney General. . . . It started with Mr. Brownell, but Mr. Rogers got promoted the day after I saw him as Assistant. See, I got him promoted."

Within a few minutes, the scope of the Consultantship had expanded beyond anything heretofore contemplated, by anyone other than Frost, at least. The questions, answers, and badinage continued for a good hour.

It was Frost's opinion that we should "do something about bringing poets and presidents and things together. Wouldn't it be terrible if this country went down in history, like Carthage, without anybody to praise it?"

Everyone had a most enjoyable time, but Frost obviously the most enjoyable of all. He was being consulted!

The reception that followed was lavish by Library of Congress standards, since Frost's publishers, Henry Holt and Company, Inc., were the co-hosts. Many distinguished Washingtonians were invited and most of them came, but, in view of later developments, it is interesting to note that neither of the Senators from Massachusetts was on Frost's guest list, although the New Hampshire and Vermont delegations were invited, and came.

During the summer, preparations were made for Frost's assumption of his official duties in October. Requests for appointments, as well as letters enclosing manuscripts for the Consultant to criticize and asking all kinds of advice, piled up, and it was necessary to devise form replies explaining why the Consultant could not personally reply to all. When Frost arrived on October 12 to spend his first week in residence, both his office schedule and his social schedule were full. He was consulted officially by the Department of State and the Army, as well as by professors, students, and poets. He read his poems to an invited audience of high school honor students and their teachers—his favorite event— and held another press conference, this time sparsely attended. When told that President Eisenhower had called a press conference at the same time, he remarked, "First things first. I'll have to say something to him about that when I see him." When introduced to the reporters by the Deputy Librarian of Congress with an explanation that the conference had been called because the Consultant's crowded schedule could not accommodate all the requests for individual interviews, he protested with good humor, "Now *you* decided all this. I ought not to be called poetry consultant. I ought to be called poet-in-waiting." He remarked that "one reason I'm here is my ambition to get out of the small potatoes class." He wanted "somebody in the Cabinet for the arts."

This conference rambled over American poetry, with pungent comment on Pound's *Cantos,* as well as American painting, especially Frost's liking for the work of Winslow Homer, Andrew Wyeth, Thomas Eakins, and James Chapin. He had a painting by each in mind that he thought would suitably decorate the walls of the Consultant's office. But he wouldn't want his working conditions to be too sumptuous. "If I had a beautiful studio, I'd never paint. I'd have ladies visiting."

During Frost's October visit, there was a welcoming luncheon for him in the Whittall Pavilion, attended by Gertrude Whittall, a delegation of Library staff, and Kingsley Amis, who was giving a reading in the Whittall series that evening. Another day, Frost consented to a recorded interview with two Library officials, David Mearns and Robert Land, on the "release from St. Elizabeths that he secured for Ezra Pound," with the understanding that the recording would be restricted during the lifetimes of Frost, Eliot, Pound, Hemingway, and MacLeish.

Now, of course, the tape may be audited in a listening booth at the Library's Recorded Sound Reference Center. The restriction hardly seems justified. Frost said nothing abrasive about Eliot, Hemingway, or MacLeish. Recalling his encounter with Pound in England before World War I, he was reproachful, even caustic. "I was repelled, annoyed, by his ego." Frost took for granted his own preeminent role in getting Pound out of St. Elizabeths. "I have no mercy for the kind of thing he did. I have only magnanimity. I don't care about seeing him." He never did.

On November 9, Frost was in Baltimore to read at the Johns Hopkins University Poetry Festival, which had been subsidized by the Bollingen Foundation. He shared the program with MacLeish, Ransom (replacing Williams, who had had another stroke), Yvor Winters, Marianne Moore, and Cummings, all reading from their work. As a reporter observed, "The poets were not enthralled by one another. There was among them a core of something between tolerance and friendliness."

If Frost's schedule did not keep him busy enough in October, it can be said that it kept several members of the Library staff more than busy enough, but to everyone's delight. When he returned for his tour of duty in December, an equally hectic schedule was observed, with a public lecture and reading, "The Great Misgiving," interviews, conferences, luncheons, dinners, and by Frost's request, another press conference.

As reported in the newspapers with the headline "Frost Complains of Lack of Work," he began, "I summoned you." He wondered if he had not come to Washington on a misapprehension, to be consulted not only about poetry but about politics, religion, science—anything. "But I've been consulted only three times by the White House, only once by the Supreme Court, and not at all by Congress. I think something ought to be done about it."

He admitted to being an expert on education. "I have long thought our high schools should be improved. . . . A lot of people are being scared by the Russian Sputnik into wanting to harden up our education or speed it up. I am interested in toning it up at the high school level. I would rather perish as Athens than prevail as Sparta. The tone is Athens. The tone is freedom to the point of destruction. Democracy means all the risks taken, conflict of opinion, conflict of personality, eccentricity."

Did he feel the present Administration sympathetic to the arts? It was "much more so before a recent sad event." Sherman Adams had departed from the White House. About his old friend he said, "He really cares about the arts."

A high moment of Frost's December week in Washington was the arrangement for presentation to the Library, by his friend and long-time correspondent Louis Untermeyer, of several hundred letters, which are in effect a large slice of Frost's autobiography. (They were published, as edited by Untermeyer, in 1963.) The promised gift—which Frost not only approved of, but had requested—was celebrated at a luncheon in honor of the two poets.

There was another presentation during the December visit. He gave a party in the Poetry Room on the 10th, attended by Mrs. Whittall, the Mumfords, the Biddles, and a few others. His invitation: "Wouldn't you find it whimsical to come and ask a hard question or so of the consultant I am supposed to be?" Frost and Mrs. Whittall, peers as they were, had a particularly good time together. Afterward, Frost wrote out a copy of a new poem, with the inscription "To Gertrude Clarke Whittall who has given us all so much." Her note in response: "Dear Mr. Frost, Your precious manuscript 'Away' will be taken to the Library of Congress tomorrow morning to be held in Protective Security. I hope you will approve of this disposition of a page of 'Frost Wizardry,' by a very grateful Gertrude Whittall." The two documents are now in the Library's Whittall Collection of Literary Manuscripts. A somewhat different social event failed to come off: a visit from Allen Ginsberg and LeRoi Jones, who were coming to read their poems at Howard and George Washington universities in mid-January. Jones wrote Frost asking if they could meet. A Library official, Henry J. Dubester, wrote Jones to say that Frost wouldn't be in town then but he hoped he would try again. "I am sure that . . . Mr. Frost would be interested in talking with you and the other young poets in your group." On February 27, Ginsberg and his companion Peter Orlovsky turned up and recorded a reading of their poems, and on April 17, Jones recorded—the first black poet to record for the archive. On May 1, Langston Hughes recorded. Basler arranged those readings. Frost wasn't around.

Frost's complaint that Congress had not taken sufficient note of his presence had borne fruit by the end of March. A Senate Resolution, sponsored by sixty-two senators, extended birthday greetings on his eighty-fifth anniversary. The day was celebrated with fanfare, not in Washington but in New York, where his publishers, by then called Holt, Rinehart & Winston, arranged a dinner at the Waldorf-Astoria, which was attended by eighty-five guests—many literary and scholarly lights of the nation and not a few political figures. Among those who sent their regrets along with birthday greetings was Senator John F. Kennedy. "The major speaker of the evening," Lawrance Thompson has reported, "was Lionel Trilling, whose carefully considered remarks in praise of certain 'terrifying' elements in the poetry of Frost unintentionally created a teapot tempest. . . . Trilling . . . sent a copy to Frost expressing the hope that the speech and the subsequent hubbub had not distressed him." Frost responded, "Not distressed at all. Just a little taken aback or thrown back on myself by being so closely examined so close by. . . . You weren't there to sing 'Happy Birthday, dear Robert,' and I don't mind being made controversial. No sweeter music can come to my ears than the clash of arms over my dead body when I am down."

At a press conference held in the publishers' New York offices, Frost quickly got into politics. "Somebody said to me that New England's in decay. But I said the next President is going to be from Boston." When pressed to name the man, he replied, "Can't you figure it out? It's a Puritan named Kennedy." The comment made the headlines across the country.

Frost's week at the Library began on March 30. It included his usual public lecture and reading at the Library as well as one at the Folger Shakespeare Library; a seminar for graduate students from the local universities held in the Wilson Room; several luncheons, one at the Federal Trade Commission, and one in the Whittall Pavilion, attended by President Eisenhower's Special Assistant Frederick Fox and several members of Congress. But not Senator Kennedy.

Shortly afterward, however, a cordial letter reached Frost from Kennedy, sending warm birthday greetings and observing, "I share entirely your view that the New England heritage is not a fading page but that it has continuing vitality and a distinctive future." Frost again entertained in the Poetry Room, at what he called a soirée, on the afternoon of April 1. His guests this time included the Walter Lippmanns and the Alexis Legers and Mrs. Whittall.

Frost's final week's visit as Consultant in Poetry began on May 18, with a talk and a reading that night to which only members of the Library staff and their families were invited. The limited seating capacity of the Coolidge Auditorium (around five hundred) had been inadequate for every public reading Frost had given, and it was felt that on this concluding performance the staff, many of whom had not been able to hear him at all, should be given priority. The auditorium was filled to overflowing again, and Frost received the accustomed ovation.

The next day, Randall Jarrell was at the Library, having interrupted the translation of Goethe's *Faust* he was working on in Greensboro. (He never finished it.) He had requested an interview with Frost in the Recording Laboratory. What he hoped for was a talk about the theme of extinction, death, the disappearance of a man or of mankind, as Frost had dwelt on it in poems. At Jarrell's prompting, Frost "said" or read many poems, but others he refused to deal with. "Some things are too near, too inside me." He talked to Jarrell of the circumstances in which he had written some of the poems, and the people who had brought them to mind, even sixty years before. The conversation often touched deep feelings. Basler hoped to bring out a record of it, but that never came about.

Frost was in the laboratory again, two days later, for two hours, recording some forty of his poems for the "Talking Books for the Blind." Next day, at a reception in the Whittall Pavilion, his consultantship was feted by the largest turnout of dignitaries and their consorts yet—Ambassadors, White House officials, Supreme Court Justices, Representatives, and Senators—among the latter John F. Kennedy, who almost "slipped" in, and out, after the briefest of handshakes, so that few in the crowded pavilion besides Frost would remember, later on, just when it was the two men first met.

On May 21 Frost had a talk with Armstrong, Dubester, and Land about his views of the year at the Library. "This year," he said, "I have quarreled with the title of my position, 'Consultant in Poetry.' As I have said before, I think it should be Poetry Consultant and this would mean consultant in everything—poetry, politics, religion, and the arts. The Poetry Consultant should certainly not be concerned only with poetry, for then he would become just like a reader of theme papers. He should not take up his time with poems sent in for him to read. These should be treated slightly, because you cannot correct people into poets. So many of those who rhyme 'flowers' with 'bowers' and 'showers' are little people who want to be fussed over. They should go out and live to improve their poetry. . . . Last night I had a real consultation with some Members of Congress. There were three, all intelligent men interested in literary matters, too. We talked about poetry in relation to other things. I was not defending or even talking particularly about poetry. There were things I wanted to hear from them and they from me. We discussed politics and the affairs of the nation. . . . Poetry can become too special, isolated and separate a thing. The connection should be closer between Government and the arts. Wouldn't it be wonderful if there could be something for the arts like the Morrill Act was for education in establishing the Land Grant colleges? The Government could use it. . . . Congressmen should personally be interested in this consultantship. The Consultant must have a broad vision for Congressmen and take an interest in what they think. The Consultant should be someone the Government consults as part of the Government." Frost remarked that there were a few times in his life, perhaps two or three, which were like renewed emancipations; his year at the Library was one of these.

On Frost's last night, May 23, before he boarded the sleeper bound for Vermont, some of the Library people who had worked most closely with him gave him a dinner at the Hay-Adams Hotel. He was especially pleased when Mumford invited him to continue in the capacity of "honorary consultant." Four days later, with the approval of the Librarian of Congress, Basler wrote Frost proposing that he serve the Library in the capacity of "Honorary Consultant in the Humanities." His reply was "Won't it be capital for us all to get together next year." And so it was. His new appointment was not announced, however, until August 27, 1959, in order not to detract from the publicity given the appointment of his successor in the Chair of Poetry, Richard Eberhart.

✳

The overwhelming presence of Frost was complemented, if not rivaled, by the literary program that continued under the Whittall Fund during 1958–59. The poets who read included George Barker, John Hall Wheelock, Allen Tate, and Padraic Colum. Eudora Welty, Kingsley Amis, and James T. Farrell read from their fiction. Three momentous birthdays were celebrated: Cleanth Brooks lectured on Housman in observance of the poet's one hundredth; Robert Hillyer on Robert Burns, for his two hundredth birthday, in tandem with the baritone John Brownlee, in kilt and tam-o'-shanter, singing Highland ballads; and Carl Sandburg appeared in a tribute to Lincoln on his 150th anniversary. Mark Van Doren contributed a reading of his new play about Lincoln. And Richard Wilbur lectured on Poe and read some of Poe's poems. In July, from his farm in Vermont Frost wrote to Quincy Mumford:

I am honored by the summons of your appointing me consultant in the humanities which I more or less arbitrarily take to mean practically everything human that has been brought to book and can be treated in poetry—philosophy, politics, religion, history, and science. Everything, everything.

This mark of friendship is more to me than an award. It sets me up mightily that my venture into the capital of my country wasn't for nothing.

❊

During Richard Eberhart's two years in the Chair of Poetry, the post arrived at a tone, a pattern, that with few exceptions the Consultant-ships thereafter have maintained. Eberhart had been on the brink of the appointment since the Aiken time, when, as he recalls, he was approached unofficially. In the spring of 1956, Quincy Mumford sounded him out after he had read in the Whittall series, but Eberhart was at the point of accepting a professorship at Dartmouth College and, after several years of moving about, wanted to settle down for the sake of his children. In July 1958, after Frost had been chosen for the year to come, Eberhart was asked if he would consider the Chair for the term following. Dartmouth granted a leave of absence, and in the fall of 1959 he began what he considered two of the best years of his life. He negotiated a raise in the Consultant's stipend, furthermore, to $10,850. (Richard Wilbur, who had also been under consideration, declined because the education of *his* children had been constantly disrupted by moves and travels.)

Tate's comment on Eberhart's poetry in *Sixty American Poets* a dozen years earlier is a little baffling, even if one knows which Thomas Wolfe he had in mind: "Eberhart's *Reading the Spirit* [1937] was one of the most promising books of the thirties, and Eberhart remains a poet of great potential power. But he has little control and his performance is unpredictable: there is some reason to see him as the Thomas Wolfe of contemporary poetry." Tate and Eberhart had a cordial if not very close friendship. They shared the experience of having been mentors of the young Robert Lowell—Eberhart as Lowell's teacher at St. Mark's School, in Massachusetts, during the mid-thirties, when Lowell was writing his first poetry. Eberhart's association with I. A. Richards, William Empson, C. P. Snow, and Kathleen Raine at Cambridge University several years earlier gave him an edge of literary sophistication over the other masters. He helped and advised Lowell with both literary and personal problems, and they kept in touch after Lowell, in summer 1937, went to Tennessee to stay with the Tates. Lowell sent poems for Eberhart's criticism, but by 1938, according to his biographer, Ian Hamilton, "It was clear to Lowell that he had already outgrown Eberhart." It was in that year that Eberhart arranged for W. H. Auden (whose early work he had discovered while in England) to come to St. Mark's for a month as "guest member of the faculty," a lively time for the school and for him. He and Auden talked poetry constantly and criticized one another's poems. After he left, Auden wrote Eberhart "to thank you for the joy of your company at St. Mark's; it would have been a bad month indeed without you. But Remember GET OUT OF THERE QUICK." Eberhart later observed, "Auden's coming to America may prove to be as significant as Eliot's leaving it."

Eberhart found the bureaucratic routines of the Library of Congress better than tolerable, even congenial. His four years as a naval officer in World War II and subsequent six years as a businessman must have case-hardened him, though he was far from stiff-backed. At his first press conference he had a kind word for beatnik poetry: "I think the so-called San Francisco school of poetry was the liveliest manifestation of social poetry in years. It burst like a bombshell." Reporters infallibly commented on Eberhart's unpoetic persona: "A stocky, vigorous man with a ruddy complexion who once ran the 100-yard dash in ten seconds. . . . He looks like a jolly salesman or an affable floor manager. . . . He walks with a slightly rolling gait and might possibly be a sailor. . . . Looks as unlike Byron as one can get."

In September, soon after beginning the Consultantship, Eberhart in line of duty met the Soviet novelist Mikhail Sholokhov, in the entourage of Premier Khrushchev, who had come for a meeting with President Eisenhower at Camp David. Through an interpreter they discussed narrative technique. Eberhart observed that, while Sholokhov treated action on a vast, panoramic scale, depth motivations of character were scanted. "His unexpected, pithy reply was that 'I give the roast beef, not the hamburger.' " Soon afterward, from the Soviet Embassy, Eberhart received a heavy package "which I thought was a bomb," but which contained a four-volume English translation of Sholokhov's Cossack epic, *The Silent Don*. Eberhart reciprocated in kind. The following spring, when the poets Yevgeny Yevtushenko and Andrei Voznesenskiĭ came to Washington to read, the Eberharts entertained them at home in Georgetown. The three poets engaged in a reading bout. "Only the memory of Dylan Thomas reading his poems could match the Russians reading theirs," Eberhart recalled, "although we couldn't understand the words." Other guests from overseas whom the Consultant received were the King and Queen of Nepal and the King and Queen of Thailand. The former monarch was, he himself admitted, a "sometimes" poet. The visit of the latter ruler had a special relevance for Eberhart, who in 1930–31 had tutored the sons of the then-King of Siam and of the Siamese ambassador when both boys were in the United States. Neither of his pupils achieved the crown. Perhaps taking a cue from Mrs. Whittall, the King of Thailand, Bhumibol Adulyadej, who was a composer, presented to the Library a set of ten Thai musical instruments; the Librarian reciprocated with five albums of American folksong recordings. As Eberhart recalled, "His Majesty and his beautiful wife walked out the front door, down the steps, and stood before forty or fifty of his countrymen assembled to see their King. . . . He stood there for perhaps twenty minutes in a silence so profound that I have remembered it ever since, then slowly walked back into the Library."

Still another event of an international cast occurred when an official of the Treasury Department asked Eberhart to write a "good-will ode on inter-allied Latin American banking amity" to be read by the Secretary of the Treasury at a dinner for representatives of twenty-three Latin American countries meeting in El Salvador. "I recalled that in the Hispanic Foundation we have a young poet, William Rivera, who knew Spanish; in less than the required time he wrote a fine occasional poem on the subject in English and Spanish and it was delivered by special messenger. When the party returned from El Salvador we learned that the poem added a great deal to the occasion."

An innovation of Eberhart's was a series of five poetry seminars in the Library's Woodrow Wilson Room, one for black poets and professors from Howard University, others for students and teachers from George Washington, American, and Catholic universities and the University of Maryland. All of these were recorded for the archive. Eberhart gave a class for the students in the Capitol Page School, next door to the Poetry Office. (The pages are teenagers appointed by Senators and Representatives to serve on the floor of Congress.) He discussed the poems of Yeats, G. M. Hopkins, Dylan Thomas, and Empson, as well as his own. And he saw an important recording through production: Oscar Williams's *Album of American Poetry,* comprising seventy-eight poems read by forty-six American and British poets.

In the service of the muse Eberhart had three adventures during November. On the fourth, with Phyllis Armstrong he attended the twenty-fifth anniversary dinner of the Academy of American Poets at the Waldorf-Astoria Hotel in New York and witnessed Léonie Adams receiving the fifteenth $5,000 Fellowship of the Academy. Then he went on to Chicago for a two-day fund-raising festival being held by *Poetry* magazine, featuring T. S. Eliot and his wife. Before an audience of three thousand in Orchestra Hall, on November 6, Eliot "in his inimitable voice" read ten poems, ranging from "Maccavity" to the chorus from *Murder in the Cathedral.* Afterward, Patrick J. Lannon, a wealthy Chicago bibliophile, gave a party for the Eliots, and Eberhart renewed an acquaintance with Eliot of nearly thirty years before, when he was a Harvard graduate student. Next evening there was a subscription dinner for several hundred at the Arts Club, followed by a benefit auction of donated books, manuscripts, and memorabilia (e.g., two bottles of Chateau Lafitte—empty, one assumes—served to the Eliots and inscribed by the poet: $55). Five of Eliot's "Landscapes," which he had freshly copied, were bid in for $1,300 by Oscar Williams on behalf of Hy Sobiloff, who immediately presented them to the Library of Congress. Within a week after coming home, Eberhart journeyed first to Maine to give a reading and then to "Steepletop," the former home of Edna St. Vincent Millay, near Austerlitz, New York. In 1924, when she read her poems at Dartmouth, Eberhart had written that "she supplies all I need in poetry"; she was for him "the mysterious, the unknown feminine." Now, accompanied by a Library official, Joseph Vance, Eberhart was to discuss with Millay's sister Norma Ellis the Library's interest in the poet's papers and early notebooks. The evening was memorable, as Mrs. Ellis read twenty-five unpublished poems of Edna

Millay's "on her reactions to Eliot." The acquisition came to nothing at the time, but in the 1960s, through the efforts of John C. Broderick, the Millay papers at last were donated to the Library of Congress.

Among the occupants of the Chair, Eberhart may have been, unlike his predecessor, the kindest respondent to the incoming mail. He managed an encouraging word in reply to every letter and cheerfully got involved. To a poet in Alaska: "You have flights of pure imaginings. I would be glad to see more from you." To another, on Martha's Vineyard: "I wish you had told me whether your name stands for a man or a woman. In either case your poem is lively and refreshing. You have a dynamic in the lingo you use. Send others if you wish to." Still another: "Your somewhat verbless poems get up a speed by pouncing on nouns or only using participles. It makes for a kind of static emblematic quality. Thank you . . ." He struck up a correspondence with a poet in India, not only about his verse and essays but about Rabindranath Tagore, and invited him to continue writing to him after he left Washington. Eberhart's good will was boundless. When Huntington Cairns drove the Eberharts, Robert Richman, and Sir Charles and Lady Snow to Baltimore to meet H. L. Mencken's brother and dine sumptuously at Miller Brothers, it was Eberhart who, on the turnpike at night in a snowstorm, changed a flat tire. "A poet changing a tire!" Sir Charles exclaimed. "Extraordinary!"

In spring 1960, when Eberhart was appointed for a second term, the spotlight at the Library of Congress was preempted by Frost, who had been booked to make his first visit as Honorary Consultant in the Humanities the first week of May. The opening event, on the second, was a luncheon in the Whittall Pavilion. Again, Roy Basler, a fast friend not only of Frost but of Carl Sandburg as a fellow Lincoln scholar, has told the story.

✵

It was pretty obvious to Basler that Sandburg was neither Frost's favorite poet nor his favorite historian. Nevertheless, when he learned that Sandburg was in town on the day of the Frost luncheon, the opportunity to bring the two together seemed too good to miss. They probably hadn't met since Elizabeth Bishop's tea party in 1949. Over the telephone, Basler proposed to Sandburg that he join the luncheon if he were free. There was a pause, then—"Why should I come to a luncheon for Robert Frost?" Basler realized in the moment that Frost was a subject he and Sandburg had never had occasion to discuss, and he sensed that perhaps the feeling was mutual between them. "I'd like to get you two guys together," he told him, "and I'll never have a better chance."

As Sandburg came into the Pavilion, a wool scarf about his neck and a black fedora on his head, he paused at the threshold. Basler greeted him and turned to Frost, who was chatting with a semicircle that included Quincy Mumford and Eberhart. "Robert, here's Carl Sandburg come to lunch."

Frost, with a glint in his eye, grinned without moving or offering his hand. "Don't you know enough to take your hat off when you come in the house?"

Sandburg chuckled as, with an exaggerated flourish, he doffed his fedora. The familiar silver Sandburg forelock fell over his eye.

Frost: "Don't you ever comb your hair?"

Another Sandburg chuckle, as he reached into his coat pocket, brought out a comb and lifted the silver lock into place, where it stayed only for a moment. Finally, the two poets did shake hands.

The luncheon group of about twenty-five persons, including two visiting poets, Oscar Williams and Hy Sobiloff, was fortunately large enough for each of the two elder statesmen of letters to have his own semicircle. When everyone sat down, the two were placed on either side of the Librarian, near enough to each other by all odds, but with Basler and Oscar Williams facing them, to keep the quips flying without any absolute necessity of smashes or kills at the net. For as they broke away from their initial greeting, Frost had brushed off his well-worn witticism to murmur, "I'd as soon play tennis with the net down as write free verse."

As Basler was well placed to observe, Sandburg was a sublime egoist, wholly indifferent to, if not wholly unaware of, the display of sparks that Frost's terrific if pettily competitive instinct was generating. The hilarity was immense because everyone was aware of how close the party was skating to the thin ice that might break and dunk them all from exhilaration into dismay.

When Mumford finally tapped his glass with his spoon and made his customary announcement—that while this was a merely social occasion, if either of the distinguished guests felt any compulsion to speak, he was sure there were those who would be glad to listen—Frost said, "Let Carl pay a tribute to me. He oughta praise me, my poetry."

Everyone roared, Basler recalled, and Sandburg shook out his throatiest prolonged guffaw to decline this gambit. Whereupon the Librarian adjourned the affair.

That evening, on the Whittall Fund, Frost gave a talk, "The Next Five Hundred Like the Last Five Hundred (Years, I mean)," to a large general audience in the Coolidge Auditorium. Sandwiched in, he "said" many poems, from memory as always. He gave his own soirée in the Whittall Pavilion next afternoon. On the night of May 4, there was another mixed reading—rather, "saying"—and talk to Members of Congress and their families. That was a near fiasco. A protracted debate in the House of Representatives on an important bill detained many Congressmen, and when Frost came to the podium he found only a scattered few Congressional kinfolk. He was obviously miffed, but "he warmed to his task," as Basler put it, "and gave a very fine performance. . . . For those who came, if not for him, the evening was a success." The next morning Frost testified before the Education Subcommittee of the Senate Committee on Labor and Public Welfare on a bill proposed by Senator Francis Case, to Establish a National Academy of Culture—the first stirrings of legislative action that led to the Kennedy Center and the National Foundation on the Arts and the Humanities. Frost in his testimony made it evident that he wanted poetry declared on a par with big business, science, and scholarship. His best hope was for a Cabinet post devoted to the Arts. Another piece of legislation then alive would not have required Frost's testimony: a bill introduced by Senator Saltonstall authorizing the President to award Frost a gold medal. (The bill was signed into law by Eisenhower in September, but its framers had neglected to provide the necessary appropriation, $2,500. The medal was eventually presented two years later by the next President.) Frost's Library friends gave him a farewell dinner at the Occidental Restaurant. The tab was picked up by the Harry Scherman Gift Fund, another source that was available for random cultural expenses.

During that year, the literary programs that Roy Basler directed under the Whittall Fund brought a colorful range of talent to the Coolidge Auditorium. Sophistication and a broader view were evident. The poets who read included William Meredith, Stephen Spender, and Stanley Kunitz—all future occupants of the Chair of Poetry. The actress Dorothy Stickney performed a three-act recital of Edna St. Vincent Millay's poems and letters that recreated the poet's life. Three European scholars—Alain Bosquet, Hans Egon Holthusen, and Eric Heller—joined in a lecture series on recent French and German literature. Vincent Price presented a dramatic reading drawn from the works of Whitman, Whistler, and Tennessee Williams. The perennial Arnold Moss and his company performed *King Lear.* Another theatrical personality, who proved to be as perennial a feature of the Coolidge stage, made a debut in March 1960: the producer Lucille Lortel, who under the auspices of the American National Theatre and Academy (ANTA) presented one-act plays by Paul Vincent Carroll and Sean O'Casey.

❋

During Eberhart's 1960–61 year, the Library's recording program achieved a goal: the transfer of all poetry and literary recordings from disc to tape. The Whittall series carried on with its new splendid variety and liberality, already venturing far beyond the donor's confines: Lowell and I. A. Richards, Lin Yutang and Agnes de Mille, Vincent Price, W. D. Snodgrass, Louis Untermeyer, W. S. Merwin, and Frank O'Connor. Two of Conrad Aiken's plays, *The Coming Forth by Day* and *The Kid,* were presented by Lucille Lortel for ANTA. For Mrs. Whittall's special delectation, Arnold Moss and his company performed a concert reading of Robinson's *Tristram.*

Eberhart gave his seminars this year for local high school students, and again taught the Congressional pages. He gave some thirty readings and talks here and there—more than sixty in his two years. Like Jarrell, he delivered the Elliston Lectures in Cincinnati. The poets whose recordings he brought in included Gwendolyn Brooks, Daniel Hoffman, Maxine Kumin—those three would be Consultants in future years—and Phyllis McGinley, Ned O'Gorman, Anne Sexton, and Mark Van Doren. Altogether, in Eberhart's two years, the voices of ninety poets were added to the archive. Besides his exertions at the Library, Eberhart was also serving as a member of the President's Advisory Committee of the Arts, to help plan for the National Cultural Center.

In league with Basler and other officials, Eberhart opened a campaign to bring in an additional $5,000 per year to help support a realistic salary policy for the Chair of Poetry. A rather tentative approach to the Ford Foundation in January 1961 attracted no interest whatever. Library staff then compiled a strong memorandum, quoting Herbert Putnam's 1937 statement of philosophy and aims for the Consultantships, showing how the Consultant's stipend had risen, in reflection of the national economy, from $3,200 in Auslander's time to $12,000 for Eberhart, explaining how the fixed conditions of the original Huntington Fund put a ceiling on its income from investment, and stating a "serious question as to whether the Chair of Poetry could function with the freedom it now enjoys were it to be conceived as an official position paid for by government [i.e., appropriated] funds." In March, Eberhart submitted that document, with an eloquent letter of his own, to the Bollingen Foundation, through Huntington Cairns. "The Consultantship," he wrote, "affords the one official poet's job where anybody in our democracy can ask relevant questions about poetry and receive a professional reply. It is a stable office and should be kept so, not having to stop for a year or two to catch up on monetary accruals. The Chair is a living witness to the fact that the Library of Congress recognizes and values poetry as a vital part of writing in English." Despite Cairns's support and the Foundation's demonstrated friendliness to poetry, its deliberations moved in so stately a fashion that only in December (months after Eberhart had left the Chair) did the President of the Foundation respond to his letter, with a boilerplate "not in a position" letter. All was not lost, however. Fate provided other means for sustaining the Consultantship. And the Bollingen Foundation was soon to prove its concern for poetry in another way.

The Eberharts were among the artists and writers invited to John F. Kennedy's inauguration, on January 20, 1961, and to the Inaugural Ball that evening, "which also included free Presidential champagne and kept us up most of the night," Eberhart wrote to a friend. "The Tates were our house guests and we took the Lowells and Katherine Anne Porter and got in toward dawn as if it were back in the old days. Auden came to supper along with Madame Perkins who originated social security. It was all quite gay." (In a later recollection, Eberhart remembered it a bit differently: because of the rainy weather, Porter was unwilling to get her "little red slippers" wet, and she and Auden passed up the Ball and stayed at the Eberharts' house.)

The Consultant's ceremonial farewell was his reading on the night of May 15, from his recently published *Collected Poems*. The *Washington Post*'s man, Thomas (nowadays Tom) Wolfe, reported that Eberhart told a space-age parable. "Let a group of scientists take a good solid cleancut crew-cut all-American boy, put a glass bubble over his head, and rocket him into space—and what does he turn into? A poet . . . like Alan Shepard, whose first words from over the rainbow were: 'What a beautiful view!' When Shepard uttered those words, he had a poet's perception of the world. . . . It's an illustration of how much poetry has in common with science in its upper reaches. When science jumps a great gap in our knowledge of perception of life, in some mystic way it does the same thing as our greatest poets have done." (A festive note: Basler requested of the Librarian, and received, approval to serve punch and cookies in the courtyard after the reading; cost defrayed from the Scherman Fund.)

In Eberhart's official report for the second year of his appointment, this cogent proposal appeared: "Considering the weight and national character of the Library it might be a good idea some time to promote a week's Poetry Festival. . . . This could be a cultural item . . . in line with this Administration's awareness of our arts as vital to the country."

And this valediction: "I shall prize every day spent here in memory, regretting only that these two exciting years passed so quickly."

The news that Frost would play a part in the inauguration was in the papers on December 18, 1960. The *Washington Evening Star* commented: "In a sense, Senator Kennedy will be paying off a campaign debt too. All through the primaries he quoted from . . . 'Stopping by Woods on a Snowy Evening.' Inevitably . . . he bade farewell to his audience with these lines:

> 'But I have promises to keep,
> And miles to go before I sleep . . . ' "

The man Kennedy appointed Secretary of the Interior, Stewart L. Udall, who had proposed Frost's participation in the inauguration, had become a close friend of the poet during his own time in Congress. Udall, in the Kennedy Administration, continued to be active in arranging occasions in honor of Frost. The inaugural ceremony itself—outdoors on an exceedingly cold day, after a heavy snowfall, in brilliant sunshine—has become a historic episode. The account by Herbert A. Kenny, in the *Boston Sunday Globe,* recreates the scene:

> Over-all, [Frost] never had a better time in his life. . . . His lone regret for the day was his inability to read his lines of dedication—the first occasional lines he had ever written.
> The brilliant noonday January sun turned the surface of his paper to the sparkle of a diamond. Vice-President Lyndon Johnson leaped forward to proffer his tall silk hat as a shield.
> "It shut out all the light," said Frost, "and I decided not to try to finish the dedication."
> He launched into "The Gift Outright," the most nationalistic poem he has ever written, a favorite with him, as it is with President Kennedy. The words [as he "said" them] rang out on the bitterly cold Washington air and reverberated, not only over the heads of a spellbound audience but in their hearts. The faces of two Presidents and Vice-President Nixon caught by the television camera were the faces of men who were deeply touched.
> Until Frost complained of the light, and then took the Texan's hat with an audible, "Here, let me have that," the program had

been stilted. Frost brought New England simplicity into it all. . . . [His] difficulties turned the crowd into a family. . . . Presidents and Vice-Presidents alike, wives of Presidents, Secret Service men, and others moved around to see how they could help. Mrs. Kennedy, with all the instincts of a perfect hostess, moved uneasily forward to lend a hand.

Frost paused after his reading, and then explained that the lines he had tried vainly to read were lines of dedication, written especially for the occasion . . . saluting President Kennedy for giving the arts a place at the Inaugural.

In the new poem that Frost had written for the inaugural occasion— was, indeed, still writing the previous night—he "presented himself as laureate of the new age," William Pritchard has observed, "by projecting on it the vocabulary of prowess and performance and play he now used as second nature. It was some kind of ultimate finding of felicity in publicity. . . . At [the] moment of disaster, he called on some resource and rose to a level in every way superior to the pumped-up one of the new poem's advertisement. . . . He fell back on an old [poem] he knew perfectly, and . . . his performance thus attained a dramatic, even a heroic quality, which it would otherwise have lacked if things had gone off perfectly."

After a trip to Israel, Greece, and England in March, Frost returned to Washington in May, though not merely for his annual reading in the Coolidge Auditorium as Honorary Consultant. As Basler said, "he no longer belonged primarily to us." Udall, on behalf of the entire Cabinet, had arranged "An Evening with Robert Frost" on May 1 in the State Department Auditorium, a black-tie occasion, for an audience once again including Ambassadors, Supreme Court Justices, Cabinet members, poets and scholars, and other VIPs. Next morning, as Tom Wolfe told it in the *Post*, "America's unofficial poet laureate invited the Washington press over to the Library of Congress . . . for 'just a little informal coffee hour.' Some coffee hour. The old word wizard became so quotable so fast, the poor scriveners had to reach for the notebooks and lose a shot at some sociable china-balancing." Wolfe's story was a flurry of Frostian wit. At Frost's reading on the Whittall series, the evening of May 7, Quincy Mumford announced that he had reappointed him to serve another three-year term as Honorary Consultant in the Humanities. Frost told the audience, "I've become part of the Library, haven't I? Almost a book."

Properly, Frost's reading should have occurred on May 1, in observance of the tenth anniversary of the Whittall Poetry and Literature Fund, but Secretary Udall had preempted that date. On the third, however, the Library celebrated the anniversary with a luncheon, attended by Frost, in Mrs. Whittall's honor. Librarian Mumford presented her with a bound volume of letters of tribute to her from many of the poets, actors, novelists, critics, and lecturers who had participated in the programs—130 of them—during the ten years. The first letter bound in the book was Frost's: "Having you there in Washington is like having seeds of fire on the hearth that only needs a scrap of manuscript for tinder to burst into flame with the passing breath of inspiration." Mrs. Whittall (she was 93) said, "The years . . . have gone like a dream—I only wish they could begin all over again—without anything tomorrow. It's been all beauty."

In early 1961, the composition of the Honorary Consultants in American Letters had shifted slightly. Bishop and Ransom, their appointments having expired, were replaced by the historian Catherine Drinker Bowen, the poet Babette Deutsch, and the "poet and poetry anthologist *extraordinaire*" (as the Library's press releases liked to describe him) Louis Untermeyer. Now, toward choosing Eberhart's successor in the Chair of Poetry, the Librarian asked for advice from the Honoraries, offering fifteen names to mull over, and inevitably received a superabundance of opinion. Deutsch opted for W. S. Merwin ("That he was engaged to tutor the children of Robert Graves is, I feel, a recommendation") and added a list of alternatives, including Kunitz, Meredith, Howard Nemerov, and MacLeish. In Untermeyer's view, "the only name on your list which elicits my immediate and complete enthusiasm is that of Stanley Kunitz," but he looked favorably also on Nemerov, Meredith, and several others. So it went. Mumford offered the post to William Meredith, who happened to have an advocate in Robert Frost, but who replied, "No, not at this time. . . . There are personal reasons, as I suggested in our interview yesterday, protective of a life which lets me write poems." Next in line was Merwin, but he had other commitments, presumably in Majorca. The Librarian was able to settle the appointment only in midsummer: Untermeyer, who at seventy-six was scarcely considered out of the running. He had demonstrated his vivacity in December 1958, when he was at the Library to negotiate the gift of the letters he had received from Frost over nearly a half-century, and again in March 1961, when he kept a Coolidge audience smiling with a lecture on "Play in Poetry." Untermeyer's acceptance has the ring of an oath of office: "I expect to devote not only my time but all my thought to the position, to ideas and projects which might benefit the cultural program and, in particular, the spread of poetry in the United States. I expect to enjoy myself hugely, but I won't derive any enjoyment from the position unless I am of service."

The announcement, in August, of Untermeyer's appointment provoked an amiable piece in the *Post* by Tom Wolfe, still on the Capitol Hill beat. "Voluble, voluminous man o' letters . . . Untermeyer is so well-known, so prolific an anthologizer of poetry, that would-be and never-were poets write him inquiring 'How much do you charge per page?' . . . He gave the Burma Shave Co. and its anonymous poets the broadest palm in all their years of roadside publishing . . . 'good rhymes, perfect rhythm, which could not be better if Pope himself had written them.' . . . But beneath the shock wave was a serious appeal to coy avant garde poets to quit shadow boxing among the begonias and start turning out some solar plexus verse: 'We are caught between the highbrows being derisive of popular poetry and the people being derisive of highbrow poetry. Until we realize that both the so-called high and low brow poetry have the same impulse, we won't get anywhere.' "

Simultaneously, however, almost ten years after the noise of Fulton Lewis and Senator McCarthy, a Congressman wrote protesting Untermeyer's "consistent record of affiliation with Communist causes," as a constituent of his had reported. Mumford responded defending the appointment and sent a statement by Untermeyer: "I have offered to state before any . . . Congressional Committee which might want to question me [that] I have always been, and will continue to be, opposed to all forms of dictatorship, whether from the extreme left or the extreme right. An old-fashioned liberal, I am—and always have been—opposed to Communism." The issue of Untermeyer's political past flared up now and again, and his testimonial was useful more than once.

The Librarian, Quincy Mumford, had offered Untermeyer what one might call a two-on two-off arrangement. The Consultant and his wife, Bryna (she was his fourth wife but the marriage was his fifth, inasmuch as he had been married twice to Jean Starr Untermeyer), usually spent about two months in Washington alternating with about two months in their Newtown, Connecticut, home or their Adirondacks retreat. During his Library shift Untermeyer was befittingly industrious. He seemed to do the job in a lighthearted, even sporty style. Citing Frost's advice to him, he remarked that "I was meant to act as a poetic radiator, radiating a love of poetry over as many miles as possible." In the elevated prose of the Librarian's annual report, Untermeyer's "indefatigable energy and urbane wit brightened the Washington scene for adults, and his enthusiasm and ability to communicate gave life to poetry for many school children of the area." He wrote cordial, even courtly, notes to the authors who sent him their verses for judgment. To a woman in a small Indiana town, "I am happy to add your lyrics to my collection as another instance of the continued creativeness of the Indiana Muse." For the Archive of Recorded Poetry and Literature he issued invitations to some fifty poets and netted about a 50 percent return. (Regarding a prospect whose work he evidently had discovered while working at home in Newtown, he wrote to Phyllis Armstrong: "I want to invite an American girl who married an English poet. She is Sylvia Plath. . . . She has had increasingly good notices." Plath didn't get to Washington; she was dead in little more than a year.) He gave the customary public lecture on October 2: "What Makes Poetry Modern." A talk he gave later in the season, to the Women's National Press Club, drew a rather mixed press. His topic, "Do Americans Speak English?," which dwelt on the advantages of American slang, entertained the *Post*'s reporter but not the *Star*'s—the sardonic Mary McGrory, who compared the Consultant uncharitably with Frost, as the Inaugural Poet, and Sandburg, who a few weeks before, on the occasion of the Civil War centennial, "swept into town and gave a convincing day-long demonstration that poetry and politics are not incompatible." (His final appearance at the Library of Congress, incidentally.) Untermeyer, McGrory thought, "served very light fare . . . the standard talk of the ladies' luncheon. . . . Mr. Untermeyer will find out that while here and now it is good to be a poet, it is not enough. You've got to do something."

Among the things of some political consequence that Untermeyer *did* do was to attend a White House luncheon for the poet Léopold Sédar Senghor, then the president of Senegal. Untermeyer sat between two friends, Langston Hughes and J. Saunders Redding, opposite Walter Lippmann and Roy Wilkins. President Kennedy paid tribute to Senegal as one of the youngest of republics and to Senghor as one of the most creative of presidents. Later, Untermeyer and Senghor, in a poetic tête-à-tête, compared their experiences as anthologists. On November 8, Untermeyer left for India, where at the request of the Department of State he was the American delegate to international literary conferences, organized as part of the Rabindranath Tagore centenary celebrations, in New Delhi and Bombay. He gave two talks—on Tagore's impact on contemporary literature, and on the role of the poet in the world today, in which he dwelt on the continual pendulum-play of convention and revolt in all the arts. Among his climaxes: "If the writer— and particularly the poet—loves nothing else, he must have a sure, though often shaken, love of this life. A poem is, first of all, an act of faith, an affirmation, a power which permits the poet to see, as Eliot saw, 'beneath both beauty and ugliness, . . . the horror and the boredom and the glory.' " (He apologized later for his obvious platitudes.) Untermeyer radiated his characteristic amiability to the novelist R. K. Narayan, the poet Umashankar Joshi, and other Indian delegates, Isaiah Berlin, Aldous Huxley, the Soviet novelist Vsevolod Ivanov, Ambassador John Kenneth Galbraith, and others from the West. Beyond his conference obligations he cheerfully gave extra talks, some on the air. A journalist reported: "One person who preached the message of love on the radio last week was the distinguished American poet Louis Untermeyer. . . . He spoke with passion and fluency and, despite his advanced age, seventy-five, showed a remarkable mental agility." Untermeyer liked the Indians he met but had reservations about India. A

Westerner, he observed, "could not walk the streets of Bombay without a shudder of compassion, a desire to do something about it, and a knowledge that nothing could be done, at least not in his lifetime."

Upon returning to Washington, Untermeyer was to be debriefed by members of the Department of State. "I knew my role was not of real importance . . . [but] I rather expected questions about . . . the attitude of Indian intellectuals toward America, whether I had been heckled by students about our racial problem . . ." and other topics of moment. He was dashed, however, to find that the debriefings were perfunctory. "I was closeted for the final session with one of the authorities on Far Eastern affairs. 'I have a rather special question,' he said. Here it was at last, something probing, something significant. 'I'll try to answer it,' I said, summoning what I had experienced and observed, and hoping to communicate something of value. 'I promised my wife I'd ask you this,' he said. 'What's your honest opinion of Henry Miller's *Tropic of Cancer?*' "

The frontier between the Whittall Fund programs and the Chair of Poetry had continued to be an issue for the Library, though the degree of acrimony had dropped far since Aiken's time. In the fall of 1961 the Library's Information Officer, Helen-Anne Hilker, complained in a memorandum to the Librarian that "I have a terrible time trying to keep photographers from taking pictures of the Poetry Consultant (or any Poetry Consultant) in the Poetry Room. They all know of its existence, it provides excellent photographic background, what with the Capitol and all, and they are simply incapable of understanding why the Poetry Consultant is not related to the Poetry Room or why they shouldn't speak of it as his domain. I can hardly explain to them that the donor of the Room considers it her personal property and that we can never be certain when she will approve or disapprove of its use." Photographers objected bitterly to shooting in the Consultant's office—a narrow cubicle, the window view giving on green copper roofing—"not only lousy for photography, but it looks like a cell. . . . Some Consultants simply overrule me and *go* to the Poetry Room; Mr. Jarrell and Mr. Untermeyer are more considerate and have always deferred to suggestions. . . ." As long as the donor survived, so did the problem, which had still another facet: when the Poetry Room was depicted or described in the press, in all its elegance, the public were likely to assume that taxpayers' money, not Mrs. Whittall's, had provided such splendor.

The programs on the Whittall Fund continued to deviate imaginatively from the donor's original canons of taste. During 1961–62, there were poetry readings by a Consultant-to-be, Howard Nemerov, and an Honorary Consultant, Babette Deutsch, and a series of three lectures on "The Imagination in the Modern World" by another Consultant-to-be, Stephen Spender. Santha Rama Rau delivered a lecture entitled "New Voices of the Far East." It was a strong season for theater. A troupe from ANTA, directed by Lucille Lortel, performed plays by Eugène Ionesco and Edward Albee, and on each night there was a symposium—"Avant-Garde Theatre—Real or Far Out?" A Parisian company did another Ionesco piece and Jean-Paul Sartre's *Huis-Clos*. The Canadian Players, of Stratford, performed Christopher Fry's *The Lady's Not for Burning*. The Dublin Gate Theatre did an adaptation of *Moby Dick,* and another of Ireland's treasures, Michael Mac Liammoir, gave a dramatic reading called "The Importance of Being Oscar" (Wilde, that is). Arnold Moss and company served tradition with a concert presentation of *Macbeth*. A Chinese drama, *The Butterfly Dream,* was done in English translation by the Institute for Advanced Studies in the Theatre Arts.

The culminating feature of the Whittall season was Robert Frost's reading, on May 7, which was also the capstone of a special exhibition marking his eighty-eighth birthday, March 26. On that day, President Kennedy, at the White House, presented Frost with the Congressional Gold Medal that had been awarded two years before; that evening, several hundred public figures, domestic and foreign, and assorted friends, attended a resplendent birthday dinner at the Pan American Union, arranged by Secretary of the Interior Udall and by Frost's publishers. The exhibition, which opened at the Library of Congress on the same day, displayed some fifty manuscripts, books, and photographs and included a number of items from the Frost collection that Untermeyer had given to the Library in 1960. (A few May days later, Frost and Untermeyer joined in a ceremony at Dumbarton Oaks Park in observance of the one hundredth anniversary of Thoreau's death. As they strolled along a birch-shaded stretch of path, Frost: "This is a place Thoreau would have

loved." Untermeyer: "I should think he would have been a bit stag-
gered.") Another exhibition that could only have pleased Gertrude
Whittall had opened on September 20, 1961, to honor the centenary of
Herbert Putnam's birth.

In April 1962 the Library had announced Untermeyer's reappoint-
ment for another year. At a press conference he said he intended to
continue working to break down the "ridiculous picture of the poet as a
vague kind of dreamer, with no sense of reality—what the lawyers call
incompetent, irrelevant and immaterial." He also took a swipe at the
beatnik poets, who had "taken poetry out of the classroom and put it in
the men's room"—but gave them their due as lively reflectors of the
current confusion.

☀

In any case, Untermeyer, as the anthologist extraordinaire who had
done signal service in making modern poetry widely known, was indis-
pensable for what was ahead. Eberhart, at the end of his term as Con-
sultant, had urged the Library to undertake a national poetry festival.
Such a vision had actually been simmering in Basler's thoughts for even
longer, "as an appropriate recognition by the Library of Congress," he
observed, "not only of the numerous poets who had served as Consul-
tant and/or Fellow, but of the remarkable burgeoning of American po-
etry in general during the first half of the twentieth century, continuing
from, if not actually beginning with, the establishment of Harriet Mon-
roe's *Poetry: A Magazine of Verse* in 1912. The . . . fiftieth anniversary
of that event seemed to afford an especially appropriate date."

His target for funds was, once more, the Bollingen Foundation,
through the local conduit of Huntington Cairns, who took at once to the
idea when Basler and Untermeyer called on him to propose it in Decem-
ber 1961. They acted at just the point when the Foundation's president,
John Barrett, had turned down Eberhart's attempt to kindle a grant to
help carry the Chair of Poetry. It may seem quixotic, but Barrett re-
ceived Basler in January and responded warmly to the picture he
painted of a festival of American poets, omnibus in character. (Festivals
seemed to go down well with the Bollingen Foundation, which had
funded a second one at Johns Hopkins University a couple of months

FOUR: 1956 TO 1963

before. The poetry readers had included Eberhart, Jarrell, Wilbur, Lowell, and a future Consultant, Josephine Jacobsen.) Mumford's formal proposal followed within the week—objectives, possible participants, tentative events, and a $15,000 budget. The Bollingen trustees approved the grant to the Library in March. They also approved a grant of $5,000 to *Poetry* for expenditures in connection with the festival. (The Foundation had previously given the magazine $77,500, over the years 1947–53, to enable it to continue publication.) On May 1 the Library announced that the National Poetry Festival would take place on the three days of October 22–24: its general theme would be "Fifty Years of American Poetry," marking the fiftieth anniversary of *Poetry*.

Basler put together the program and the invitation lists, in consultation with Untermeyer and the editor of *Poetry*, Henry Rago. The responses and regrets began to come in. Carl Sandburg would be reading in Seattle, probably couldn't make it, and didn't. (He told Basler, "I don't want to celebrate poetry with all those people.") MacLeish wrote, "How happy it makes me to see the Library of Congress engaged in the recognition of contemporary poetry. I have never forgotten the fact that when I became Librarian, the Library had almost none of my books. Nor the additional fact that I discovered upon inquiry that the same thing was true of the rest." He would be too caught up in writing a poem about Lincoln's Emancipation Proclamation to attend. Eliot: ". . . simply out of the question for me to be in America next October," but "cordial good wishes." Mark Van Doren, who had been invited to give the keynote speech on the first night, declined: "I don't know the field in either the broad or the deep way that is indicated; in other words, I am not a historian of contemporary poetry." But he would, and did, read. Instead, Jarrell gave the address—"Fifty Years of American Poetry." Lowell, invited to speak on the poet and the public, declined, but he would be willing to read. By October, Lowell had had one of his attacks and was a patient at the Institute for Living, a psychiatric hospital in Hartford. As late as September, Auden declined the invitation to give the closing lecture, because he couldn't get back in time from his summer house in Austria. Through the good offices of the Bollingen Foundation, Herbert Read agreed to take Auden's place. (Read had been close to the Foundation for many years, as an author, a consultant, and a member of the editorial boards of the C. G. Jung and S. T. Coleridge collected editions.) He wrote the address while traveling and lecturing on the Continent, and his last-minute change of title, from "A View of American Poetry from Abroad" to one he hoped was "a little less colourless," "American Bards and British Reviewers," barely made the final proofs of the program.

The Bollingen officers had no desire to influence the festival plans, though Jackson Mathews, a vice-president of the Foundation and, as editor of the Paul Valèry edition, the one most involved with poetry, had expressed intramurally his own disquiet over the possible "handling" of two poets who, in vastly different ways, were concerns of the Foundation: Ezra Pound and St.-John Perse. Because of Pound's importance in the early history of *Poetry,* Mathews felt that Eliot (or Tate, Ransom, or MacLeish) should talk about him at the opening meeting "so as to forestall any impromptu remarks." And it was essential to invite Perse, in view of his earlier post at the Library and his publications in the magazine. Alexis Leger was, in fact, in France at the time of the festival, intent on studying the wildlife of the Camargue, and unable to accept the invitation.

Nearly one hundred poets had been invited to the festival; some eighty attended; thirty-five (poets and a few introductory critics) participated in readings, lectures, and discussion. Those in the last category had their expenses reimbursed by the Library. The invited guests included Gertrude Whittall, who attended most of the sessions, in her usual seat, with her electric hearing device turned up so loud that some of her neighbors complained. The principal officers of the Bollingen Foundation—John Barrett, Vaun Gillmor, Huntington Cairns, Jackson Mathews—were present at most sessions, and Paul Mellon came to the opening reception. Complimentary copies of the fiftieth-anniversary issue of *Poetry* were distributed to all the participants and guests—a double number, dedicated to Harriet Monroe, comprising some 150 pages of *new* poems by fifty-seven poets. (Two thousand more copies were bought by the U.S. Information Agency, for distribution overseas.) The participants were also given blue leatherette briefcases, "which," a reporter observed, "made them look like a group of actuaries."

Other logistics: There were morning, afternoon, and evening sessions on each of the three days. In view of the limitations of the Coolidge Auditorium, tickets and name badges were obligatory and the seats were apportioned strictly: the first six rows of the center section for programmed participants and their spouses, and those behind for the press and invited guests. When all those had been seated, upon a signal from Phyllis Armstrong, the ushers threw open the doors to the unticketed public. When every seat was occupied, the overflow audience could sit in the Whittall Pavilion and hear but not see the festivities (closed-circuit television had not yet arrived at the Library). All the places were taken at each session, and people thronged the corridor besides. Nothing like it had ever occurred at the Library of Congress unless, possibly, Frost's SRO readings.

Of course, all of the previous Consultants had been invited. Lowell, as noted, was absent. For Elizabeth Bishop, now living in Brazil, the distance was too far to travel. Warren was in the hospital for a checkup. Aiken was ill in Savannah (Hy Sobiloff's generosity had made it possible for him to move back to his home town). Williams too was in failing health, but it's doubtful he would have wanted to attend. Joseph Auslander was invited, but a trip to Washington would have been out of the question for him. His wife Audrey Wurdemann had died two years earlier, leaving him to care for their two young children. He was working as a night clerk in a Miami Beach hotel, but he was a personage in Miami's literary world. Occasionally, though ill with heart trouble, he read his poems or gave a talk. In the further reaches of poetry he kept in touch with Marie Bullock and with Frost, who spent part of each winter in Miami.

When the festival opened, on the morning of Monday the twenty-second, Rago's introductory remarks contained an allusion that (even though fortuitous) carried a certain adumbration: a line from a poem in the anniversary number of *Poetry* by the Lallans (Scottish Lowlands) poet Tom Scott, "Tak hame your Polaris, send us your *Poetry!*" (Basler recalls a quiet awareness of large portents in Washington, but he and others saw the happy irony of a poetry festival convening a stone's throw from the Capitol. For several weeks the increasing flow of Soviet military and economic aid to Cuba had intensified pressure on the Kennedy administration to take some direct action against Fidel Castro's government.) Rago also made forthright mention of Ezra Pound, the only contributor to the anniversary issue (with an unpublished canto) who had also contributed to the first number of the first volume. "Civilization not a one-man job" was the not irrelevant quotation. Pound's name sounded often during the festival, though there were none of the "impromptu remarks" that Mathews had been anxious about.

To give a full account of the festival would inflate this chronicle intemperately. Rather, regard will be paid chiefly to the poets who have held the Chair of Poetry and some of the other participants whose names are significant in the story. (The complete proceedings, based on a transcript of the tapes that were assiduously recorded, were published by the Library as a book two years later and widely distributed. It is a unique and decisive literary document.)

Rago, that first morning, introduced Harriet Monroe's successor as editor of *Poetry*, Morton Dauwen Zabel, who spoke of the founder herself and the career of the journal, giving due weight to its first foreign correspondent, Ezra Pound—who, when Monroe died in 1936 while traveling in Peru, wrote that "no one in our time or in any time has ever served the cause of art with greater devotion, patience, and unflagging kindness." The next two speakers addressed, in a general way, "The Role of the Poetry Journal," both of them, Louise Bogan and Stanley Kunitz, having published often in *Poetry*. Bogan, indeed, had had her first publication there. (The journal was the vantage point of that day. In the Coolidge Auditorium lobby glass cases held the earliest issues and facsimiles of the manuscripts of classic poems *Poetry* had first published.) Open discussion followed the talks, certainly impromptu and occasionally querulous, but in the main constructive, rising to small peaks of highmindedness.

The day's reception was held in the Great Hall of the Library, among still more exhibition cases, displaying manuscripts, books, and photographs of nearly all the poets on the program. Jarrell's sense of the event is conveyed by what his wife Mary has written: "Among the guests who greeted him, Ransom was fond, Shapiro was sunny, newly met Ogden Nash was a friend at first sight, and wily Frost was playing the Grand Old Man. Wilbur was mannerly, and Muriel Rukeyser and Eberhart ungrudging. Untermeyer's two former wives, Jean Starr and Virginia Moore, both poets, were sociable, but the Tates were aloof. Léonie Adams and Louise Bogan were civil, but Oscar Williams refused contact with Jarrell by hand, word, or eye." (Jarrell had once written that Williams's poems seemed "to have been written on a typewriter by a typewriter." Williams thereafter excluded Jarrell from his anthologies.)

Matinee of readings, introduced by Basler: Adams, Meredith, Nemerov, Ransom, Rukeyser, Schwartz, Shapiro, Van Doren, and Untermeyer, who lightened and closed the afternoon with one of his parodies—"The Old Woman Who Lived in a Shoe" as Edgar A. Guest would have rewritten it.

In the evening, greetings to the convocation were delivered by a man whose post, created by the new Administration, seemed a sure consequence of Robert Frost's preachments in Washington: August Heckscher, Special Consultant on the Arts to the President. The keynote address—that politicizing term seems inescapable, but Quincy Mumford's introductory phrase, "assessment and review," might be safer—belonged to Randall Jarrell. Four years later, Shapiro remembered the occasion: "All the poets sat on the edge of their seats while Jarrell, who everybody had to admit had earned the right to do so, put together the jigsaw puzzle of modern poetry in front of our eyes. When I was finally fitted into place, with a splash of color, I felt a relief that I fitted, and a regret that that puzzle had been solved."

Jarrell's historical and critical premise: "If in 1912 someone had predicted that during the next 50 years American poetry would be the best and most influential in the English language, and that the next generation of poets would be American classics, men who would establish once and for all the style and tone of American poetry, his prediction would have seemed fantastic. Yet all this is literally true of the generation of American poets that included Frost, Stevens, Eliot, Pound, Williams, Marianne Moore, Ransom"—and the first three he believed were the greatest of this American century. The sequence of his program, thereupon, was a blend of the historical and critical, from Robinson forward.

Frost: "In his poems men are not only the glory and jest and riddle

[239]

of the world but also the habit of the world, its strange ordinariness, its ordinary strangeness, and they too trudge down the ruts along which the planets move in their courses." (Frost sat smiling in the front row.)

Pound: "His style comes to us, mostly, in beautiful fragments or adaptations; it is surprising that a poet of Pound's extraordinary talents should have written so few good poems all his own." Jarrell balanced due praise with one of the few references to Pound's shadow side at the festival: "The *Cantos* are less a 'poem containing history' than a heap containing poetry, history, recollections, free associations, obsessions. . . . His obsessions, at their worst, are a moral and intellectual disaster and make us ashamed for him."

Williams: "Anyone would apply to him such adjectives as outspoken, warmhearted, generous, fresh, sympathetic, enthusiastic," and fifteen more. "If his poems are full of what is clear, delicate, and beautiful, they are also full of what is coarse, ugly, and horrible. . . . In his best poems . . . the humor and sadness and raw absurdity of things, and the things themselves, exist in startling reality."

Eliot: "Won't the future say to us . . . : 'Surely you must have seen that Eliot was one of the most subjective and daemonic poets who ever lived, the victim and helpless beneficiary of his own inexorable compulsions, obsessions? From a psychoanalytic point of view he was far and away the most interesting poet of your century. . . . So far as Eliot is concerned, your age can be satisfied with itself.' "

Aiken: "The accomplished body of his work—which has been at once respected and neglected—is something you read with consistent pleasure, but without the astonished joy that you feel for the finest poetry. . . ."

Tate: "Another respected but somewhat neglected poet . . . But the best of his harshly formed, powerful poems are far more individual, unusual, than even the best of Aiken's."

MacLeish: "The smoothly individual style that he developed makes such a poem as 'And You, Andrew Marvell' beautiful in just the way that a Georgia O'Keeffe painting is beautiful. . . . His later work . . . is almost more conscious of the impressiveness of what it says than of what it says."

Elizabeth Bishop: "The future will read [her] almost as it will read

Stevens and Moore and Ransom. . . . The more you read her poems, the better and fresher, the more nearly perfect they seem. . . ."

Warren: "He is at his best in one of the only good long poems of our century, 'Brother to Dragons,' . . . a terrible but sometimes very touching poem, one of extraordinary immediacy, strength, and scope."

Adams and Bogan: Jarrell placed them in the tradition of feminine verse that included Wylie and Millay, though they "have produced . . . poems more delicately beautiful than any of [theirs]." (He here inserted a parenthetical smile: "One thinks with awe and longing of Millay's real and extraordinary popularity: if only there were *some* poet—Frost, Stevens, Eliot—whom people still read in canoes!")

He clustered some other Consultants, past and future. Among the "interesting and intelligent," Nemerov; among the "charming, individual or forceful," Dickey; among the "respected," Kunitz, Eberhart, and Untermeyer—and then resumed extended comment with Shapiro, finding his poems "fresh and young and rash and live . . . their hard clear outlines, their flat bold colors create a world like that of a knowing and skillful neoprimitive painting. . . . He loves, partly out of indignation and partly out of sheer mischievousness, to tell the naked truths or half-truths or quarter-truths that will make anybody's hair stand on end, he is always crying: 'But he hasn't any clothes on!' about an emperor who is half the time surprisingly well dressed." (Painting was never distant from Jarrell's critical imagery.)

With Lowell, he delivered an envoi in somber and affectionate tones, in which he alluded to the shadow over Washington during those days: "Most poets . . . no longer have the heart to write about what is most terrible in the world of the present: the bombs waiting beside the rockets, the hundreds of millions staring into the temporary shelter of their television sets, the decline of the West that seems less a decline than the fall preceding an explosion. Perhaps because Lowell's own existence seems to him in some sense as terrible as the public world—his private world hangs over him as the public world hangs over others—he does not forsake the headlined world for the refuge of one's private joys and decencies. . . . You feel before reading any new poem of his the uneasy expectation of perhaps encountering a masterpiece."

That Monday had closed with President Kennedy's address to the nation announcing that American policy demanded the withdrawal of the ballistic missile bases the USSR was building in Cuba, the quarantine of offensive military equipment bound for Cuba, and the alert of the armed forces to any eventuality. The poets' reactions took a variety of forms. Not a few dealt with panic in the bars. Basler recalls that Delmore Schwartz embarked on a pub crawl that ended in the loss of his wallet, so that next morning he had to ask Basler for an advance of his expense reimbursement. (True, the same misfortune might have befallen Schwartz without a missile crisis.) Mary Jarrell remembered that "Rexroth rebooked on an earlier flight to San Francisco, and Ogden Nash holed up in his room with the television, not to be seen again until his own reading. Frost spent the day in bed with the curtains drawn, his companion, William Meredith, reported; but rumors flew that this was not from fear of nuclear attack but from grief at losing the Nobel Prize to Steinbeck."

Tuesday morning, the phase entitled "The Poet and the Public" was opened by Basler, who announced that Richard Wilbur would pinch-hit as chairman for Warren, who was in the hospital. The first speaker under that rubric, Babette Deutsch, observed that "the speech from the White House last night would seem to obliterate every other matter for consideration." Yet, she believed, the topic of the morning's discussion had some relevance to the situation. The passage in Deutsch's speech that the press tended to single out was this: "If two Americans, strangers to each other, are sitting next to one another on a plane or in steamer chairs or on bar stools, one may ask his neighbor: 'What's your line?' If the other's 'line' is poetry, he will be embarrassed to confess it, and his companion, in most instances, will be more than half embarrassed to learn it. . . . With us there is a kind of reciprocal contempt felt by the poet and the public." Howard Nemerov, next at the lectern, spoke on "The Muse's Interest." Noted and notable: "The public for poetry is made of multitudes, of generations, incalculably transformed by the stuff, often without having read it. A new inflection of the voice may be the seed of new mind, new character; and many persons still to be born will enact in their lives the poet's word. Ours is a power the more immense for not being directed to a specific or immediate end other than the poem itself." Karl Shapiro finally put the topic in a Shapirovian skeptical perspective: "Without being ponderous, I will be slightly prophetic. What we are honoring here is, I take it, the dawn of American poetry—a poetry which will someday bear a relationship to a great American poetry, such as Anglo-Saxon bears to modern English literature. We are in our Beowulf years. That is why it seems absurd to me for our poets to pretend they are the jaded heirs of prosody and culture. We would look much better to paint our bodies blue and butter our hair." Discussion followed, often anecdotal, sometimes reproving and rebutting. The speakers impromptu could be remarkably keen and witty and, above all, articulate. Item, Langston Hughes: "I am what you might call the public kind of poet in that I do write for a public, I write primarily for the Negro public, I try to say something that my own people want to hear—that they are beautiful, that they are oppressed sometimes, that they have problems they can fight about. I try to interpret and make a bridge between one section of our American public and another, so I do write public poetry." Hughes also gave young poets a tip: as poems are paid for by the line, you can cut four long lines in half and make eight.

Jacqueline Kennedy had invited everyone on the festival program with their consorts to a reception (a sherry party it was reported to be) at the White House at noon of Tuesday, and buses were to pick them all up at the main entrance of the Library. But the party was canceled, along with all of the Kennedys' social engagements that week. An official spokesman explained that all those guests couldn't be "received in the White House when every entrance was being used by high-level advisers trying to avoid the press. That place was a beehive of secret meetings."

Another matinee of readings: Berryman, Bogan, Gwendolyn Brooks (thus the first black poet to read publicly at the Library of Congress since Paul Laurence Dunbar in the 1890s), J. V. Cunningham, Eberhart, Paul Engle, Henry Rago, W. D. Snodgrass, and Tate (he included "The Swimmers," his great lynch poem in terza rima).

On Tuesday evening the star turn was Robert Frost. Lines of would-be listeners had begun to form at 5 P.M. and eventually filled the front corridors as never before. Mary Jarrell thought Frost "seemed touchingly broken, and Jarrell was irate at the disrupting late arrival of Snodgrass, Berryman, and Schwartz, who were full of spirits and rude remarks." The transcript gives no hint of Frost's being either broken or disrupted. His old friend Untermeyer made the introduction, mentioning his discovery of the poet's work fifty years before, how Frost's "casual lyrics and colloquial monologues came as a distinct shock," and reminding the audience that Frost's was "a penetrating, mind-provoking and heart-shaking poetry in which words have become deeds."

Frost said, "I won't follow any particular theme tonight. I'm going to read right and left. Let's see." As Untermeyer later recalled, it was a matter of "circumambulating without an apparent objective, yet somehow centered." The themes *were* there: his recent encounter in the Soviet Union with Khrushchev—"he agreed with me that the great thing was to make the issue great, not to have petty squabbles decide it"— and with the Russian poets who translated his poems as he said them, "fine fellows and very amiable"; Matthew Arnold and the Dover Beachcombers; "And here . . . tonight—when such great things are happening for us, to us, such magnificent things. Playing a great world game; some style, I tell you. And so many people want to belittle it by something: qualms and squeams . . ."; Ezra Pound, "he's been a rather faithful friend . . . that I owe much to"; Harriet Monroe, "a great little lady . . . she wanted to be thought as good a poet as anyone, and she didn't get that recognition . . . she just hid her poetry by being such an editor. . . . But that's what we're celebrating." Among all of his conversation with the audience he said some fifteen poems, from earliest to latest. Basler observed, "If anyone present had doubts that Frost was *the national poet,* his talk and reading on the night of October 24, in the midst of the Cuban Crisis, dispelled those doubts in a moment."

The last morning of lectures was the brainiest, if not the headiest. Its subject was "The Problem of Form." After an extended introduction by Ransom, discoursing learnedly on Valéry and on a nursery rhyme, Tate gave an unexpectedly brief lecture, equally learned, dwelling on "The Rape of the Lock," synecdoche, and Jung's concept of the shadow, followed by Léonie Adams and then J. V. Cunningham, both still charitably brief and austerely learned. The audience by now, and accordingly the discussion, had somewhat fallen off. Among remarks that were noteworthy, one by Muriel Rukeyser: "This Festival itself may be

thought of as a form imagined by Mr. Untermeyer; and these prolifer-
ations, this wish for form, are what binds us all together, however far
apart we may sound." Many may have felt that, as Mary Jarrell re-
marked, "if this was the END, they preferred to meet it at home." On
this day, President Kennedy's quarantine of Havana-bound shipping
was to take effect, and a military confrontation with the Soviet Union
was conceivable.

The afternoon's readings opened with Basler's acknowledging a
weight that lay on his conscience. "In preparing this Festival, we antic-
ipated that an era so variously rich in poetry as our own could not be
fully represented in the three days which were at our disposal. There
are many fine poets who will not have appeared on this stage. But the
Library of Congress does not expect to abandon its role as a center for
poetry when this Festival is at an end." The readers, then: Blackmur,
Katherine Garrison Chapin, Deutsch, Langston Hughes, Jarrell, Kun-
itz, Ogden Nash, Rexroth, Wilbur, and Oscar Williams. Many in the
audience thought it the most *enjoyable* afternoon of readings.

Richard Eberhart introduced the festival's one Englishman, Sir Her-
bert Read, on "American Bards and British Reviewers" with an "ana-
lytic profile" that outlined Read's literary development. Read closed the
festival on a fresh and reconciling note. He surprised his audience, after
saying that "to each nation is given one towering archetypal figure, one
representative poet," and enumerating Greece's Homer, England's
Shakespeare, and so on, by announcing that the United States possesses
a poet of such universal significance: "I refer not, as might be antici-
pated, to Walt Whitman, but to Henry James." Read argued, demon-
strated, and for a great many listeners convinced them, that English and
American poetry are part of the same stream. "American poetry in our
time, indeed ever since the time of Whitman, has been a great poetry
because it has renewed the spiritual vitality of the English language—
'made it new.' . . . The achievement [of American poets] is to have
approached, more nearly than their British contemporaries, the grace,
the realism, and the intensity that were always the proper virtues of an
English verse."

As a coda, one welcomes the skeptically observant eye of Bogan, in
a letter to a friend after the event. "What a coming and going! What an

array of poets: bearded (R. Jarrell), plain (no names!), dark, light, snowy polled (Shapiro, surprisingly, and Nemerov, prematurely); fat (Rukeyser); thin (J. V. Cunningham, Kunitz, and *me*); learned, foolish, hung over and sober as judges.—The librarians, I must say, in all echelons, fell over themselves to be courteous. . . . The [first] afternoon reading went on, all of a lump—too much of a good thing, but fascinating, none the less.—I passed up a reception that evening, and just ate and went to bed. . . . A 'tea' at Mrs. Biddles . . . , whereat I saw Katie Louchheim, looking v. beautiful in red furs (to match her hair)—just back from Germany—an assistant Secretary of State!! . . . [At] the Frost reading, . . . Frost was pretty maudlin: painful!—A party was given, later, by the Udalls, to which I was not invited, and this festivity, I have just heard . . . , was followed by 1.) Delmore Schwartz tearing up his hotel room, and being nabbed by the police and 2.) John Berryman going to Delmore's rescue, and also being nabbed!—So, you see, there was a touch of the Dionysian, after all. No more, perhaps, than in a convention of brassiere makers, but still a touch. . . . The Capitol, lit up at night, was exquisitely lovely; and we walked back and forth to the Library, through its park, with those great old trees. Washington is really becoming a lovely place. Fountains play. And the weather was as balmy as spring."

❊

Untermeyer, writing afterward to his friend John Hall Wheelock, whom illness had kept away from the festival, was satisfied that the event "achieved its objectives: exchange of ideas, wide diversity of forms, idioms, and personalities, and, perhaps best of all, public responsiveness." It was a "spectacular success" despite some inconsistencies: "poets who couldn't attend, poets who were not invited and should have been, and poets who should not have been asked." To another friend he wrote that the festival was "a welter of work—a cross between an Eisteddfod and a rat-race (with, of course, very cultivated rats)." He summed up:

> As a veteran anthologist, I had brought many of these poets together between the covers of a book. I had never seen so many of

> them in the flesh at one time—a living anthology, an extraordinary collection, extremely diverse and, at times, even dangerous. . . . [Nevertheless] a rapport between the poets and the public was quickly established. . . . It was a refutation of the often-repeated charge that the modern poet was writing only for himself and for a few other poets. It was also an affirmation of the hope that poetry was—and is—essentially a communication, a reaching out by the writer and a ready acceptance by the reader.

Words from the White House—that is, from August Heckscher—to Quincy Mumford: "Looking back upon the past week with all its great and fearful events in the public scene, I remember the National Poetry Festival as a bright and somehow wonderfully fitting interlude. No one could have foreseen that this gathering would have fallen in the same week as the Cuba crisis, and no one would have planned it that way. But now that it is over, we can all feel that these readings and discussions by America's outstanding poets reminded us of the real meaning of the struggle being carried on at other levels."

The officers of the Bollingen Foundation, too, were happy about what their donation had wrought. Encouraged, Basler (with Mumford's agreement) submitted another project for Bollingen support: the recording of poets on color sound film, on a budget of $70,000. Jackson Mathews was enthusiastic, but after a silent year, the Foundation declined with regret, and also declined Basler's request for $3,500 to defray the cost of publishing the festival proceedings. It wasn't yet known that, in 1963, Paul Mellon had decided to bring the Foundation's work to a close within five years; no new grants of money would be considered. The Andrew W. Mellon Foundation took over the subsidy for the Bollingen Prize in Poetry at Yale and eventually endowed it. And, thanks to Basler's encouragement, the Bollingen Foundation gave its archive of papers to the Library's Manuscript Division.

❊

The other happenings in Untermeyer's second year as Consultant were not entirely crowded out by the festival. On the Whittall Fund, there was again considerable attention to drama and the theatrical. Four actors gave solo recitals: Burgess Meredith (his fourth time at the Library), Bramwell Fletcher, Vincent Price, and Arvid Paulson, reading from his translations of Strindberg. The Canadian Players performed Shaw's *Arms and the Man;* the Institute for Advanced Studies in the Theatre Arts gave a play of Lope de Vega in translation; Arnold Moss and company put on a Shakespearean evening; Elmer Rice lectured on "Show Business." Saul Bellow gave a talk on the writing of fiction, Kay Boyle read from her prose and poems, and Ogden Nash read *his* poems in a program he called "The Portable Nash." Aside from the Whittall events, Untermeyer gave his annual lecture in April, "Edwin Arlington Robinson: A Reappraisal," thus returning that poet to the spotlight. In the Great Hall during the weeks following there was a comprehensive exhibition of poems, letters, and first editions of Robinson's, drawn largely from the Whittall Collection of Literary Manuscripts.

Frost was to have given his spring "talk" for the Whittall series on May 6, 1963. After the Poetry Festival, he had said to his friends at the Library, "I don't like to say goodbyes. I shan't be gone long. Think of me as just being away." In December 1962, Frost underwent an operation at the Peter Bent Brigham Hospital in Boston; two days before Christmas he suffered a heart attack. Allen Tate takes up the account, in a lecture he gave at the Library for Frost's centenary:

> On January 5, 1963, I was at Yale, in the library, as a member of the jury for the Bollingen Prize of 1962. Up to that time the Bollingen juries tacitly assumed that to award Robert Frost the prize would carry coals to Newcastle. But in 1963 we knew he was dying in a Boston hospital. There was no time left for him to get the Nobel Prize. The jury—composed of Robert Lowell, John Hall Wheelock, Richard Eberhart, . . . Louise Bogan, and myself—voted unanimously to award him the prize. Would he accept it? I was appointed to telephone him and ask. I did; his feeble voice came through distinctly. "Is this Allen?" he said. I said, "Yes, and we hope you will accept the Bollingen Prize for 1962." After a brief silence he said, "I've wondered where you fellows stood."

FOUR: 1956 TO 1963

"One new reason to live," Frost called the award. "The committee's unanimity is magnificent. . . . Poets one and all of the first esteem." Untermeyer went to see him. "We recalled the National Poetry Festival and how it separated the true poets from the poetry-vendors, the self-adulators, and exhibitionists. Enjoying ourselves, we were particularly malicious about one of the contingent who was an unconscionable opportunist. After a while Robert said with mock contrition, 'We ought to be ashamed of ourselves. We should be more charitable to a fellow-poet who happens to push himself forward.' 'Why?' I asked. 'Because,' he said—and he could not resist a word-play even on his deathbed—'we are all so near the Day of Doom that everyone, even Gabriel, has to blow his own trumpet.' " He died on January 29, 1963. It had been evident for many years, of course, that Frost's poetry and his voice would remain a permanent part of the Library; but what its staff members would remember, above all, was the man, who, as one of them said, "was so genuine in his humanity." In his last public appearance, in Boston on December 2, Frost had read the poem he had given Gertrude Whittall, "Away!," from his last volume—"which," as William Pritchard wrote, "felt as if it were about something besides going for just another walk and which ended with the following instructions":

> Don't think I leave
> For the outer dark
> Like Adam and Eve
> Put out of the Park.

> Forget the myth.
> There is no one I
> Am put out with
> Or put out by.

> Unless I'm wrong
> I but obey
> The urge of a song:
> "I'm—bound—away!"

And I may return
if dissatisfied
With what I learn
From having died.

Little more than a month later, on March 4, William Carlos Williams died at his home in Rutherford. Shortly afterward he was awarded the Pulitzer Prize and the Gold Medal for Poetry of the National Institute of Arts and Letters. He would have—could have—known what Robert Lowell had written of him a year before: "He loves America excessively, as if it were *the* truth and *the* subject; his exasperation is also excessive, as if there were no other hell. His flowers rustle by the superhighways and pick up all our voices."

❈

In his last fortnight in office, during late May, Untermeyer arranged one final recording session of ten over the year. The poet was MacLeish, and Untermeyer, who had been anthologizing MacLeish for forty years, couldn't resist contributing his own marginal comments. The next week, through the hospitality of Mrs. Whittall, there was a reception in the Pavilion for Untermeyer and his wife and his successor in the Chair of Poetry, Howard Nemerov, with his wife Margaret. Altogether, the Library connection had been more than agreeable for Untermeyer, and he was pleased to learn he would serve still another year as Honorary Consultant in American Letters, with five newly appointed Honorary Consultants—Saul Bellow, Eberhart, Katherine Anne Porter, Elmer Rice, and John Steinbeck. The Untermeyers' final Washington obligation was to attend a briefing session in preparation for a lecture tour of Japan in July and August, arranged by the Department of State. The trip came off; Japan, unlike India, was a hit; and the Untermeyers were a hit in Japan.

❈

The 1950s were colored by the abrasions of the William Carlos Williams episode, the Fellows' disenchantment with Luther Evans, and the bewilderment of the four Chairless years that followed. Those troubles were offset by Gertrude Whittall's endowments, Roy Basler's arrival as director of the enhanced literary programs, and his success, with the help of Phyllis Armstrong, in carrying them on despite the empty Chair. The appointment, then, of so popular, enthusiastic, sardonically witty, and *brainy* a poet/critic as Randall Jarrell brought in a Consultant who exerted himself to give structure to the post. That structure, of course, was immediately put in abeyance by the appointment of Frost, for whom the terms of the office were drastically adapted. But Frost's admirable year was lively and newsworthy; the Consultant was constantly in the spotlight, and the Consultantship acquired a national prominence, even a kind of glamour. Eberhart restored the lines of Jarrell's structure and brought a welcome calm and goodwill to the job. Through Basler's tactful enterprise, the Whittall programs became more sophisticated and variegated. Upon Frost's occasional return visits to the Library, Eberhart gracefully stood out of the glare.

Untermeyer combined the prestige of a senior man of letters already familiar to the public for his anthologies with a display of vigor and imagination that would have done credit to a much younger man. Through the mixture of his and Basler's inspiration and savvy, *Poetry* magazine's fiftieth birthday, and the Bollingen Foundation's money, the National Poetry Festival in 1962—sharing the scene, if unequally, with the Cuban missile crisis—brought the Library's poetry program to larger national attention. The friendly interest of the Kennedy Administration, without a great deal of precedent in Washington, was a nurturing influence toward the close of these years. Paradoxically, that influence found a representative voice in the eldest among the poets, the one who was nearest to the traditional—Frost, altogether the dominant figure in this phase of our story, which ends with his passing in 1963.

Howard Nemerov, fall 1962

Reed Whittemore at the Goddard Space Flight Center, near Washington, with the painter Morris Graves and an official of the Center, 1964

Stephen Spender and W. H. Auden, March 28, 1966. Behind Spender, a portrait of Gertrude Clarke Whittall

Evgeny Evtushenko, reading to an overflow audience in the Library's snack bar after his performance in the Coolidge Auditorium, spring 1967. To his right, his translator, Barry Boys; to his left, the second man is James Dickey.

James Dickey with Reynolds Price and John Cheever, on the Coolidge Auditorium stage, March 4, 1968

William Jay Smith, fall 1968

Jorge Carréra Andrade (center), of Ecuador, with his translator, John Malcolm Brinnin, and (right) William Jay Smith, during the International Poetry Festival, April 1970

William Stafford, at an escritoire in the Poetry Room, fall 1970.

Josephine Jacobsen with a visitor, Robert Hiner, poet and businessman, of Indianapolis, October 14, 1971

Supper in the Library's Great Hall, at the conference on the teaching of creative writing, January 29, 1973

Daniel Hoffman, May 14, 1974

*Seated in the Wilson Room: Stafford, Dickey, Jacobsen, Bishop, Hoffman;
standing: Whittemore, Eberhart, Hayden, Smith, Spender, Kunitz, Shapiro, Nemerov*

The Consultants' Reunion, March 6, 1978.

William Jay Smith and Daniel J. Boorstin

Seated clockwise: Bishop, Nemerov, Nancy Galbraith (the special assistant in poetry), Jacobsen, Roy P. Basler, Eberhart, Ruth Boorstin (guest poet), Kunitz

Kunitz and Stafford

John C. Broderick and Robert Hayden

Luncheon in the Whittall Pavilion

Five

1963 TO 1971

In the parlaying for an incumbent in the 1963–64 Chair of Poetry, the Library administration took account of all the poets who had participated in the National Poetry Festival, after eliminating those who had already served and those who had permanently declined an invitation. The rather lengthy slate of candidates included for the first time two poets who were black, Gwendolyn Brooks and Langston Hughes, along with more than a dozen others disposed broadly in age, experience, temperament, stability, publication, renown, proficiency, conformity, availability, personality, and the other aspects that come into the decision. There is evidence that Wilbur and Meredith had been invited and had declined for the present. No records survive to reveal how the accolade happened to light on so happy a choice as Howard Nemerov, a mensch in cynic's clothing, or what part Untermeyer had played.

When, in April 1962, Nemerov was in Washington to read his poetry on the Whittall series and had to face a press conference, he readily won the affection of the reporters, in particular the *Washington Post*'s man, Phil Casey, who found him "to fumbling interviewers as daylight is to a coal miner." Nemerov "faced calmly his interviewers' ignorance of him and inundated them with quotable answers"; e.g., to "Why don't your books sell better?" he responded, "People just don't buy them," and to "What do you think of other poets?" "I'm a decent union man. All the competition is great." In spite or perhaps because of that experience he informed the Library's Information Officer, before he arrived in August 1963 to take over the Chair, that he'd prefer to skip the customary press conference. He had already ruffled bureaucratic feathers, even before he had reported for duty, by declining to speak gratis to the Washington Chapter of the National Society of Arts and Letters, though willing to return half of his minimum fee of $200 for the annual scholarship program. His letter to the chapter's president, describing the economic basis of his premise, was that of a decent union man. Nemerov later received avuncular advice from Quincy Mumford, who was on the chapter's advisory council. "We have found that the energies devoted by the Consultant to addressing various groups have been beneficial to the Library's cultural programs . . . though each invitation has to be considered in relation to obligations."

Nemerov was the latest-born Consultant to date, though not so junior upon assuming the Chair as Lowell and Shapiro had been. He came from New York via Harvard, where he was a student in Robert Hillyer's writing class. After Hillyer died, in 1962, Nemerov in a memorial publication remembered him as "a wonderful teacher, though his sort of distinction is not easy to describe. . . . [Hillyer's] reputation as a poet suffered, toward the last of his life, from a fashion which allowed very little to the models he had formed himself upon, and he died neglected by a world he had earlier praised and prized." (On balance, one may take note of Nemerov's reply, while a Consultant, to a correspondent who was fuming over the Academy of American Poets Fellowship of $5,000 awarded to Ezra Pound. "I should be much disinclined to make a fuss over such things. . . . Remember too that apart from his wartime behavior Mr Pound is an old and ill man who suffered much, who is probably in need of money, and whose poetry and critical writings have been, for many years longer than you have been on the earth, a source of inspiration to many intelligent, learned, and gifted men and women.")

Nemerov went through the Second World War as a pilot, in the Royal

Canadian and then the United States Air Force. Afterward, he taught at Hamilton College (alma mater of both Pound and Thorp) and at Bennington College; with Reed Whittemore he helped to edit the literary journal *Furioso*. In 1947, on *Furioso* business, he got to know Allen Tate, who ten years later recommended Nemerov, Jarrell, and Joseph Frank for the editorship of the *Kenyon Review*, from which Ransom was retiring. The appointment went to Robie Macauley. Subsequently, Nemerov was Tate's choice to fill his chair at Minnesota during a year's absence. When he was offered the Consultantship, Nemerov was on leave from Bennington and, as he had already been away a year as the writer-in-residence at Hollins College, in Roanoke, Virginia, he agreed to stay but one year in the Chair.

Almost the first assignment that fell upon Nemerov was to make a study of the Archive of Recorded Poetry, not the happiest task for one who "regards the tape recorder as a demonic instrument enabling people to waste the same time twice." Asked to speak to certain specific questions, Nemerov reported that the effect of the tape recorder on the art of poetry was "great, and bound to be greater, but not necessarily good. Bound to encourage, as it has already done, every mouthy rhapsodist in the land." He found the present use of the collection "very little, partly because . . . no one has a clear idea of what would be an appropriate use or how the machinery for it might be set up." He conceded that records ought to be made available of, at least, the famous poets now dead, though "there is something sad, hoarse, ghostly, and unliving about such performances." Nemerov came away from the exercise with the determination that "I should prefer not to have recordings made of my own readings. Maybe a purely formal, rather solemn, and deliberately stilted reading for the record—maybe. But not in a crowded hall, where the poet's feeble compound of vanity and apology, his helpless humor, the auditors' feeble coughs and gasps, produce an effect of the drowned commiserating with the hanged." As for the use of recordings in teaching, "It makes for a spirit of fake reverence which is the worst spirit in the world in which to approach the art work. . . . A teacher who would make routine use of these materials, taking up time which might have been given to the exploration of a poem, is doing something lazy and a little bit dishonest. I would not encourage these qualities in teachers by making these things widely available." Basler tolerantly commented, "I think we must not let our activity lapse, but I understand Mr. Nemerov's position and see no reason why his activity as Consultant needs to concentrate as much in this area as have the activities of his recent predecessors."

Nemerov brought in only ten poets to record for the Archive. He himself, in spite of himself, did make a recording in the Laboratory, though expressly for the "Talking Books for the Blind"; and he is represented in the Archive by at least four other recordings of poetry readings—thus his voice is not lost at all. At the end of his year, Nemerov's pessimism had been tempered somewhat. "Although I do not think much of the tape recorder as an instrument of education in poetry . . . I take this occasion to point out the pity of allowing all this material to lie inert and useless on the shelves, chiefly because schools . . . are not made aware of its availability. . . . The Library should consider seriously the desirability of issuing, on a regular schedule, discs made from the best recordings of the best poets." (In December of Nemerov's year the Archive issued, on Hy Sobiloff's Ambrook Fund, a record that had originated with Untermeyer: "Nine Pulitzer Poets Reading Their Own Poems," twenty-nine poems, read by MacLeish, Kunitz, Warren, Wilbur, et al.)

Scarcely a month after Nemerov arrived, the persistence of the question asked by his friends and the public at large—"What does the Consultant in Poetry do?"—compelled him to clarify the matter in a private essay under that title which is an amalgam of Borges, Mark Twain, Nabokov, and Nemerov. As a unique picture of the Chair—some of Nemerov's successors have thought it so—it is made available to the reader here in an appendix.

Nemerov found the bulk of the incoming mail—or of the poetic submissions that incumbered the incoming mail—particularly vexatious. Undoubtedly most of the Consultants feel the same way, but Nemerov made the case in Swiftian terms. "I have found it to be a primary obligation upon the Consultant to develop an epistolary manner that shall be tactful, even amiable, while at the same time giving absolutely no encouragement to people's poetic pretensions. . . . A few salient memories . . . : the man who telephoned to say he wanted to start a salon, and did the Poetry Office have any advice to give him (no); the lady who sent her elegy on the President, with the news that it had been read to great effect from the pulpit of her church, and the request that the Poetry Office arrange for it to be recorded with the United States Navy Band playing 'Anchors Aweigh' in the background. . . ." He formulated two general rules for the guidance of his successors: "1. Real poets do not consult an official about their poetry. That leaves the others. 2. Except for real poets, persons writing poetry in America are either under twenty-three or over sixty; what they do in the intervening thirty-seven years is not known, except that it is not poetry." He dwelt on this part of his activities because it was "time almost entirely wasted, of no possible use to anyone except, perhaps, as a demonstration to the Consultant of the appalling misunderstanding of the nature of poetry spread through America by pernicious education. . . ." In spite of all this seeming contrariety, Nemerov's files contain not a few constructive replies to petitioning poets, such as one to a young man at William and Mary College, where he had gone to read: "Sitting here in the scholarly quiet of the Library—sirens whining, pneumatic drills reverberating through the marble corridors, workmen shouting cheerfully ('Okay, Jack?' 'Okay') as they drop one more steel filing cabinet in an echo chamber nearby—well, anyhow, sitting here I have been reading your poems." Three pages of careful analysis follow.

It was, indeed, the educational aspect of his work that interested Nemerov most. "It is almost always worthwhile talking with the young, who may possibly learn something (and very likely teach something, too . . .). It is upon the whole less worthwhile talking with the grownups, who are already full of belief that they know about poetry and who in any event are supposed to be aware that they live in a society based on money, and hence prepared to pay for what they value." Clubs (such as the Washington Chapter of the NSAL) were disinclined to pay lecturing fees, Nemerov observed, and he spoke before none of them and to very few grownups—a lawyers' club, women prisoners in the penitentiary at Lorton, Virginia, a P-TA. But he did talk with a good many high school and college students from the District and environs. With the cooperation of Dorothy Goldberg (the painter, who was the wife of Arthur Goldberg, an Associate Justice of the Supreme Court) and Charlotte Brooks (chairman of the English department for the D.C. public schools) he gave four seminars on poetry in the Library's Wilson Room to teachers and young students, many of them from the impoverished black section of Southeast Washington. When he gave his poetry reading in May he suggested that a block of maybe a hundred tickets be set aside for District of Columbia high school students. Over the year he traveled to nearly three dozen schools and colleges around the country for lectures and readings. "In a country so very generally supposed— with some reason, too—to value poetry not at all, it is very affecting to learn what a welcome subject it is, how much young students especially want to know more of it and about it, and how very clearly they grasp what it's all about. . . .[Yet] such a care for poetry may subsist right alongside the most dreadfully routine and imagination-slaying classroom procedures, graduate studies, &c."

For the Forum Series of the Voice of America, Nemerov coordinated a series of lectures, for broadcast abroad, by nineteen American poets "whose various styles, ages, and degrees of achievement give a fair representation to the whole range of what is presently being written." They included Aiken, Eberhart, Whittemore, William Jay Smith, James Dickey, and himself, from the roster of Consultants, besides such exemplars as Marianne Moore, Berryman, Corso, and Theodore Weiss. The frequency of poetry quoted in the lectures gave the collection the character of an anthology, and it was eventually published as a book, *Poets on Poetry.* As for his own poetry, he had not expected to write any while in the Chair. "Being in some sense National Poetry Administrator . . . , one would not expect to write poems oneself; there would be something a little ludicrous in that. One's physical position, sitting on the top right-hand corner of the Collected Dreams of Humanity, level after level descending deep into the earth, was somehow not quite right for adding a few more small dreams to the stack. . . . And, after all, as to poetry, I didn't absolutely not write any; a few samples will be appearing from time to time. . . ." Nemerov did write a poem, though not an elegy, on President Kennedy, whose death occurred on November 22, 1963, a day when Nemerov was at Lawrence College, in Wisconsin, participating in a symposium with Harlow Shapley and Bruno Bettelheim on the theme of science and the humanities. When a publisher asked him to contribute to an anthology about Kennedy's death, he replied, "I did indeed write a poem on that occasion . . . but the result strikes me now as having been rather willed, although sincerely so, than fully imagined, and I am not willing to see the piece reappear in your anthology."

As the Great Society gained momentum, Nemerov found himself included in a planning conference, chaired by Eric Goldman, assistant to President Johnson, which sat for five hours on the question of what the President might do for education in the arts. "Not a great deal, I should have said as a result of that meeting; but maybe it's too early to tell." Nemerov, at any rate, found a title for a group of poems in his next volume, which included one poem entitled "The Great Society, Mark X":

> The engine and transmission and the wheels
> Are made of greed, fear, and invidiousness
> Fueled by super-pep high octane money
> And lubricated with hypocrisy,
> Interior upholstery is all handsewn
> Of the skins of children of the very poor,
> Justice and mercy, charity and peace,
> Are optional items at slight extra cost,
> The steering gear is newsprint powered by
> Expediency but not connected with
> The wheels, and finally there are no brakes.
>
> However, the rear-view mirror and the horn
> Are covered by our lifetime guarantee.

This Consultant's relations with Mrs. Whittall aren't recorded. On December 4, 1963, he was speaking at a Unitarian church in Fairfax, Virginia, and therefore was unable to attend a luncheon given for her by the Librarian of Congress, in the Pavilion. The event followed a ceremony in the office of a District of Columbia commissioner, Walter N. Tobriner, who bestowed on Gertrude Whittall the Meritorious Public Service Award of the District, in appreciation of her gifts of music and literature to the people of the United States and of the Capital. Mrs. Whittall, then ninety-six and still faithfully attending *her* events at the Library, returned the tribute with the words "If my book of life were written—the Library of Congress and its enchanting associations and memories would be recorded in letters of gold."

With Nemerov it became usual for the Consultant to introduce some of the Whittall Fund programs, further breaching a rather pointless barrier. He presented Marianne Moore, when she finally read in the Coolidge Auditorium on October 21 (and was fêted at a reception in the Pavilion); the English novelist T. H. White, presenting a lecture entitled "Poets Unfashionable" on December 2; and Reed Whittemore, reading his poetry on March 9. Ralph Ellison and Karl Shapiro were paired as lecturers on "The Writer's Experience"—each telling of his literary development in a singular American context. Ellison talked on January 6, Shapiro on January 27. Untermeyer returned to the Library on March 23 for a memorial lecture, "Robert Frost: A Backward Look," and a reading from his late friend's work. By all reports he held an overflow audience spellbound. The acting companies that had become welcome fixtures in the Whittall series gave performances chiefly Shakespearean, though the ANTA troupe, under Lucille Lortel's aegis, varied the pattern with Jean Anouilh's *Medea*. Nemerov, in his Consultant role, gave a lecture entitled "Bottom's Dream: The Likeness of Poems and Jokes" in early October and read his poetry toward the end of his term, the following May.

Picking Nemerov's successor—after he resisted Basler's and Mumford's friendly insistence that he stay a second year—was the Library's concern in January, and again the festival roster was mulled over. Nemerov nevertheless made a strong case for Whittemore: "a [man of] most skillful and literate intelligence . . . [who] might give the post the sort of relevant substance that I fear I've not been able to do." He was plainly trying to sense what Basler and the bureaucracy were looking for, when he made his comments on, e.g., Berryman, "of whom I know much less . . . a gifted writer, marvelous witty talker, said to be immensely learned . . . whose presence would make for a lively year, one way & another." Other "reckonable poets, who may be over-young," were W. S. Merwin and James Dickey. "Reading Dickey's poetry during the past year, . . . I have the sneaky feeling that this lad may be it, a real poet, maybe even the real poet." Nemerov also suggested considering "a side of the country rarely represented here," the West Coast. The decision went to Whittemore.

✳

"A 'poor man's' orchid tree stands outside the white-gated Joseph Auslander house in Coral Gables. It was planted there in memory of Robert Frost and often reminds Auslander of his friend." So began a feature article in the *Miami Herald*, about Auslander's winning the Robert Frost Poetry Award on January 23, 1964, for a poem entitled "Two That Unlatched Heaven," on the subject of a domestic quarrel. The prize, being given for the fifth and last time, was announced at the 54th anniversary dinner of the Poetry Society of America, in New York. More than thirteen hundred poets had competed for the award: $1,000, underwritten by Frost's publishers, Holt, Rinehart & Winston. Auslander's words to the reporter, "The deliberate obscurantism of the new crop of poets today is a sign of immaturity. It's a kind of emotional measles. The sickness of modern people is that they don't love people—Frost did." Auslander didn't travel north for the dinner. He said his doctor advised him the excitement would be too much for his heart. Another prize-winning poet made it to the dinner from Portland, Oregon—William Stafford, who got the Shelley Memorial Award of $1,400.

✳

As the Consultant in Poetry during 1964–65, Reed Whittemore brought an unprecedented kind of experience and interest to the Library of Congress; his stretch proved to be of mutual value to the Library and to him. Typologically, he seems to have had something in common with his predecessor; the word used sometimes to describe him was "undeceived." As sophomores at Yale, in spring 1939, Whittemore and his roommate, James J. Angleton, had started the literary magazine *Furioso,* whose Volume I: Number I opened with a letter from MacLeish and closed with an essay by Pound, blasting usury (not quite the contribution the editors of a poetry magazine had hoped for). MacLeish's communiqué contains a stark admonition aimed at young poets: ". . . the poets take in each other's poetry. The critics criticize each other's criticisms. The critics, because they have no other expression, and often no other life, live on the expression of the poets. The poets because they have no other audience, write for an audience of critics." The issue also contained work by W. C. Williams, Cummings, Eberhart, and other contemporaries. That summer, Pound paused in New Haven after visiting Washington and New York. He met his young editors, and Whittemore's parents put him up for the night. Neither Pound's uppishness that evening and next day, when Angleton and Whittemore drove him to Cambridge to visit Theodore Spencer (while Pound belted out lines of Canto One), nor MacLeish's warning, discouraged *Furioso*. It continued for a few irregular issues, was dormant during the war while Whittemore was overseas in the Army, and revived in 1946, when Whittemore came into a small bequest that enabled him to carry it. After a spell of graduate work in history at Princeton, he began teaching English at Carleton College, in Northfield, Minnesota, in 1947; *Furioso* went with him and survived until 1953. Like many little magazines, it had begun as a protest against commercial publishers, but "we discovered that nobody had even the good manners to acknowledge that we were at war with them. . . . Thereafter . . . *Furioso* took arms against the academic world, the new criticism, the writing world, the advertising world, General MacArthur, and the production of H-bombs with the same results. . . ." After *Furioso*'s demise, it was succeeded by *The Carleton Miscellany*, under Whittemore's editorship until he assumed the Chair of Poetry.

Whittemore was one of the founders of the Association of Literary Magazines of America, acronymically ALMA. Thus his first memorandum to Basler, who asked him for suggestions for the Consultant's activities, proposed a meeting of literary magazine editors, possibly under the auspices of such a patron as the U. S. Steel Foundation or the Carnegie Corporation. Encouraged to pursue the idea, Whittemore proposed as a basis a meeting of ALMA ("now nearly defunct") that might lead to its rejuvenation, coupled with a symposial gathering of editors. The scheme won approval quickly, provided the funding could be obtained. So it was: a grant of $14,500 from the Carnegie Corporation of

New York, through the interest of Peter Caws, a professor of philosophy at the University of Kansas, on leave to do foundation work, who also would participate in the symposium. The event was set for the following April. (The Carnegie Corporation had for some years been a generous benefactor of various of the Library's programs. This was its first gift in the area of aesthetics.)

For his lecture, on October 12, Whittemore took as his text a reference in Nemerov's report, cited heretofore, to the "appalling misunderstanding of the nature of poetry." Under the title "Ways of Misunderstanding Poetry" he aimed to adjudicate between two somewhat contradictory notions of poetry—as the final repository of most worldly wisdom (the poet-as-seer principle) and as something having nothing to do with anything and suitable only for dissemination in poetry magazines and the Coolidge Auditorium. His disarming lecture and a social event soon afterward helped to introduce him to Washington as an unexpected variety of Consultant. Dorothy Goldberg gave a large reception for him, at which he proved to be, in the view of a *Washington Post* writer named Ellen Key Blunt, "not a ponderous eccentric spewing murky profundities" but "a lovely, lively, lilting, lyrical fellow . . . a mild-mannered English teacher whose shoes and socks match." Surely Whittemore was feeling better about opting for Washington instead of taking his family abroad for this sabbatical year.

On November 29, he found himself reading out of the Bible in the National Cathedral during a celebration of Shakespeare's 400th birthday, in which C. Day Lewis, Roland Mushat Frye, and William Jay Smith also participated. The Whittemores spent New Year's Eve with the Biddles. On January 5, 1965, he was on the radio reflecting about the life and the death—the day before—of T. S. Eliot. As a "reluctant long-time admirer," Whittemore wrote, "it is difficult even to meditate in silence about this poet's death without employing some of the poet's own 'terms.' . . . He now lives on, for his admirers, in the quotation-ridden thoughts they entertain about his death, they having learned a good deal of what they know and feel about death from him, learned of growing old with their trousers rolled, of dying with a little patience, of shoring fragments against their ruin, of dancers gone under the sea, of captains, bankers and eminent men of letters fading off into the dark." In the same dour month Whittemore received four Soviet writers (Bondarev, Kudryavtseva, Ryurikov, and Zbanatsky) and their State Department escort-interpreter in the Poetry Room and, with his wife, attended President Johnson's inauguration and the concomitant luncheons, suppers, and dances. The President had invited fifty Americans prominent in the arts and letters as his special guests. (On the clear snowy morning of the inauguration, the Poetry Room, with its direct view of the East Terrace of the Capitol, where the ceremony was taking place, was closed and guarded by Secret Service men, though the Poetry Office staff, including Whittemore, were allowed to sit on the balcony and watch.)

A poem came out of Whittemore's time in the Capital, "Washington Interregnum":

> When politicos of the old life have departed,
> Movers enter, and painters,
> And sometimes fumigators,
> To help get the new life started.
>
> In the halls there are boxes and echoes.
> There is rain on windows.
> Inside windows,
> Framed by taxpayers' marble,
> An occasional lingering face in its lostness mellows.
>
> Newcomers straggle up and down in the wet,
> Waiting in elegant duds on alien corners,
> Calling for taxis, searching out parties,
> Questing for something obscure, unnamed, unmet.
>
> The something decided not to attend the Ball,
> Nor grace the Parade.
> It failed to appear and perform in the grandstand charade
> On the Hill.
> Maybe it hides in an old box in a hall?

Maybe not. Anyway, there are offices, empty.
There is rain.
There is marble.
There is also the rust and ruin of parting pleasantry—
There is also the new paint, in all the empty.

Whittemore's relations with governmental Washington were perhaps more energetic than those of the run of Consultants. He "set out to stir up a cultural storm, suffering the consequences . . . and became convinced that all poetry consultants hereafter should do the same. I am, however, confident that should the next Consultant choose to live in splendid isolation in his third floor retreat, the kindly Library officials would smile as sweetly upon him as they have smiled upon me as a greenhorn bureaucrat." With moral support from Dorothy Goldberg, Michael Straight, and Paul Goodman, he arranged two informal meetings of officials in various governmental agencies about the possible roles of artists and writers in government. "The Useful Arts" was his topic. "The poet's bent is language. The good poet is a master of language. The language of Washington (for example) could use poets." Ideally, the President should appoint consultants in art and literature at strategic places in the government. No conclusions were reached, no plans were drafted, but Whittemore felt that "the climate in Washington is such as to produce . . . jobs like the Library's Consultantship in other agencies in Washington, and perhaps other substantial evidence of artistic subversion of the bureaucracy."

As a private and practical experiment in the fostering of "useful arts" in government, Whittemore, at the request of the National Park Service, wrote the text of a new pamphlet for the Thomas Jefferson Memorial, which was approved and issued, with credit, exactly as he wrote it. "The enforced anonymity of bureaucratic prose produces . . . a diffuse, evasive, and strongly uninformative expository literature. . . . To reinstate the writer as author . . . without being constrained by protective agency specifications—this was the core of the experiment." Whether or not Whittemore's experiment was a catalyst, the literary style of Park Service pamphlets is today a decided improvement on what it used to be. It was important, Whittemore also thought, to sell poetry to the ordinary civil servant, and he gave readings in such venues as the cafeteria at the Department of Agriculture. Whatever the purpose may have been, Whittemore and the painter Morris Graves were invited to the Goddard Space Flight Center, outside Washington, to talk to astronomers on the staff, a three-way encounter he enjoyed. His response was entirely skeptical, however, to a two-day conference run by the University of Texas in Austin, whose subject turned out to be "What to Do with the New Government Foundation for the Arts and Humanities." "Everybody talked a great deal but settled little. . . . My own private feelings are that . . . no government program encouraging things as they are would serve any purpose not now being served by private funds, and . . . any program encouraging radical changes in the teaching and general promulgation of our humanistic culture would be met with cries of dictatorship."

The symposium on the little magazine and contemporary literature, held April 2 and 3 in the Coolidge Auditorium, brought to Washington, from as far away as Pakistan and Alaska, a hundred or so editors, representing some sixty magazines, plus several literary scholars. There were three sessions, chaired by Whittemore; each one involved papers by two speakers followed by a panel and then a general discussion. William Phillips, one of the editors of the *Partisan Review*, spoke first, on the present state of literary publishing. He was followed by Karl Shapiro, who after holding the Library's Chair of Poetry had edited *Poetry* and then *Prairie Schooner*, in Nebraska; he talked about the campus literary organ. "Institutions," he said, "whether the newspaper, the university, the foundation, or the government, can only deaden or paralyze art. . . . No academy should ever be put in the position of having to arbitrate and establish the values of works of art. This great and glorious Library had its knuckles rapped many years ago when it started to give out poetry prizes. And a good thing, too." Allen Tate (who was the honorary president of ALMA), speaking on subsidized publication, argued for foundation help but warned against the legislative powers of foundations, excusing the Guggenheim and Bollingen foundations from that vice. After alluding to foundation support of cancer research, he pointed to "an equally sinister disease, the corruption of language by Madison Avenue and Washington . . . the foul suppuration of political and advertising rhetoric which daily corrupts the body social and politic—a spiritual cancer that the literary magazine might be expected to . . . perhaps do something towards extirpating." Whittemore was next, still taking "the gloomiest view of the state of our literature and literary publications," yet ready to contemplate radical literary ventures, such as collaboration or merger or synthesis of magazines, like to unlike, as a means of salvation. The talks at the last session were on the teaching of contemporary literature; the speakers were Wayne Booth, a professor of English at the University of Chicago and an editor of the *Carleton Miscellany,* and the philosopher Peter Caws. A persistent and summarizing thread in the conference was funding, which continued at the business meeting of ALMA that followed.

Though the divergence of views was extraordinary and noisy ("Little Mag Editors in Dither," as Geoffrey Wolff headlined his story in the *Post*), Basler calmly reported that "the Symposium made its point, not only about the nation's indebtedness to little magazines as hotbeds of literary talent, but also about their comparative neglect at the hands of the public and the sources of support." When the symposium proceedings—penetrating, often witty, explosive, rapid-fire, even raunchy— were published for the Library of Congress in 1966 by the Modern Language Association of America (on the Carnegie grant), Whittemore summarized his impressions of his handiwork.

It was hoped that from this group some worthwhile proposals would float forth for redeeming or restoring to health a kind of publishing now, it seems evident, in real trouble. This hope was not realized. Though a number of proposals were in fact made— I, for example, made a perfectly magnificent one—none seemed to take hold. Most participants left the conference persuaded of the difficulties of joint efforts at restoration and mightily impressed by the extraordinary absence of agreement.

It was an exciting meeting. Maybe the disagreements are in themselves instructive. "Back to the drawing boards," cry the world's architects when their roofs leak, their bridges fall down. The architects of little magazines can now go back to their drawing boards too—and perhaps project another conference.

Two years later, when Whittemore returned to Washington to work for the National Institute of Public Affairs, he took the lead in organizing the Coordinating Council of Literary Magazines, which replaced ALMA and continues today, with support chiefly from the National Endowment for the Arts, to minister to the little magazines from an office in New York. It would appear that the "New York crowd" in some sense seized CCLM, when Whittemore was immobilized with a grave illness in 1967. "The Consultant in Poetry has to put up with the patronizing attitude of the New York literary community," Whittemore felt at the time. "They look at Washington contemptuously as a hick town, the way Henry Adams saw it. It's something to reckon with."

The White House Festival of the Arts, on June 14, 1965, inevitably drew the Consultant, in his bureaucratic situation, into its net. When an assistant to Eric Goldman, who as a "special consultant" to President Johnson was in charge of the festival, asked Whittemore for a list of the heads of prominent organizations in the country directed to the furthering of poetry, he obliged while dissenting with the principle of planning the event around the "most familiar front-men for the arts." "The life of the arts is not with these men, alas, except in a few rare, happy instances, and you cannot, it seems to me, run an intelligent arts festival around them without managing to misrepresent the whole world of art." Besides the "front-men"—among whom were such rare, happy instances as Marie Bullock, Robert Richman, and Lewis Mumford— the eventual invitation list included, for "literature," Mark Van Doren, Saul Bellow, John Hersey, Edmund Wilson, Robert Lowell, Dwight Macdonald, and of course Whittemore.

Goldman later conceded that the festival was, to some extent, "a tool to quiet opposition to the Vietnam War," though he doubted that the President took it very seriously, but probably thought of it as "the sort of thing a President ought to do in view of all the interest in art around the country." Lowell at first agreed to come and to read his poetry, but soon afterward he reconsidered and wrote an open letter to President Johnson, refusing the invitation because of his "dismay and distrust" over the Administration's foreign policy. The letter, published in the *New York Times,* infuriated Johnson, and it also spurred twenty writers and artists to sign a telegram to him expressing a similar dismay and their support for Lowell. Among the signatories were Stanley Kunitz, W. D. Snodgrass, John Berryman, Robert Penn Warren, and Dwight Macdonald. Edmund Wilson brusquely refused the invitation, as did several others, but Macdonald decided to accept, and he brought with him a petition that read: "We should like to make it clear that in accepting the President's kind invitation . . . , we do not mean either to repudiate the courageous position taken by Robert Lowell, or to endorse the Administration's foreign policy." In the Rose Garden of the White House, Macdonald collected nine signatures, including Whittemore's. As Whittemore later observed, "Not only do I share the doubts of Robert Lowell and others about Vietnam . . . , but I am also opposed to many of the statements made by the President about the role of art in the culture." Whittemore felt obliged to apologize to Goldman for his indiscretion in audibly describing as "canned" a speech that Goldman made in the Rose Garden. His comment had been picked up by the vigilant ear of Mary McGrory. "My unmannerly word," Whittemore went on, "was an inadequate description of my deep conviction that the hopes expressed in the . . . speech are not attainable by patronage, subsidy, even White House benevolence toward the arts—or in other words of my conviction that the difficulties run deep and are if anything merely accentuated by gestures like the Festival, at least so long as the notion that art and politics can be dealt with separately prevails."

That Whittemore called on Mrs. Whittall in her apartment at the Shoreham may have been as much his good manners and innate friendliness as it was evidence of the closing of the old gap between the Whittall programs and the Consultantship. He was, it appears, the only Consultant who made that civil gesture since the programs began (though some of the others would surely have been welcome). On the other hand, Whittemore didn't introduce the poets who read that year in the Coolidge Auditorium—James Schevill, Jean Garrigue, Howard Moss, and Muriel Rukeyser. The events on the Whittall Fund included a showing of three movies in which poems by Hy Sobiloff were read by actors—Ed Begley, Jason Robards, and David Wayne—against appropriate pictorial backgrounds. (Within the year, Sobiloff made another gift for the poetry programs, this time $10,000.) There were lectures by Gore Vidal, on "The Novel in the Age of Science," and by Erskine Caldwell, on his own writing. ANTA, under Lucille Lortel's direction, brough Margaret Webster to the Coolidge two nights to perform a dramatic reading, *A Coward Soul,* about the Brontes. The Whittall Fund also supported a Dante Symposium, on May 1, 1965, marking the 700th anniversary of the poet's birth, with lectures by J. Chesley Mathews, Francis Fergusson, and John Ciardi.

Gertrude Whittall was in the audience on April 12, 1965, for the performance (by the Actors Studio Workshop, which Lortel now directed) of Mark Van Doren's play, *The Last Days of Lincoln,* in the Coolidge Auditorium, and at the reception afterward in her Pavilion for the playwright and the cast. On April 23, she attended the last concert of the season by the Juilliard String Quartet, on the music foundation she had established. Soon afterward, pressed by friends to forego, at the age of ninety-seven, some of her lifelong independence, she left Washington to go and live at Juniper Hall, formerly her mansion at Shrewsbury, Massachusetts, which she had endowed in 1922 as a retirement home and presented to the Grand Lodge of Masons of Massachusetts in memory of her husband. She spent less than twenty-four hours at Juniper Hall and returned to her Washington hotel. Her apartment had already been let, and she was sitting in the lobby waiting for a new assignment when her old friend Harold Spivacke, chief of the Music Division, came to be of help to her. She waved her hand about her and said, "*This* is for me." In Basler's words: "Not long afterward she slipped, as all of us had feared she would for ten years or longer, fell hard, and broke her hip. She died at George Washington Hospital some days later—on June 29. When visited near the end, she is reported to have whispered, 'I think it's time to go.'" Her Library friends remembered best what she said at a luncheon in her Pavilion in summer 1958: "When I die and go to heaven, if I don't like it there, I'll come back to the Library of Congress."

Like Archer Huntington, Gertrude Whittall gave away her entire fortune. She had gradually been adding to her gifts to the Library of Congress, and even in 1965 she gave an extra $5,000 "for the entertainment of literary visitors," to make certain that receptions were properly catered. At her death she bequeathed to the Library of Congress, in investments and cash, a total of $677,728.72, with the stipulation that it be divided equally to augment the principal of the Whittall Foundation (for music) and the Whittall Poetry and Literature Fund. Her benefactions to music at the Library of Congress came to approximately $1,478,812; to poetry and literature, approximately $960,187—altogether $2,439,000. The additional capital not only enabled the literary and musical programs to be very much augmented, but afforded funds to bolster the income, then about $10,000 per year, available for the Chair of Poetry from the Huntington endowment. The Consultants' stipends could thereafter be maintained at a level realistically on a par with academic salaries. Mrs. Whittall had verbally approved such a disposition several years before her death, when Basler had discussed the probability with her.

Besides the capital sums represented by the Foundation and the Fund, Gertrude Whittall gave the Library tangibles of far greater value: the Stradivari instruments and Tourte bows, the Pavilion and its contents, the sculptures in the courtyard, the furnishings of the Poetry Room, the many literary manuscripts, and the collection of music manuscripts that "has no parallel in the Western Hemisphere."

Quincy Mumford, in his *Annual Report* for fiscal 1965, called Mrs. Whittall "a close and valued friend" and "a wise as well as a generous woman, [who] made her gifts freely and set no restrictions which would limit their usefulness in the future." He quoted a sentence in a letter she had written in 1945, the basic policy statement governing her Foundation for music: "I do not wish to burden future generations with burdensome stipulations since I am aware of the fact that it is impossible to foresee what conditions may be like in the future."

❋

Joseph Auslander died in a Miami hospital on June 22, 1965, after a heart attack. He was sixty-seven. His death received extensive notices, rehearsing his career, in the New York and Washington papers. People came into his Coral Gables house and helped themselves to some of Auslander's manuscripts, before his elder daughter, Blossom, could arrive from Seattle. She took his and Audrey Wurdemann's two children, aged ten and twelve, back with her, adopted them, and brought them up.

※

In February 1965, Basler had begun to ponder the next year's appointment to the Chair. Whittemore's leave from Carleton College couldn't be stretched and, in any event, he had other projects in view. Basler sent the Librarian a set of lists, as usual: nine good possibilities who had been held in reserve, including Dickey, Donald Hall, Denise Levertov, and Rukeyser; poets who had said no fairly definitely; nine repeatedly recommended names that he mentioned for the record— Auden (beside whose name someone jotted "homosexual"), Berryman, Kunitz, Snodgrass, Schwartz, Deutsch, Peter Viereck, Langston Hughes, Alan Dugan. Mumford wrote some more names in the margin: Carolyn Kizer, Michael Straight, Stephen Spender. Then he offered the Chair to Snodgrass, who was teaching at Wayne State University in Detroit. But Snodgrass was in the midst of a psychoanalysis and loath to interrupt it. The matter drifted, until Basler got a fresh hint from Whittemore. In April, in line of duty, Whittemore agreed to serve on a committee to try to make a go of International Cooperation Year, or ICY, which had been designated by the United Nations in recognition of the twentieth anniversary of its founding. There was to be a White House Conference on International Cooperation during November 30 to December 2, 1966. "The difficulties of sponsoring a significant effort in international cooperation while our government deploys and employs military forces all over the world seem very great," Whittemore had to say. "I've proposed that we try to set up a series of East-West dialogues about aesthetics and encourage greater East-West exchange of university persons concerned with the arts." An "international" appointment came into view.

Mumford wrote Spender in late April, "Perhaps the time has come to consider the possibility of inviting a distinguished English poet, especially if he could be one who has become almost as much 'at home' in the American scene as one of our own. It would be particularly appropriate during International Cooperation Year." Indeed, Spender had been in the United States frequently, and for long periods, since the

1940s, lecturing, reading, teaching, visiting his numerous American friends, ranging from Michael Straight through Joseph Alsop to Muriel Gardiner. "I've spent a good third of my life in the States since the War," he has recalled. "I acquired rather quickly an American point of view and was in Europe, during the most anti-American decade, a pro-American. . . . I suppose that I became unconsciously American." At the Library of Congress, he had recorded his poetry first in 1948, Lowell's time, and had read and lectured in 1959 and 1962. And being a British subject seemed no impediment; poetry in English was the concern of the Chair. Spender accepted the appointment eagerly enough, with the understanding that he could meet obligations he had previously made, to teach a course during the year at Northwestern University, to give the Clarke Lectures at Cambridge University in February, and, in a subdued way, to act as an "editor abroad" for *Encounter* (having originally been coeditor).

So Spender arranged to rent Conrad Aiken's house on Capitol Hill, and his wife Natasha was able to join him. He had felt, before arriving in Washington, that the Consultant should involve himself in some worthy project that would enhance the reputation of the Library, and he proposed a conference of the translators and the translated. The idea had grown out of a conversation in London a year or two before with the Russian poet Anna Akhmatova, who had found that translations of her great poem "Requiem" by English poets were quite inaccurate, but when an interpreter attached to her produced an accurate translation it was unpublishable. Such a problem deserved addressing. Furthermore, Spender stated in his report at the end of his term, "behind the Iron Curtain a new generation of poets is emerging who attach more importance to the appearance of their poems, translated, in other countries than in their own countries, where the intellectual climate is so oppressive and conformist, and there is no vital discussion of poetry except along the lines of whether it is political or antipolitical. . . .The question of translating . . . has become a very living and urgent problem to writers in other languages." Spender's proposal didn't appear to interest anyone; nothing came of it during his year, though it may have helped bring about the International Poetry Festival two years later, from which, ironically, Spender was absent. Reflecting some years later on the Chair of Poetry, he said, "It could well be made a great *international* honor, not only for poets writing in the English language but for poets of the eminence of Brodsky, before he became an American citizen, or Neruda."

Going on with his view of the appointment, Spender wrote, "The Consultant should regard himself as being in the 'gift' of the Library of Congress. . . . For this reason, I accepted almost all invitations to speak at schools, to attend prize-givings, to make commencement addresses, etc." The work in schools Spender found the most engaging part of his term—"having a close look into the life of Washington at a time of action and integration." Thus he helped judge a poetry contest in the secondary schools: "The poems were quite good—good enough to publish in the small magazines." And he arranged to give seminars for high-school students in the Wilson Room. Late in his term he went to a White House reception for prize scholars from all over the country. "As most of the scholars seemed to have no idea why they had been chosen from their states, and to be in a stunned condition, this was altogether charming, and there was a great air of spontaneity." That occasion diverted him more than another at the White House, when he was invited to be present when President Johnson signed into law the National Foundation for the Arts and Humanities Act, on September 29, 1965. (That legislation owed much to the efforts of Senator Jacob Javits, who as a young Congressman had played a role in the controversy over the Bollingen Prize award to Pound.) The President gave Spender one of the ballpoint pens he had used, stamped with the Presidential autograph.

The peripatetic aspect of the Consultantship was never more urgent than in the Spender year. The calendar of his engagements is exhausting just to look through. Sample: In early October, after recovering from the Whittall Pavilion reception for him and his wife, Spender flew next morning to Rochester, New York, for a college lecture, flew back next day for Katherine Anne Porter's lecture at the Library, got up and flew to Boston for another college talk, came back via Caldwell, New Jersey, for still another, and arrived home in time for dinner at the British Embassy. Meanwhile, he had been writing his expected lecture, appropriately called "Chaos and Control in Poetry," which he delivered in the

Coolidge Auditorium on October 11. Of course, nearly all the Consultants have gone through the same exertions, but seldom at such a fever pitch. Most of them would recognize as a model what Spender wrote in his journal after a trip to a small college in Ohio:

> Sometimes on these flying visits there is a feeling of complete unreality, as though an old movie is being run through for the thousandth time. One gets out of the plane and walks into the airport lobby. There is a wild feeling that perhaps no one will be there to meet the plane. I am still free, perhaps I will take a taxi to the hotel, lie down on the bed, read a book, write a poem, look at T.V. . . . But no, a pallid young instructor . . . or two or three embarrassed giggling students, appearing out of nowhere, say: "Are you Mr. S? We weren't sure we'd recognize you," and I am led off to the car. . . . During the drive to the "school," which can take anything up to four hours, frantic efforts are made to "communicate." Plans for the day are broken to one: the coffee hour with the students; lunch in the cafeteria, then a question hour, then an hour or so to "rest up"; then a select dinner at "the only moderately decent restaurant down town," with a few of the faculty, then . . . after the lecture, a party for graduate students and faculty. At this point I am struck by their extraordinary generosity, their real kindness and considerateness. We treat each other as though we are friends, with a sad feeling underneath that we will forget one another as soon as the occasion is over. . . . There is, in the end, a kind of magic of mutual appreciation and interest which works.

Among Spender's happier experiences on the lecture circuit, an encounter at a Southern university was reported by an acquaintance who was with him. After his talk, to a large and cordial audience, Spender was approached by a small elderly woman who stood by shyly until he smiled and spoke to her. She murmured that she'd like to recite a poem she had written about him. With slight apprehension, he said he'd be delighted. The lady drew herself up proudly and declaimed:

Stephen Spender,
Splendor.

Then she bowed and went on her way.

Randall Jarrell's death, on October 14, severely shook all those who had come to know him at the Library. Jarrell had been in a hospital at the University of North Carolina Medical School, in Chapel Hill, for treatment of a wrist injury, the result of a suicide attempt some months earlier during a siege of depression. The prognosis for the wrist treatment was favorable, Mary Jarrell has written. While taking an evening walk along a narrow, one-lane road, Jarrell, dressed in dark clothing, was sideswiped by a car and killed instantly. Suicide appeared to be a possibility, but the coroner gave a verdict of accidental death. Spender, in his journal, recorded that "everyone from the reference division (to which the poetry consultant is attached) seemed upset. They asked me downstairs into an office where we stood round listening to the Librarian's remarks about Randall, which were broadcast." Spender telephoned Lowell in New York to learn more about the tragedy. He sent flowers to Mary Jarrell: "For Randall Jarrell—Poet, Friend, and my colleague as poetry consultant." Later, he wrote in his end-of-term report: "I did not hear about Jarrell's funeral until after it took place, and I very much regretted not attending it, both for my own personal reasons, and because I thought it would be a nice gesture for the incumbent poetry consultant to attend a service for a previous consultant. For the same reason, I was disappointed not to be invited to the Yale gathering in which papers were read honoring Randall Jarrell." At the time, Spender had raised the question of the role the Consultant might have, in being invited to represent the Library on occasions such as these.

As for the White House Conference on International Cooperation, the inevitable summons came on November 5, when Spender learned from the Department of State that "we all think that a poem written and read by you will adorn the occasion." Here was an instance when the Consultant in Poetry had to perform like a Poet Laureate. Spender composed a work entitled "Poem for a Public Occasion" ("an immense labor, and probably not worth it"), which he read at the opening program of the Conference, on November 28. He served at two other Laureate-like occasions: for the annual dinner of the Oxford-Cambridge Boat Race (on the Potomac), he wrote a poem which proved to be a sequence of limericks; and he gave a poetry reading for the opening of the first village center at the satellite town of Reston, Virginia, which he enjoyed famously.

It is not news that Spender was a political radical in his youth, and at the time of the Civil War in Spain had a brief adventure with the Communist Party. Subsequently his politics were centrifugal; when he was a coeditor of *Encounter,* the journal was opposed to fascism and communism equally. (And when, in 1967, Spender discovered that the journal was financed indirectly by the CIA he resigned from its staff.) In 1953, when Spender was appointed to a professorship at the University of Cincinnati and he was refused a visa, Senator Robert A. Taft, aware that Spender had arrived at an anti-Communist position and was not going to *teach* communism, intervened, and the visa was approved by waiver. Notwithstanding, Ralph de Toledano, a right-wing journalist, soon after Spender got his first Washington press coverage as Consultant, questioned the "importation of a minor poet with dubious political sentiments," and reviewed Spender's "fashionable" party membership thirty years earlier. "Why, if the Library of Congress feels compelled to import a British poet, did it not select W. H. Auden, a man of infinitely greater talents who has become an American citizen and participated in this country's literary life? . . . Someone of considerable importance must have intervened to get Mr. Spender over that hurdle [of his past party membership]." Ineluctably, the Librarian heard from Congress: Senator Everett Dirksen, Senator Wayne Morse, and several others questioned the appointment, as much because Spender was not an American as because of his erstwhile politics. Mumford made an eloquent reply (drafted by Basler): in view of the ICY, "it seemed appropriate to appoint a citizen of the nation which has been our longtime friend and ally . . ."; "the post is not supported by appropriated funds"; the man has had numerous American involvements and honors; his "forthright stand, his penetrating analysis of the glaring contradictions and weaknesses of Communism [described in *World within World* and *The God That Failed*], was, of course, known to us. . . . His appointment [is] to the great credit of poetry in English and to the common heritage."

※

The Whittall programs did not much involve Spender, though he met and visited with most of the visiting poets and lecturers, as his published journal entries attest. The events in the fall, which reflected Basler's planning the previous spring, opened with a wryly reminiscent lecture by Katherine Anne Porter, "The Long War. Recollections of a Writer's Beginnings." Upon the publication of her novel *Ship of Fools* two years before, Porter had become at seventy-five a popular writer, indeed a glamorous celebrity, and she attracted a full house. She began her talk with a tribute to the late Gertrude Whittall, whose ninety-eighth birthday fell on the next day.

The first poet to read that season was also the first poet to appear on the Whittall series who happened to be black, Melvin B. Tolson. Basler had wanted to invite Tolson to the National Poetry Festival. He wasn't invited, Basler has written, "because he was not well enough known among the literati who had adulated Eliot and Pound for a generation. . . . That the committee was all white was not the trouble, for even if it had been a committee of all Black poets the verdict would probably have been the same." Tolson, of Missouri birth, had been gravely neglected, though he had been made Poet Laureate of Liberia (a country he never visited) and his ode *Libretto for the Republic of Liberia* had been introduced by Allen Tate when it was published in 1953. (Neglect has persisted, since Tolson's death, in 1966, at the age of sixty-eight.) The other poets who read that fall were Rexroth (the first member of the Beat Generation to achieve a Whittall engagement), Dickey, and Philip Booth. When Dickey came to read, on November 9, Spender dined with him, and wrote up the evening in his journal. (He published the entry and tactfully but recognizably disguised the poet as "K——.") The talk turned to Jarrell. "K—— said 'the younger generation' took no interest in his poetry or him. He had been a force, earlier on, whose unsparing criticisms destroyed reputations. Perhaps he had lost too many friends by writing such attacks. . . . [K——'s] reading was odd, fascinating to me as someone who also gives read-

ings. He had a stylized anecdote . . . attached to each poem, often more
absorbing to the audience than the poem itself. They reacted to the
anecdotes, they merely listened politely to the poems. All the anecdotes
were autobiographical and the poems seemed to be straight autobiog-
raphy."

In the new year, the British "outsider" Colin Wilson delivered a lec-
ture entitled "The Revolution in Literature." On two nights at the end
of January, after a spectacular blizzard, *An Evening's Frost,* a dramatic
portrayal of the late poet, written by Donald Hall, was performed to
large audiences. ANTA and Lucille Lortel were responsible for the pro-
duction. The role of Robert Frost was played by Will Geer, who had
portrayed Jeeter Lester in *Tobacco Road,* during later years was black-
listed for his radicalism, and in the 1970s as television's Grandpa Wal-
ton became almost as familiar an American icon as Frost had been. Two
other theatrical events featured plays of Racine and Shaw. The poet-
readers were Henry Rago, on February 7, and William Jay Smith (then
the writer-in-residence at Hollins College, Virginia), on March 21. The
Annual Report of the Librarian of Congress rose to an unusually lyrical
pitch in describing the events soon afterward: "'March . . . goes out
with a peacock's tail' wrote the essayist, and the last week of March
1966 proved his words by displaying a brilliant array of people and
programs . . . representing in capsule the color and variety found in a
year's programs." Auden was the star on March 28. Spender introduced
his poetry reading, which was attended by some seven hundred people,
occupying every seat and step in the Coolidge Auditorium and over-
flowing into the Whittall Pavilion, where a public address system car-
ried the proceedings. The following evening another capacity crowd
heard the Soviet poet Andrei Voznesenskiĭ read his poems in Russian,
with William Jay Smith reading English translations. This time the
overflow was accommodated in the snack bar, and after the formal pro-
gram Voznesenskiĭ and Smith made their way to this outpost and read
three more poems. The brilliant week continued with a visit by Gregory
Peck, who came to investigate the Library's motion picture holdings,
and ended with a concert by the Juilliard String Quartet. Spender's own
poetry reading, on May 2, drew another full house. As his last official
act at the Library, Spender received the Chilean poet Pablo Neruda,

who had come to record his famous revolutionary poem "Las Alturas de Macchu Picchu" in the Laboratory, to examine Walt Whitman manuscripts, and to be honored at a luncheon in Mrs. Whittall's Pavilion.

In accordance with what had become custom, at the end of his term Spender was invited to become an Honorary Consultant—in English Literature, however, not in American Letters—and he accepted the three-year appointment. Among the Honorary Consultants in American Letters there were triennial shifts in 1966. The terms of Bellow, Rice, and Steinbeck expired; the new appointees were Katherine Garrison Chapin, Ralph Ellison, and Robert Penn Warren. Mumford had also invited Vladimir Nabokov to serve. Though an American citizen, Nabokov had been living for some years in Montreux, Switzerland, and rarely visited the United States. In 1966 he was deeply into the writing of his novel *Ada, or Ardor: A Family Chronicle.* He replied to Mumford, first to tell him "how deeply honored I feel by the invitation," then going on to say: "With reluctance and regret, I must decline this honor. I lack the necessary energy and aptitude to be of any practical use to the Library. I would not be able to acquit myself properly even of the very limited duties you outline; and my conscience forbids me to accept your offer while knowing that I should not be able to force myself to write a single letter or read a single book beyond those that nature compels me to write or read. Let me add that I lead a very secluded life and have very little contact with either American or foreign writers."

※

James Dickey's reading in the Coolidge Auditorium on November 8, 1965, had the force—whether or not intended so—of a trial flight, which impressed the principalities and powers at the Library of Congress to the end that, only a few weeks later, he was offered the Consultantship. He accepted by return mail, "with pride and humility . . . in the name and spirit of the American poets of my generation." His record was appealing. It echoed that of some of his predecessors in the Chair while introducing novelty. Southern born—in Atlanta, 1923; a post-Fugitive Vanderbilt graduate; an Air Force pilot in World War II (eighty bombing missions over Japan) and a training officer in the Korean War; six years an advertising copywriter, on Coca-Cola, potato chips, fertilizer, Delta Airlines; a high-hurdles champion, weight-lifter, and archer; Guggenheim and *Sewanee Review* fellowships in Europe; five volumes of poetry published; master of the guitar; several English instructorships (his first at Rice Institute, where Willard Thorp, visiting there, looked with interest at his poetry) and poet-in-residencies. In 1965–66 he was the p.-in-r. at a state college in Northridge, a suburb of Los Angeles, and at the University of Wisconsin; he was committed to the same post the next year at Hollins College, but Hollins understandingly released him to Washington.

It was Dickey's good luck that he could bone up on the Chair of Poetry at a quasi skull practice that Basler arranged on January 22, 1966. Not that Basler planned the event to coach Dickey, who was an eminently quick study. Thanks to the much enhanced Whittall money, Basler was able to arrange a reunion of Consultants, including the Honorary Consultants in American Letters, for the purpose of discussing the conduct of the Chair and, in particular, the Whittall poetry and literature programs. He invited the previous, present, and prospective incumbents for an expense-paid visit to Washington. Besides Spender, Dickey, and Basler, the participants were five past Consultants—Aiken, Eberhart, Nemerov, Untermeyer, and Whittemore (the seven other survivors declined)—and two of the current Honorary Consultants, Katherine Garrison Chapin and Babette Deutsch. They met all day long in the Whittall Pavilion, while Phyllis Armstrong and her assistant Nancy Galbraith (who had come onto the force the previous year) superintended the recording microphones, discreetly hidden behind potted plants. Galbraith's painstaking transcript of the day's discussion ran to some forty-thousand words, almost a book. Basler had prepared a nine-point agenda and had distributed a confidential memorandum on the history of the Whittall Fund, one of the more interesting disclosures being the statement that the endowment at 4 percent was bringing approximately $34,760 into the operating account. The recommendations that arose under Basler's agenda headings were as follows:

A. Though it would seem a matter for administrative rather than consultative concern, the group expressed consensus on the need of supplementing the inadequate Huntington income for the Chair with amounts as needed from the Whittall Fund. There was also a cry for "gaining access to the huge funds now available for Culture" (Eberhart), meaning the recently created National Foundation on the Arts and Humanities. If big money *did* come in, why not have a Consultant in Fiction, a Consultant in Literary Criticism, and so on, to which Nemerov murmured, "They could play bridge on the top floor." Or why not have several creative writers at the Library, to which Untermeyer, "It would begin to look like a MacDowell Colony."

B. Opinion was diverse on the sort of programs the Whittall series should present. Most everyone favored more poetry readings by poets and lectures on poetry by poets and critics, but dramatic programs should be curtailed. Deutsch: "Actors reciting poems do a disservice to the poems." Untermeyer: "It's nothing more than exhibitionism." And how to bring many more poets to read? Untermeyer had a list of a hundred prospects. He suggested having two appointments, a peregrinating poet and a sedentary poet. Spender cut through all this, urging that Dickey be consulted at once about the next year's program which he would have to be involved in. (Yes, Basler aimed to do that.) Then, Spender offered, a poet reading should talk less about himself and his poems and more about poetry in general. Foreign poetry, and translations thereof, ought to be encouraged—translations the foreign poet accepts. And poets of contrasting views could be presented together; the academy vs. the Beats. Dickey, who had mostly been listening, began to open up. "Setting two people of opposite schools in public controversy with each other seems to diminish the importance of the poetry, as the personalities become important instead." Basler threw in the idea of another poetry festival, featuring people who had never appeared at the Library of Congress. Whittemore approved of that but was against poetry readings as a genre: "I can't think of anything as a genre that's much sicker than the poetry reading. It tends to drive people off . . . when it's not done well."

Katherine Chapin (always "Mrs. Biddle" in the Library context) put in a plea for doing plays *by poets*, mentioning Aiken's and Van Doren's. She harked back to "the good old days" when she thought the Consultant had more to do. (Mystifying, that.) Nemerov made an eloquent pitch for seminars with local high school students. Aiken spoke, as of old, for a lecture series. Eberhart recalled how impressive Arnold Moss's dramatization of E. A. Robinson's poems had been. Spender liked university dramatic troupes. Someone else thought they were too amateur. Both Spender and Eberhart mentioned the International P.E.N. congress in New York the next summer: the Library should get involved in that, perhaps invite the delegates down to Washington.

C. Everybody agreed that efforts should be made to extend and expand the audience for poetry readings by lending the Library's tapes for educational radio and classroom use. But should the poet get a fee if his tape were so exploited? Nemerov strongly believed so. "Otherwise it just gets out on tape, you don't own it any more, you have no more protection from copyright law." Basler: "The element of book-keeping and disbursing almost scares me to death." Deutsch proposed distributing to the audience mimeographed copies of the poems being read. "They'll enjoy them more if they can follow with their eyes." Untermeyer: "Babette, how would your publisher feel?" Whittemore: "This happened to me in Arizona last week. I found it very depressing, because, at the height of my eloquence, everyone would turn the page." Dickey: "It distracts them from you reading your own poem." Nemerov: "If you're still there next morning you can walk to breakfast on a carpet littered with your poems!"

D. A proposal to begin making video tapes, kinescopes, or talking pictures of the poets reading, for the archive, was met with both enthusiasm and misgivings. Basler remembered Frost saying, "Oh, they don't come to hear me, they come to see me." And Dickey remembered seeing an old film of F. Scott Fitzgerald, just sitting at a table with Hemingway in the South of France. "It was a wonderful new dimension of the man. Because no amount of still photographs, or even disembodied voices coming over the airwaves, is ever going to convey that sense of the living presence." Mrs. Biddle had never seen a good film of a poet, but Deutsch thought a film about the late Theodore Roethke (who had died in August 1963) was magnificent. To Nemerov, oneself on TV is like an effigy. "By the time one gets up on the platform one has already consented to become a vaudeville comic. Now with TV in the matter, it raises the question of how professional a vaudeville comic, how much time you must take from poetry to practice your audience appeal. Enough is enough." Mrs. Biddle mentioned "that dreadful film of Archie MacLeish and Mark Van Doren wandering around among the brooks and the trees. . . . I think they looked so—" Untermeyer broke in: "It was praised by everybody except the people who looked at it."

Nemerov was wonderfully wound up. "The tape recorder is a way of wasting the same time twice. I don't have much sympathy with the whole business of stacking the archives. There are an awful lot of records now in an awful lot of archives and files, and the past is growing heavier by exponential increases every year. It has crossed my mind that a great library can confer immortality. And that we find we are running a mausoleum." Whittemore picked it up. "If you're going to keep it from becoming a mausoleum you have to have somebody going through those caskets occasionally and choosing those things that might be imagined to live. A lot of it *is* dead."

E. A proposal to issue a new series of long-playing records was pretty thoroughly rejected. Though the Library had done the pioneer work of making and marketing records of readings, the commercial companies had now taken the lead. Records of the Yale Series of Poets, which Lee Anderson had begun making, had been bought out by Decca. The Library couldn't compete with such companies; it lacked the distributing facilities. As for the Decca records, Eberhart complained that the company wouldn't bring them up to date. His record (made at Yale) was five years old, and he'd like new poems added; but Decca told him they'd bought the Yale records lock, stock, and barrel and couldn't afford to alter them.

F. A proposal to make, experimentally, some sound movies of poets reading (as against mere videotaping, as in D) got a mixed reaction. There was the cost, to begin with—the Roethke film, generally admired as a model, cost around twenty-eight thousand dollars; grants from foundations would be necessary. If such a film were made, for example, about Marianne Moore, Untermeyer observed, "it might be a rather negative result. Whatever her qualities are, she's probably the worst reader in America—dull, heavy, monotonous—and the poems lose a great deal." In the Roethke film, Basler said, the director put "a great deal of sea beach and whispering leaves and whatnot into it besides Roethke. Suppose he directed a film around Moore. What would be the result?" Deutsch: "You might get a baseball game into it." Dickey: "At least a visit to the zoo." Untermeyer, in any case, spoke for "a perfectly straightforward presentation of the poet reading. I would love to have seen Walt Whitman read 'Song of Myself.' Without any appurtenances. You wouldn't have to see him pedalling down Mickle Street in Camden!"

G. After a sandwich lunch, discussion resumed on a proposal to commission poetic or dramatic works. It was rather thoroughly scrapped. (Its only defender was Spender.) Untermeyer: "Let us keep back our hoots of derision and try to be orderly and decent about the whole thing. I suppose there have been one or two great odes in the English language, written on purpose with malice aforethought, to celebrate an occasion. But even for money, it's rather difficult for a poet to sit down and write an occasional poem for recitation or performance." A parallel was drawn between a commission and a prize. The Congressional Joint Committee had ruled out such awards as the Bollingen Prize, but Basler believed that commissioning might be acceptable. Untermeyer (throughout the day, the most vocal of the party): "Frost commissioned himself to write a poem for the Kennedy inaugural; it was probably the worst poem he ever wrote—a long pseudo-history of America in what I can only describe as doggerel. Nature was very kind to him; it prohibited his reading it, what with the sun and the wind. . . ." He went on: "A commissioned poem could also put a terrific burden on the judge. Suppose this were a very fine poem in the, let's say, Robinson Jeffers manner, cursing Creation, Christianity, democracy, and so forth. What would the judge do. . . ?" Spender put in that he rather liked the poem he'd been commissioned to write for the ICY, and Basler complimented him on it. Dickey: "In a sense, every poem you write you commission yourself to write. . . . We ought to commission Howard to write a play about a bunch of eminent poets sitting around a table trying to decide. . . ." Nemerov: "A play called 'The Committee Meeting.' It wouldn't have much action."

H. Annotated bibliographies, anthologies, or an annual of the best poems of the year (suggested in order to "give the Consultant something to do"—Basler) received a lukewarm to cold reception. Dickey: "I would be *ag'in* all this! I just don't cotton to that kind of a thing." Untermeyer, constitutionally, argued for the anthology idea—drawn from the poetry of all the Consultants. Dickey (now): "We could live with that kind of an anthology."

The talk turned to the popular confusion of the post of Consultant in Poetry with that of Poet Laureate. Spender: "When Masefield was first made Poet Laureate, he took the trouble to invite young poets to stay with him for weekends and tried to encourage them. He didn't do this *as* Poet Laureate but *because* he was in that position. No one felt that 'this is a great rubber stamp on me from the government.' One can use this post [the Consultantship] to encourage other people, rather as a pedestal you happen to've been put on than a rubber stamp you've been equipped with."

I. Basler's last item was the idea of awarding prizes. There was little enthusiasm for that, but contradictorily it was unanimously recommended that the question of the Bollingen Prize be reopened by the Librarian with the Congressional Joint Committee and that the Bollingen Foundation and Yale University be requested to consider returning the Prize award to the Library of Congress. As Eberhart put it, "This institution should not be dispermitted from giving prizes, both in music and in literature, if it wants to." Basler duly passed the recommendation along to the Librarian as part of his report.

The discussion meandered on for another hour. Several more recommendations emerged: The Consultant's tenure should be for more than one year (even five years, some thought). The Library should try to secure large funds to expand its literary activities, either directly from Congress or from the National Arts Foundation. An annual convocation of the Honorary Consultants in American Letters should be reinstated. (Aiken was for reconstituting them as Fellows. "Things aren't like they used to be.") Nemerov: "I don't know how Jim feels, but I would have been very grateful for having been invited to a briefing of this sort before taking up the Consultantship." Finally, it was agreed that a memorial program for Randall Jarrell was appropriate. Basler had already invited Robert Lowell to lecture on and read some of Jarrell's poetry the following October.

Last murmurings: about Carolyn Kizer, in charge of the poetry office at the N.E.H. Nemerov: "Say, 'Carolyn, suppose we pool our resources: your money and our wits.'" Eberhart: "She has $65,000,000 to give away, as I understand it." Basler: "No, no. I don't know how much. . . ."

✳

That spring, before he got to Washington, Dickey compiled three more honors—the Melville Cane Award of the Poetry Society of America, the National Book Award in poetry for his last book, *Buckdancer's Choice,* and a National Institute of Arts and Letters grant in literature, $2,500. He moved his wife, Maxine, and two sons, Christopher and Kevin, into a Federal house in Leesburg, Virginia, an hour west of Washington. His first official act was to hold a press conference in the Poetry Room, dwelling on healthy egos, LSD (which he had found disappointing), the Presidency, big sports cars, Beatnik poems ("ludicrously inept"), Theodore Roethke ("immensely superior to any other poet we have had in this country"), Madison Avenue, Vietnam, Watts, and poetry. Almost immediately, like one of his predecessors, Dickey was in hot water over the question of a fee. He allegedly insulted the president of the League of American Penwomen, who offered him fifty dollars for a speaking engagement. He replied, "You would not expect to consult Dr. Paul Dudley White and pay him with peanuts. My fee is $700.00." The offended president complained to her friend Raymond Swain, the president of the Poetry Society of New Hampshire, who wrote angrily to both his senators, who complained to the Librarian, who defended Dickey: "He is paid from gift funds . . . can accept or decline invitations . . . is frequently paid $700 . . . has often read and spoken to school children without a fee. . . ." Dickey nevertheless salted Swain's wounds in a reply to his "pompous letter, impugning my motives and questioning my character, . . . plainly intended as an insult," and offering to "take the matter up on a personal basis when I come to your part of the country." The following spring, when Dickey published his poem "May Day Sermon" in the *Atlantic*, about a Georgia girl raped by her father, Swain addressed his outrage (at a poem that was "anti-Christ, anti-God, filth filled") to Senator Herman Talmadge, of both Swain's own and Dickey's native state. Talmadge relayed the protest, in spades, to the Librarian. Mumford's firm and courteous reply only inflamed Swain, who wrote him, "If Dickey is your idea of a poet, then, Sir, I have no respect for you whatsoever. . . . Perhaps we should start a movement to remove you. . . ." Swain erupted again when he read Dickey's famous poem "The Sheep Child" and reported he had received 1,722 letters of congratulation (from Cardinal Cushing and Senator Karl Mundt, inter alia) for his courageous attacks on Dickey.

Contrariwise, Dickey's extremely busy program of reading and lecturing, with guitar accompaniment, brought an unprecedented abundance of fan letters. A sampling: ". . . the absolute magic with which he takes over a student audience . . ." (Bethesda, Maryland); ". . . his depth of personality and his humility . . . outstanding spokesman for American letters, and a true and gentle person . . ." (Valparaiso, Florida); ". . . highlight of our poetry series, which has included Ransom, MacLeish, Wilbur, Van Doren . . . lucid, witty, and exciting . . ." (Bethany College, West Virginia); ". . . magnificent as both poet and reader . . . a charming *and* frank person . . ." (Hotchkiss School, Connecticut); ". . . outstanding contribution in poetry readings and discussions . . ." (Adelaide, Australia); ". . . the standing ovation from our junior high-school students said best how much your visit was appreciated . . ." (Alexandria, Virginia); ". . . the most memorable days in our college's history . . . everyone went away with something new and important in their lives . . ." (Rockland College, New York).

In spite of Dickey's attendance at Basler's meeting in January, he declared in his first annual report that "I had in the beginning little idea as to my duties . . . , and even less idea of the vast penumbra of personal associations, opportunities, trials, difficulties, and pleasures that surrounds the office." Dickey accepted nearly every invitation to speak, "whether or not it entailed payment." His usual style, when appearing at schools in the Washington area, was half guitar concert and half poetry reading, "being best received by the very young children, among whom there were not so many who could play better than I can." His voyaging around the country seemed, in retrospect, terribly taxing, but "gratifying almost beyond belief." As for the plague of poetic manuscripts coming over the transom, Dickey devised the most graceful rejection letter so far: "I do not criticize unsolicited manuscripts, because I believe that often an external evaluation of a poet's work distracts him from his necessary spontaneity, and from the pleasure which he may derive from the creation of his work." For the Theodore Roethke Memorial Foundation, however, he consented to be involved in its first triennial Roethke Poetry Award. The Foundation, in Roethke's home town, Saginaw, Michigan, had requested that the Consultant in Poetry choose three judges, one of which could be himself. Dickey named John Malcolm Brinnin, John Frederick Nims, and himself, and in May 1968 the judges gave the prize, $3,000, to Howard Nemerov's *The Blue Swallows*.

Dickey, in agreement with Basler, introduced two innovations in the Whittall literary programs at the Library, both of which had been chewed over at the January meeting: the videotaping of the performers for the archive and a format for poetry readings wherein there are two participants instead of one. The first event that combined both features was a reading on December 3 by Louis Simpson and James Wright, moderated by Dickey. Each visiting poet read and all three engaged in a literary conversation. The program was televised on station WETA, of the Greater Washington Educational Television Association. (These procedures soon became standard for the programs.) The Whittall season had opened on October 17, when Karl Shapiro delivered his indelible memorial lecture for Randall Jarrell. There was another pairing of poets on March 6, 1967: Donald Hall and William Stafford, under Dickey's superintendence. (This time the stage was set to represent a living room, with armchairs, a coffee table, and on the walls reproductions of paintings borrowed from the National Gallery of Art.) Once again, Yevtushenko read in Russian, with translations by Barry Boys. The literary lecturers that year included P. L. Travers, Herman Wouk (who asked the Library to retain half his stipend for the Whittall entertainment fund, and pay the other half to a charity he chose), Allen

Curnow (a New Zealand poet/professor, lecturing on his country's poets), Allan Nevins and Catherine Drinker Bowen (the two historians on "The Art of History"), Anaïs Nin, Sir Tyrone Guthrie, and John Barth. An ANTA troupe put on *Portrait of Emily Dickinson,* written by Norman Rosten. Kim Hunter was a very moving Emily. Outside the Whittall *temenos* were Dickey's own reading and lecture ("Spinning the Crystal Ball: Guesses at the Future of American Poetry"—he predicted a return to simplicity, to the "language of life") and a program of readings by the first recipients of grants in poetry from the National Endowment for the Arts, including Consultant-to-be Maxine Kumin.

Dickey's expansive and gregarious manner earned him many friends around the Library. No Consultant, other than Frost perhaps, had been so well-liked and well-acquainted. In a Library report he was said to "leave the vivid and lasting impression of a man in motion and of graceful expression." To general congratulation, Mumford reappointed Dickey. The Consultant and the Poetry Office staff were able to plan the entire next year's series of programs.

The pairing policy was first applied in 1967–68 to writers of fiction (all were *New Yorker* writers, as was Dickey) on two evenings, with Dickey moderating and leading a three-way discussion: in November, Peter Taylor and John Updike each read one of his short stories; in March, two novelists, John Cheever and Reynolds Price, read and talked about their work. The poetic programs, on the same pattern, presented Ben Belitt and John Frederick Nims in October, Josephine Miles and Elder Olson in March. In February, a reading from Edna St. Vincent Millay's collected poems was given by her sister Norma Millay Ellis, with the actor Roscoe Lee Browne. Concurrently the Library mounted an exhibition of the poet's manuscripts, which Mrs. Ellis had deposited in the Library. In January, Mark Van Doren gave a lecture in memory of Carl Sandburg, who had died the previous year at the age of eighty-nine; and in the North Gallery there was a memorial exhibition of Sandburgiana from the Library's collections. A week later the television writer and producer Rod Serling lectured on "The Challenge of the Mass Media to the 20th-Century Writer," preceded by a troika of discussants—Dickey, Serling, and Bernie Harrison, a local TV critic— whose conversation was telecast. Dickey himself lectured in December on "Metaphor as Pure Adventure" and closed the season on May 6 with readings from his most recent work.

In his second year Dickey rented an apartment near the Library as a *pied-à-terre* for entertaining visiting poets more easily than he could at Leesburg. (At a memorable party there in November 1967, after the readings by Taylor and Updike, the guests included Senator Eugene McCarthy, who had just announced his candidacy for the Democratic presidential nomination.) During that year, Dickey estimated, he traveled twice as much as in the first. He ranged widely, reading, talking, and strumming, in the United States and Canada (and found time for a week of bow hunting in the Alleghenies during the fall). For most of March 1968 Dickey was in the Southwest Pacific. The Department of State sent him as an official representative to the fifth annual Adelaide Festival of the Arts, in Australia. En route he paused in New Zealand to visit the poet Allen Curnow and lecture and read. ("He didn't look frail enough to handle delicate stuff like poetry," observed an Auckland reporter.) At the Adelaide Festival he gave the opening address and fraternized with delegates from the rest of the world, including writers from the Soviet Union and a surprising bonus: Marlene Dietrich. In several Australian cities, Dickey read at factories, schools, Rotary Clubs. On the way home he stopped to read and talk in Hong Kong, Osaka, Kyoto, and Tokyo. "I came out of the trip with the profound conviction that the more American writers visit these—or indeed, any—foreign countries, the better will be America's 'image' in what TV newscasters call 'the world picture.'" A month later, with his wife, he went to London to participate in a conference on contemporary British and American poetry held at the American Embassy and to sit for a BBC interview. Dickey summed up, in the report of his second year: "I consider these trips my outstanding contributions to the office of Poetry Consultant."

Composing expressions of condolence is another contribution the Consultant has often to make. While these have an official weight, Dickey's telegrams were notably personal in feeling. In 1967, to the family of the late Poet Laureate of Great Britain: "It was with great regret and a sense of personal loss that I heard of the recent death of John Masefield. Indeed, his going is a grievous diminishment of all men and women who love the English language, and respond to the moving sea and the still earth." (In due course Dickey cabled congratulations to Masefield's successor in the Laureateship, C. Day Lewis, who responded, in some confusion: "I was so delighted to get your telegram . . . I believe that the Librarian of Congress is an equivalent to our Poet Laureate—and I hope gets a higher salary . . . Best wishes.") On April 5, 1968, to Mrs. Martin Luther King, Jr.: "I pray, with you and your husband, who is still praying, that the great work may not falter, but go on." And on June 7, at the end of his time in the Chair, to Mrs. Robert F. Kennedy: "Sincerest condolences. I am as speechless as the rest. I hope you will understand the depth of feeling that underlies the dumbness of the man of words."

Dickey, upon retiring from the Chair, was appointed an Honorary Consultant in American Letters; MacKinlay Kantor and Marianne Moore also accepted appointments, along with Conrad Aiken, who was gratified to renew a connection with the Library. Dickey resumed academic life the next year—a semester at Georgia Tech, then a permanent appointment as professor of English and writer-in-residence at the University of South Carolina, in Columbia. He had enough free time to finish his novel, *Deliverance,* which he had begun while in the Consultantship.

Even earlier than usual, in July 1967, Basler and Mumford addressed the question of a successor to Dickey. Only two candidates were considered, both familiar to the Library because they had appeared on Whittall programs: William Jay Smith and William Stafford. "Both . . . have been exemplary citizens, Smith being perhaps the more energetic in civic and public affairs and Stafford in religious and educational affairs. Both are good family men and especially fond of their children"—so read an interoffice memorandum. Mumford's Solomon-like decision was to choose both. Smith, being immediately available, would serve first, then Stafford, if he could come. The appointment was announced in December.

Smith's background was out of the ordinary. He was born in Louisiana and grew up mostly at Jefferson Barracks, near St. Louis, Missouri.

His father was an Army corporal—a clarinetist in the Sixth Infantry Band; on his mother's side there was Choctaw Indian ancestry. Smith earned B.A. and M.A. degrees in French from Washington University, in St. Louis, where poetry entered his life. (Smith, with Thomas Lanier—i.e., Tennessee—Williams, and other aspirants, formed what they ambitiously called the St. Louis Poets Workshop.) During World War II, as an officer in the United States Navy, he performed liaison duty aboard a French warship in the South Pacific and was commended by the French Admiralty. (The islands of French Polynesia, he once remarked, evoked for him the Guadeloupe of St.-John Perse's *Eloges,* which even that early had influenced Smith's poetry.) After the war: *Poetry's* Young Poets Prize in 1945, graduate work at Columbia University, a Rhodes Scholarship at Oxford, and two years of study at the University of Florence, where he added Italian to his armament. Later, Russian. And, along the way, Spanish. During the 1950s and 1960s Smith was variously poet-in-residence at Williams College and at Hollins College, served two years as a Democratic member of the Vermont House of Representatives, and, while writer-in-residence at the Arena Stage in Washington under a Ford Foundation grant, wrote a comedy, *The Straw Market,* that was performed both at the Arena and at Hollins. In 1966 he was twice on the Whittall series, as poet and as translator from the Russian.

In May 1968, Smith (as Consultant-to-be) and Robert Lowell were sounded out, via the Department of State, by the organizing committee for the Olympic Games, to be played in Mexico City later that year: would they write poetry for the International Seminar of Poets, which was somehow correlated with the Games? They were to recite "in choice public places." Nothing came of *that.* Smith arrived in Washington in July, with his wife of a year, Sonja, for a month's teaching appointment at George Washington University, and at once began work at the Library of Congress.

The idea of a television film about poets, which had been mooted at Basler's 1966 gathering of Consultants, was realized in Smith's first year. He and Basler worked with television station WETA, the Library's prints and photographs division, and the two poets whom the film featured: Robert Hayden, of Ann Arbor, and Derek Walcott, of Trinidad—after M. B. Tolson, the first black poets who read on the Whittall series. They gave a dual reading, moderated by Smith, on October 21, and repeated their reading next day in the WETA studio. The program, entitled "Middle Passage and Beyond," with Smith's introductory remarks and other visual contents, was assembled afterward. Smith's appraisal: ". . . although it suffers from certain technical flaws (poor filming in parts), it is, I think, a most impressive film and one which shows how the resources of the Library may be put to use to help bring contemporary poetry to a large audience."

On November 16, Smith was moderator for another dual reading, by Louise Bogan and J. V. Cunningham. He and Bogan had been close friends since 1947. While she was visiting him and his first wife, the poet Barbara Howes, in North Pownal, Vermont, Bogan and Smith made up their minds to collaborate on an anthology of poetry for young people, which was published in 1965 as *The Golden Journey.* Smith, who had retained a link with Hollins College, arranged for Bogan to spend the month of January 1969 there as the poet-in-residence. On the way back northward, she paused in Washington to dine with her old friends Katie and Walter Louchheim, the Smiths, and Senator Eugene McCarthy. She was at the Library again on May 5, for a celebration of the thirty-fifth anniversary of the Academy of American Poets. Bogan and five other Chancellors of the Academy—Elizabeth Bishop, Robert Fitzgerald, Robert Lowell, Allen Tate, and John Hall Wheelock—read from their poetry in the Coolidge Auditorium. Smith introduced them; the event was presented in the Whittall series. Bogan, who had been in depressed spirits, wrote of the evening as pleasurable, in a letter to a friend, and commented that Smith "has done a fine job of giving life to that consultant job. After J. Dickey, things had fallen rather low." (A puzzling observation, as it was Smith who came after Dickey. According to Dickey, by the way, *The Golden Journey* "may well be the best general anthology of poems for young people ever compiled. [The poems] could have been selected only by poets as distinguished as these and by human beings who realize that to make the wrong concession to children is injurious to them.")

Two events gave the Whittall series an international cachet that year. The French scholar Pierre Emmanuel lectured on the poetry of St.-John

Perse—by which time Alexis Leger, in his eighties, had retired from Washington to his villa in the south of France. And Garson Kanin gave a talk and a reading based on his memoir, *Remembering Mr. Maugham,* in the course of which the actor Dennis King took the part of Maugham—who had died three years before at the age of ninety-one at *his* villa in the south of France.

Smith's interest in poetry for children—he had written or edited a dozen books of poetry for young people—led to the proposal that he and Virginia Haviland, head of the Children's Book Section of the Library, compile an annotated bibliography in the field: *Children and Poetry,* which was published in November 1969, coincident with a Poetry Festival in the Coolidge Auditorium to celebrate the fiftieth anniversary of National Children's Book Week. Smith (whose appointment as Consultant had been extended another year), Bogan, and William Cole, also an anthologist, took part in a discussion of the making of anthologies, and in the evening the Irish poet Padraic Colum joined the others for a panel on children's poetry. "We had a *packed* audience," Bogan wrote her friend, "with P. Colum pulling long poems out of his 89-year-old memory. Fantastic!"

Smith's own calendar, his first year, was as crowded and wide-ranging as every Consultant's was now likely to be. On October 7 he read his poems in the Coolidge Auditorium. On November 16 he spoke as a poet (standing in for Allen Tate, who was unable to come) at a memorial service for his longtime friend Francis Biddle, in the National Cathedral. On December 18, at the unveiling of a bronze bust of Robert Frost, by the Puerto Rican sculptor José Buscaglia, at the National Portrait Gallery, he talked of his Vermont acquaintance with Frost (having introduced the bill that made Frost the poet laureate of Vermont); next day flew to Paris with his Parisian wife for Christmas; flew back on January 6, and immediately celebrated Twelfth Night at Katherine Anne Porter's, with the R. P. Warrens and other literati. During March, the Australian poet A. D. Hope was at the Library to lecture, read his poetry, and advise on the holdings of Australian belles lettres. (Thin; Hope recommended two hundred missing titles for acquisition.) Smith arranged a lecture tour for Hope and took him around for joint readings in New York, Williamstown, and elsewhere. He moderated a paired reading and conversation by Malcolm Cowley and Theodore Weiss on April 7, and two weeks later gave the Consultant's customary lecture— his subject, "The Making of Poems." Then, after being briefed by the Department of State, Smith, with his wife, left on May 6 for a six-week lecture-and-reading tour of Japan, Korea, Singapore, Cambodia (for the sightseeing), and Indonesia, under the American Specialists Program. Everywhere he described the changes that had occurred in the United States with respect to poetry since World War II: the increase in its publication in both "little" magazines and the big ones; publishing houses and university presses bringing out books of verse; prizes, awards, grants, fellowships; no college or university "of any standing . . . without its poet in residence"; poetry readings everywhere. Besides which, the Chair of Poetry had been created "specifically to call attention to the fact that poetry in the United States is a national art." And into this (Utopian) picture the government itself had stepped, with the National Foundation for the Arts. "I met more poets, it seemed at times," Smith reported, "than there are images of the Lord Buddha, and every one of them presented me with a volume of his works." He handed out mimeographed copies of the poems he read, some of his own, some by representative poets who had come into prominence since 1945, such as Roethke, Wilbur, Bishop—"poems in which I felt the language would not be too difficult to follow. . . . Where I felt the level of English comprehension was high I used a poem or two by Robert Lowell." Beyond the poetic orbit, the high point of the trip was Angkor Wat, the low point the parsimony of the per diem.

Early in October 1968, Roy Basler became the chief of the Manuscript Division and assumed the Library's Chair of American History. In both posts he succeeded David C. Mearns, whom MacLeish had once described as "the rarest treasure of the Library of Congress," and who now, retiring after fifty years in the Library's service, was appointed Honorary Consultant in the Humanities, the post that had been created for Frost. Basler, who continued to be responsible for the Library's poetry programs, in his new responsibility oversaw a signal event: the Library's acquisition of the unparalleled Walt Whitman collection—numbering over twenty thousand items, including manuscripts, letters, memorabilia, and books—that Charles E. Feinberg, of

Detroit, had been assembling for more than forty years. An exhibit of some two hundred items from the collection opened in the Great Hall of the Library on May 31, 1969, the sesquicentennial of Whitman's birth. (Another major body of materials acquired that year, in the Motion Picture Section, was the RKO Film Library, holding more than seven hundred feature films and many short subjects. An optimistic concern for both categories of accession—Whitmaniana and cinema—went back to the time of Auslander and MacLeish.) Also in the fall of 1968, the Katie and Walter Louchheim Fund, originally established to support the taping of musical performances, was increased by $10,800, to support the audio- and videotaping of poetry readings for educational dissemination. The Louchheims had, of course, long been warm local friends of poetry and poets at the Library; Katie Louchheim had recorded her poetry, with Dickey introducing her, in January 1968.

Smith, upon resuming life in Washington after the East Asian adventure and being debriefed by the Department of State, gave his first attention to his concern for juvenile poetry (that is, poetry *for* children). He recorded some seventy of his poems of this kind in the Laboratory, the preponderance from his book *Mr. Smith and Other Nonsense*, which was also the basis of another program made by WETA, under a grant from the National Endowment for the Arts. Smith read a great many poems, which were illustrated by drawings especially executed. The film had its first showing on Christmas Day, 1969, and a few months later won a National Educational Television Award (the same award that had been given the previous year to "Mouse Tales," made by the Library and WETA, with Rumer Godden, under a similar grant). "Mr. Smith and Other Nonsense" is still a popular item on public television.

On December 31, Stewart Udall, the former Secretary of the Interior, who had become a close friend of Robert Frost, presented to the Library the manuscript of the poem "Dedication" that Frost had unexpectedly written for Kennedy's inauguration on January 20, 1961. Kennedy and Udall had understood that Frost was going to recite "The Gift Outright"; he had always refused to compose commemorative verses. The night before, however, he had written the new poem, and he handed Udall the manuscript, which he was still revising. It was nearly illegible. At his office, Udall had a fair copy typed and placed in a folder with the handwritten copy. When the time came to read, Frost had both copies in his hands. And when the reading began to go wrong, he was, mercifully, able to recite "The Gift Outright" from memory. Later, he gave Udall the original manuscript.

❋

The Children's Poetry Festival, with Bogan, Cole, Colum, and Smith, in the fall of 1969, has been noted already. Still another Library of Congress festival was now in prospect: an International Poetry Festival, set for April 13–15, 1970. Such an event had been proposed four years earlier by Spender; now it was Smith who ventured the idea, with Basler's support (and the appreciating Whittall funds to make it a reality, as part of the Whittall series). As momentum gathered for the event, the National Endowment for the Arts arranged a complementary occasion: a reading by American poets in the Granite Gallery of the National Collection of Fine Arts, to welcome the international poets. That program included Maxine Kumin, Stanley Kunitz, Denise Levertov, Howard Nemerov, Anne Sexton, Louis Simpson, Smith himself, A. B. Spellman, and Mark Strand; and then Michael Straight, the deputy director of the NEA, invited the entire throng home to dinner.

The International Poetry Festival brought eight foreign poets and five translators to Washington (a ninth poet who was invited and hoped to come, Andrei Voznesenskiĭ, wasn't allowed by his government to leave, though he had made other literary visits to the United States). The readings were spread over three days: first the English translation was read, then the visiting poet's poem. The participants were Jorge Carréra Andrade, from Ecuador (translator, John Malcolm Brinnin); Nicanor Parra, from Chile (translator, Miller Williams); Yehuda Amichai, from Israel (translator, Smith); Francis Ponge, from France (translators, Donald Finkel and Serge Gavronsky); Philippe Thoby-Marcelin, from Haiti (translator, Smith); Vasko Popa, from Yugoslavia (translator, Smith); Zulfikar Ghose, from Pakistan, reading in English; Shuntaro Tanikawa, from Japan (translator, Harold P. Wright). Two venerable former Consultants also participated. Allen Tate delivered a lecture on the influence of permissiveness on creativity and the poet's need for rules and boundaries. "We are now in an age of great translations," he said. "I think this is indisputable but . . . good translations are never obsolete. George Chapman's rhymed decasyllabic translation of the *Odyssey* is as good as it was in 1615, and I submit that Robert Fitzgerald's free blank verse translation is as good as Chapman's. Do we need both? I think we do. . . ." On Wednesday morning, Louis Untermeyer led a panel discussion on the difficulties of transmitting the magic of poetry in translation. The audience included poets, teachers, and editors from all over the country. On the Wednesday afternoon, a tour of the White House and tea with Mrs. Nixon were the feature, and the First Lady's staff had consulted the Poetry Office about a suitable gift for the visitors. Smith suggested copies of a facsimile edition of *Leaves of Grass* that had been published by the New York Public Library, at thirty dollars each. The White House considered this outlay excessive, and finally decided to present copies of Elizabeth Bishop's collected poems, newly published and prominently reviewed. The publishers contributed eight copies, which Mrs. Nixon autographed and handed to the visitors as she greeted them, lined up alphabetically in a receiving line. Some of the poets weren't aware they were meeting Mrs. Nixon and supposed she was Elizabeth Bishop. Fortunately, there were no gaffes. The press in attendance found the occasion rather unexciting. One reporter suggested that someone come up with a poem. Untermeyer, ever resourceful, offered an impromptu "Ode to the Miniskirt":

> I think that I shall never see
> A poem as lovely as a knee.

To which Smith added:

> And if the miniskirt should fall
> I may not see a knee at all.

Still, it was a successful festival, in spite of a bit of political embarrassment for one participant when a photograph of him shaking hands with Mrs. Nixon was published in his country. The spirit of the occasion is communicated in a note to Smith from John Malcolm Brinnin, sending "a word of thanks for the chance to be part of the Festival and its occasions—& for the effortless continuity of things you & your colleagues provided. It's uncommon, at least in my experience, to find an event of this nature concluding in palpable harmony, & even cross-currents of affection, but this one *did*."

Another accompaniment to the festival was the April 1970 issue of *The Quarterly Journal of the Library of Congress,* planned by its editor, Sarah L. Wallace, in collaboration with the Consultant, to appear (as it did) at the same time. The feature of the issue was, in miniature, the Consultants' anthology that Untermeyer had urged at the 1966 meeting: "Consultants' Choice," presenting one or two poems by each one of them, from Auslander through Smith, preceded by a poem of Mac-Leish's, "In and Come In," specially written. The other contents were appropriate: essays on "The Making of Poems" by Smith and on "The Frontiers of Literature" by the Australian visitor A. D. Hope; a profile by Katherine Garrison Chapin of the Biddles' close friend St.-John Perse, "Poet of Wide Horizons"; "The Greatest Whitman Collector and the Greatest Whitman Collection," a detailed account of the Library's Feinberg Collection and other Whitman holdings, by John C. Broderick, then the assistant chief of the Manuscript Division; and catalogs of the Whitman Exhibition then on display and of the Library's poetry publications and recordings. Another article written on request for the issue didn't appear—"Poetry and the Library of Congress," by Roy P. Basler. The Librarian of Congress had vetoed its publication, because Basler had quoted from closed administrative files on the Pound and Williams cases. As Helen-Anne Hilker explained on Mumford's behalf, "the publication of this much of the story will certainly occasion additional demands to see the files . . . [which] contain information about persons still living. . . ." Furthermore, "the paper opens up old wounds. . . . It airs, once again, unfortunate situations that did the Library no good at the time and would do it no good now. It would simply bring a new generation of newspaper reporters to our door . . ." The Librarian would prefer a summary "picturing the accomplishments of the poetry program. . . . Someday, a complete history will, of course, be compiled. . . ." Basler put his article away until 1974, when he published it as "The Muse and the Librarian" in a volume of his collected literary essays under the same title.

✺

To account for the other events in the Whittall series during Smith's second year in the Chair: There were more programs of paired readings than usual, five, each moderated by the Consultant—Gwendolyn Brooks (a future Consultant) and Katherine Garrison Chapin; Julia Randall and May Swenson; John Malcolm Brinnin and Daniel Hoffman (another future Consultant); Dannie Abse and Tony Connor; and Lee Anderson and Josephine Jacobsen (still another). Arnold Moss and his company again presented their dramatic reading about Edwin Arlington Robinson. Lillian Gish gave a lecture on her film career, illustrated with movies (and she changed into her costume in the Poetry Office, Smith's assistant, Helen Handley, remembers). Rumer Godden gave a reading from her fiction. There were other dramatic presentations, by Richard Wordsworth and by ANTA (Lortel's production again: "A Round with Ring," i.e., Lardner's stories in a musical and dramatic performance by Orson Bean and others). In this unprecedentedly busy time for the Poetry Office, the entire third floor of the Library was in a state of chaos, because of remodeling, the installation of air-conditioning, and, at Christmastime, a heavy snowfall that brought the plaster down, flooded the rooms, and damaged Mrs. Whittall's furniture, though not her treasures. To his struggling colleagues on the third floor Roy Basler offered solace: "Nuns fret not at their convent's narrow room."

Louise Bogan died suddenly on February 4. For Smith's last lecture, on May 4, Smith's subject was "Louise Bogan: A Woman's Words," a recollection of her life and poetry and his friendship with her. Among tributes to Bogan he quoted the one in *The New Yorker*, as whose poetry critic she served for nearly forty years. It closed with Bogan's lines, written in 1938, in defense of the true artist:

> Come, drunks and drug-takers; come perverts unnerved!
> Receive the laurel, given, though late, on merit; to whom and
>   wherever deserved.
> Parochial punks, trimmers, nice people, joiners true-blue,
> Get the hell out of the way of the laurel. It is deathless
>   And it isn't for you.

Two days later, Smith and his wife departed for a visit of two and a half months, again under the American Specialists Program of the Department of State, to the Soviet Union, Poland, Romania, Hungary, Cyprus, Israel, and Turkey. He was the first American writer in three years to be sent to the Soviet Union under the cultural exchange agreement, and the first one ever to visit the Academic City in Novosibirsk, where he read and spoke at the Institute of Nuclear Physics and at an American educational exhibit that had been mounted there.

❋

When Smith returned to Washington in late summer, he was surprised to learn that Phyllis Armstrong had retired. "It is virtually impossible to think of the Poetry Room without her," he wrote, in his end-of-term report. Phyllis Armstrong had come to the Library of Congress in 1938, as a member of the Law Library staff. She was on military leave from 1941 to 1945, serving with the Women's Royal Naval Service. In 1946, in the Shapiro time, she was appointed the first Special Assistant in Poetry. Fourteen Consultants had the benefit of her guidance, common sense, political tact, and ministration; and during the hiatus of 1952–56, after the Williams episode, Basler and Armstrong virtually *were* the Chair. She was a close friend of Gertrude Whittall, and this enabled her to maintain an invaluable liaison between Mrs. Whittall and the Poetry Office. At a farewell party for Armstrong on June 18, Mumford mentioned some of the other special ways in which she had served: "If Robert Frost liked to write letters from an armchair, she could design a lap desk and get it made. When Arnold Moss wanted a stage prop at Sunday rehearsals, Phyllis was there to see that he got it. If a popular Russian poet drew an overflow audience, she could handle it. If fifty poets gave nine programs for a festival that lasted three long days and three long nights, she could handle that, too. And in spite of all she did as a handmaiden on Mount Parnassus, she managed to devote some part of her energies to her own poetry." Roy Basler announced that Phyllis Armstrong had been awarded the Amos R. Koontz Memorial Foundation Distinguished Service Plaque "for her outstanding performance of duty in the Poetry Office. . . . For 24 years she has provided continuity to a vital literary function. She has helped immeasurably to bring poetry and people closer together." Armstrong was also presented with a recording of her own poetry—some fifty poems she had recorded in the Laboratory ten years earlier, at Richard Eberhart's behest. A volume of her own poems, *A Witness in Washington*, was published subsequently, with a foreword by Katherine Garrison Chapin, also a close friend since the early days. Several poems were tributes to poet friends: "A Note from a Balcony," for Randall Jarrell; "No Soft Evangel for Conrad" and "The Dreamer and the Dream," for Conrad and Mary Aiken; and "Moon Landing," for Robert Frost.

Nancy Galbraith, after several years with the Central Intelligence Agency, had first joined the Poetry Office staff in 1964, then spent a year as a bibliographer in the Copyright Office. In August 1970 she was appointed to succeed Armstrong as Special Assistant for Poetry. She was that rarity, a native of Washington. At Bryn Mawr (B.A. cum laude) she had dipped herself deep in the life, language, and literature of Chaucer and Shakespeare. She, too, wrote poetry. At the Poetry Office, she quickly found her footing in the strategies of working with the poetic temperament.

❄

In the summer of 1969, when it appeared unlikely that William Stafford would be able to come east for the Consultantship, Basler suggested to Mumford that the post be offered to Gwendolyn Brooks, "at present probably the most widely known and respected Negro poet." The Deputy Librarian of Congress, John G. Lorenz, and the Assistant Librarian of Congress, Elizabeth E. Hamer, also recommended the appointment. Lorenz had met Brooks at a dinner in Cleveland, where she had received an award, and had been "much impressed with her sincerity and intelligence." Mumford vetoed the appointment, and the matter floated until December, when he offered the Chair to Robert Hayden. Hayden, for a complex of reasons, declined. Then it transpired that Stafford *could* accept.

He was the first Midwestern native and the first West Coast resident to have the Chair. Born in mid-Kansas, with an Indian stripe in his ancestry, raised in little Kansas towns like Liberal and El Dorado, he had worked his way through the University of Kansas at jobs in an oil refinery, in the sugar-beet fields, and in construction. During the war, as a pacifist, he spent four years in C.O. camps, fighting forest fires, building trails and roads, and terracing eroding land. When he was assigned to a camp run by the Church of the Brethren, he went to listen to a sermon and met the minister's daughter, Dorothy, who in due course became his wife (and the Brethren his church). His Ph.D. was *echt* Midwestern—the State University of Iowa. Since 1948, Stafford had taught at Lewis and Clark College, in Portland, Oregon. (The only other Consultant with Midwestern credentials, and not watertight ones, has been William Jay Smith, who grew up in Missouri. Those who taught in Minnesota—Tate, Warren, and Whittemore—scarcely qualify. The only other Consultants the West Coast can tenuously claim are that native of San Francisco Robert Frost and the emigré Shapiro.) Besides the Shelley Memorial Award from the Poetry Society of America, Stafford received a National Book Award (1963), a Poetry Magazine Award, and a Yaddo Foundation award. When Stafford read on the Whittall series in 1967, Dickey, in his introduction, declared him to be "a fine outdoorsman, a good guitar player and singer, a good shot with a bow and a lively raconteur. He is said to be 'America's most prolific poet,' and that is probably true." (The guitar part is a kindly exaggeration, Stafford told a friend.) He is also a photographer of mark, who loves the refuge of his darkroom. Back in Lake Oswego, the Portland suburb where the Staffords live, when the Library of Congress offer came through for certain, his wife Dorothy, also a teacher, four children, and Stafford took a poll. The vote for Washington, D.C., included only one nay, which was Stafford's; he knew he'd miss the openness of life in Oregon, the country roads he could cycle to work on. The Staffords, fortunately, found a house to rent in the woodsy Virginia country near McLean. The poet set up his darkroom.

In the spring of 1970, when the appointment was announced, Stafford was interviewed in Portland by a United Press reporter, Gordon MacNap, who asked him what he thought of the "trend toward four-letter words in literature." "I feel negative toward it," Stafford said. "My own background is more genteel than that. But the language people speak belongs to everyone and society will determine what people say. The whole language is changing and society is accepting things it did

not before." The reporter paraphrased him: readers should get what they
want. The *Miami Herald* picked up the story and headlined it, "4-Letter
Words What Readers Want." The director of the National Poetry Day
Committee, Inc., Dr. Frances Clark Handler, of Miami Beach, got off
a heated letter to the Library of Congress: "Since that statement this
office has been deluged with complaints. . . . Mr. Stafford's statement
is very very far from the truth. Because a few avant-garde, off-beat
poets, capitalize on the 'shock treatment' of filth in their work, do not
place this label on the entire writing or reading public." From Mum-
ford's office, a mollifying reply: "Mr. Stafford's own poetry and the
recognition it has received from critics and readers alike indicate that
there is a large body of readers who admire the beauties of landscape
and character that he portrays." Nothing more came of that, and in April
Stafford went to the Poetry Society of America's annual dinner again,
to claim the second annual Chicago Tribune Poetry Award, $1,000, for
a clean-cut poem about a swing, the moon, and some haystacks.

Some two-thirds of Stafford's office time as Consultant, he estimated,
was spent in reading and answering mail. On Basler's advice he got
into the office for about twenty hours a week unless on the reading-and-
lecturing road. Several of the letters he received—and answered—
stayed in his mind. A teacher in the South wanted advice for her stu-
dents "interested in poetry, but unsure of their abilities"; how could the
work be assessed for promise, how could the successful efforts be mar-
keted? Stafford replied with two and a half rambling, sage pages. "I've
purposely rambled," he wrote, "for the issue in your letter is one that
requires a human interchange, not a formula. The question each writer
has about his own work will never be solved, even if he has 'success,'
for who is to say when the awarding has been right? I believe each of
us should try out our attempts in the environment near us and harmo-
nious with our backgrounds and expectations. Then we can attempt to
enter larger and larger contexts, as we feel confident. We should not
feel competitive, but just right, near, congenial. When we feel right,
near, and congenial with the next circle outward, we should attempt to
move there. . . . You make me brood about my own moments of an-
guish. I hope my brooding relates to your inquiry." Then there was a
Congressman whose daughter was coming to Washington and would be

grateful for guidance about what books in the Library of Congress might be pertinent for her term paper on Shelley. A New York publication was compiling a list of current writers and their addresses and wanted a reaction. A writer planning a lecture tour asked for help in lining up engagements along the trajectory. The last three applicants got far briefer replies than the first, but constructive ones. When a government employee asked for an unbiased opinion of poems by his niece and her father, Stafford avoided a critical judgment. He thanked the man "for the human gesture you make in letting us share the feelings indicated in those poems. . . . These two people have put into language a sustained attention turned toward helpfulness and trust; I can't help feeling that such sustained attention will lead them and those around them to have better lives." To a man who wanted to know whether to encourage his high-school son's poetic efforts: "Speaking as a father, I hazard the idea that we should welcome our children's confident entry into sustained creative activity. We shouldn't make too much of each effort, I believe, for we do not want to induce an assumption of competitive stances; but welcome and rejoicing are in order every time, I say."

To the standard request "What advice would you give young poets to help them achieve success": "William Blake said, 'I give you the end of a golden string, Only roll it into a ball; it will lead you in at Heaven's gate Built in Jerusalem's wall.' Follow the golden string of your own nature; accept the impulses and the language that are near and ordinary parts of your life. Write every day, at least a little . . . have hope, but do not presume on 'success.' This way, whatever you do accomplish will be your own, and within the content of your own life it will be worthy."

Soon after Stafford's arrival, he was involved with the U.S. Information Agency in planning a tour abroad by a poet who would represent the literary scene in the United States. To his surprise, he was then asked to take the tour himself. He sought Basler's advice, which was "By all means go, if you'd like to." Stafford felt his obligation to the Chair was to stay mostly in it; and he didn't want to leave his family during this year they had set their hearts on. Instead he recommended another Northwesterner, the poet David Wagoner, at the University of

FIVE: 1963 TO 1971

Washington. So it was settled, and Stafford carried on with help in the planning. The USIA laid groundwork for the eventual trip by commissioning a short film, for which Wagoner came east and, before the camera, engaged in a discussion of the current state of American literature with Stafford and the poet William Claire, publisher of the literary journal *Voyages*.

Stafford's own domestic touring was in accord with custom. His first junket took him to read at Dartmouth College, at the invitation of Richard Eberhart, by then a professor emeritus. In November, a circuit in North Carolina, another in New York City, and then Minnesota. In the spring, he made a loop through Texas and New Mexico, and later another around familiar haunts in Kansas, then Idaho and Utah; Florida; Rhode Island; Maine; Tennessee. Toward the end of May he was the commencement speaker at Oberlin College, in Ohio, and received an honorary LL.D. The students had chosen him. "His insights penetrate our past, our present, and our future," the citation stated, "and his poems show how our lives, even in their ordinary moments, are lit by extraordinary meanings." (Another recipient of an honorary degree was a member of President Nixon's staff. The events in Vietnam—and just then, the trial growing out of the My Lai incident—were the national preoccupation. At the moment of the award, the graduates, as one, opened their academic gowns and released a cloud of black balloons.)

And in and around Washington, Stafford's calendar was full. At a meeting of the District of Columbia Commission on the Arts he got to know May Miller Sullivan, the doyenne of the city's black poets, and took part in poetry workshop gatherings at her apartment. Indeed, Stafford made an unwonted rapport with the local community of poets, three of whom, Linda Pastan, Myra Sklarew, and Ann Darr, staged a big cocktail party for him and his wife. He was asked to judge the entries in a limerick contest, sponsored by a local public radio station, WGMS, on the occasion of Beethoven's two hundredth birthday. As the contest culminated in the award of a prize (a trip abroad), Library policy had to be consulted. The involvement was deemed personal rather than official. Stafford read hundreds of limericks (how many rhymes with Beethoven *are* there?) and, for his trouble, was given an album of Beethoven's quartets.

POETRY'S CATBIRD SEAT

On December 2, Robert Penn Warren was the focus of a paramount literary event in the Coolidge Auditorium: the award of the 1970 National Medal for Literature of the National Book Committee. Stafford made the principal address in appreciation of Warren as novelist, critic, and poet—whose poems form a "wonderfully impressive body . . . varied, alive with surprises, often moved along by narrative in a way unusual in current poetry." James Dickey and his wife came up for the occasion, and the Staffords gave a dinner party, memorable to those Midwesterners for Southern table talk as strange as possum stew, rich as pecan pie.

The Whittall series of poetry readings opened in October with Barbara Howes and a Consultant-to-be, Anthony Hecht. Though Stafford performed the by now usual office of moderator, he initiated the innovation of having the visitors introduce each other to the audience. Margaret Atwood and Galway Kinnell made up the next program. "Before he read," Stafford recalled, "Kinnell opened with a little talk along these lines: 'When I was invited to come to Washington in times like these, I came because I like and respect those who invited me, but I didn't really want to come because I don't like what's happening in Washington. My fee will be paid over to the War Resisters League.'" The spring readers, recommended by Stafford, were Hollis Summers with Raymond Patterson and Nathaniel Tarn with Robin Skelton. (Some of Stafford's other nominees who didn't get on the list in his year were Ted Hughes, Adrienne Rich, Wendell Berry, Robert Bly, and Jane Cooper.) The artist Maurice Sendak gave a lecture for National Children's Book Week; readers of their prose were N. Scott Momaday and Kurt Vonnegut, Jr. Rob Inglis gave an ambitious solo presentation of Chaucer's *Canterbury Tales*. The season closed with a presentation, for two nights, of "To Be Young, Gifted, and Black; A Portrait of Lorraine Hansberry in Her Own Words." The Chicago playwright had died in 1965 at the age of thirty-five.

While bibliographies had not been a concern of the Consultant for a good long time, Stafford elected to compile two modest ones, in response to inquiries that came in the mail. One was a list of poetry anthologies for a school of nursing in North Carolina (a pleasant thought, nurses reading poetry to patients, or to themselves in the sol-

FIVE: 1963 TO 1971

itude of night duty). Mark Van Doren's *Anthology of World Poetry,* "the richest collection I have found," led the list, which included "appealing" collections by Untermeyer, Donald Hall, and Oscar Williams. For the Conservation Foundation he compiled a list of readings on environments and human values. A more direct service to poetry was Stafford's nomination of judges for the second triennial award of the Roethke Memorial Prize: Josephine Miles, David Wagoner, and (as a nod to the East) Richard Wilbur. Wagoner withdrew, because he had published a book of poems during the period of eligibility. Perhaps in deference to him, the other judges decided to make no award.

An interviewer asked Stafford. which contemporary poets he felt some sort of affinity with. "I like Thomas Hardy and feel much more affinity with him than with any contemporary poet I can think of. . . . I get a kind of feeling of elation out of him. . . . Of the men writing now, I think the most significant is Robert Lowell by quite a distance. . . . I feel congenial about Galway Kinnell." As for Robert Frost: "I can't help thinking that part of Frost's centrality in American life comes from qualities that are not necessarily good, or not necessarily important for poetry. He lived a long time, he showed up well in photographs, and you know, he came from the right part of the country. . . . I don't feel he was wise at all, his political advice seemed to me poisonous, and his influence on politics, if he had any, just seems to me a feedback of stereotypes. So I don't consider him a seer at all or wise man or prophet or anything like that. But he was a tenacious old guy who wrote some interesting poems."

On May 3, Stafford gave his expected lecture in the Coolidge Auditorium. It had the force of a farewell speech: he entitled it "Leftovers: A Care Package." The leftovers were the memories he carried away of the meetings he had had during the year with strangers—other writers, arrived ones and hopeful young poets, people who sought him out at his office or met him at social gatherings. He said he soon learned that, in such meetings, "there can be a reaching out of the spirit in a man that goes beyond the point of the meeting." There was one more public function in Washington. At a librarians' dinner he introduced his friend Senator Eugene McCarthy, who gave a reading of his poetry.

The Stafford family drove home cross-country, back to Lake Oswego, the darkroom, and the students of Lewis and Clark College. A year later, when it happened that David Wagoner could not go on with the Department of State tour that Stafford had helped to plan, Stafford substituted for him and spent two months reading his poetry and talking to USIA information centers and cultural institutions in Egypt, Iran, Pakistan, India, Nepal, and Bangladesh.

Six

1971 TO 1980

Josephine Jacobsen: born Josephine Boylan of American parents in the summer of 1908 on the Canadian shore of Lake Ontario, where the family was vacationing; brought up in Baltimore; was writing poetry as far back as she can remember ("nothing I have subsequently published has brought quite the visceral and voluptuous thrill which struck me when I set eyes on my first published poem, in *St. Nicholas Magazine"* —which awarded her its gold and silver medals); at eighteen, she mailed poems to Harriet Monroe, who published them in *Poetry;* played leading roles in experimental and imported plays in the Vagabond Theater, the oldest little theater in the country; planned a theatrical career until, in 1932, she married Eric Jacobsen, a tea importer; and only in the early 1960s, after what she calls "long years of a very fitful apprenticeship," entirely clear of the academic, began to regard herself as able to be a truly professional woman of letters. By spring 1970, when she read her poems on the Whittall series (the Consultant then, Smith, had warmly reviewed *The Animal Inside,* the book that brought general recognition of her poems), she had published four volumes of poetry, two of literary criticism (with William R. Mueller, on Beckett, and on Ionesco and Genet—playwrights then in the vanguard), and a number of short stories, which were beginning to show up in anthologies. She was, of course, the first woman in the Chair of Poetry since Elizabeth Bishop left it in 1950. Basler's telephone call sounding Jacobsen out left her incredulous but eager. When she went down to the Library and got the first briefing, any doubts she may have had disappeared. (She was mindful of a special weight of responsibility: the Maryland House of Delegates had passed a resolution of congratulation on her appointment and declared her, "for all practical purposes, the unofficial Poet Laureate of Maryland.") Baltimore remained home base; her routine was to give Mondays and Tuesdays to the Poetry Office (the intervening night at the Congressional Hotel) and again Fridays, with working trips on the train. But often, she stayed most or all of the week in Washington.

Taking a cue from Stafford, Jacobsen in her annual report gave a week's sample of her mail, in depth: "Three books to be evaluated; three little magazines, ditto; a letter from a poet who recently recorded here, to say why it had been a good experience; a letter from a Washingtonian interested in the inter-influence of poetry and theater; one of the always pathetic letters asking for impossible help in publishing unpublishable poetry; a small sheaf of poems (limited by my own rule) from a very talented young poet who has been visiting the Poetry Office during the winter and has just had his first acceptance from a university review; a 'statement of poetic position' by a well-known foreign poet who is going to be introduced to a Washington audience by the Consultant; an inquiry from a young poet, who doesn't know anyone seriously writing poetry, to ask if there are any groups reading and discussing their poetry in the Washington area; a batch of incredible poems from someone's niece; a letter from a Ph.D. candidate asking for an appointment to discuss her thesis on a poet-playwright; a letter from a mediaman, interested in promoting poetry on TV but, unsurprisingly, without funds to do so; a letter describing (probably in somewhat gilded terms) the reactions of school children to a poetry reading; two or three self-promoting letters from harmless screwballs; a request from a poet to read; a letter expressing pleasure in a recent program; two requests to record . . ." and so on. Of all that agitation, Jacobsen's view: "These are people who are, naively or more knowledgeably, concerned with some aspect of poetry; they have the conviction that the Library has put a Consultant there partly to serve them, and I think they are perfectly right."

As for visitors to the Poetry Office: "this aspect of the job shows the value of the Consultant's actual presence . . . more clearly than anything else. . . . Very few utterly futile interviews take place." What surprised and pleased her was the number of young poets and tyro-poets of whom there was a steady come-and-go. She had expected the like of them to be turned off by the "establishment" label. She met with young hip students off the street, and in one case helped a young poet who had been on drugs and living the commune life. With Jacobsen's encouragement, he began to publish. What disappointed her was the rarity of black faces among her visitors and in the poetry audiences. "A tender matter which has concerned me as Consultant is the question of the truly honest, effective, and long-range view of the matter of representation of black poets in our recordings and in our public readings." The Poetry Office should, Jacobsen firmly believed, continue to make sustained and energetic efforts to bring talented black poets into both programs and recordings, and the Consultant should attempt to make contact with that most difficult person to reach, "the young non-academic black poet."

The fall 1971 season opened with Jacobsen's reading of her own poetry in the Coolidge Auditorium. Her fellow townsman John Dorsey, in the *Sun,* gave the picture: "Smoothly, silently, electrically, the doors at the back of the stage glided apart and through them stepped, liquid in lavender, Josephine Jacobsen. Her day had begun with work in the morning, a long, formal cocktail and luncheon party, a technical rehearsal in the afternoon and more cocktails and dinner; after that, Mrs. Jacobsen still had to give her reading and stand in a receiving line for an hour. Yet she looked as full of life as if she had just been out for a morning walk after ten hours' sleep. It was her eyes that managed the deception. Bright and alert as a bird's, they darted quickly around the auditorium, then alighted upon John Lorenz, deputy librarian of the Library of Congress. He introduced her. . . . When Mrs. Jacobsen rose, the applause, from the surprising crowd of more than two hundred (the largest ever for the opening of the poetry series) was more than polite. . . ." She ended the evening with a new poem, "The Planet," describing how the Earth might, seen from the moon, seem a paradise of beautiful lands, clear waters and love, an "innocent planet / shining and shining." She left her audience, Dorsey wrote, "with the admonition to discover what she pointedly didn't say."

Another observer, William Holland, of the Washington *Star,* depicted the setting somewhat differently. The Coolidge stage he found "an incredibly cold and barren one . . . but somehow the poets have managed to . . . erase that intimidating, naked forum from the consciousness of the audience and replace it with a setting of their own." William Stafford had often made it "a cottage in the woods, a back porch facing open land. . . ." Jacobsen transformed it into "a sunny place, not so much a place of sunshine, but where things can be plainly seen for the things they imply."

The events in the Whittall series—one of the most various yet—began with a duo from England, D. M. Thomas (then an unknown name, well before *The White Hotel*) and Peter Redgrove. The other pairings that year: Isabella Gardner and John Logan; Elliott Coleman and Mona Van Duyn; David Ray and Robert Watson; George Garrett and Brendan Kennelly. John Ciardi read his poems solo. Alex Haley (another unknown name, five years before *Roots*) drew from his material a lecture on "Black Heritage: A Saga of Black History." Joan Aiken, Conrad Aiken's British daughter, talked on children's literature during National Children's Book Week. Arnold Moss, on his eighteenth appearance at the Library, with a company of Broadway actors, presented "7 X Malamud," dramatic readings of seven stories of Bernard Malamud's. On February 21 and 22, Lucille Lortel, for the Matinee Theatre Series, presented Sam Dann's play about the Washingtons, *Sally, George, and Martha.* Ruth Gordon gave two performances of "An Evening with Ruth Gordon." The Soviet poet Andrei Voznesenskiĭ, again free to leave Soviet terrain, read his poems, with William Jay Smith back to read translations.

"Poetry continues to be the most undersupported, ignored, and underprivileged of the arts in Washington," Jacobsen wrote, in agreement with Whittemore, "a ridiculous if familiar situation." She hoped

to see the Consultant consistently in touch with those figures in govern-
ment who have evidenced a serious interest in the arts—"a group not
in danger of overcrowding the Poetry Office." Toward strengthening the
local cadre of poets she met several times with a group hoping to estab-
lish a Washington Poetry Society. With two in particular, May Miller
Sullivan and Katherine Garrison Chapin, she had lasting friendships.
She arranged Sullivan's recording for the archive, among more than a
dozen poets. Jacobsen echoed Dickey's vehement appeal for a perpet-
uating fund to continue recording poetry and literature, and Nemerov's
belief in the importance of regularly issuing discs of the best recordings
of the best poets. She shared Spender's feeling that the Poetry Office,
whenever possible, be represented at a public tribute to a distinguished
poet after his death. Two of the great poets died during Jacobsen's time
in the Chair: Marianne Moore, on February 5, 1972, and Ezra Pound,
on November 1. She was invited to neither the memorial service for
Moore on February 8, at the Lafayette Avenue Presbyterian Church in
Brooklyn, nor the "Quiet Requiem" for Pound, held by the Academy
of American Poets at the Donnell Library in New York on January 4,
1973, at which the speakers included Robert Lowell and Richard Wil-
bur. On April 3 there was a gathering in Washington to honor Pound,
at the Corcoran Gallery, which Jacobsen did attend in her capacity as
Consultant. Reed Whittemore was among the speakers, braving the cli-
mate of adulation to remark that "it is a sort of Poundian fallacy to
imagine you can separate Pound's poetry and his politics." (Pound him-
self, a number of months before he died, had mourned the death of
Marianne Moore, at a memorial service at the English Church of Ven-
ice, by reading her poem "What Are Years?")

Still, Jacobsen did pay honor to Marianne Moore in the course of her
closing lecture, on May 1: "From Anne to Marianne: Some Women in
American Poetry." Anne of the title was Bradstreet, the pious and
learned poet of seventeenth-century Massachusetts. A procession of
women poets followed, culminating in Moore. Jacobsen sought to ex-
amine "the atmosphere [often undermining] in which they worked, to
attempt to understand a little of its pressures and permissions." Among
her subjects was Muriel Rukeyser, who, in the fall of 1972, as a partic-
ipant in an anti-Vietnam War demonstration in Washington, was ar-

rested and locked up in the Women's Detention Center. Jacobsen wrote her: "I have learned from Gene McCarthy of your situation. Not knowing you personally, I wouldn't feel the right to intrude upon you; but I have been thinking of you so much and wanted to send you this talk, which I gave at the Library last spring, in which I quoted your marvelous 'This Place in The Ways,' which seems to me to explain more deeply the creation of a poem than almost any lines I know. We owe you so much for poetry, and for being the brave person you are."

❊

The composition of the Honorary Consultants in American Letters shifted more or less every year, though in virtual silence. Beyond being listed in the *Annual Report of the Librarian of Congress* (along with twenty or so other Honorary Consultants, including Charles A. Lindbergh in Aeronautics and Donald C. Holmes in Photoduplication) they appeared to be no more than respected lilies of their field, unconsulted and unsummoned. Mumford, one of his staff remarked, enjoyed appointing the Honorary Consultants but didn't enjoy seeing them. In 1972, the group had shrunk to the recent ex-Consultants Dickey, Smith, and Stafford; the venerables Aiken, Kantor, and Wheelock; and three relatively young writers, Bernard Malamud, William Styron, and John Updike. The next year saw the venerables gone and four more new names added, Gwendolyn Brooks, Clare Boothe Luce, James Michener, and Wallace Stegner. As custom ordained, Josephine Jacobsen joined them at the end of her term.

❊

During Jacobsen's second year in the Chair, three areas of her domain gave her a sense of accomplishment. Besides, there was the good of starting the season already in training, an advantage that every twice-around Consultant has remarked on. For one thing, the programs under the Whittall Fund had, in the main, been her suggestions. The pairs of poets who read were Anne Sexton with X. J. Kennedy, Samuel Allen with Ned O'Gorman, Lucille Clifton with Owen Dodson, and Donald Justice with Carolyn Kizer. Arnold Moss put on a program honoring John Donne's four hundredth birthday. Ian Hamilton (who only a few years later was to write Robert Lowell's biography) lectured on recent British poetry, and a Danish writer, Erik Haugaard, talked on Hans Christian Andersen, to celebrate the tenth anniversary of the Children's Book Section of the Library. Also under Whittall sponsorship, the Conference on Teaching Creative Writing was the responsibility of the Poetry Office, and of this event more will be said.

Second among the Consultant's satisfactions was the initiation, expansion, and ultimately the warmth of her relations with a number of black poets. "This year the atmosphere has totally changed. . . . Black poets living in Washington have invited the Consultant to their homes, and discussed black and white relations in the world of poetry and of the arts in general; others, visiting Washington, have called her for lunch or dinner to talk about poetry . . . and have seemed to find the Poetry Office and the position of Poetry Consultant appropriate to their interests and work. . . . It is hard to overestimate the value to the Library's human relations of this positive and friendly attitude." She mentioned the reading by Clifton and Dodson, "a very dramatic and unusual occasion, complete with a talented young singer and dancer [David Bryant] who chanted and danced to some of Owen Dodson's poems." There had been amiable contacts also with Michael Harper, Samuel Allen, May Miller Sullivan, Léon Damas, and Sterling Brown. Jacobsen set hopeful plans in motion for a record of readings by black poets from the Library's collection, to be put on sale.

A third source of the Consultant's gratification was an upswing in the poetry scene in Washington. Jacobsen herself read, talked, and propagandized conspicuously in the District and its environs. (She roamed less than most Consultants, however. Her only distant excursion, in May, took her to St. Louis and several California cities for readings.) Locally, she persuaded the Smithsonian Institution to begin a poetry-reading series and lent support to planning one at the Textile Museum. She was on the board of the Mayor's Committee for Poetry in the Schools. Two other of her projects were, as she reported, "barely seeded": readings in the parks, and programs at the Kennedy Center for the Performing Arts, which so far had presented, as its solitary contribution to the celebration of American poetry in the nation's capital, Rod McKuen.

[331]

The Conference on Teaching Creative Writing, on January 29 and
30, 1973, was the brainchild of Roy Basler, reinforced by John Brod-
erick and by Jacobsen, who chaired the conference. More than five
hundred people attended—most of them teachers of creative writing
from colleges and universities. Basler recruited the directors of the four
pioneer writing programs in the country, each of whom led one of the
panels and set it going with a formal paper. Elliott Coleman, the found-
ing director of the Writing Seminars at the Johns Hopkins University,
led the opening panel, "A Perspective of Academic Programs in Crea-
tive Writing." The voices called upon for discussion included the writer
George Garrett and Theodore Morrison, who had directed the Bread
Loaf Writers' Conference from 1932 to 1955, and whose wife Kather-
ine had been Robert Frost's right hand in his late years. Richard Eber-
hart turned up in the audience and, upon being called upon, made an
immediate assault upon the term "creative writing," instead of which he
proposed "imaginative writing," though with faint hope. "As in govern-
ments and Presidents, we will get what we deserve." Incidentally, Cole-
man had described *his* Writing Seminars, which he had founded in
1945, as "seminars in imaginative writing"; Hopkins has its standards.
At the first seminar meeting, Coleman reported, "in the back of the
room there sat a young veteran from the Navy by the name of Russell
Baker." Louis D. Rubin, Jr., John Barth, and Anthony McNeill (from
Jamaica) were also out of Hopkins, and were at the conference.

Paul Engle chaired a panel entitled "The Writing of Poetry." He had
been director of the Program in Creative Writing (founded in 1930) at
the University of Iowa until shortly before. Coleman generously called
it "the most extensive and the most famous university writing program
in America." The discussion drew in the poets Michael Dennis Browne,
from the United Kingdom, Anthony McNeill, N. Scott Momaday,
Miller Williams (who translated Spanish poetry), Jacobsen, and many
nameless voices from the audience. A panel on "The Writing of Fic-
tion" was in the hands of Wallace Stegner, abetted by John Barth, Ralph
Ellison, Ernest J. Gaines, George Garrett, Robie Macauley, and Mar-
garet Walker. Stegner had directed the writing classes at Stanford
University since 1945. This was the session, strong on audience partic-
ipation, that seemed to have the most excitement, much of it turning on

the contrasting work of black and white writers. John Ciardi, who had directed the Bread Loaf Writers' Conference of Middlebury College from 1955 until 1972, led "The Writing of Nonfiction Prose." The discussants were Ellison, Jacobsen, Momaday, Rubin, Stegner, and William J. Lederer (co-author of the novel *The Ugly American,* which had originally been a work of nonfiction prose). William Jay Smith, who had dropped in, also lashed out at the term "creative writing." To no avail; the college catalogs had frozen it as academic/administrative jargon. Ciardi voted for merely "Writing."

On the second and final evening, "the readings . . . turn out to be the life's blood of the convention," as Momaday commented later in a Santa Fe newspaper. "They bear directly, vitally, on all the foregoing discussion, but it is questionable whether or not the discussion bears directly upon them. And that is as it should be. I sit on stage, listening to a young Jamaican poet, Anthony McNeill, read from his work, and because I am not attuned to his accent, to the rich, slow motion of Creole, I have to concentrate, to listen hard. And so it is when I listen then to Michael Dennis Browne, an Englishman, and to Ernie Gaines, who reads, as he writes, out of an experience of plantation life in Louisiana. It is the variety of language and literature that I am reminded of on this occasion, and I come away having been refreshed in my mind and spirit." And Jacobsen remembered that "something happened that night as an entranced audience listened"—to an American Indian, a young Englishman, a black Jamaican poet, a black American novelist—"which was extremely rare. I have a cold and unsentimental eye for professional evenings, . . . and I believe that an empathy of audience with readers extremely unusual in my experience took place. Each reader was aware of that rapport, and it seemed exhilarating that it took place in 1973, and at the Library of Congress."

Despite that exhilaration, Jacobsen subsequently told an interviewer that "it's a dangerous situation where poetry meets institutions. There's something deadly dangerous about the conjunction of poetry and bureaucracy. The grave peril is that poetry, a very intransigent, frequently violent, and utterly incontrollable force, could get swamped by an enormous, prestigious, global sort of organization. This is the kind of thing that so far has been avoided. Where protocol, or politics, or bureaucracy, or prestige, or international recognition or *anything* impinges on poetry, poetry has got to come out unarguably on top." In her lecture that closed her second year, "The Instant of Knowing," Jacobsen projected the same urgency. No poet in the Chair had defended the domain so vehemently. But, in protection of the Muse, she could regard her own kind harshly, as in a poem she wrote while Consultant:

> When the five prominent poets
> gathered in inter-admiration
> in a small hotel room, to listen
> to each other, like Mme. Verdurin
> made ill by ecstasy,
> they dropped the Muse's name.
> Who came.

> It was awful.
> The door in shivers and a path
> plowed like a twister through everything.
> Eyeballs and fingers littered that room.
> The floor exploded the ceiling
> parted
> and the Muse went on and up; and not a sound
> came from the savage carpet.

�֍

A few days after the Conference on Teaching Creative Writing, Roy Basler, with his wife, Virginia, flew to New Zealand, where, on the invitation of Allen Curnow, he spent the antipodal autumn lecturing on American literature at the University of Auckland (where both Curnow and his son Wystan were professors of English) and elsewhere in those islands. During the long absence, John Broderick—"a special and potent source of help and advice," in Jacobsen's words—looked after the Library's poetry machinery.

SIX: 1971 TO 1980

❉

In the fall of 1972, Quincy Mumford invited Gwendolyn Brooks to take the Chair of Poetry in 1973–74 (on Basler's recommendation). Brooks declined with thanks; she was unwilling, at that point in her life, to move her family and her work from Chicago to Washington. She suggested some prospects—May Miller Sullivan, Diane Wakoski, Robert Hayden, and others—but Mumford's eye next fell on Donald Hall. He declined; he was working on a long and complicated book, dangerous to interrupt. In March 1973, acting again upon the recommendation of Basler, supported by Jacobsen, Smith, and others, the Librarian announced the appointment of Daniel Hoffman, poet-in-residence and professor of English at the University of Pennsylvania, author of five published books of poetry, a Columbia product through to the Ph.D., with three years out for the Air Force. He also had published a good deal of criticism: on Stephen Crane, Yeats, Graves, Muir, myth, fiction.

After the war, when Hoffman was back as a graduate student, he was one of a group of young Columbia poets, including John Hollander, Allen Ginsberg, and Louis Simpson, who were influenced by Auden's poetic example, his precise views on the writing of poetry. Hoffman devoted his M.A. thesis to a study of the legendary American lumberjack Paul Bunyan. Possibly his interest had been whetted when, as an undergraduate, in May 1941, he saw the première of Benjamin Britten's opera *Paul Bunyan*, with a libretto by Auden, performed by the Theater Associates of Columbia University. (In 1952, Hoffman published a book, *Paul Bunyan: Last of the Frontier Demigods*, based on the thesis.) Rather more to the point, in 1954, Auden as editor of the Yale Series of Younger Poets chose Hoffman's *An Armada of Thirty Whales* as the winner of the annual competition for the best manuscript of a first book of verse. Their literary acquaintance began with that event. Two days after Auden died in Vienna on September 29, 1973, Hoffman was interviewed about him for the Voice of America, and that evening he gave the customary Consultant's poetry reading in the Coolidge Auditorium—an occasion for what must have been the first public words of tribute to the deceased Auden. "The look of our literature is suddenly different," he observed, writing to a friend. "We now have only minor poets of varying heights: all foothills, no mountains." Two days later, after a reading at the University of Louisville, Hoffman flew to New York and represented the Library of Congress at a memorial service for Auden in the Cathedral of St. John the Divine. "Sumptuous," he described it, "with all the pomp, pageantry, incense, and especially music that would have pleased Wystan so much." And, on December 14, when with Spender he participated in a memorial program at the Smithsonian Institution, Hoffman spoke and played a recording, made during the Columbia presentation in 1941, of some of Auden's choruses in *Paul Bunyan*.

Hoffman's year, it seemed, was overshadowed by memorials and ceremonies. Almost the first official act that he had to perform as Consultant, on September 25, was to write a letter to the Embassy of Chile, conveying "to the literary community and the people of Chile the sense of loss felt by all Americans who are lovers of poetry on learning of the death of the great Chilean poet, Pablo Neruda."

In March 1973, the governor of Georgia, Jimmy Carter, appointed Conrad Aiken the state's poet laureate. Scarcely five months later, on August 17, Aiken died in a Savannah nursing home, where he had been laid up for some weeks after a fall. He was eighty-four. A few days before his death, Aiken had dictated a letter to a high school student who had written to praise his poetry: "I don't have any great notion about where I stand as a poet. That will be taken care of by those wiser people who come later on the scene than we do. Thus, as in their turn, those opinions too will be revalued over and over. None of us knows in what direction poetry and the other arts will turn—that's part of the cruel fascination of being interested in the arts." In the early 1960s, the poet and patron of poetry Hy Sobiloff had bought the old house in Savannah that adjoined Aiken's boyhood home, restored it, and given right of occupancy to Aiken for his lifetime. Hoffman, while Consultant, upon learning that there was no historical marker identifying Aiken's house, wrote the Georgia Historical Society, in Savannah, urging such commemoration "of one of the greatest American poets of this century." Hoffman's voice joined the voices of other advocates in Aiken's home state, and in 1980 the marker was placed—actually, between the two houses in which Aiken had lived at the beginning and the end of his life.

Hoffman joined in planning most of the Whittall poetry programs that occurred under his aegis, though not the season's opener, which had been booked well before: the perennial Arnold Moss, reading from Ben Jonson in honor of the poet's four hundredth anniversary. Next, a pair of contemporary poets, Daryl Hine and George MacBeth, reading and discussing their work. On November 26 Hoffman presented his Columbia classmate John Hollander, paired with another friend of his, the West Coast poet Gary Snyder, who was expected to turn up in exotic if not hippy garb but wore a three-piece suit, with his father's watch chain across his vest and his boots smartly polished. In March, the readers were another Columbia graduate, Richard Howard, and the Irish poet Richard Murphy; in April, Elizabeth Bishop and James Merrill; and, in May, as some kind of culmination, one more Columbian, Allen Ginsberg, with Ishmael Reed. The Ginsberg engagement had its complications. Some Library officials were apprehensive—presumably of uninhibited behavior by the poet's followers, or even by the poet, in the auditorium or at the usual wine-and-cheese reception in the Pavilion. To reassure them, Hoffman took personal responsibility for his old classmate's decorum. Ginsberg would be glad to come, he said when Hoffman reached him at his pad in New York. He had wanted to accept an invitation to read at the Textile Museum, which paid no fee, whereas the Library paid a comfortable one; now he could read at both places on one visit. Basler, however, had to enforce the "sixty-day rule": Whittall readers could not read elsewhere in Washington sixty days before or after. A fortunate compromise was reached. After the reading at the Library, the Textile Museum gave a reception for the two poets, at five dollars a head, to support its own poetry program. The event was jammed, not only with fans of Ginsberg but with fans of Reed, who according to Hoffman had been an "electrifying presence," an exemplary foil for Ginsberg.

The central event of the Whittall series that year was a celebration, on March 25 and 26, of the centenary of Frost's birth. Basler had planned the affair with the assistance of Hoffman, who had the idea of inviting Allen Tate to give the principal lecture. A scintillating aspect of the occasion was the presentation (under Lucille Lortel's auspices), on two evenings, of a performance by the dancer and choreographer Jean Erdman's Open Eye Company of "Robert Frost, with Rhyme and Reason," a medley of his poems and his *A Masque of Reason*—recited, mimed, sung and danced to music. (Before and afterward, the Open Eye Company toured its Frost show all over the country, to the acclaim of audiences sometimes innocent of Frost's poetry.) On the twenty-sixth there was a symposium, chaired by the Consultant. During the morning, three lecturers composed the program, each linked to Frost in a different way. Helen H. Bacon, professor of classics at Barnard College, was the daughter of the poet and translator Leonard Bacon, a longtime friend of Frost's; her subject was Frost and the classics. Peter Davison, poet and publisher, had known Frost in his old age as a friend, "closer than casual but not close enough for intimacy." He spoke on Frost's crucial years of self-realization, 1911–12, after the time of depression and inanition on the farm he unsuccessfully worked, near Derry, New Hampshire. Robert Pack, the director of the Bread Loaf Writers' Conference, which Frost had founded in the 1920s, lectured on Frost as a teacher and preacher. The afternoon was given to Tate's lecture on Frost as a metaphysical poet. Tate had first been introduced to Frost by Herbert Read, in London in 1928, and had last been with him in 1962 at the National Poetry Festival. (Hoffman has recalled that Tate, seriously ill with emphysema, lectured seated in a chair. The Library had a nurse in waiting, backstage at the Coolidge Auditorium. Tate's young family had come with him from Sewanee, and his little boys, Ben and John, spent the afternoon in the Poetry Office in the care of Jennifer Whittington, the poetry assistant, while their mother, Helen Tate, attended the lecture. "Never before have such well-behaved and handsome young men been seen in these chambers," Hoffman wrote their father.) On the twenty-sixth, the post office at Derry inaugurated the first-day issue of the Robert Frost commemorative stamp, which Hoffman had joined Marie Bullock and many others in pressing the United States Post Office to approve.

During his year as Consultant, Hoffman was involved in something that wasn't actually a Library of Congress matter, though the Library approved his giving time to an endeavor that served the cause of poetry.

The story begins with Copernicus and Petrarch. The Copernicus Society of America had been established by Edward Piszek, of Philadelphia, who had immigrated to the United States from Poland as a child and had become a notably successful entrepreneur in the frozen food business. (Mrs. Paul's Kitchen, Inc., was his firm.) The Society's first benefaction had been made in 1973, for an observance to celebrate the four hundredth anniversary of the Polish astronomer Nicholas Copernicus. The Society (under the direction of Piszek's then legal adviser Ernest Cuneo, a man of literary inclination) was also supporting the World Petrarch Congress, in April 1974, arranged by the Folger Shakespeare Library and the Library of Congress to mark the six hundredth anniversary of the death of Francesco Petrarch. The previous autumn the Society had proposed to the Folger's director, O. B. Hardison, Jr., the idea of an annual prize in contemporary American poetry. Since the Folger was dedicated to the Renaissance rather than to the present day, Hardison invited Hoffman to come and discuss the proposal on behalf of the Library of Congress. What Piszek had in mind was a $20,000 prize for a poem celebrating these United States, where an immigrant boy could become a wealthy man. Hoffman, aware that the Library of Congress was prevented by law from making prize awards, suggested that the Academy of American Poets, of which he was a Chancellor, be invited to organize and administer the project.

So it came about. Hoffman, with Marie Bullock and the Academy's director, Elizabeth Kray, persuaded Piszek to modify the prize program in a way that would be "most conformable to the needs of the community of poets in this country." Accordingly on April 10, as a feature of the Petrarch Congress, a jury composed of Elizabeth Bishop, James Wright, and Hoffman made two awards, in the Shakespeare Theater of the Folger (rather than on the steps of the Capitol, as the Society had first proposed): the Copernicus Award of $10,000, recognizing the lifetime achievement of a poet over forty-five, to Robert Lowell; and the Edgar Allan Poe Award, of $5,000, recognizing the continuing development of a poet forty-five or under on the occasion of a new book of poems, to Mark Strand. A third award was announced: it was named for Walt Whitman (Hoffman had suggested that the two awards be named for the great American poets who had lived in the Philadelphia area) and would be given to the winner of a competition open to American poets who had not yet published a book of poems. The winning manuscript—to be chosen by a single judge, that year William Meredith—would be guaranteed publication, the Academy would buy and distribute 1,500 copies, and the author would receive a cash award of $1,000. The competition opened in the fall of 1974; Meredith's choice was Reg Saner.

The Copernicus Society agreed to sponsor the awards for the next five years, with an option to renew. The Consultant in Poetry, the Academy's Chancellors, and the past winners of the Copernicus Prize nominated each year's jurors. In 1975, the winners of the Copernicus and Poe awards were respectively Kenneth Rexroth and Charles Simic; in 1976, Robert Penn Warren and Charles Wright; in 1977, Muriel Rukeyser and Stan Rice. Before the 1977 presentations could be made, however, the Copernicus Society, for a complex of reasons, abrogated its agreement with the Academy. The Academy raised the prize money, which Piszek later reimbursed. The Copernicus and Poe awards were abandoned, but the Academy has continued to make the Walt Whitman Award on its original terms, with support from other sources.

And still other memorials. The triennial poetry award of the Theodore Roethke Memorial Foundation fell in May 1974; Hoffman invited Nemerov and Warren to join him as jurors, and they bestowed the award on Donald Finkel (who had participated as a translator in the International Poetry Festival) for his book *Adequate Earth*. In June, Hoffman and Muriel Rukeyser made a videotape for the United States Information Agency, in which each of them read a poem that had been inspired by music of Charles Ives. The recording was part of the USIA's "thematic program package" for the Ives centenary on October 20, 1974, which was sent to all its offices abroad.

For the Recording Archive Hoffman arranged tapings by twenty-some poets. One of these was Robert Fitzgerald, reading from his translation of the *Odyssey;* and Hoffman arranged for the archive to exchange a copy of the *Odyssey* tape for Yale University's tapes of Fitzgerald reading from his translation of the *Iliad*. At the start of his term, Hoffman was interested in realizing Josephine Jacobsen's hope for preparing a record of black poets reading. When Basler made it clear there were no funds for making new recordings for sale, Hoffman had the inspiration (with Basler's agreement) of sounding out the 3M Corporation of Minneapolis, whose tapes were used in the Recording Laboratory, for a donation. Nothing came of that; the corporation apparently felt that such a gift would receive too little exposure to the public eye. Hoffman then approached the Rockefeller Foundation, but a grant for recordings of poetry was, in foundationese, "outside the scope of our current program activities." Undeterred, a few months later Hoffman wrote asking Helen Vendler to consider selecting and introducing a long-playing record of American women poets reading their work, chosen from what there was in the archive. He sent a list and offered a token honorarium of one hundred dollars. What he had in mind was "a sober, historical-minded excursion into the sounds of women's voices and verses." Vendler replied with a cordial No. She wasn't turned on by the lists, she said. "If the poets are good, their best poems aren't there"; she had never liked some of the poets; in any case, she would have to listen to all the women's recordings in the Archive, and for a very token honorarium.

Hoffman took satisfaction in having worked in collaboration with the Authors Guild to seek remedies for the income tax law revision of 1969 that limited authors' deductions for gifts to libraries of their own literary papers to only the cost of writing materials, instead of fair market value, which any other donor of such papers could still claim. As he observed, "This worked a hardship on many poets and writers (also composers, artists, etc.), to say nothing of libraries whose gifts of this sort had fallen away to nothing. It meant also that the future study of contemporary poets would be made more difficult through the dispersal or loss of their papers which might otherwise be conserved together. I took this concern as a legitimate expression of the Consultant's responsibility to represent the literary community." Hoffman's and the Authors Guild's efforts were in vain.

In January, with the Library's blessing, Hoffman planned to attend a literary conference in Germany, with Vonnegut, Dickey, and Jerzy Kozinski, but the event "came apart at the seams," as Hoffman wrote Basler, when the others opted out for various reasons. He was invited, also, to make a literary visit to the Soviet Union, which he declined because "it would give countenance to their persecution of Solzhenitzin and other truth-sayers for an American writer to go over there at this time." His domestic travels were fairly confined; Montgomery, Alabama, was the farthest remove. Hoffman was content to stay close to the Library and, in his own time, do the research that was the basis of his long poem *Brotherly Love* (published in 1981), which he described as "a reverse image of Washington-on-Watergate"—about William Penn, his friendly treatment of the Indians, and his conception of an ideal commonwealth.

Hoffman gave the customary lecture on May 6: "Others: Shock Troops of Stylistic Change," taking off from the ground-breaking poems by the then little known young poets Sandburg, Eliot, Pound, Moore, Stevens, Williams, in *Others: An Anthology of New Verse,* edited by Alfred Kreymborg in 1916. "They changed the modes by which poetry is conceptualized, expressed, and read. . . . [Those] shock troops of sensibility . . . [were] responding to the blasting apart by the Great War of the complacent arrangements of the preceding era." Agreeing with Louise Bogan, Hoffman found the shock troops of his own time wanting. "Poets must, of all people, in their work as in their deepest feelings, keep alive the possibilities of order, the resonances of emotion, the allusiveness of cultural richness. They must dramatize the relationship between the personal and the public life, between the pressures of reality and the importunity of visionary truth. It is on these that great literature has always been founded."

※

Hoffman put Stanley Kunitz's name at the top of a short list of suggestions for the next occupant of the Chair of Poetry: "An elder statesman of the Republic of Letters whose appointment would add lustre to the office . . . [and] a capable man of affairs." (Kunitz was sixty-eight.) Basler seconded Hoffman—"a good and viable suggestion"—and the announcement was made in April. In the news coverage Kunitz's biography was highlighted. His parents were Russian-Jewish immigrants who had settled in Worcester, Massachusetts; he was born after his father, a garment manufacturer, had committed suicide (leaving an extensive library, in which the boy steeped himself); his mother, "an intense person of great vigor and natural untutored intelligence," carried on and became a prosperous manufacturer of children's dresses. "Although I . . . heard a foreign tongue in my home and my neighborhood, I early became enamored of 'the great and noble English tongue,' collecting words as other boys collected stamps and marbles, and resolving to make myself master of this beautiful instrument." He won a four-year scholarship to Harvard, where he became "an advocate of the Modern, from Hopkins down to Joyce and Eliot." After earning an M.A., in 1927, Kunitz worked as a reporter for the Worcester *Telegram* and covered the Sacco-Vanzetti case, at the time when a new trial had been denied by the Massachusetts supreme court. As it was for many writers, the case became Kunitz's cause; after Sacco and Vanzetti were hanged, that August, he left for New York in hopes of publishing Vanzetti's letters, didn't succeed, and stayed on in the city. One of his first literary friendships was with Lewis Mumford, who arranged for Kunitz to be invited to Yaddo, the artists' and writers' retreat then recently established at Saratoga Springs. There he met Alfred Kreymborg, who opened more doors.

For many years, as a livelihood, Kunitz wrote and edited *Twentieth Century Authors* and many other publications on literary biography for the H. W. Wilson Co. He worked from old farmhouses that he himself restored, in Connecticut and Bucks County, and settled down eventually in Greenwich Village and Provincetown. In 1930 Kunitz sent the manuscript of his first book of poems over the transom to Doubleday Doran. It was accepted in a fortnight by the editor John Farrar, having been spotted by a first reader, Ogden Nash. He published his second book, *Passport to the War,* in 1944, after he had been drafted in the Army. As a pacifist Kunitz had accepted service on the premise he would not bear arms. The Army assigned him to latrine and k.p. duty (under surveillance) for two years, then allowed him to start a camp paper, provided he edit it on his own time. When his paper received an award as the best camp publication in the Army, he was assigned to information work with the Air Transport Command in Washington, was offered a commission, but preferred a promotion to staff sergeant. After the war, Theodore Roethke helped him into a teaching post at Bennington College. Thence followed a steady recurrence of academic appointments, fellowships, awards, and honors as Kunitz's literary work was recognized.

Kunitz has always placed a high value on being a free agent; he believes that "it's stultifying for young poets to leap immediately into the academic life." When at Eberhart's invitation Kunitz read at the Library of Congress in March 1960, Tom Wolfe, interviewing him for the *Washington Post,* cited his outrage at "sales-crazy hucksters" overrunning the arts in America, converting culture into a "commodity." Poetry is one of the last forms of uncorrupted art, he told Wolfe, "because it has one great advantage—no market value." And, in October 1974, newly in Washington, he told Mary Hanley, a UPI reporter, that a poet must be "an adversary spirit in the modern world, out of the mainstream of ambition, power and money, apart from the usual touchstones of power." He cringed at the thought of being a poet laureate. "That's a vestige from a monarchic age which doesn't fit in with the adversary concept. There's nothing worse than a domesticated poet." (In December, Kunitz achieved a comparable honor: election as one of the fifty members of the American Academy of Arts and Letters. He succeeded to the chair that had been held by John Crowe Ransom, who had died on July 3, 1974.)

At the time Kunitz took the Chair of Poetry, he was an adjunct professor of writing at Columbia, in its School of Arts, and editor of the Yale Series of Younger Poets. He took leave from the former and suspended work on the latter (often five hundred book manuscripts a year) while he was in Washington, where he stayed in the historian Constance M. Green's house, at 19 Second Street N.E., at the Library's back door. (Green offered to sell the house to the Library as a permanent residence for the Consultant, but that didn't come to pass.)

In the 1974–75 Whittall series, Kunitz inherited only the New Zealander Allen Curnow, to whom Basler had made a commitment; Curnow read along with the English poet Thom Gunn. Kunitz nominated all the others: Maxine Kumin with Alan Dugan, Jim Harrison with Mark Strand, Philip Levine with David Wagoner, Edward Field with Michael S. Harper, Louise Glück with Robert Haas and Gregory Orr, and—the writer who attracted the largest audience of the season— Joyce Carol Oates, reading her poems and discussing her fiction. (One poet whom Kunitz, "as an old political dissenter myself," invited to read was Adrienne Rich. He was encouraged to try her by his feeling "that this is a different historical moment from the previous occasions of your refusal." But once again refuse Rich did.) Ursula K. Le Guin gave the annual lecture for National Children's Book Week. The theatrical event, in spring 1975, was a performance, arranged by Lucille Lortel, of dramatizations of some of John Steinbeck's short stories in *The Long Valley*.

Kunitz's view of the poetry readings was that "we should be somewhat adventurous in our programming and not restrict ourselves to booking twosomes of established poets," but he also wondered "whether we ought to be so rigid about not inviting poets back for a second reading. There are some older poets whom we ought to hear again before the opportunity is lost forever. . . . In the post-reading discussions I have tried to initiate an intimate and relaxed conversation . . . that will disclose each speaker's special persona. Not all poets are able to feel at ease in this setting and a few are notoriously inarticulate when sober. . . ."

Roy Basler retired on December 31, 1974. His successor as chief of the Manuscript Division and ringmaster of the poetry activities, John C. Broderick, arranged a retirement program in the Coolidge Auditorium on December 9: an evening of readings in Basler's honor by three former Consultants representing the three decades of Basler's service, Eberhart, Jacobsen, and Whittemore, reading their own work, and by Arnold Moss, reading from Basler, Lincoln, and Shakespeare—Moss's final appearance at the Library, after twenty years on the Whittall series. Besides many members of Basler's large family, the audience included a number of out-of-town friends: Hoffman and Meredith, Lillian Gish, Lucille Lortel, Jay Saunders Redding, Mrs. Sean O'Casey among them. In the auditorium foyer was an exhibit comprised of Basler's writings, letters about them, and photographs of him with Consultants and other literary friends. (One photograph showed Basler in feather headdress and warpaint, portraying Chief Powhatan in a staff drama production.) To gild his departure, the Librarian appointed Basler the first Honorary Consultant in American Studies. On the same date, L. Quincy Mumford retired as Librarian of Congress, after a twenty-year career, and John G. Lorenz, the Deputy Librarian, became Acting Librarian of Congress.

Broderick hailed from Memphis; his A.M. and Ph.D. degrees, in American literary history, were from the University of North Carolina. After nearly a score of years as a professor of English in several Southern universities, he joined the staff of the Library's Manuscript Division in 1964 as a specialist in American cultural history. The next year he became assistant chief of the division. Broderick was—and is—a member of the editorial board of the *Writings of Henry D. Thoreau* and general editor for Thoreau's *Journal,* a compendious work in progress.

❉

The incoming mail presented a new species of problem for Kunitz. As he explained, "The incontinent circulation of interviews attesting to [my] interest in young and unrecognized writers led to my being inundated with manuscripts and requests for advice and criticism from all parts of the country. Most of the material submitted was—alas!—hopelessly incompetent." As the easiest and kindest solution, he concocted a noncommittal form letter for the signature of a member of the staff: "Mr. Kunitz has asked us to thank you for wanting to share your poetry with him. However, he no longer has time to read and comment on the unsolicited poetry sent to him and still conduct his official duties at the Library. Please forgive the use of this form letter, but the volume of material he receives precludes his making personal replies." The tide receded, then rose again when a syndicated story of the same kind appeared the next year. Kunitz also received an unusually large throng of visiting foreign writers, usually steered to the Poetry Office by the USIA. Over his time in the Chair, they came from Argentina, Barbados, Bulgaria, Colombia, Cyprus, Dominican Republic, Germany, Ghana, India, New Zealand, Pakistan, Senegal (President Senghor again), South Africa, the USSR, the United Kingdom, and Venezuela. For the USIA, in turn, Kunitz supplied a selection of poems on American themes for an exhibition of photographs to be circulated internationally during 1976, the bicentennial year.

Because of his known involvement with the visual arts—his wife, Elise Asher, is a painter, and he was a founder of the Fine Arts Work

Center in Provincetown—Kunitz was consulted about American painting by curators at the Hirschhorn Museum, the Renwick Gallery, and the Smithsonian Institution. In January, when S. Dillon Ripley, the Secretary of the Smithsonian, canceled the Institution's literary evenings— reportedly in order to exclude "controversial" writers, and particularly Allen Ginsberg, who had been scheduled to read—Kunitz was among those who wrote him in protest. "Poets . . . are not easily domesticated, they are sometimes impolite, and they can be outrageous; but they are also the idealists and visionaries whose presence is needed throughout history to clear the air of corruption and hypocrisy, to mock oppressors, and to challenge spiritual apathy." But the Smithsonian evenings weren't reinstated. In April Kunitz was master of ceremonies at the Folger for the bestowal of the Copernicus Award on Kenneth Rexroth and the Poe Award on Charles Simic—judged by Donald Hall, Anthony Hecht, and W. D. Snodgrass.

On May 12, Kunitz gave his expected lecture, "From Feathers to Iron," a title from Keats. At a nodal point he observed: "One of my convictions is that at the center of every poetic imagination is a cluster of key images which go back to the poet's childhood and which are usually associated with pivotal experiences, not necessarily traumatic. Poets are always revisiting the state of their innocence, as if to be renewed by it. Carl Jung has observed that 'no one can free himself from his childhood without first generously occupying himself with it.' . . . When fresh thoughts and sensations enter the mind, some of them are drawn into the gravitational field of the old life and cohere to it. Out of these combining elements . . . poetry happens." And at another: "Poets told the ghastly truth about Vietnam long before the public had ears for it. Indeed, future chroniclers may record that the turning point, the peripeteia, . . . in the drama of our nation's commitment to the war occurred on June 14, 1965, when poets and artists converted the White House Arts Festival into a passionate fiasco. I am happy to confess I played a role in the planning of that episode."

In June, having completed his year in the Poetry Office and accepted another year's appointment, Kunitz went to London to participate in Poetry International 1975 and to attend a meeting of the Arts Council Committee for the Bicentennial Poetry Tour, a project which, in collaboration with the Library of Congress and the National Endowment for the Arts—such was hoped—would involve exchanging poets from the United States and the United Kingdom for readings in the host country. (The Library, as Broderick remarked, blushed to acknowledge that the idea for this bicentennial event had originated with the mother country.) The U.K. sponsors were definitely committed and had raised sufficient funds. "I trust that we can catch up with them in the fall," Kunitz remarked.

On June 20, 1975, President Ford nominated a new Librarian of Congress: Daniel J. Boorstin, a scholar and author of wide reputation, most recently honored for his work *The Americans,* which was awarded the Pulitzer Prize in History in 1974. He was the senior historian of the Smithsonian Institution, but not a career librarian. On July 4, the American Library Association, at its annual conference, in San Francisco, adopted a resolution opposing the nomination because his "background, however distinguished it may be, does not include demonstrated leadership and administrative qualities which constitute basic and essential characteristics necessary in the Librarian of Congress." Meeting in the same venue thirty-six years earlier, the ALA had opposed MacLeish's nomination on similar grounds. The Senate Committee on Rules and Administration began hearings on July 30 for two days, recessed, then resumed and concluded them on September 10, and reported in unanimous favor of the Boorstin nomination on September 25. Next day the Senate confirmed the nomination. On November 12, in the Library's Great Hall, in the presence of the President, the Vice-President, and the Speaker of the House, Boorstin took the oath of office as the twelfth Librarian of Congress.

※

Kunitz opened his second season in the Coolidge Auditorium with the customary autumnal reading, not only of some of his own work, but poems of Hopkins, Hardy, Yeats, Eliot, Stevens, Marianne Moore, W. C. Williams, and Roethke, to which he gave the best of his strong, lucid, resonant style—in a platform tradition no longer often enough heard. (At the start of his 1960 reading, Mrs. Whittall, listening through her apparatus, proclaimed in a high, shrill voice, floating over his own, "That young man reads loud, thank God!") The houses were larger, younger, and more responsive this year, Kunitz observed, and he wondered if a contributing factor may have been the improved design he had suggested for the program notes sent out on the mailing list: with a photograph, a poem or two, and biographical and other matter of interest, attractively printed. (Still the design these days.) The success could equally have been laid to the variety and interest of the readings Kunitz had helped to arrange, chiefly of younger poets: Richard Hugo and Diane Wakoski; John Ashbery and Charles Simic; Denise Levertov and James Tate; Robert Bly and Samuel Hazo; Robert Duncan and Jerome Rothenberg.

The signal event of the fall season—and, Kunitz felt, of his Consultantship—was a Conference on the Publication of Poetry and Fiction, on October 20 and 21, which Kunitz, thinking primarily of the plight of poetry, had proposed to John Broderick the previous year as an item for the Whittall Fund. The NEA, besides supplying a grant, suggested considering also the almost equally sad state of affairs with serious fiction. The audience, most of whom stayed with the meetings both days, numbered some 250 concerned writers, publishers, magazine editors, and other members of the literary community. There were four panels, with thirty-two participants, on trade publication, publication by university and small presses, publication in magazines, and "Survival of the Writer," i.e., support by organizations and foundations.

In a comprehensive report on the discussions, *Publishers' Weekly* commented: "When Stanley Kunitz said that the publishing industry is in a state of crisis, he set the keynote for the rest of the discussion. 'Most publishers who care about literature—and there are *some*,' he said, 'agree that the American publishing industry is not very well.' Cutbacks in the number of books published have been announced, Kunitz pointed out, and although some might be welcome in a year which has produced four 'definitive' biographies of Judy Garland, many of the cuts will come in poetry and fiction. . . . In 1974 some 120 first novels were published, compared to 200 in 1973. Drawing a 'grim' conclusion, he said authors of poetry and fiction are unable to make a

living and must write as a precarious labor of love. 'What we are dis-
cussing here is more than the economics and logistics of publishing.
What we are really discussing is the survival of the life of the imagi-
nation in this country.'"

In the *New York Times Book Review,* Doris Grumbach summarized
some of the more practical suggestions offered at the Conference:
"Since 86 per cent of the poetry now being published comes from small
presses and university presses, a holy alliance between the trade people
and the small presses was proposed, which might result in a better dis-
tribution of books of poetry, a sharing of the largesse realized from
popular publishing with the struggling publishers of good young poets.
Stanley Kunitz was enthusiastic about instituting a farm-system, with
large publishers supporting smaller ones. . . . The willingness of poets
to give readings, in a sense to sell their own books by their presence
and the live sound of their poetry, was regarded as hopeful, as well as
the ability of the small presses beyond the Eastern Seaboard to contact
their regional audience through their lists and the local press: these were
regarded as causes for cautious optimism.

"Without some positive, imaginative action, the future for the pub-
lication of short fiction and poetry is dismal."

Complementing the talks and discussions—notably articulate; the
published proceedings fill more than 150 pages—there were poetry
readings by Ai (pen name of Florence Anthony, a young black poet),
Clayton Eshleman, Don L. Lee, and Maura Stanton one evening, and
a prose reading by the novelist Donald Barthelme the other.

Among more than a dozen publishers of small presses who were
present and heard from, one was notably absent: Lawrence Ferlinghetti,
the publisher of City Lights Press. He had written, in response to Kun-
itz's invitation to join a panel: "My alienation from the U.S. Govern-
ment has widened, rather than narrowed. . . . I am less willing than
ever to participate in any way (whether it is at the Library or in the
National Endowment for the Arts) with a Government which conducted
such a disgusting war in Vietnam and financed the overthrow of the
Allende regime in Chile (thereby indirectly contributing to the death of
Pablo Neruda . . .)." Responding, Kunitz said he understood and re-
spected his feelings, but he was mistaken in identifying the Library

with Administration policy; the Poetry Consultantship and the readings were in fact privately funded. "Peace and love!"

The director of the Literature Program for the National Endowment for the Arts, Leonard Randolph, who participated in the conference, expressed interest in the appointment of an "action committee" to carry on the work of the conference. That didn't come to pass, but something else eventually did. One of the members of the panel on university and small presses was Daniel Halpern, publisher of the Ecco Press, which for several years had been bringing out the National Poetry Series, comprising two books a year, distributed through Viking. Halpern proposed a realignment of the series, with the cooperation of several university presses for publication, the NEA for funding, a commercial publisher for distribution, and arrived poets, including the Consultant in Poetry, as judges. The plan would yield five books of poetry a year, in quality paperback format. At the conference the proposal fell flat; the NEA didn't cotton to the idea of funding. When the proceedings of the conference were published two years later, by the Library of Congress, a copy came into the hands of James Michener, who upon reading it telephoned Halpern and offered to endow the series along the lines of his proposal. Michener's view was that successful and prosperous writers like himself ought to help out the less fortunate of the profession and, specifically, poets. He channeled his remarkably generous gift through the Copernicus Society, and his friend Edward Piszek joined in the contribution. The program continues successfully, with a shifting consortium of commercial, university, and small publishers. In some years the NEA, after all, and the Ford Foundation have supplemented the endowment income. The Consultant is not officially involved in the judging, though some poets who have had the Chair—Hecht, Kunitz—have served as judges.

On January 5, 1976, Kunitz departed for a visit to West Africa under the auspices of the Department of State. In Senegal, where he was received hospitably, he read and discussed modern American poetry at the University of Dakar and called upon President Senghor at the Presidential Palace. Senghor promised him he would give a public reading at the Library of Congress during his next visit to the United States. (Senghor hasn't as yet fulfilled this promise.) In Ghana, though the country was between coups, Kunitz encountered unrest. At the University of Accra, when he went to read, hostile students seized the microphone and were opposed by loyal students, and Kunitz read instead at the U.S. Embassy. Finding that no course in American literature was offered, he helped the faculty prepare a syllabus for such a course. In Kumasi, the students wanted to recite *their* poems, or a grandfather's poems. Kunitz learned of the secret arrest and incarceration of the poet Kofi Awoonor, who had taught in the United States. Returning to Washington, he called on the Ghanaian ambassador and expressed his concern at Awoonor's fate. The Ghanaian government announced he would be tried as a political conspirator; but in the fullness of time Awoonor was freed and allowed to travel again. (He eventually read his poetry at the Library of Congress in January 1986. Awoonor was then his country's ambassador to Brazil.)

As a result of Kunitz's criticism of the literary content of the "core collections" in USIA libraries he had visited abroad—among the missing, besides himself, were Bishop, Bogan, Jarrell, Plath, Snyder, and Warren—he was asked to bring the poetry titles up to date, and he made up new lists.

In February, soon after returning, Kunitz arranged (on the Whittall series) a program in observance of Afro-American (the preferred term is now *black*) History Month, in which Gwendolyn Brooks, Michael S. Harper, and Robert Hayden read from their own works and those of other poets. Hayden's appointment to the Chair of Poetry for the year following was announced. Harper had drawn up an outline for a record of black poets reading, the project originated by Jacobsen and pursued by Hoffman and Kunitz through their tenures. Persistent delays continued to stall this design.

On April 7, Kunitz received a party of Soviet writers—Aleksandr Ovcharenko, Sergei Makashin, Lidia Gromova, Lidia Spiridonova-Oposkaia, and Vladimir Baskakov. Though he had heard Russian in his childhood he hadn't learned to speak it. But, after an extensive lecture tour of the Soviet Union in 1967, during which he got to know Andrei Voznesenskiĭ, he acquired a literary mastery and published translations of the poems of Voznesenskiĭ as well as Akhmatova, Yevtushenko, and Mandelstam. The visitors came with greetings from his Soviet friends.

Two events on the Whittall calendar evoked the bygone. On March
29, Archibald MacLeish, then eighty-three, read his poetry to the larg-
est audience of the year, bearing out Kunitz's contention that "there are
some older poets whom we ought to hear again before the opportunity
is lost forever." At a press conference before the event, MacLeish (or
the questioning press) had dwelt on the political, philosophical, poetic,
and personal: human liberty, war, poetry, old age. During his five years
as Librarian, he said, he managed precisely one poem. "President Roo-
sevelt's idea that you could run the Library of Congress while shaving
turned out to be not quite true," he said. The Library to which he re-
turned at night from the world of "challenged facts and debated figures"
was "a presence where in those darkening days a man could feel and
almost see the Republic." Now he was involved with the Bicentennial:
his verse play *The Great American Fourth of July Parade* (commis-
sioned by Samuel Hazo, the director of the International Poetry Forum,
in Pittsburgh, where it had first been presented a year before) was to be
broadcast nationally in the summer. (In the drama, John Adams and
Thomas Jefferson return to comment, as John Broderick has said, "on
a shrunken, fearful, Nixonian America. The last hopeful line of the
play, however, echoes John Adams: 'Thomas Jefferson still lives.'")

Michael Kernan, in the *Washington Post,* observed that, at the press
conference, MacLeish "to each questioner . . . gave total, clear-eyed
attention, as though no one else were in the room. His voice and skin
had the smooth tension one might expect in a man of 50. . . . His words
rang. Not many people are making words ring these days."

On May 3, the silver anniversary of the establishment of the Gertrude
Clarke Whittall Fund was celebrated in the Coolidge Auditorium with
a memorial lecture—reflective, affectionate, anecdotal—by Roy Bas-
ler, back for the occasion, and a reading of poems by the archetypal
Whittall performer who had inaugurated the series in 1951, Burgess
Meredith.

Kunitz's close friendship with Theodore Roethke found gratifying
expression the same spring when the Roethke Memorial Foundation, in
Saginaw, asked him to nominate the judges for the third Roethke Poetry
Prize. Kunitz asked Donald Justice and Carolyn Kizer to do the honors
along with himself. Their choice was Richard Hugo, for his volume

What Thou Lovest Well, Remains American, published in 1975. (Because of organizational problems, the Roethke Foundation has been inactive over the succeeding decade; thus, after Kunitz, other Consultants have not been concerned with the Roethke Prize.)

During the fall and winter of 1975, Kunitz and Broderick had continued to pursue the project of a bicentennial exchange of British and American poets. The National Endowment for the Arts declined to fund the exchange. An approach to the English-Speaking Union was unavailing. It was finally the Folger Library and the Academy of American Poets who came through, to supplement a partial share from the Whittall funds. Six American poets were sent to Great Britain for a two-week reading tour, culminating in a performance on June 29 at Queen Elizabeth Hall, in London, as a feature of Poetry International 1976. They formed two teams, one consisting of Michael Harper, Galway Kinnell, and Denise Levertov, the other of Louise Glück, Philip Levine, and Mark Strand. (Gary Snyder and Richard Hugo had been on the original list but had to withdraw.) In October, two comparable teams of British poets would visit the States for a three-week tour concluding at the Library.

The Muse attended only sporadically during Kunitz's time at the Library, he told an interviewer. The distractions of the job, "an oppressive sense of the weight of the bureaucracy," worked against its being a "high creative period." He wrote only one poem of significance, but he couldn't have written it, he said, unless he had been the Consultant. It was "The Lincoln Relics," inspired by an exhibit in the Great Hall, during February 1976, of the contents of Lincoln's pockets the night he was assassinated, together with the Gettysburg Address and other documents and memorabilia. (The pocketed objects, which had been placed in the Library many years later, were made public in 1975.) From the poem, this contemporary and local apostrophe to Lincoln:

Mr. President,
in this Imperial City,
awash in gossip and power,
where marble eats marble
and your office has been defiled,

I saw the piranhas darting
between the rose-veined columns,
avid to strip the flesh
from the Republic's bones.
Has no one told you
how the slow blood leaks
from your secret wound?

Kunitz's farewell to the Consultantship, traditionally a lecture, took a different and appealing form: a valedictory evening, which he entitled "A Poet's America." He read from his late mother's journal, from Walt Whitman, and from his own work, reminisced, and conversed with the audience.

What *does* the Consultant in Poetry do?—indeed.

❋

"What does the Consultant in Poetry *do?*" Robert Hayden opened the annual report of his first year with the persistent refrain. He arrived at the Library in August, somewhat earlier than required, in order to get the "feel," as he wrote, "of the psychic and physical environment." He confessed to starting out with a certain apprehension, "since I came to the Library in the glare and blare of publicity that few of my predecessors, I imagine, have experienced. . . . As the first Afro-American to become Consultant . . . I was a news item (however minor) in the United States, Europe, and Africa. I suddenly became 'public.' . . . I began to feel more and more alarmed as the notoriety swirled around me. I did not want any of this, for it had little to do with me as an artist and far too much to do with me as a member of an ethnic minority. I felt trapped in sociology and politics. I am, of course, enough of a realist to know that, given the racial dilemmas in our country, the situation could hardly have been otherwise. Cold comfort indeed. . . . I am glad to remember how emphatically I insisted that it was my intention to do what I could for *all* American poets without regard to ethnic backgrounds."

Robert Hayden: born 1913 in Detroit; raised by poor foster parents, in Paradise Valley, the "colored world" of Detroit; in spite of poor sight (as an adult, he was legally blind), he wrote his first poems in grade school and read adventurously; discovered Sandburg, Millay, Countee Cullen, Hughes, and recognized his own vocation; after college in Detroit, worked on local black history and folklore for the Federal Writers Project; 1940, his first book of poems, his marriage to Erma Morris, a concert pianist; 1941–44, graduate study at the University of Michigan, in Ann Arbor, and a writing course under Auden, who stimulated and helped him. Soon afterward, the Haydens joined the Baha'i faith, which teaches the essential oneness of all people, the basic unity of all religions. In 1946, reluctantly, Hayden accepted an assistant professorship at Fisk University, in Nashville. (That year, at Mardi Gras time, he was in New Orleans and happened to meet Mark Van Doren, who, "meditative, ironic, richly human," was another source of encouragement. Hayden's poem "A Ballad of Remembrance" depicts that encounter.)

Nashville was his first experience, and his family's, of the segregated South. Conversely, during the 1960s, as activist black students became rebellious and intolerant of traditional studies, Hayden was attacked as an Uncle Tom, an Oreo, for not identifying with the militants. He regarded himself as "a poet who happens to be a Negro." At a Black Writers' Conference at Fisk in spring 1966, he was criticized and humiliated. His fine sentiments were rebuked even by M. B. Tolson. In the same year, ironically, Hayden's *A Ballad of Remembrance* brought him the Grand Prize for Poetry at the First World Festival of Negro Arts, in Dakar, Senegal. (Christopher Okigbo from Nigeria and Derek Walcott from St. Lucia were also in the running.) That fall in New York, when President Senghor bestowed the award, Langston Hughes, who had been one of the judges in Dakar, congratulated Hayden. "[He] came over to chat with my wife and me after the presentation and asked me to autograph my *Selected Poems* for him. I was deeply moved somehow, and I remember saying, as I tried to hold back the tears, 'Well, Langston, it's a new day when you ask *me* to autograph a book for *you.*' Behind my words . . . was the memory of that afternoon years and years ago, when I was a young hopeful with a sheaf of bad poems to show him." In fall 1968—at the time he and Walcott were filming "Middle Passage and Beyond" in Washington—Hayden left Fisk and returned to Ann Arbor; the next year he was appointed Professor of English. To have accepted the first offer of the Chair of Poetry, in 1969, would have meant an immediate leave of absence from the new position. In the militant 1960s, furthermore, there might have been some special pressures upon him as the first Afro-American Consultant, pressures that had moderated a few years later. The second invitation, in fall 1975, had been strongly supported by both Kunitz and William Meredith, who wrote to Boorstin that the appointment "would be a wonderful gesture for the bicentennial year. It will also confirm your own position, which was, I thought, maligned during the hearings." That year Hayden was elected the 1975 Fellow of the Academy of American Poets, "for distinguished poetic achievement." With the award came a stipend of $10,000. He had been through an exhausting illness, and the windfall enabled him to have a restorative sojourn, with his wife, in the Virgin Islands.

Introducing Hayden at his first reading, on October 5, in a crowded Coolidge Auditorium, Boorstin called him "our remembrancer" whose poetry has "a simplicity, directness, and conversational quality which can use the exotic subject to tear away the veil from the familiar." The date was also the birthday of Hayden's daughter Maia and of President Senghor of Senegal; he read poems in honor of each. Appropriate to the bicentennial season, he read poems about Phillis Wheatley, the eighteenth-century Bostonian slave poet; Crispus Attucks, the black man who led the attack on the British in the Boston Massacre; John Brown, Paul Laurence Dunbar, Frederick Douglass, and a boxer of his youth named Tiger Flowers. His encore, right for the time, was a humorous poem, "Unidentified Flying Object." (Hayden's handicapped eyesight made readings from the Coolidge podium difficult for him. Evalyn Shapiro, Karl Shapiro's former wife, for many years a member of the staff of the Library's Service for the Blind and Physically Handicapped, provided an experimental visual aid for him—a magnifier on an armature. Hayden didn't care for it, however, and preferred to bring his text close to his eyes.)

On November 1, the Bicentennial Poetry Program opened the Whittall series. Hayden introduced readings by the British poets who were on this side for a tour: Patricia Beer, Adrian Henri, Pete Morgan, Peter

Porter, Charles Tomlinson, and Kit Wright. (During the preceding after-noon, the visitors had engaged in a discussion of the poetry exchange with the American poets who had read in Britain: Louise Glück, Mi-chael Harper, Philip Levine, and Mark Strand. Also joining in: Eliza-beth Kray, for the cosponsoring Academy of American Poets, Broderick, and Kunitz.) The other Whittall events included poetry read-ings by Kenneth Koch and Jay Wright, May Miller Sullivan and Duane Niatum (a Native American poet), and Radcliffe Squires and Chad Walsh. Larry McMurtry read and discussed his work in progress. Lu-cille Lortel's White Barn Theatre gave two presentations: in December, "Love Is A . . . ," theater and dance based on the poetry of Sandburg, Millay, and Plath; and in February, "Walk Together Children," dramatic recitations by Vinie Burrows of poetry and prose by black writers, in observance of Afro-American History Month. In the spring there was an evening of English music and poetry, cosponsored by the Whittall music foundation, and "This Italy of Yours: Andante," with Michael Del Medico as Maxim Gorky, in cooperation with the Italian American Foundation. Hayden closed the season with a talk, "From the Life: Some Remembrances," drawn from his autobiographical work in prog-ress. A member of the audience described it as "alternately heart-breaking and hilarious, with its bittersweet recollections of his child-hood and youth." The calendar of the visitors to his office was notably international: literary people from the USSR, Hungary, Bulgaria, Can-ada, Japan, Yugoslavia, Portugal, Venezuela, and Trinidad; and, in his second year, Cyprus, Malaysia, Pakistan, and Poland.

In November 1976, the Library opened a major exhibition of avant-garde publications that show the tie between poetry and the visual arts in works by such poet-artists as Marsden Hartley, E. E. Cummings, Djuna Barnes, and Ben Shahn, and by poets and artists working to-gether. The show's title was straight from Ezra Pound: "Making It New." It stayed on view, as a bicentennial side-dish, into the following spring.

An innovation of Hayden's was a series of gatherings he called "Cof-fee with the Consultant," in the Poetry Room on intermittent Thursday afternoons, to which he invited local poets and their friends. Upon this pleasant sort of occasion hung a near contretemps. In December, Hayden wrote to the Librarian: "I have recently learned that you are planning to use the Consultant's reception room for luncheon meetings, and I am therefore writing to ask if this means that the room will no longer be available to me for my Thursday gatherings and other activities of the Poetry Office. . . . It is your prerogative, of course, to use the facilities of the Library as the needs of your programs require. But I feel that my needs as Consultant have been disregarded. It is my understanding that the use of the reception room by all my predecessors was never a point at issue, as now it seems to be. As one who takes the Chair of Poetry here seriously and not as a sinecure, I do not find the present situation reassuring." It was amiably resolved, however; and shortly afterward, Boorstin invited Hayden to stay for a second year, at an increased stipend. "I have been especially impressed by the way in which your appointment and your service here have been received in the community and in the nation at large," the Librarian wrote in his official letter, and he added a handwritten postscript: "It would give me special pleasure if you are able to accept. . . . Best to Erma."

During the week of President Carter's inauguration, in January 1977, Hayden and Whittemore were among the poets who participated in celebratory readings at the Folger Library. In reply to a note of appreciation signed "Jimmy," Hayden responded, "As a poet, I wish to thank you for what you have done to encourage a wider recognition of the value of poetry in our culture and that poets 'too sing America.'" Possibly he was alluding also to James Dickey's reading of an inaugural poem, "The Strength of Fields," during the Inauguration Eve Gala at the Kennedy Center, which was televised nationally. Dickey had been chosen, according to a spokesman for the President, because Carter considered him "the best-living American poet he knows." Dickey told a *Washington Post* reporter, Donna Landry, that though he didn't usually do occasional poetry, this request, when it came in early December, was "special" because he believed that "Jimmy Carter is the man destiny has cast in the role of deliverer." The poem, he explained, was about "the enormous political power that this man has drawn from the strength of his context, from the land—whether it's from peanuts or not doesn't matter." The news story was inevitably headlined "Poet Laureate of the Carter Administration."

"The knotty problem . . . for any Consultant," Hayden wrote, in his annual report, "is to give a full measure of work to the Library and at the same time keep enough energy for writing, which is, after all, an essential part of the job." He finished a series of poems on John Brown, which the Detroit Institute of Arts commissioned in connection with an exhibition (in 1979) of Jacob Lawrence's paintings dealing with the abolitionist, and he worked on *American Journal,* a new collection of poems, many of them growing out of his roots in Paradise Valley. He gave a number of readings at Howard University and elsewhere in the neighborhood and traveled as far as Colorado and Detroit; but he found that "such 'barn-storming' makes it extremely difficult to keep abreast of my work at the Library and go on with my writing."

In January, Hayden presided over a seminar in the Poetry Room at which two Bulgarian poets (who were also bureaucrats: Ljubomir Levchev, the First Deputy Minister of Culture, and Luchezar Elenkov, the Secretary of the Union of Bulgarian Writers) read their poems and met local writers. It was perhaps this encounter that led to his receiving, in April, an invitation from the Bulgarian ambassador to attend an international writers conference—a "meeting and dialogue on peace"—in Sofia in June, combined with a tour of the country, all expenses paid. Among the others invited were Voznesenskiĭ, Yevtushenko, Sholokhov, Denis Ritsos, Yasar Kemal, James Aldridge, Ana Maria Matute, and, from the United States, Erskine Caldwell, Denise Levertov, John Cheever, John Updike, and Gore Vidal. With some of the others, Hayden signed a call to the conference. The American Embassy in Sofia telegraphed the Department of State, pointing out that Hayden, "prize-winning *black* poet," would attend. Hayden declined the invitation, because—as he wrote to a Department of State official in Washington— "I feel that my presence might very well place me in a false position. I regret signing the conference 'appeal' only insofar as my action . . . apparently has been misconstrued as representing a political stance. Yet I cannot truthfully say that I am sorry to have added my name to those of the other American writers who believe, as I do, that we should all be deeply committed to the cause of international peace and to world unity. I am naive enough to believe that these considerations transcend political ideology."

SIX: 1971 TO 1980

⁂

Hayden returned to the Library of Congress to begin his second term as Consultant on September 12, the day on which Robert Lowell died of a heart attack, at the age of sixty, in a New York taxicab. At the requiem mass for Lowell in Boston, and at the memorial tribute for him on September 25 at the American Place Theater in New York, the Library was represented by neither the Consultant nor, officially, anyone else. On October 12, however, a program in the Whittall series was dedicated to Lowell: a reading by Voznesenskiĭ, with translations by William Jay Smith, sponsored jointly with the Kennan Institute for Advanced Russian Studies. Hayden absented himself from the program, and gave this explanation in his annual report: "The Voznesensky reading last fall was the most ineptly handled of all the season's programs. I hope it will be made clear in the future that when an outside organization co-sponsors a poetry event with the Library, it should inform the Poetry Office of its plans and should certainly not ignore the Consultant. Since I was not asked to take part in this program, despite my interest in and rather extensive knowledge of Russian poetry, I had no choice but to refuse to attend it. And although this might seem, on the surface, bureaucratic pettiness, I considered my action a way of emphasizing the significance of the Consultantship and of honoring the office." John Broderick introduced the program, and Senator Edward Kennedy introduced Voznesenskiĭ. In May 1978, the Library remembered Lowell again with the publication of a memorial album containing two discs comprising his readings of sixteen poems, recorded over a number of years—the first records to be issued for sale since those of William Jay Smith reading his poems for children. (The album of black poets reading, to which several Consultants, including Hayden, have given their time, is still in prospect.)

The Whittall series in Hayden's second year continued the international emphasis begun with Voznesenskiĭ. During the fall, there was an afternoon of Danish literature, with the poet Klaus Rifbjerg and the literary scholar Torben Brostrom; an evening of Hungarian poetry readings by Ferenc Juhász, Amy Károlyi, István Vas, and Sándor Weöres, introduced by Miklós Vajda, with translations by Daniel Hoffman and

William Jay Smith; a lecture by Alan Paton, on the tragic dilemmas of South Africa (to Hayden, the "most memorable" event in the series); a celebration, with readings and tributes, of the centennial of the poet and thinker Sir Muhammad Iqbal, who wrote in Urdu and Persian and is honored as the national poet of Pakistan; and Kimon Friar, lecturing on modern Greek poets. In the spring, an evening of Chinese poetry and music, with the poets Chang Ch'ung'ho and Huang Po-fei, musicians, and William Jay Smith in his customary role; and an evening of readings in honor of the early Honorary Consultant St.-John Perse (Alexis Leger), who had died in France in 1975 at the age of eighty-eight—Pierre Emmanuel read the poet's work in French, and Richard Howard read English translations, to an audience that included Leger's widow.

During October 1977 the Whittall series presented four dramatic programs recreating Federal Theatre Project plays of the late 1930s—a series Hayden took special pleasure in, because of his work as a young man with the WPA Federal Theatre Project in Detroit. On January 5, there was a celebration of the centennial of Carl Sandburg's birth, with a lecture by Daniel Hoffman, "'Moonlight Dries No Mittens': Carl Sandburg Reconsidered," and folksongs and readings from Sandburg's prose and verse by Beverly and Rufus Norris. The less exotic and reminiscent features of the year's programs were readings by Robert Huff and Ann Stanford, Dudley Randall, Patrick Galvin, A. Poulin, Jr., and David R. Slavitt, Katie Louchheim and Henry Taylor, and Beth Bentley and Nelson Bentley.

Perhaps the crowning literary event of the Hayden Consultantship—as we observed at the outset of this chronicle—was the Consultants' Reunion, on March 6, 1978, an inspiration of John Broderick's, though as resident Consultant Hayden had a central role to play. Twelve of the former Consultants joined him for a discussion with Library officials and also Roy Basler. The talk dwelt on the Consultantship, its history, its outlook, ways and measures of strengthening the appointment, and the influence upon American letters of the poets who had held it. (Hayden was less than certain of the success of the discussion. "We did not really come to grips with the topics . . . , particularly the question of the role of the Consultant today. What did emerge . . . was a reaffirmation of the significance of the Consultant's position in relation to American poetry.") There followed a gala luncheon and a press conference. The evening event was a reading by the thirteen poets, in the order of their terms in the Chair: Shapiro, Bishop, Eberhart, Nemerov, Whittemore, Spender, Dickey—then an intermission—William Jay Smith, Stafford, Jacobsen, Hoffman, Kunitz, and Hayden. (Of the surviving Consultants, only Tate, Adams, and Warren couldn't be present.) Hayden wrote that its three hours provided "the literary event of a lifetime." He found Spender's reading of "I Think Continually of Those Who Were Truly Great" the most profoundly moving experience of the evening. As Smith said to Spender, "We all grew up with that poem." And as Hayden summed up, "We who had participated in the reading felt that it was an historic occasion, and, too, that maybe poetry does mean something to Americans, after all."

Several of the participants in the reunion wrote the Librarian of Congress in appreciation. Eberhart, teaching at the University of Florida in Gainesville, took the occasion to suggest poets for the next appointment: he listed twenty-three in all, his first choices being Muriel Rukeyser, Gwendolyn Brooks, Michael Harper, James Wright, Donald Hall, and Maxine Kumin. "I think of my taste as catholic. I love them all!" Smith proposed N. Scott Momaday, "three-quarters Kiowa . . . , a gentleman, whose gracious manners have delighted a wide range of people throughout the world." Hoffman proposed Meredith, "one of our most considerable poets . . . a man of the world widely acquainted in the literary and academic communities"; and of the readings he wrote that "few foresaw that monster turn-out . . . or the cheers for the biggest serial poetry reading on record." Nemerov: ". . . just to walk into your library once again brought back the feelings almost of awe, and now accompanied by nostalgia, that always attended even my daily entrance into the place when a consultant." Boorstin, writing each Consultant "to tell you how much your presence meant to us," observed: "Seeing this group together has suggested that we should consider the former Consultants in Poetry to be a Council of Poets for the Library and the Nation. And we hope we will be able to have similar gatherings from time to time in the future."

�֎

Hayden's many public readings, radio and television appearances, and press interviews—particularly one interview for an extended feature article in *Ebony*, with photographs of Hayden, Nancy Galbraith, and Jennifer Whittington in the Poetry Room—sharply stimulated public awareness of the Consultantship. Hayden was deluged with letters and manuscripts (even from prison inmates) and invitations to read. "There is the assumption," Hayden observed, "that the Consultant is a 'public servant' whose primary function—indeed, obligation—is to assist and encourage the pursuit of poetry and the 'literary' life." In order to attend to his responsibilities at the Library, Hayden therefore accepted fewer reading engagements; he did read at Yale, Wesleyan, Phillips Exeter Academy, Alabama State, the United States Naval Academy, and local schools. And he accepted an appointment for the year as poet-in-residence at Howard University and was on campus one day a week, teaching a seminar in contemporary American poetry and conferring with student poets. Hayden's time would have been even more heavily obligated if an idea of his had come to something during his Consultantship: a conference on science and literature, growing out of his interest in the literature of science fantasy. The Library made overtures to several persons thought to be essential to such a conference; most of them were unavailable at a suitable time, and the conference was deferred.

When Broderick asked Hayden to suggest prospects for the next appointment to the Chair, there had apparently been a consensus that it should be a woman. Hayden accordingly recommended, in order, Muriel Rukeyser, Carolyn Kizer, Josephine Miles, Ann Stanford, Isabella Gardner, and Maxine Kumin; but he added, "I personally would hope that Bill Meredith could be asked again. I think I could convince him to accept."

The Honorary Consultants in American Letters were slowly vanishing by attrition. The custom of appointing a Consultant in Poetry to the honorary group, as a bit of lagniappe at the end of a term, was allowed to lapse, and new appointments were no longer being made. In 1978 there were but five survivors: Jacobsen, Kunitz, Luce, Michener, and Updike. Basler's Honorary Consultantship in American Studies also ended. A new entity, the Council of Scholars, replacing the various Honorary Consultantships, was in prospect.

※

William Meredith had had the special regard, from the early 1940s, of MacLeish (who, in a manner of speaking, discovered him), Tate (likewise), Auden, Lowell, Blackmur, Frost (who, twice his age, made a pal of him), Eberhart, Hayden—the list of poets who liked and encouraged him, or whom he encouraged, might go on and on. Tate, directing the first Creative Arts Program at Princeton in 1940, told Meredith that his was "easily the best class poem I have ever seen, and it leads me to suspect that your other verse must be very promising indeed." After graduation, Meredith stayed on a year as an assistant and collaborated with Willard Thorp in planning an anthology, *Princeton Verse Between Two Wars,* which Tate edited. Tate's choices included several poems of Meredith's, one of which was dedicated to Muriel Rukeyser, whom he had come to know through Thorp. Thus the web widens. As we have observed, Meredith was launched when MacLeish, thanks to Rukeyser, chose his first book, *Love Letters from an Impossible Land,* for the Yale Series of Younger Poets in 1943, while Meredith was a Navy pilot, on antisubmarine patrol in the Aleutians. The title poem in that volume won the Harriet Monroe Lyric Award the next year. His second collection, *Ships and Other Figures,* appeared in 1948, when he was teaching creative writing at his alma mater. He went back and back to Princeton, as resident fellow in creative writing, during the 1950s and 1960s; was recalled to flight duty in the Korean War, 1952–54; taught at the University of Hawaii and Carnegie-Mellon University; wrote opera criticism; during five summers was on the faculty at the Bread Loaf Writers' Conference; in 1955, established himself at Connecticut College, in New London, and rose (amid a steady accretion of fellowships, grants, awards) to a chair of English; for ten years ran an Upward Bound program for inner city youths; and intensively supported the Union of Concerned Scientists. When, at Eberhart's invitation, he read at the Library in October 1959, Tom Wolfe of the *Washington Post* remarked, not surprisingly, on Meredith's un-Beat attire: "impeccably turned out in a conservative brown suit and cordovan shoes," not bothered by "the temptation to strike the pose of an inspired madman." Meredith told him, "A poet is distinguished by his verbal experience; what is new is the world." As for beatniks, "they tend to be alert and interested in poetry, which is a recommendation in itself. But they do have some erroneous concepts of originality."

Meredith was appointed to the Consultantship despite agitation by the Poetry Society of Alaska, supported by some senators, in behalf of Alaska's poet laureate, Jeno Platthy. On the Librarian's part, John Updike had been under consideration; he declined.

During Meredith's first year in the Chair, what most gratified him were the seminars he held for teachers of poetry in schools in and around Washington—enthusiastic teachers who brought in poems they had found successful in the classroom and made an informal anthology of them. In the department of good works, he wrote to James Michener in December congratulating him on taking the lead in donating funds to the National Poetry Series. "Those of us who make poems take great pride and comfort . . . and fortunate poets will take publication and money from the fact that you have put your money where your mouth is. What you are doing is something of a landmark in American literature. . . . [This is] an unofficial letter, but perhaps the most appropriate one I have yet composed on this letterhead." Another letter on that letterhead encountered difficulties. Addressing President Carter, on December 7, Meredith wrote: "There are now eleven defendants on trial in the Superior Court for an act of protest on the White House grounds. . . . If these people—including the gifted and patriotic writer Grace Paley—had unfurled a nazi banner on the White House lawn, I would throw them on the promiscuous mercies of the Civil Liberties Union. But since they are supporters of the cause of anti-war and anti-nuclear armament—a cause you and I share—I would be grieved to see their action misjudged as a crime. So would future Americans, if I read history right. Please do not let the prosecution of these serious patriots distort their deliberate protest to appear a crime." He had written on "Poetry Room stationery ordered years ago for . . . my friend Robert Frost, [who] might have felt that the matter was an appropriate concern for a Poetry Consultant." A Library official reviewing Meredith's correspondence deemed the letter "personal and inappropriate for official correspondence." Meredith rewrote it on the letterhead of Connecticut College (to little effect; the codefendants were convicted and fined.)

Another interest Meredith pursued, where appropriate and opportune, was to attract foreign writers to come to the Library and talk about their own national literatures. Such a program had been arranged by the Library administration before he arrived: on October 31—actually on the eve of *Todos los Santos*—two Mexican poets, José Emilio Pacheco and Tomás Segovia, read their poems as part of a "Mexico Today" observance, with translations by Meredith and by Alastair Reid. (Earlier that day he had arranged a recording by the Australian Aboriginal poet Kath Walker.) In the spring, the Irish poet Seamus Heaney read. And at the end of the season, supporting an observance of "Japan Today," there was an evening of Japanese poetry—Makoto Ooko reading his poems, Donald Keene translating. The Whittall Fund's domestic presentations, in which Meredith played the customary role, were exceptionally copious: James Alan McPherson and Tim O'Brien; Maurice English and Frederick Morgan; Roland Flint and Linda Pastan; Jane Cooper and Louis O. Coxe; June Jordan; Alice Walker; Ann Darr and Gloria Oden; Gary Gildner and William Matthews; Toni Morrison; John Irving (from a novel in progress, *The Hotel New Hampshire);* Romulus Linney (from his plays) and May Sarton. Two dramatic programs were offered: the British actress Elizabeth Morgan portraying Samuel Johnson's friend Hester Lynch Thrale, and the American actress Peggy Cowles in a dramatic study of Anna Dickinson. Besides managing a fair number of poets coming in to record, in the spring Meredith honored an earlier commitment by loyally commuting every Thursday to Princeton, where he taught a workshop in modern poetry.

In fall 1978, Meredith went out to the International Writers Workshop, at Iowa City, and met German, Irish, and Bulgarian poets who subsequently visited the Library. The focus of this interest of Meredith's was sharpened when, in February, Boorstin, Broderick, and he met the director of the United States International Communication Agency, John Reinhardt, and discussed ways the Library and the ICA could cooperate. In March, Meredith assembled for the ICA a brief anthology of American poetry on the theme of freedom, for display at a Latin

American conference on international law. Soon afterward, the ICA invited him to lead an American delegation of poets to the eighteenth annual poetry festival at Struga, in the southwest corner of Yugoslavia. Meredith and the others attended the festival and toured around the country in August 1979; afterward, during September, he traveled on to Bulgaria and Israel, where he visited writers and American Cultural Centers.

Meredith's reappointment had evidently been a foregone conclusion. He wound up his official duties on May 7 with a lecture, "Reasons for Poetry" (which proved to be the first half of a diptych, of which the second half, "The Reason for Criticism," was his lecture a year later). Before leaving the Poetry Office, on June 4, he wrote to the Librarian on two counts. He urged the appointment of his replacement in 1980 as far as possible in advance. Second, he suggested that Boorstin consider "very seriously" appointing Allen Ginsberg to succeed him. "Looking back over the last 13 appointments, since Robert Frost, I see a kind of Establishment pattern, of which I am perhaps a good example. As visible as this position is, here and abroad, I think it ought to be *representative*. The excellence of Ginsberg's work is pretty much agreed on now. His role as a social critic and prophet has run its course, as far as being radically offensive to many. He has become a responsible member of such organizations as the American Institute of Arts and Letters. He has set up a small foundation from his earnings from which such poets as Basil Bunting have received help." He knew Ginsberg was interested in the Consultantship. And he proposed inviting him for a talk. "I think you and John would be surprised at what a good Consultant he would prove. More than that, I think it would do wonders to expand the terms in which people have come to think of the Consultancy." The appointment went to Maxine Kumin. Meredith, though entirely partial to Kumin, considered her stigmatized with the same "Establishment respectability" as he himself was, and he renewed his case in a later report. The Consultantship ought to be "aesthetically, geographically, ethnically, and sexually representative. I think the most important advice I have given . . . was that Allen Ginsberg should be appointed. I will continue to recommend him."

SIX: 1971 TO 1980

✳

Under the twelfth Librarian of Congress, Daniel Boorstin, organizational changes comparable to those in the MacLeish era were reshaping the Library's administration. The post of Assistant Librarian for Research Services had been created in 1978, holding sway over a wide range of divisions and offices, including the Manuscript Division and the Poetry Office. At the beginning of 1979, John Broderick was appointed to the post; he carried along to his new office the responsibility for both the Poetry Office and the Consultantship in Poetry that he had inherited from Basler.

The Archer M. Huntington Trust, which its donor had established in November 1936, stipulating that its income be used half for the Library's activities in the Hispanic field and for the maintenance of "a Chair of Poetry in the English language," half for the American Academy of Arts and Letters, had continued to be managed in accordance with the provisions of the original trust. In 1977, the Library of Congress Trust Fund Board approved a request that cy pres action be sought from the U.S. District Court for the Huntington and two other "Chair" funds administered in behalf of other programs in Research Services. (In the law of charities, the doctrine of cy pres [legal Anglo-French, "so near"] provides that when it becomes impossible, impracticable, or illegal to carry out the particular purpose of the donor, the Court will frame a scheme to carry out the *general* intention by applying the gift to closely related purposes.) Writing to the Bank of New York, which administers the Huntington trust, Boorstin observed with some asperity that the rate of return on the trust was "the least attractive of all the investments held for the Library of Congress: . . . a disappointing 4.9 percent." On January 25, 1979, the Court approved cy pres action to expand the purposes for which income from the Huntington Fund could be used. (Similarly, in due course, for the Benjamin and Guggenheim funds.) The Bank of New York thereupon agreed to change the Huntington trust portfolio in order to generate a yield of about 7 percent. The Court's action had made it possible to spend accumulated surpluses in the fields of interest originally favored by the donors.

✳

With Meredith's help, the fall 1979 issue of the *Quarterly Journal of the Library of Congress* was planned by its editor, Frederick Mohr, and associate editor James Hardin around three features. One was an article by Kurt S. Maier on the friendship of Thomas Mann, Agnes Meyer, and MacLeish. (MacLeish had, of course, appointed Mann an Honorary Consultant in German Letters in 1941, and Agnes and Eugene Meyer had funded the post.) Secondly, Meredith inaugurated (or hoped he did) a feature called "Consultants' Choice," a listing of recent books of poetry recommended and briefly reviewed by Consultants. Eight had responded to his invitation; seventeen books were included. In the heat of the day, "Consultants' Choice" didn't survive. The third feature would be an eightieth-birthday tribute to Allen Tate, the centerpiece of which was a "pictorial introduction" to Tate's novel *The Fathers*: photographs of Alexandria, Georgetown, and Washington during the Civil War, with legends from the novel, arranged by Hardin (who walked the streets to identify fictional locations); and a scholarly essay on *The Fathers* by Thornton H. Parsons. Tributes to Tate were forthcoming from Malcolm Cowley, Cleanth Brooks, Louis Coxe, Eudora Welty, William Jay Smith, and Meredith. (Meredith had kept in touch with Tate over the years. In October 1976 he wrote Tate to comment on a newspaper article about him, which he felt was "no proper estimate of the generosity of your life towards other writers, especially your juniors—Cal, John [Berryman], Louis Coxe, Howard Nemerov, Reed Whittemore, me, dozens of others. We know, though.")

When the news came of Tate's death in Nashville on February 9, 1979, after his long siege with emphysema, the birthday issue became a memorial. Present tenses became past, and the photographic portrait of Tate at the front of the *Journal* was framed with a black border.

✳

At the Library, the fall 1979 season opened on October 2 with a commemoration of the fortieth anniversary, to the day, of MacLeish's assuming the Librarianship of Congress. MacLeish, eighty-seven, was present in strength. The event centered on a panel discussion in the Coolidge Auditorium that morning, led by Boorstin, before an audience including Luther Evans and L. Quincy Mumford, and carried on by five veterans of the MacLeish era: Robert Penn Warren, the second Consultant in Poetry whom MacLeish had appointed; Frederick R. Goff, who had been assistant and acting chief of the Rare Book Division; Ernest R. Griffith, director of the Legislative Reference Service; Lewis Hanke, director of the Hispanic Foundation; and Herman H. Henkle, director of the Processing Department. Each man talked of his work at the Library in MacLeish's day, reminisced, paid tribute, endorsed the historic fact that MacLeish effected a profound change in the Library's relationship to the nation and the world. Evans and Mumford added their appreciations. MacLeish had the penultimate word. "I have been touched, moved, excited, amused, and delighted by this conversation." He had one aphorism to utter: "The crucial thing with a library is that it should be a library. . . . A glimpse of Red Warren going up the steps, working here for a year, writing poems here, as part of the Library, is more of the purpose of this Library than any canon I ever set up." And he told a story to illustrate what his aphorism came down to. When he brought the exiled Alexis Leger to the Library in 1941 "to see what he could do about our holdings in French literature, which were not very admirable," Leger accepted but, "clicking his heels like a dragoon," said he would never return to his work as a poet. A year later—and during that interval Leger had quietly been performing valuable bibliographical and advisory work—he handed MacLeish the manuscript of his poem *Exil.* "That is what the Library of Congress is." Warren closed the session by reading MacLeish's poem, "You, Andrew Marvell"—"so that we shan't forget *that* aspect, which will be as immortal as any other aspect of his achievement, and (do I have to gamble on it?) more immortal."

After luncheon in the Pavilion, the feature of the afternoon was a showing in the Poetry Room, for those of the celebratory party who could manage it, of an hour-long color film, *Those Paris Years,* produced by Samuel Hazo. In the course of an interview Hazo had conducted at the farm in Conway, MacLeish recalled his life in France during the 1920s and recited some of the poems he wrote then, "voice-over," with photographs of Paris in those days. The evening event was the Consultant's customary reading, introduced by his "discoverer" of some thirty-five years earlier, MacLeish.

On October 6, 1979, a year and a half after her last, rather reticent visit to the Library for the Consultants' Reunion, Elizabeth Bishop died suddenly at her home in Boston, where she had been living for nearly ten years, since the death of her close friend in Brazil. She had been teaching writing classes at Harvard and M.I.T. There was no memorial gathering at the Library, though her death was mentioned—almost without precedent—in the Librarian's annual report.

To survey, only briefly, the poets, speakers, and other performers in the 1979–80 Whittall series: Richard Dyer-Bennet, reading three excerpts from Robert Fitzgerald's translation of the *Odyssey*, with lute accompaniment; William Heyen and Peter Viereck; W. S. Merwin, cosponsored by the Folger Shakespeare Library; Sandra McPherson and James Welch; Myra Sklarew and Edward Weismiller, both Washington poets; Wendell Berry; Sterling Brown, also a Washington poet, introduced by Michael S. Harper; John Peck and Ellen Bryant Voigt; an evening of Australian poetry—Vincent Buckley, David Malouf, and Les A. Murray; Christine D'haen, Belgian poet, part of an observance of "Belgium Today." The novelist Herman Wouk lectured on "War and Remembrance: the Paradox of Historical Fiction." (He retained his fee this time.) In a joint observance of the centennial of two stunningly different poets, Vachel Lindsay (d. 1931) and Wallace Stevens (d. 1955), A. Walton Litz presented a lecture entitled "Wallace Stevens: The Poetry of Earth" and Anthony Howard read from the works of Lindsay. Ernest J. Gaines read from his fiction. The Royal Shakespeare Company, cosponsored by the Folger and the Kennedy Center, presented three evenings of Shakespeare and one entitled "Murder Most Foul." Sir Peter Pears gave an evening of English poetry and song, cosponsored by the Whittall Foundation.

On December 6—moving further into the new organization of the Library—the Librarian invited 140 guests from the world of scholarship to a "Circle of Knowledge" dinner in the Great Hall, at which he announced the formation of the Council of Scholars and introduced the concept of the Library as a "Multimedia Encyclopedia." The Council, in a sense a successor to and extension of the Honorary Consultants, is a group of some twenty-five persons representing a spectrum of academic fields and disciplines, charged to "advise the Librarian about the relationship between the Library of Congress and the world of scholarship" and to "sponsor programs which will examine large intellectual questions affecting scholarship and public policy." MacLeish was appointed the Council's honorary chairman. The current and the designated Consultants in Poetry are automatically members; thus, at the outset, both Meredith and Maxine Kumin were on the Council.

Meredith, however, was absent from the "Circle of Knowledge" dinner. As a guest of the Bulgarian government, he flew to Sofia on the fourth for two weeks, to receive one of the Nicola Vaptsarov prizes newly established by the Union of Bulgarian Writers. Vaptsarov, revolutionary poet, Resistance fighter against the German occupation, had been shot by a German firing squad in 1942, at the age of 33. On this seventieth anniversary he was being honored as a national martyr-poet. The Vaptsarov Prize, awarded the same year to poets from Italy, Poland, Cuba, and Lithuania, carried a purse of 4,000 lev (about $2,750), a gold medal, and a bronze trophy in the shape of a winged horse. The American writers invited to the event included Cheever, Updike, Caldwell, Saroyan, and the Consultant-designate, Maxine Kumin. Meredith delivered a speech on the occasion, invoking our own American Revolution, Walt Whitman, the time when "American and Bulgarian resistance heroes were comrades in arms against a common foe," the need for "constant vigilance for freedom," and "the brotherhood of free artists." After coming home, Meredith urged the other Americans who had been in Sofia to join him in sending copies of their books to the National Library of Bulgaria as a token of gratitude. (Later Meredith joined Updike, Barbara Tuchman, I. M. Pei, and others in signing a letter to Leonid Brezhnev, expressing strong concern over the fate of Andrei Sakharov and quoting lines of Bella Akhmadulina.)

Another literary/political event: On the afternoon of January 3, 1980, Rosalyn Carter, the President's wife, invited twenty-one poets to the White House for a "Salute to Poetry and American Poets": readings of their poems to invited guests (largely other poets), in seven rooms, three poets to a room. To account just for the Consultants and Washingtonians who took part: Maxine Kumin (with Sterling Brown) was in the

China Room; Lucille Clifton in the Green Room; James Dickey in the Red Room; Kunitz, Jacobsen, and Hayden in the East Room; Gwendolyn Brooks and Richard Eberhart in the Blue Room. (Among the poets on the guest list were Hoffman, Shapiro, and Whittemore. May Miller Sullivan was present, too; in the crush she fainted, but recovered. Meredith was absent, still abroad.)

When Robert and Erma Hayden arrived at the White House gate, Hayden found himself without any identification whatever. Broderick has told the story: "Because of his reliance upon the faithful Erma, Robert did not always burden himself with a wallet. He had no driver's license because of his eye trouble. Admittance to the White House is carefully controlled, of course, and the guard was merely exercising proper caution. Suddenly, Robert remembered that the book he was carrying, and from which he would shortly read, carried his picture on the dust jacket. The likeness was recognizable; the guard was convinced. On with the show!"

Few knew that Hayden was then ill with cancer. After returning home to Ann Arbor, his condition worsened. On February 24, the Center for Afro-American and African Studies at the University gave a "Tribute to Robert Hayden"—readings, drama, music, discussions. He was unable to attend, but after the tribute, some of the participants came by the house to see him. "His daughter Maia helped him dress," a friend wrote, "and he went downstairs to greet his guests. Soon he had them laughing with his deft wit and loving manner. The next day, Robert Hayden died." Meredith, in a statement to the press, said, "Robert Hayden lived and died ahead of a reputation that could only lag behind his accomplishments. He set himself a standard of excellence that leaves his life and work beautifully clear."

There was an unhappy sequel to the White House readings. More than four months later, Meredith wrote to John Simon, the cultural journalist: "I have just read, with sorrow and anger, the ungenerous words in the May issue of *Vogue* about Robert Hayden in your piece about the White House reception. . . .I replayed a tape made at the reception (which I did not attend) of Hayden's reading of 'The Night-Blooming Cereus.' Your sentence, 'A bulging, disheveled, thickly be-spectacled man, he had to hold his text an inch from his nose, and couched his uncommunicative verses in an impenetrable delivery'—that sentence, to anyone familiar with the man Robert Hayden, his life, his physical courage, or the poem 'The Night-Blooming Cereus' (even as read under the unfavorable conditions you describe) will always seem a very inaccurate piece of criticism. Chiefly its inaccuracy is the inaccuracy of values: nothing in the sentence suggests awareness of what the event we know as Robert Hayden was worth."

A sampling of Meredith's preoccupations during the last days of his term, after giving his closing lecture, "The Uses of Criticism": (1) In answer to a high school student's asking what his feelings were about the future of poetry in the United States: "It will sooner or later come up from the basement of popular songs and vulgar McKuenism, and down from the attic of intellectual and surreal elitism, and meet in the living room of a wide American audience. Josephine Miles speaks of this kind of poetry when she says it should be 'recitable, quotable, usable by everybody.' As a seer, I see this, but my crystal ball doesn't have a digital clock." (2) Advice to the Friends of the Kennedy Center about plans for poetry readings in the Terrace Theater there: a list of a dozen and a half recommendations, in order of urgency, beginning with MacLeish and Warren; mourning the absence from the list of Hayden, Bishop, and Muriel Rukeyser, losses of the recent past; advising the inclusion of minority, women, mid-West, and western poets. (3) Attending President Carter's presentation of the Presidential Medal of Freedom to Robert Penn Warren and others at the White House.

An event that did not much involve the Consultant in Poetry was the dedication, on April 24, 1980, of the James Madison Memorial Building, which had been under construction since 1971 on the entire block south of the original Library of Congress. (It is considered to be the largest library building in the world.) The symbolic key to the building was handed to the Librarian by the Architect of the Capitol, George M. White, who had been in charge of construction. Boorstin and the Speaker of the House, Thomas P. O'Neill, offered toasts. Concurrently there were alterations of the names of the library buildings. The "Annex" to the east, which had been opened in 1939 and had been officially named the Thomas Jefferson Building in 1976, now became the John Adams Building, and the original, monumental Library of Congress building of 1897 was renamed the Thomas Jefferson Building, appropriately honoring the President who had been the Library's most prominent advocate and whose personal library became its nucleus after the holocaust of 1814. The Poetry Office and the Consultant's office retained their eyries on the topmost floor at the northwest corner of the Jefferson Building; the Coolidge Auditorium and the Whittall Pavilion, on the ground floor, are still the focus of the public and nonpublic events that concern poetry and literature (though an occasional program occurs in the Mumford Room of the Madison Building); and the office of the Assistant Librarian for Research Services, John Broderick, who continued to oversee the Poetry Office, remained on the Jefferson Building's main floor. Whatever collections and files related to the Library's poetic and other literary activities, however, have found new quarters in the Madison Building—in the Manuscript Division, on its ground floor, or in the Central Services files (not ordinarily available to the public) on an upper floor.

Because Kumin couldn't take up her appointment until January 1981, Meredith stayed on into December. After returning to the Poetry Office on September 18, he left the next day for Bulgaria again. The Writers' Union had invited him, along with Denise Levertov and John Balaban, to an international conference on "The Contribution of Writers to World Peace" allied with a Parliament of Peoples for Peace. He was back in Washington for his last reading in the Coolidge Auditorium on October 6. The program included a work written during his time in the Chair—"On Jenkins' Hill," that being the old name for Capitol Hill (now preserved in the name of a neighborhood bar):

The weather came over this low knoll, west to east,
before there was a word for leaf-fall, before
there were any leaves. Weathers will nuzzle and preen
whatever earthwork we leave here. And we know now,
don't we, that we will be leaving, by fire or ice,
our own or His, or at the very worst, nobody's.
May that be a long time off. Now,
it is our hill for debating.

The dome at the top of the hill, heavy with reference,
is iron out of the soil, yearned up as if it were white stone,
the way for a time our thought and rhetoric yearned upward.
Here our surrogates sit. It is almost too much for them,
some days, to make the world go around.
They are urged to clean it, to sully it more grandly,
to let it alone. We have elected them, they are our elect.

If only we knew what to ask, there are trees, white oaks,
not far from here that have seen the whole thing.
Year after year they have put on new growth, dropped leaves.
I can tell you this much: it is a badly informed citizen
who stands on this hill and scoffs.

On the Whittall Fund, Meredith was in charge of three dual reading programs: Michael McClure and Ira Sadoff; Patrick Galvin and Thomas Kinsella, from Ireland; David McAleavey and Susan Shreve; and, on December 9, Carolyn Heafner in a program of poetry and music commemorating the 150th anniversary of Emily Dickinson's birth, cosponsored by the Whittall Foundation. Of most particular concern to Meredith, on November 17 he introduced an evening of Bulgarian poetry, in the Mumford Room of the Madison Building, in which his friends Bojidar Bojilov, Georgi Djagarov, Luchezar Elenkov, Vladimir Golev, and Ljubomir Levchev read their poems, and Vladimir Philipov and Meredith read translations. Next day Meredith attended a reception for the Bulgarians given by the Academy of American Poets in New York, and on the day after that he was back at the Library for a two-day conference on Creativity, the first to be sponsored by the Council of Scholars (and supported by the Carnegie Foundation and the Standard Oil Company of California). Meredith departed the Library on December 16, after supervising a recording in the Laboratory by the Washington poet and friend of the Library Katie Louchheim.

❅

The 1960s and 1970s witnessed the silencing of the voices that, by consensus, had been recognized as those of the lights of twentieth-century Anglo-American poetry: Eliot, Frost, Pound, Moore, Williams, Auden, Lowell, Bishop, Tate, and as anthologist Untermeyer. Who would fill their places? The question perplexes us still. Over those decades, ten American poets brought a variety of traditions, styles, ages, homegrounds, to the Chair. The appointment of a Consultant who was not an American citizen, Stephen Spender—himself a member of a distinguished tradition—might have inaugurated a new pattern of inviting an occasional poet from abroad to take the Consultantship, but that was not to be. During the same decades, however, international poetry became a standard in the series, through a festival, frequent visitations, and special programs planned by the Library administration. Drama was represented with greater range and professionalism than ever before. The Washington public for poetry was growing, too, in numbers and sophistication. And the Library's example had encouraged poetry readings and lectures on the poetic art at other cultural centers in Washington.

The color line—obtuse and disgraceful in a governmental institution—had been breached just before and during the National Poetry Festival, and the determination to bring a black poet to the Chair was fulfilled in the bicentennial year with the appointment of Hayden. A woman Consultant, absent from the post for twenty years (despite a continual murmuring hope), reappeared in 1971 with the happy choice of Jacobsen. The notable patrons of the poetry program—Huntington, Mrs. Whittall, the Bollingen Foundation—left the scene, but through fortunate and shrewd husbanding of the endowments, the Chair and the Whittall series enjoyed far better than adequate funding. More and more poets in the English language, particularly the young, were brought to read at the Library.

What had been an ineffectual rumor for several years—the idea of an American poet laureate—was to gather strength toward realization in a way unforeseen by either its advocates or its adversaries.

William Meredith, October 1978

Herman Wouk (left) at a luncheon in his honor, October 29, 1979, with Daniel J. Boorstin and Senator Claiborne Pell of Rhode Island

Maxine Kumin in the Poetry Room with a fourth-grade class from a Washington elementary school, December 11, 1981

Josephine Jacobsen, Anthony Hecht, and Maxine Kumin, in the court-
yard adjacent to the Whittall Pavilion, spring 1982

Celebrating the fiftieth anniversary of the Academy of American Poets, November 14, 1983. Seated: Fitzgerald, Nemerov, Marie Bullock, Kunitz, Meredith; standing: Eugene McCarthy, Jacobsen, W. S. Merwin, John Hollander, James Merrill, Mark Strand, May Swenson, David Wagoner, Hoffman, Hecht, Mona Van Duyn, Warren

Robert Fitzgerald, at Harvard University, 1975

Reed Whittemore, September 1984

Gwendolyn Brooks, 1985

Brooks at a reception in her honor as Consultant, in the courtyard of the Whittall Pavilion, September 30, 1985. John C. Broderick was introducing her to William McGuire (left) and to James Hutson, chief of the Manuscript Division.

Robert Penn Warren, the first Consultant to hold the additional title of Poet Laureate, at a press conference in the Poetry Room, October 6, 1986

Seven

1981 TO 1986

Maxine Kumin, the twenty-fifth Consultant in Poetry, was the fifth woman in the Chair in its forty-three years. As she later said to an interviewer, she must have appeared to be a "very safe, heterosexual, middle-class, middle-aged woman poet, the kind who wasn't going to disgrace anybody." When, at a meeting of the Council of Scholars, she found herself "among all those eminences grises, all of whom were male, I said I felt as if I had stumbled into a stag club and ought to leap out of a cake." Kumin, during her membership on the Council (until spring 1982, when she disengaged herself from the Council's activities for the remainder of her term as Consultant in Poetry), continued to be an audible voice, not merely on the issue of female representation, and she was a notably articulate occupant of the Chair of Poetry. (Female representation on the Council improved somewhat after Kumin's term, and, as will be seen, another female poet did soon take the Chair of Poetry.) In her judgment, the Library of Congress was a "gentility-ridden, traditional, hidebound place," though in the end she found many aspects of her time there "quite wonderful," particularly the out-reach programs and her brown bag lunches for women poets in the

Poetry Room—which, she felt, made a difference by helping to de-mystify poetry.

Kumin was born Maxine Winokur, 1925, in Philadelphia, where, as she put it in a memoir, "my father owned the largest pawnbroking establishment in the city, and I grew up in an environment where status was a preeminent consideration." Her family were "non-immigrant, non-orthodox Jews," and her early education was in a parochial school. She had been "a closet poet from the age of eight"; Radcliffe College, an M.A., an early marriage, three children, from 1958, jobs teaching English and writing at a range of Eastern colleges; first book of poems, 1961, first novel, 1965. Since 1963, Kumin and her husband, Victor, a consulting engineer, have run a working farm near Warner, in southern New Hampshire. "As my belief in the perfectibility of man has eroded before my recognition of human depravity, I find myself digging in ever deeper to accept the natural world. I hope to live out my life on the land, raising horses and turnips and making jam from the wild berries."

Meredith had suggested Kumin as his successor to the Chair. When the Librarian's invitation reached her, in March 1980, she was teaching at Princeton and had already committed herself to a full schedule of readings and lectures during the fall—thus Meredith stayed on until December and Kumin arrived at the Poetry Office on January 23, 1981. On the very day, she gave a reading and judged a poetry contest at a local college. For her new job she had been armed with her friend Nemerov's "funny, iconoclastic, and hard-headed" advice about the Library of Congress. She brought her mare, Boomer, down from Warner in a horse trailer and boarded her at a farm in Maryland. Every morning at seven she drove out and rode Boomer, before going to the Poetry Office, which she did nearly every weekday, exceeding the customary half time. Within the first week (just as "the hostages are rounding the bend to the Capitol," she wrote a friend) she opened the spring literary session with her own reading in the Coolidge Auditorium; recommended Adrienne Rich, "our most eminent contemporary woman poet," for a professorship at Cornell; and went off to Memphis to hold a poetry workshop. The next week, Tucson. As she wrote in her annual report, "I have chosen, at least in this first 'semester,' to focus on women poets whose work seems to me to merit the attention of a sym-

SEVEN: 1981 TO 1986

pathetic and sophisticated Library of Congress audience. Next year I would like to see us grow somewhat more adventurous. . . . Poets west of the Mississippi frequently complain that the Eastern Establishment ignores them; perhaps we can cast a wider net geographically." The poets that read that spring included Cynthia Macdonald and Ruth Whitman; Rod Jellema and Dolores Kendrick; Ruth Stone and Constance Urdang; Marvin Bell and Shirley Kaufman; and, on April 7, after having declined six times to read at the Library, Adrienne Rich. "The five-hundred-seat Coolidge Auditorium had been sold out for weeks," Michael Kernan wrote, in the *Washington Post*. "We could fill a stadium. It is always this way when Adrienne Rich gives a reading. She presents for many the cutting edge of the feminist movement. . . . It was a powerhouse evening. There couldn't have been more than fifty men in the overflow audience. [Not so, many more, says a witness.] 'I write as woman, lesbian and feminist,' Rich said. 'I make no claim to be universal, neuter or androgynous.'" The event, Kumin observed, was complicated "by the fact that Rich's arthritic knees have reduced her to traveling by wheelchair any distance longer than across a room."

Two weeks later, Kumin went to Worcester to do an Emily Dickinson reading for the American Antiquarian Society. "The day after that," she reported, "we trailered Boomer three hours northeast of D.C. to do her first-ever competitive trail ride, a thirty-miler, which was a day full of high drama. . . . She completed the ride in good condition; she was enormously excited by the other forty-four horses on the ride and gave me five hours and five minutes of some angst."

The Whittall programs also presented an evening of the Chilean poet Gabriela Mistral's work, read by Doris Dana; a lecture by Paul Theroux, on "The Uses and Abuses of Patronage"; and a play, "Chekhov in Love," by Tom Rothfield, produced by Lucille Lortel's White Barn Theatre. On May 4, the Library celebrated the thirtieth anniversary of the Whittall Fund. Cleanth Brooks, who had lectured on the first Whittall program, in 1951, returned to lecture on "American Literature: The Past Thirty Years," dwelling on the fiction of Bellow, Ellison, and Updike, the poetry of Lowell, Bishop, and Warren. The occasion was embellished by the presence of several former Consultants in Poetry, and Roy Basler, and—yet again—Arnold Moss. The next evening in the Coolidge Auditorium belonged to Maxine Kumin: her lecture as Consultant, entitled "'Stamping a Tiny Foot against God,'" devoted to some of the American women poets who wrote between the two wars. Her title was taken, wryly, from a statement by Theodore Roethke, leveling his guns at poetry by women in general. Kumin dealt principally with Amy Lowell, H. D., Teasdale, Millay, Marianne Moore, Rukeyser, and Bogan, and reflected on the ironies of how women poets were perceived by their male peers.

In her brief first "semester" at the Library, Kumin introduced some innovations. She arranged for the sales shop in the Jefferson Building lobby to remain open an extra hour on evenings when there was a poetry reading, so that the poets' books (usually unavailable in local bookstores) could be purchased in time to obtain the poets' autographs. "As a way of evading the long business lunch," she occasionally invited visiting poets from the provinces and Library people to tea in the Poetry Room. In the same civilized demesne, she conducted workshops for high school English teachers and inaugurated the "brown bag lunch," at first for established poets of the Washington area, who were invited to bring a student, friend, or disciple. "Discussion of the individual Xeroxed poems was lively, intelligent and compassionate. . . . The energy generated might well have lighted the Great Hall."

Toward the end of May, Kumin wrote to friend, "Our office is as busy as an ant heap. . . . We all have a marvelous feeling of accomplishment as the spring schedule winds down—so many good workshops, good readings, gatherings of poets and audience—picking up again in the fall will seem quite natural. . . . Having the horse to go to at end of day has provided me with a safety valve, a sane center." And to another friend, May Swenson: "I'll have the whole summer free. Poem ideas sail right past me now but I hope I can gather them in when there's space and steadiness again."

❋

The gradual—and in some respects the sudden—transformation of the Chair of Poetry and the Whittall programs through the 1970s and 1980s came out of an unpredictable synthesis. The Whittall and Huntington funds, invested, each, by the Trust Fund Board and the Bank of New

York under surprisingly improved terms of investment, had appreciated in a spectacular way. The Chair and the Whittall series no longer were bound by the budgetary asceticism of the earlier years. The Library of Congress could take for granted many more seasonal programs; stipends and honoraria that had kept pace with inflation and, in general, better than matched those of the academic world, the theater, and the lecture circuit; a more sophisticated and liberal view of content; and a public that often came in overflow crowds, keyed up, expectant, knowledgeable, critically initiated in a Washington no longer provincial.

Kumin's fall 1981 season, however, began with a familiar sort of commotion. Outraged citizens complained to their congressmen, who passed the outrage on to the Librarian of Congress, about poetry of Kumin's in *Harper's* that contained explicit references to human unmentionables. ("Sperm," a family chronicle, and "Heaven as Anus," a theological and antivivisectionist statement.) A woman in Skaneateles intended to withhold her tax dollars. The Librarian replied, appealing for tolerance; in any case, tax dollars were not involved in a Consultant's poetry. The upset settled down.

As Kumin had promised, the season of readings (after her own reading on October 5) opened on the twenty-sixth with two poets from the West, Richard Shelton (from Arizona; he had run writers' workshops in state prisons) and Leslie Marmon Silko (a Pueblo, from New Mexico) and continued to bring poets from other areas remote from the Eastern Establishment: Madeline DeFrees (Montana) and Patricia Goedicke (Michigan). Smaller audiences, Kumin observed, came faithfully to readings by somewhat less public poets—Hayden Carruth, Eleanor Ross Taylor, Charles Wright—and had a better opportunity to talk to the poets afterward. Also: Audre Lorde and Marge Piercy; Irving Feldman and Lisel Mueller; and two locals, Joyce Kornblatt (a short-story writer) and Lloyd Van Brunt (a poet). Two recent Nobel laureates attracted "almost dismayingly enormous audiences": Isaac Bashevis Singer offered readings, anecdotes, and comments; Czeslaw Milosz read his poems, introduced by William Jay Smith. The Viennese actress Luise Rainer gave a dramatic reading of, unexpectedly, Tennyson's *Enoch Arden,* on a stage draped in black. The centennial of James Joyce's birth, February 2, was celebrated March 10 with a lecture on the writer by Richard Ellmann—followed in successive years by three more annual lectures Ellmann delivered on other great Irish writers, Wilde, Yeats, and Beckett—and celebrated again during the same season by the Irish actress Siobhan McKenna, reading from Joyce for the Library's archive of recordings.

Kumin went forward with the brown bag lunchtime poetry workshops, refined now to embrace women writers only. Some fifty from the Washington orbit attended, ranging from published authors such as Faye Moskowitz and Linda Pastan to members of the Library staff, a closet-poet lawyer, a physicist, a magazine editor, a high-school teacher. In a valedictory summing up she said that enthusiasm for the brown bag workshops had run so high that she hoped her successor would develop a similar format for inviting outsiders to share the hospitality of the Poetry Room. (The brown-bag-lunch principle was picked up again by Whittemore and then by Gwendolyn Brooks.) All in all, Kumin was happy with the local scene. "Washington is not alien territory for the muse," she said to a reporter. "There's an awful lot of good stuff going on here . . . an extraordinary degree of amity among Washington poets. They hang together. You'd be hard-pressed to find that in Manhattan."

✳

Hayden's idea of a conference on science and literature—a dream deferred—remained on the Library's agenda. Broderick acquainted Meredith with the discussions and abortive actions that had occurred. Meredith, at first unenthusiastic, became increasingly intrigued with the possibilities. On May 19, 1980, with the assistance of James Beall, a local poet/scientist (then in the Congressional Office of Technology Assessment, later in the National Academy of Science), Meredith arranged an afternoon's seminar on the influence of science and technology on literature. The idea of a full-scale conference was appealing, but by the time such a gathering could be planned, Meredith's term had expired. The Conference on Science and Literature finally was realized during Kumin's term, on November 9 and 10, 1981, under the Whittall Fund. There were forty participants—scientists, poets from Washington and elsewhere, science writers, science-fiction writers, other writers, literary scholars, philosophers, Library staff members. The principal speakers were the biochemist George Wald, a Nobel laureate, on "Science and the World Beyond," and O. B. Hardison, director of the Folger Shakespeare Library, on "The Poetry of Nothing." The discussants included the British physicist Sir Fred Hoyle; the physiologist Paul D. MacLean; and one of the creators of "Star Trek," Gene Roddenberry. Kumin, Meredith, and Beall each moderated one of the three closed sessions; the only open public event was an evening of readings by Diane Ackerman, Philip Appleman, John Gardner, and Gene Roddenberry. (When Ursula Le Guin was unable to attend, Kumin read one of her stories. Ray Bradbury had also been invited and couldn't come. He was available to lecture at the Library in April, however, presenting "Beyond 1984; What To Do When the Doom Doesn't Arrive.")

In a preface to the publication of the conference, John Broderick commented: "The papers were mere springboards for wide-ranging reactions and counterreactions, some far removed from the topics introduced by the papers. Thus did the Conference . . . take on a life of its own and become a true *conference*. It moved in its own directions, unmindful of the efforts of its moderators to contain it. It was, at times, decidedly immoderate. Participants became peeved or disgusted, and one withdrew himself, only to return to the circle of discussion later. There were disagreements, changing alliances, and obscure harmonies in the dynamics of the meeting. At the end there were no pronouncements, as in diplomatic summits, but there was a sense of resolution and coherence, which each participant would undoubtedly express in his or her own way, in his or her own poetic or scientific vocabulary. The record of the conference is offered, therefore, not as proceedings but as the retrospective scenario of a memorable gathering . . . in which partisans of different perspectives and ways of viewing human existence shouted at, insulted, disagreed with, but ultimately *listened* to each other."

✳

On May 4, Kumin delivered her valedictory lecture in the Coolidge Auditorium: "The Poet and the Mule," a title that unnerved proofreaders looking for the muse. It was an ingenious and refreshing interweaving of scientific, historical, and mythical lore about the mule as a valuable but misunderstood hybrid, with *aperçus* from the world of poetry. Delightful as this essay is, the Library didn't publish it as a chapbook, the usual procedure with Consultants' lectures. It's pleasant to report that "The Poet and the Mule" found print in the spring-summer 1983 issue of the *Ontario Review.*

Toward the end of her term, Kumin received a letter from a young woman poet, unknown to her, who felt she was on the way to suicide. Kumin's reply is memorable. "Your letter makes me very sad—not sad, certainly, that Anne Sexton's poetry is meaningful and vital in your life, but that you see yourself on a parallel course, as you put it. Anne fought all her life to stay sane enough and strong enough to honor the Muse. She never wanted her excesses, needs, addictions to be imitated or made much of. I hope you'll get good professional help. . . . So don't admire only the flippant, narcissistic aspect of Sexton, but appreciate her courage, her talent, her desperate desire to make a contribution to the world—and get going!"

In a note Kumin wrote to a friend on her last day: "I'm going home to the horses & the garden & the blackflies & I mean to write pomes."

❄

Three former Librarians of Congress died during the fiscal year of 1981–82. Luther Evans expired at his home in San Antonio, Texas, on December 23, 1981, at the age of seventy-nine. His last visit to the Library had been on the occasion of the "MacLeish Era" celebration in October 1979. A number of Evans's colleagues from the United States and abroad gathered with his widow and his son at a luncheon in the Whittall Pavilion on April 28 and discussed his influence on the acquisitions and scholarly activities of the Library and his contributions, through UNESCO, to international understanding.

Archibald MacLeish died on the night of April 20, 1982, in Massachusetts General Hospital, Boston, two and a half weeks before his ninetieth birthday. He, too, had not returned to the Library of Congress since the festivities there in his honor. He declined President and Mrs. Carter's invitation to the poetry readings at the White House in January 1980, for the reason of advancing age, and he attended none of the meetings of the Council of Scholars, of which he was honorary chairman. He remained at his farm near Conway, Massachusetts, writing and corresponding, until early 1982, when he slipped on a patch of ice and broke his elbow. In late March, MacLeish entered the hospital for exploratory surgery unrelated to the elbow accident, and died within the month.

L. Quincy Mumford died on August 15, 1982, in Washington, where he had continued to live. He was in his seventy-ninth year. At a memorial service in St. Alban's Church, in Cleveland Park, the Deputy Librarian of Congress, William J. Welsh, delivered an appreciation of Mumford's twenty years of service. In a ceremony on December 13, a large assembly hall on the sixth floor of the Madison Memorial Building—one of the most notable accomplishments of the Mumford era—was named in his honor. Plans were announced in 1983 for honoring in similar fashion the other former Librarians of Congress who had served in this century: as renovation of the Thomas Jefferson Building proceeds, two pavilions on its second floor, which will serve as common rooms for scholars who come to the Library, will be named the Herbert Putnam Pavilion and the Luther H. Evans Pavilion, and the present Congressional Reading Room will be assigned to the Council of Scholars and renamed the Archibald MacLeish Pavilion.

The last of the Honorary Consultantships in American Letters petered out in 1982: the one Stanley Kunitz had held since 1976. Two other Honorary Consultantships were terminated by death: Frederick R. Goff's, in Early Printed Books, and Anna Freud's, in Sigmund Freud Studies. Three Honorary Consultantships survived: those of Edwin G. Beal, in East Asian Bibliography, Morris N. Young, in the Literature of Magic, and Walter W. Ristow, in U.S. Cartographic History.

❊

On September 13, Anthony Hecht began his year as the twenty-sixth Consultant in Poetry in time to participate that evening in a memorial for MacLeish in the Coolidge Auditorium. Boorstin introduced the program, speaking for the Library to members of the MacLeish family who were present; and Broderick read from MacLeish's 1943 essay "The Unimagined America." Poems of MacLeish's and of their own were

read by Julia Randall (she chose "You, Andrew Marvell," her "favorite
lyric of the century," and other early poems), Samuel Hazo (a long-time
friend; he chose "Years of the Dog," recalling Paris of the 1920s, and
the poem about Hemingway's death), William Meredith (he read some
of the late "Songs for Eve"), and Hecht (his choices included "Epistle
to Be Left in the Earth"; and he read two choruses from his own trans-
lation of "Oedipus at Colonus"). MacLeish's voice was heard in a 1963
recording, from the archive, of "Ars Poetica." The memorial evening
closed with the actor Pat Hingle reciting passages from his role as
"J.B." in the original New York production of the poetic drama, based
on the Book of Job, for which MacLeish had received his third Pulitzer
Prize (1958). Hecht's involvement was, of course, a consequence of his
appointment to the Chair; he hadn't known MacLeish and wasn't a
particular admirer of his poetry and polemics. To an interviewer, Hecht
observed that MacLeish's *The Irresponsibles,* the extended essay he
wrote during his first year as Librarian of Congress, was a notably con-
servative statement, celebrating the life force and urging a poetry of
uplift and patriotism, not too distant from what Robert Hillyer espoused
in his articles on the Bollingen Prize awarded to Pound.

One has to regard with perplexity MacLeish's attitude toward that
furiously debated award. In his Aristotelian dialogue *Poetry and Opin-
ion*—with three subtitles, "The Pisan Cantos of Ezra Pound," "A
Dialog on the Role of Poetry," and "Mr. Bollingen/Mr. Saturday"—
which he wrote at Conway in spring 1950, he seems, after rehearsing
the argument on both sides, to come down on the side of Mr. Bollingen,
i.e., the Fellows in American Letters of the Library of Congress.
Twenty-four years later, MacLeish published an essay in, indeed, the
Saturday Review of Literature: "The Venetian Grave," a kind of ironic
memorial to Pound, a year or so after his death. MacLeish gave a brief
summary of the Bollingen Prize episode: "a group of [Pound's] friends,
including a number of the most distinguished American poets of the
time, conceived the idea of a new national prize for poetry to be
awarded by the Library of Congress through a jury of notables who
would select Pound as the first recipient, thus dramatizing his situation
and putting the government, and particularly the Department of Justice,
in an awkward if not untenable position." The implication of a deliber-

ate chain of events, contrived by the Fellows to foster the establishment /
of the Bollingen Prize, its award to Pound, and consequent embarrass-
ment for the Department of Justice, is not borne out by the record and
has been repudiated by three who as Fellows had participated in the
balloting: Shapiro, Thorp, and Warren. MacLeish's statement was
quoted, along with Hillyer's *S.R.L.* articles, to support a theory of con-
spiracy in a recent study of the case, *The Roots of Treason,* by E. F.
Torrey, a St. Elizabeths Hospital psychiatrist.

All that aside, let the last word be what Broderick said in a memorial
tribute he gave to the American Philosophical Society: "Few great men
of the twentieth century were as approachable as Archibald MacLeish,
as interested in the work of those many years his junior, as unconcerned
about past achievement in the expectation of grander accomplishment
tomorrow. . . . His eye was ever on what lay beyond the next horizon.
That was his greatness, and this is our loss."

❅

Hecht brought a distinctive style to the Chair in Poetry. What a critic
(Brad Leithauser, in the *New York Review of Books*) recently said about
Hecht as poet fills out a picture: "Most of his work is 'formal' in two
senses—elevated and patterned. He is probably the grandest of our con-
temporary poets in tone and dignity. With his ramified syntax, his ven-
turesome Latinate vocabulary, and his readiness to retrieve words and
constructions that verge on archaisms, he presents a voice of unexam-
pled refinement." Hecht's rather Augustan presence, his rather elegant,
courteous, and affable address, reflected his role as University Orator
at the University of Rochester, where he had been professor of poetry
and rhetoric since 1967. The University Orator composes and, at the
commencement exercises, delivers the citations—sometimes miniature
prose poems—for the honorary degrees the university is bestowing.
New York born, Hecht in his manner reminds some of his older ac-
quaintances of John Crowe Ransom, whose courtliness and poetic ex-
ample he experienced while at the Kenyon School of Letters after World
War II (during which, as an infantry rifleman, he saw action in Ger-
many, was with the first troops to enter the concentration camps, and,
later, had occupation duty in Japan). He taught at the universities of

Iowa and Minnesota and at Washington University (St. Louis); princi-
pally, however, his academic life has been in the East, as a student at
Bard, Columbia, and N.Y.U. (under Tate—who nominated him to take
his post the next year), and a teacher at Harvard, Yale, and Rochester,
with interludes in Europe. In 1951, Hecht won the first Prix de Rome,
a fellowship given to young writers of promise for a year's residence at
the American Academy in Rome, awarded by the American Academy
of Arts and Letters. (Its rosette is visible in his lapel.) Between 1954
and 1979 he published four volumes of poetry. In Leithauser's view,
Hecht belongs to the small group of "truly accomplished contemporary
American poets . . . whose members have discovered some fruitful
way to dwell upon the special horrors of the age. A plausible case could
be made that his four books . . . record a journey from darkness into
greater darkness."

Perhaps influenced by Nemerov's pseudo-Annual Report (which
Nemerov's successors in the Chair customarily read as initiation), both
of Hecht's reports are more in the nature of satirical essays than ac-
counts of his tenure. (From the beginning he was engaged to come for
two years. Tearing his family away from home for only a year was an
unattractive prospect. His wife, Helen, is a professional writer, and
their son, Evan, was then ten.) The humor in the first report is close to
black. About the city of Washington his reactions tended to the depre-
catory. While he appreciated the art museums, the Kennedy Center and
its musical offerings, "the comparative moribundity of the city's literary
life" struck him painfully. In contrast, the advantages of New York City
for a poet and poetry-lover merited an appreciative page. "The plain
fact is that Washington does not yet furnish the sort of loyal, enthusias-
tic, and informed audience that poetry can count on in New York and
on certain first-class university and college campuses." Poets invited to
read in Washington are in danger of being "abashed by the sort of
[middle-brow] audiences they are likely to face here . . . and the Con-
sultant will in all likelihood feel some chagrin . . . in behalf of the
invited guest, as well as for the Library." A Consultant had to console
himself with the knowledge that the invited poets' readings become a
valuable part of the literary archives of the nation. Most awkward,
Hecht felt, is the misconception that "a consultant is there to be con-

sulted" and, at a public institution, to be consulted by the public.

On the Whittall series, the poets who were invited to read at Hecht's suggestion were Carolyn Forché and George Starbuck; Alfred Corn and Carl Dennis; Richard Murphy and Jon Stallworthy; and Alicia Ostriker and Dave Smith. Joseph Brodsky was also invited to read his poems, with Hecht reading translations. When Hecht fell ill, and a substitute was proposed, Brodsky declined; the program was postponed to the next year. There were two other international programs, both introduced by Hecht—Edward Kamau Brathwaite, from Jamaica, reading his poems, and an evening of Scandinavian poetry, presenting Paal Helge-Haugen, Sigurdur A. Magnússon, Henrik Nordbrandt, Pentti Saaritsa, and Göran Sonnevi, reading from their work. Two joint literary and musical presentations, both British in theme: "Music in Tudor and Stuart England," by the Deller Consort, and "An Evening with Queen Victoria," by the English actress Prunella Scales. The British theme continued with a lecture and reading by a former Consultant, Stephen Spender, a lecture by the playwright Tom Stoppard, and Richard Ellmann's second lecture in his Irish series, "Oscar Wilde at Oxford." Another former Consultant, William Jay Smith, presented a dramatization of his memoir *Army Brat*. Two American writers: Ralph Ellison, reading from his work in progress, and Donald Barthelme, lecturing. Hecht, who had already appeared on the Coolidge platform in the MacLeish memorial, opened the literary season with a reading of his own work on October 4, and closed it on May 2 with a lecture, "Robert Lowell," that took as a point of departure the biography by Ian Hamilton published earlier in the year. That poet, the sixth Consultant, Hecht said in peroration, "is, first of all, clearly and singularly, Robert Lowell—which, as a poet, is not a bad thing to be; and . . . through his constant moral and artistic endeavor to situate himself in the midst of our representative modern crises, both personal and political, he has led, for us—as it were, in our behalf—a life of Allegory; and his works are the comments on it." For Hecht himself, his year at the Library was crowned in February by the award of the Bollingen Prize in Poetry, which he shared with John Hollander. (Coincidentally, or so one assumes, Hecht and Hollander had some years earlier shared the invention of a comic prosodic form called the double dactyl, composed of two four-line stanzas in dactylic feet—one stressed syllable followed by two unstressed—with other technical intricacies. Their collection of double dactyls was published as *Jiggery-pokery* in 1967.)

During 1982–83, Hecht undertook no distant journeys for readings and lectures, but he gave generously of his time in the Washington area, reading and talking in the schools and receiving a procession of visitors, domestic and foreign, during the half of the week he spent at the Poetry Office. He joined the meetings of the Council of Scholars. He responded faithfully to the "mind-boggling" quantities of verse submitted for evaluation, "or, more accurately, for approval." "All too often," he remarked, "it comes from people terribly handicapped, and in conditions of such pronounced despair that they are forced into the desperate hope that a straightforward account of their anguish will *ipso facto* be poetry." Hecht's policy, and his advice to his successors, was "to err on the side of patience, good will, and generosity." (A sample from the file: "Your poems clearly rise out of deeply felt and compassionate convictions. May success attend your every effort.")

✢

Hecht's second year in the Chair was richer in commemoration and ceremony. On October 17, 1984, he represented the Library of Congress at a requiem service for W. H. Auden, at the Cathedral of St. John the Divine, in New York. Derek Walcott delivered the eulogy. Next day, Hecht joined twelve other poets and Christopher Isherwood in a reading of Auden's poems at the Guggenheim Museum in New York. On November 1, in the afternoon, he was moderator for a symposium on modern Greek poetry at the Library, which commemorated the centenary of the birth of Nikos Kazantzakis. In the evening of that day Hecht introduced Reed Whittemore, who, honoring another centenary, gave a lecture on "William Carlos Williams: The Happy Genius of the Household." Both Consultants mentioned Williams's abortive appointment to the Chair. Hecht: ". . . had only things turned out a little more happily than they did, [Williams] might himself have been consultant in poetry to the Library of Congress." Whittemore: "He was about as far left as Al Smith (whom he voted for in 1928), and I hope that no one at the Library now would take seriously the Red charge against him that the Librarian of Congress, Luther Evans, did take seriously in 1952. The Library had nothing to do with the charge against him, but it bent to the charge, and produced the result that he was unable to serve as a consultant at all. . . . My point is that the political allegation was a misfire. Williams did not need, did not want, the Communist party or any other party to help him be a troublemaker. He wanted to be a troublemaker on his own. That makes him a true, totally loyal American." Whittemore's tribute was brash, expert, funny, learned, irreverent (but not of WCW), and altogether touching. Thirty years had gone by in a wink.

Going on with Hecht's occasions: On November 14 and 15, he introduced the poets who read at the celebration of the fiftieth anniversary of the Academy of American Poets, of which more later. On December 8, at the American Academy and Institute of Arts and Letters, he met with the committee that discussed the Richard Rodgers awards to encourage the development of the musical theater. On March 15, 1984, he went out to St. Elizabeths Hospital and gave a paper to psychotherapists and doctors attending a Bibliotherapy Conference. He noted, on the one hand, the rise of madness among poets since the industrial revolution and, on the other, the therapeutic benefit of writing poetry, particularly of prosodic complexity, for some poets. At the end of April he chaired the Library's conference on George Orwell and *Nineteen Eighty-Four,* of which more will also be said. On May 16, Hecht attended the annual ceremonial of the American Academy and Institute of Arts and Letters, in New York. And, on June 2, he was at Alice Tully Hall, in Lincoln Center, where the New York Philharmonic performed the world premiere of *The Seven Deadly Sins,* composed by Robert Beaser with a text by Hecht.

On the Whittall series, there were readings by Peter Davison and Nancy Willard; Hecht, with the pianist Frank Glazer, in "An Evening of Literature and Music," alternating poems and compositions; Ray Handy, in a dramatic reading of David Jones's war novel *In Parenthesis;* Sydney Lea and David St. John; Shirley Hazzard, reading her prose; Amy Clampitt and Robert Pinsky; Bernard Malamud, reading from his fiction; and Joseph Brodsky, with Hecht reading translations of his poems. Richard Ellmann gave his third lecture on Irish writers: "W. B.

Yeats's Second Puberty," which induced a few sedate, Whittallesque murmurs; Northrop Frye lectured on "The Social Authority of the Writer." There were two dramatic events, each for two nights: in February, Pat Hingle in "Thomas Edison: Reflections of a Genius"; and, in March, the Harold Clurman Theatre's production (coproduced with Lucille Lortel) of three short plays by Samuel Beckett, "Ohio Impromptu," "Catastrophe," and "What Where."

Near the end of his Consultantship, Hecht told an interviewer that the only disappointment during his term had been the poor attendance at some of the literary events. "Though small," he said, "it is a faithful and a good audience, well-educated and conscientious. And undoubtedly committed in a very special way—the way in which the special audience for chamber music is committed, for example. It's not the great, mass public, but it's a big enough audience to keep art going at a very high level of performance and of practice."

✳

The celebration of the fiftieth anniversary of the Academy of American Poets, on November 14 and 15, 1983, was, after the National Poetry Festival in 1962, the Library's starriest poetic event. Hecht, who was the interlocutor, likened the occasion to certain mammoth films of the early 1930s—*Paramount on Parade, Warner Brothers' Show of Shows*—in which the studio aimed to exhibit every star under contract. Fifteen poets were in this cast. They included all the twelve Chancellors of the Academy, of whom seven had been or would be Consultants in Poetry: Fitzgerald, Hecht, Hoffman, Kunitz, Meredith, Nemerov, and Warren; the other five Chancellors were John Hollander, James Merrill, May Swenson, David Wagoner, and Richard Wilbur. The three other stars, not yet Chancellors (though each had been elected to an Academy Fellowship), were W. S. Merwin, Mark Strand, and Mona Van Duyn. The event was one of the programs in the series sponsored by the Whittall Fund, with supplements from other sources.

At its golden anniversary, the Academy—under the leadership of its president from the beginning, Marie Bullock—was a highly honored body, mature in more than the chronological sense, abreast with the contemporary currents of American poetry, whatever its "winged horse" logo might suggest. Its officers, the members of its board of directors, and its numerous sponsors had always, of course, been predominantly people of means and social status; and the Academy's fiscal position, based on its permanent trust fund, had continued to improve with the happiest sort of vitality. Thus, the stipend that its fellowship "for distinguished poetic achievement" carries, originally $5,000, was doubled in 1969. The twelve Chancellors (appointed permanently) elect the Fellows. Beginning with Edgar Lee Masters in 1946, nearly fifty poets have won the fellowship—including, among the Consultants, Frost, Williams, Aiken, Bogan, Adams (twice), Tate, Bishop, Kunitz, Eberhart, Hecht, Nemerov, and Hayden.

The Academy's other benefactions, at the present time, include the Walt Whitman Award, which supports the publication of an American poet's *first* volume of poetry, chosen by a single judge, provides for distribution of 1,200 copies, and carries a prize of $1,000 (funded originally by the Copernicus Society and now chiefly by the NEA, and won by a dozen poets since 1975) and the American Poetry Abroad Award, funded by James A. Michener and enabling the publication in England of three books of American poetry annually, chosen by three of the Chancellors, and won by nine poets, or rather books, since 1982 (including books by Robert Penn Warren twice). The Academy since 1954 has expended nearly $200,000 in sponsoring annual $100 poetry prizes at 130 colleges and universities in the United States and issuing anthologies of the winning student poems. Through grants from the A. W. Mellon Foundation, the Academy has carried on a program of inviting poetry societies around the country to become affiliates. In 1966, the Academy initiated the "Poetry-in-the-Schools" program, as a series of classroom readings for students and courses for teachers, which became nationally successful and has grown without Academy support. In New York City, the Academy sponsors a rich program of readings, workshops for children and teenagers, classes for high school teachers, and literary-historical walking tours. Of all this remarkable activity Marie Bullock had been the prime mover. That her mentor in the establishment of the Academy of American Poets in 1934 was the first Consultant in Poetry, Joseph Auslander, is a fact virtually forgotten today—though scarcely by Marie Bullock. As Hecht observed, "she has done more for the art of poetry and individual poets over the years than any institution whatever."

The celebration in November 1983 took the form of two evenings of readings, by seven poets each evening, on the fourteenth and fifteenth, in a full Coolidge Auditorium—the adjoining Whittall Pavilion, with closed-circuit television, was also full. A *Washington Post* reporter, Chip Brown, observed the events on what he called the Spartan stage, where seven poets sat in a crescent. "As each poet proceeded to the lectern, the crowd hushed. Some took notes, some followed along in copies of the poets' books. Robert Fitzgerald, the foremost translator of Homer, read of Colorado, and of his own 'minuscule part in the sway of tranquil grandeur.' Mona Van Duyn read 'letters' from her father, sick and late in life, that marked the change wrought in him by a bur-geoning passion for birds, a poem that was closed by a line in his daughter's voice: 'So the world woos its children back for an evening kiss.' The audience occasionally gasped at eloquence or insights. Pain was visible when Stanley Kunitz read his poem about a beached and dying whale in whose flesh people had carved their initials. At other moments, such as when Howard Nemerov offered a riddle, the audito-rium resounded with laughter: 'Why are stamps adorned with kings and presidents?' 'That we may lick their hinder parts and thump their heads.'" At the reception afterward, in the Great Hall, "Fans, disciples, writers and autograph hounds toting satchels of slender volumes plucked at fruit plates, sipped fizzy wine, and swarmed about the book-jacket faces. . . ." At the unpublic social occasions—luncheons, recep-tions, interludes at the bars on Pennsylvania Avenue, snacks of coffee and bagels in the Poetry Room, a grand dinner party given by Marie Bullock at the Sulgrave Club—the poets and their consorts might have been attending a class reunion, or a rather refined Shriners' convention. For one outside the Freemasonry, it seemed an intrusion to break into any conversation.

To Hecht, who had introduced each poet (and read for William Mer-edith, on stage but prevented by a recent stroke from coming to the lectern), the great thing was the punctilio, the dispatch, of the readers, observing each the twelve-minute time limit. "When so many gifted and important poets on a stage are asked to read for only a brief time, you can't be sure that temperament or self-intoxication won't take over. They all did read well, with cheerful wit and intelligence. Nobody tried to hog the spotlight." More than one member of the audience remarked on Hecht's aplomb as introducer: "as fine to listen to as some of the poems," was a remark overheard. He was, of course, a University Orator.

One imagines that Gertrude Whittall would have applauded what went on in the Coolidge that evening, though she would not have known more than a handful of the poets or have heard them read in her day. Certainly the clarity, the sonority, the volume, the theatricality, with which most of them spoke would have pleased her as much as March, Meredith (B.), and Auslander used to please her. Is it experience on the reading-and-lecture circuit, so much a part of a poet's career since the 1950s, that has raised the level of elocution, of platform persona, of extroverted communication? Still, the most effective readers at the celebration, by Mrs. Whittall's or anyone else's standards, were two of the eldest, Fitzgerald and Kunitz, who had come up in the old school.

✿

But what would Mrs. Whittall have made of the final program on "her" 1983–84 series, the Conference on George Orwell and *Nineteen Eighty-Four*? For a woman born in 1867, the date 1984 must have been beyond contemplation. Could this book, or anything that Orwell wrote, ever have caught her attention? Subjects like Burma, squalor in Paris and London, British poverty, Catalonia, Newspeak? (Aspidistra? Perhaps.) In any event, he wasn't a poet or a dramatist—not a writer who, whatever his subject-matter, conceivably could have been the subject of an early Whittall program. The Orwell conference was the decisive, the archetypal *post-Whittall* event of the Whittall series.

Originated by the Library administration—chiefly by the literary scholar John Broderick—the conference for two days considered a man, a novel, a date, a political and social worldview. The event and the year were resonant. "An annual report for the year 1984 can hardly avoid some passing reference to George Orwell's novel *1984*," the Librarian of Congress began his yearly accounting. "The Library of Con-

[407]

gress paid its respects to the (possibly temporary) public fascination with his most famous book. . . . Beyond that, so far as the Library is concerned, the parallels between the book and the year do not seem particularly apropos. The technologically oriented society depicted in Orwell's book is fixed and definite, with only the slightest opportunities for freedom of thought and action and personal initiative, and these few systematically suppressed. The Library of Congress in 1984, on the other hand, was a beehive of intellectual activity, the year witnessing the culmination of years of planning . . . and the initiation of new ventures. . . . The year 1984 and Orwell's *1984* have possibly one thing in common: widespread use of technology. . . . 'The mutability of the past' is a central tenet of the society Orwell depicts. Works of nonfiction are continually revised at the so-called Ministry of Truth, and new fictional works are composed by machines according to standards set by the Party. Not so at the Library of Congress, [which] seeks to preserve the wisdom (and folly) of the past in virtually whatever form it is recorded, an ambitious and sometimes daunting task."

Hecht, as chairman of the conference, observed that it had been undertaken "in the hope of doing both honor and justice to the man and his work." The speakers, before an audience in the Mumford Room, were a mix of British and American literary scholars—including some from one country who were pursuing careers in the other. On the first afternoon, Peter Davison, a professor at the University of Canterbury and editor of the projected *Complete Works* of Orwell, gave a paper on some textual problems of the edition. In the evening, two papers on the author's personality: Jenni (Daiches) Calder, who taught in the Education Department of the Royal Scottish Museum, Edinburgh, was concerned with "who and what is the man revealed in the writings?" and Peter Stansky, of Stanford University, talked on Orwell's "Englishness" as a member of the "lower upper middle class." On May Day morning, three scholars discussed the book itself: the Irish critic Denis Donoghue, professor at New York University, spoke on the novel as a work of "politics and fable"; Alfred Kazin, professor at the City University of New York, discussed it in the political context of its time; Jeffrey Meyers, professor at the University of Colorado, was concerned with *Nineteen Eighty-Four* in its literary setting. The afternoon's events closed with papers on the book's meaning in 1984, by Bernard Crick, professor at the University of Sheffield, and Nathan Scott, Jr., professor of religious studies and English at the University of Virginia. In the final discussions, Ezra Pound's name surfaced, perhaps inevitably in a consideration of moral and aesthetic dualism. One discussant rose to observe that, "regarding the Bollingen award . . . , Orwell said that if the judges thought Pound's poetry to have the greatest literary merit, no objection to his fascist ideas should impede the award, although Orwell added that he himself thought the poetry greatly overrated."

The conference saw print a year later, in a paperback book of 160 pages, containing the full-length addresses (which had been delivered in abbreviated versions), summaries of the floor discussions, and a 28-page annotated list of references. (The Library's "1984" event was not, of course, the only celebration of the Orwell year, not even in Washington. The Smithsonian Institution jumped the gun with a four-day observance in mid-December 1983, entitled "The Road After 1984: High Technology and Human Freedom. A Tribute to George Orwell." It opened with an academic procession across the Mall, bagpipe music, and peals of the Old Post Office bells. There were other conferences during 1984, at Stanford, Manhattan College, London, the Hebrides, Italy, and elsewhere. Few if any of them rivaled the Library's in intellectual quality and the distinction of its lecturers.)

In the Poetry Room on May 7, Hecht was honored at a dinner the guests at which included Robert Fitzgerald, his and Hecht's friends the classicist Bernard Knox and the archaeologist William MacDonald, Boorstin, Broderick, and their wives. It preceded Hecht's lecture in the Coolidge, on "The Pathetic Fallacy," a consideration of the literary device deplored (and named) by Ruskin, which, in literary use, credits nature with the feelings of human beings. The lecture again brought scholarship of a high level of refinement to the Whittall audience. The Librarian's appointment of Fitzgerald as the next Consultant in Poetry was announced on the occasion, and he was introduced to an audience many of whom remembered the reading he had given from the same stage the previous fall. His had been one of the names on a short list of prospects, and Boorstin was just then reading the Fitzgerald *Aeneid*.

✳

Fitzgerald was, of course, best known as the translator of great classics
and would have been expected to bring a new emphasis to the Whittall
programs. He was born in western New York state, the son of aspiring
actors. Both his parents had traveled in a road company that performed
a Catholic morality play, "The Sign of the Cross," before they settled
in Springfield, Illinois, where he grew up. His gift for graceful conver-
sation, for admirable platform reading, it would appear, had theatrical
roots. He lost his mother when he was three, his younger brother when
he was eight, his father when he was seventeen. Someone close to him
wrote, "A large part of Robert's patience, of his readiness to accept
people as he found them, and of his capacity to sustain a reassuring
poise in the face of difficult circumstance derived from those early years
. . . of pain and love." At the Choate School, he was a pupil of the poet
Dudley Fitts, who was also his teacher later at Harvard (as was Hillyer).
Fitts became his mentor, collaborator, and friend. After his Harvard
A.B., 1933, Fitzgerald was a reporter on the *New York Herald Tribune*
and then, 1936–49, a writer for *Time,* except for the war years spent
on Navy duty. He published his first volume, *Poems,* in 1935, and the
next year his first translation of Greek drama—Euripides' *Alcestis,* in
collaboration with Fitts. Later he translated Sophocles' *Oedipus Rex*
and *Antigone* (with Fitts) and *Oedipus at Colonus.* In 1949, after leav-
ing *Time,* Fitzgerald went to Princeton as Blackmur's assistant in crea-
tive writing and for two years played an important part in the Princeton
Seminars in Literary Criticism, of which he wrote a chronicle for the
sponsoring Rockefeller Foundation. (The seminars were the first stage
of what became the Christian Gauss Seminars, and Jacques Maritain's
contribution was to be transformed into the inaugural volume of the
A. W. Mellon Lectures on the Fine Arts, at the National Gallery of Art,
which are published in the Bollingen Series. Fitzgerald's richly com-
mentative record of the seminars, prepared for the Rockefeller Foun-
dation, dropped out of sight in the 1950s. Fitzgerald found a carbon
copy of the typescript thirty years later, and it was published only in
1985, as *Enlarging the Change.*)

Beginning in 1953, Fitzgerald with his large family lived eleven years in Italy, supported by foundation grants and publisher's advances, working on his translations of Homer: *The Odyssey*, published in 1961 (and dedicated "to my sons and daughters"), *The Iliad* in 1974, both appraised as masterpieces. During that time he also translated works of Paul Valéry and St.-John Perse for the Bollingen Series and occasionally came back to the States for teaching appointments. In 1964 he succeeded MacLeish as Boylston Professor of Rhetoric and Oratory at Harvard; his teaching was renowned. He became emeritus in 1981, and two years later published his translation of *The Aeneid*. Fitzgerald continued to write and publish his own poetry. He recorded both poems and translations for the Library of Congress in 1948, read from his *Odyssey* on the Whittall series in 1974, and joined in the Academy of American Poets celebrations in 1969 and 1983. A long friendship with Allen Tate had, in its way, also brought him closer to the Library during earlier years.

Ezra Pound he had met at Rapallo before World War II—one of the "young writers and scholars who appeared from time to time to enroll at the 'Ezuversity,'" David Heymann wrote in his Pound biography. In the 1950s, Fitzgerald's concern over Pound's ideas found expression in a series of bitter letters and finally in an article in *Encounter* (July 1956). But he was one of the signers of the statement in defense of Pound in 1958, and subsequently he went to see him after Pound's return to Italy.

Fitzgerald—according to his friend Hecht, who had strongly favored him as his successor—was at first ambivalent about taking the Consultantship. He had passed through an arduous stage of his life: had completed four years of labor on *The Aeneid;* had nearly died of cancer, and survived through radiotherapy; had been divorced and remarried; had moved from Cambridge to a suburb of New Haven. He had begun to write his memoirs—his first concern. He agreed, finally, to accept the Chair for a single year, on special terms; remaining at home in Connecticut, he would come to the Library for a week each month. He was seventy-four, the eldest poet to be appointed since Untermeyer.

Literature in general, Fitzgerald promised, not only translation, would be the focus of his Consultantship. Poetry would have pride of place. As John Hollander observed, Fitzgerald "could not have been so remarkable a translator without having been so fine a poet, and he stood out among his contemporaries for an ever-growing and deepening mastery of a high elegiac tone. . . ." And Hecht, thinking of the famous course in prosody that Fitzgerald taught at Harvard, remarked that "Fitzgerald has a keen sense of the availability of the whole range of English poetry for adaption to whatever dramatic purpose he has in mind." He cited in illustration the way Fitzgerald translated the Song of the Sirens, in *Odyssey* xii—imitative of the songs of such Elizabethans as Thomas Campion.

In early June, signs of Fitzgerald's illness reappeared. (He insisted nevertheless on delivering the commencement lecture at St. John's College, in Annapolis, and making the journey there and back by train.) By mid-summer it was evident to him that he couldn't expect to open the season at the Library, though he believed that treatment would enable him to come to Washington later. For the first time in the history of the Chair of Poetry, the Library had recourse to an interim appointment: of Reed Whittemore, who had been Consultant for the year 1964–65 and had been professor of English at the University of Maryland, in College Park, since 1968. He had retired the past spring. (On May 9, two nights after the announcement of Fitzgerald's appointment, Whittemore had been honored by a reception, sponsored by his university, at the Folger Shakespeare Library. Before a large and friendly crowd, fourteen members of the Washington poetry community—including Ann Darr, Eugene McCarthy, May Miller Sullivan, Linda Pastan, John Pauker, Henry Taylor—read their poetry, and Whittemore read his. He was praised for his singular contributions to the cause of poetry and especially of young poets in the capital.) The interim appointment was announced on September 6, and soon afterward Whittemore went up to meet Fitzgerald for the first time and talk with him about the job. "I was charmed and touched by his warmth and good will," Whittemore recalled.

On October 1, Whittemore was honored at the now traditional luncheon in the Pavilion, attended by some of his family, old friends (including Joan Mondale and James Angleton), local poets, and Library dignitaries. That evening he opened the literary season, reading from his poems and from Fitzgerald's translations and poems and a moving memoir Fitzgerald had written about his father. Next day he wrote Fitzgerald reporting on both events—something he continued to do, as the season went on. And the Library sent Fitzgerald tapes of some of the programs.

Fitzgerald had been instrumental in planning three of the Whittall programs that fall, which Whittemore now presented, drawing upon introductions that Fitzgerald had written. On October 3 the British diplomat, poet, and translator Sir Charles Johnston read from his work, including his verse rendering of Pushkin's *Eugene Onegin,* which Fitzgerald called "a literary wonder, . . . an exquisite version." His friend Annie Dillard, a lively writer from Pittsburgh via Wesleyan University, gave a reading from her fiction on December 3, during which she made a charming pitch for John Hersey's performance the next evening. Hersey read from his novel *The Call,* then forthcoming. Unhappily, forty minutes into his reading he fell over in a faint. A doctor (Hersey's nephew) and a nurse in the audience attended him within seconds; the Coolidge curtain was swung shut for the first time in some years; the rescue squad arrived promptly, and after a day in hospital Hersey was pronounced sound.

The other literary programs on the Whittall series, arranged by the Library, included a reading from fiction-in-progress by the Canadian writer Robertson Davies; a poetry reading by Russell Edson and the publisher James Laughlin (a friend of Fitzgerald's since Harvard undergraduate days); a reading and talk by Maya Angelou (vastly attended, and described by one who was there as "not so much a reading as a happening"); "Two Evenings of English Literature"—John Wain giving the Samuel Johnson Memorial Lecture on December 10 (an observance suggested by Senator Charles Mathias) and reading from his own work the next night; a reading of her fiction by Toni Cade Bambara; two local poets, Grace Cavalieri and Robert Sargent, reading their poems; Richard Ellmann, delivering "Samuel Beckett: Nayman of Noland," the concluding lecture of his four on Irish writers; Tess Gallagher and Michael Ryan, reading their poems. There were two dramatic presentations: the British actors Gabriel Woolf and Rosalind Shanks performed a program they had compiled from the writings of "George Eliot: The Female Shakespeare, So To Speak," on October 23; and, on April 22 and 23,

[413]

Lucille Lortel's White Barn Theatre—now as much a Library tradition
as Moss had become—gave "Sprechen Sie Brecht (a Brechtspiel)"—a
cabaret evening of poetry, music, and dialogue from the works of Ber-
tolt Brecht, with Kurt Weill's music, directed by David Schechter. And
Whittemore presided at two bag lunch workshops for literary program
organizers, in the Poetry Room.

The program of this ever more expansive Whittall year included three
"national" features. In late November, "An Evening of Postwar Poetry
of the Netherlands and Flanders" featured four poets, Hugo Claus, Ger-
rit Kouwenaar, Judith Herzberg, and Cees Nooteboom, reading their
work, with translations by James S. Holmes and William Jay Smith.
Coincident with the Modern Language Association convention in
Washington over the Christmas season, a program devoted to St.-John
Perse included a lecture by Edouard Morot-Sir, friend of the poet and
former diplomat, on science in the poet's work, and a reading of Perse's
poems by Jean Guillou, in French, and Whittemore, in English. The
readers had thoroughly rehearsed an experimental presentation, rapidly
switching back and forth between French and English. Whittemore,
"no great fan of bilingual shows," reported that "I had my faith renewed
in their possibilities. . . . We were (we thought) terrific." On April 2,
in the Whittall Pavilion, a two-session program on Israeli poetry today
presented the poets Karen Alkalay-Gut, Yehuda Amichai, Dan Pagis,
and Nathan Yonathan—born, respectively, in Germany, Rumania, Rus-
sia, and England—discussing with Whittemore questions of cultural
and linguistic identity, and in the evening reading their poetry. There
were two programs that interlinked the arts. In February, the two Whit-
tall funds, for literature and for music, jointly sponsored two programs
on Arnold Schoenberg's song cycle *Pierrot Lunaire:* a lecture by An-
drew Porter, the *New Yorker's* music critic, on his translation of the
work, and a concert presenting the Schoenberg work and others. In
March, in the Mumford Room, the artist Grace Hartigan lectured, with
slides, on her collaboration with the late poet Frank O'Hara, on the
abstract expressionist art scene in Greenwich Village in the 1950s.
Whittemore observed, "I had hoped that she would move beyond
O'Hara and her work with him and deal with the complicated artistic
challenge of poet-painter at large. . . . Though the result was good and

the audience . . . was in part a new one for the Whittall series, I think that the possibilities for such a program have yet to be explored."

In his end-of-year report, Whittemore wrote that "I did not this year choose for myself a special project, . . . but before the year was out I found that I had a project anyway, a translation project. It was a project that kept appearing like a ghost in the Poetry Room, brought there every week or two by visitors from abroad, writers from France, Holland, Israel, East Germany, Lithuania, Norway, Yugoslavia, Bulgaria, China, Korea, India, Quebec, Mexico, Chile, Argentina, Colombia, El Salvador, Montserrat, Peru, Uruguay, and Bangladesh. The chief subject discussed with these visitors was, always and forever, translation, and who or what in the United States was 'doing anything' about it. Here sits the Library of Congress, with probably the best international collection in the world of the world's literatures (both in print and on tape), yet the Library's role with its collection is passive only, the role of archivist. . . . During my Consultant year I made inquiries and preliminary proposals, learned of the Library's own sallies into the translation jungle, and became, slowly, a sort of fanatic on the subject." Whittemore urged that the Library consider establishing a national translation center, like the Consultantship and the Whittall series, and bringing out a translation magazine, modeled on the short-lived *Delos*, published 1968–71 by the short-lived National Translation Center, which enjoyed Ford Foundation support, at the University of Texas. "The Library is the natural place for such a center in our country," Whittemore wrote, and he submitted an informal proposal to the Library, which in the current fiscal picture could only table the idea. As of the summer of 1986, a group of local well-wishers hoped to submit the project to a consortium of Washington colleges and universities, but its prospects were inauspicious.

Another of Whittemore's unabashed proposals related to the Council of Scholars, in which he sat pro forma during his year. "The Council appears to be a replacement for the old, loose body of Honorary Consultants in American Letters and is, I am sure, a much more effective instrument than its predecessor; but aside from . . . the Poetry Consultant, it is an entirely academic body. Would not the inclusion on the Council of practicing representatives of American letters (including a

[415]

translator perhaps!) as well as of American music and art, be appropriate? I mention this possibility because the Council appears to be headed for a significant role in the Library's future, and as an old academic myself I would like to see the views of academics tempered by a few 'creators' in that future."

Two other fresh suggestions Whittemore tried out: that the Library have an internship program for young people, which would include a summertime "gopher" for the Poetry Office, who might free the rest of the staff to get on with updating *Literary Recordings: A Checklist of the Archive of Recorded Poetry and Literature in the Library of Congress,* which now stops at May 1975; and that the Whittall series include "retrospectives"—programs about the neglected dead. Ruminating over the latter, Whittemore may have free-associated forward to the subject of the lecture he gave toward the end of his term: "Poets and Anthologists: A Look at the Current Poet-packaging Process." From the Greek Anthology (circa 60 B.C.) onward to the teeming W. W. Norton & Co. anthologies of our own age, he gave a learned, comprehensive, and funny treatment of a subject of anxious concern to every poet.

Most Consultants, in their annual reports, close with a grateful word for the staff of the Poetry Office, Nancy Galbraith (who had succeeded Phyllis Armstrong as Special Assistant in Poetry the year Whittemore served his first Consultantship) and Jennifer Rutland. Whittemore's was cogent: "They have a feel for the odd dimensions of the Office and the Consultantship that no Consultant can ever have."

Fitzgerald died on January 15, 1985. At a requiem mass three days later in St. Mary's Church, New Haven, five of his children read from the Bible and from his poems, and a sixth chose as an epigraph for the program of the service something that her father had written in a letter to an aunt in 1928, when he was eighteen. "I feel very strongly and very often that if a fellow keeps away from cheap and commonplace things and does his level best to live proudly and sincerely, and never quits, then somehow, I don't know how nor why, things will turn out all right in the end." His widow Penelope spoke a moving biographical "comment" (too modest a term) that considered his life, work, and character.

On April 30, the Library, under its Huntington and Whittall funds, presented a program in memory of Fitzgerald. Richard Dyer-Bennet read—or rather, declaimed, in the classic manner—five passages from Fitzgerald's *Odyssey,* accompanying himself with a lyre made to his specifications and first used on this occasion. Poems from the volume *Spring Shade,* which Fitzgerald had published in 1971—his choice of his work up to that time—were read by Whittemore and by Seamus Heaney, who had succeeded to the Boylston Professorship at Harvard. The program closed on an exultant, joyous note: Wesley Boyd's Gospel Music Workshop Choir, composed of singers from the Washington black community, performing two choruses from *The Gospel at Colonus,* a cantata that had been adapted by Lee Breuer from the version of *Oedipus at Colonus* Fitzgerald had translated and the other Oedipus plays he had translated with Dudley Fitts. Breuer himself supervised the musical presentation and accompanied the choir.

In September 1985, Reed Whittemore was sworn in as the fourth poet laureate of Maryland, succeeding Lucille Clifton, who had moved to California. The term is three years; there is no salary. In January 1986, James Merrill was named Connecticut's first poet laureate, "a do-nothing post." Richard Eberhart served a five-year time, 1979–84, as the poet laureate of New Hampshire, and was succeeded by Donald Hall. (Eberhart had used his influence with the State Legislature to limit the appointment to five years.) Gwendolyn Brooks was in her eighteenth year as the poet laureate of Illinois. At least thirty other states of the union have poets laureate. They run a helluva gamut, as Huntington Cairns used to say.

It is worth recalling that MacLeish felt the brush of the laurel in June 1969, when President Nixon proposed that he (rather than the Consultant in Poetry, William Jay Smith) write a poem on the occasion of the projected moon landing. "I am . . . somewhat aghast," he responded. "To be asked by the President of the United States to compose a poem on a great public event is to be asked, in a sense, to speak for the Republic and the burden of such a responsibility would be very heavy indeed." MacLeish said he'd like to think it over. On July 21, the day after the landing, his poem "Voyage to the Moon" appeared on page one of the *New York Times*.

※

Gwendolyn Brooks, the twenty-seventh Consultant in Poetry, recalls that she came to the Library to record her poetry at the invitation of that "sunny-natured" poet Richard Eberhart on a date she chose, January 19, 1961, the day before President Kennedy's inauguration. The previous October, when Eberhart wrote to invite her, the Poetry Office, unable to find her Chicago address, sent the letter in care of *Poetry,* where her work had first appeared in 1944. (William Stafford, in a review in *Poetry,* remarked on her "steady view," her "insight.") Three years after Leroi Jones and Langston Hughes in 1959, she was the third black poet to read for the Archive of Recorded Poetry and Literature. (And she had been the first to win the Pulitzer Prize, in 1949, for her second volume of poems, *Annie Allen.*) When Brooks had finished her recording in the laboratory, Eberhart asked her if she'd like to meet Robert Frost, who was in town to play his part in the inauguration and had taken the Poetry Room over for the afternoon. "He was in his grandfatherly aspect," Brooks remembers. "He picked up a copy of *Poetry* from the coffee table and asked me, 'Do you know the lit-tle book?' He was so proud of *Poetry* and wanted to be sure I was aware of it." Brooks wrote Eberhart when she got home, "I am still breathless with excitement because of visiting the Library of Congress, and because I 'left me' there! . . . And I am so grateful to you for making the honor possible. I'll never forget that day."

Brooks was back in 1962, to participate in the National Poetry Festival (where her path and Frost's failed to cross), and again in 1969, when William Jay Smith was the Consultant, to read on a Whittall program with Katherine Garrison Chapin, with whom she found an amiable rapport. In the fall of 1972, when Mumford (on Basler's and Jacobsen's suggestion) invited her to take the Consultantship, she was too involved in her family and in the local black literary scene to consider leaving Chicago. She visited Washington the following April, however, when the new Institute for Arts and Humanities at Howard University gave its first formal program: a three-day celebration of Brooks's poetry, written, she has said, "out of love for blackness." From 1973 to 1976, she was an Honorary Consultant in American Letters. And, during the spring of 1976, in Kunitz's Consultantship, she joined Hayden and Michael Harper in the Coolidge Auditorium for two programs of readings of Afro-American poetry. Boorstin, who had known Brooks since a first meeting in Chicago many years before, said in announcing her appointment that she "writes in lyrics in a world overshadowed by polemics. She brings high honor and a distinctive voice to the company of Poetry Consultants."

Brooks's parents—a janitor and a schoolteacher—were Kansas people living in Chicago. Her mother went home to Topeka for Gwendolyn's birth, in 1917, and a month later back to the South Side of Chicago. Brooks grew up there, "bookish and lonely," as she told a reporter. Her family was poor; they revered education, and when her father provided her with an old desk someone had given him, her mother announced, "You are going to be the *lady* Paul Laurence Dunbar." Brooks has named Dunbar and Langston Hughes, Dickinson and Eliot, as her principal influences. Both Hughes and James Weldon Johnson encouraged her as a youngster. She graduated from a junior college, worked for the Youth Council of the NAACP in Chicago, and, with her husband, Henry Blakely, enrolled in a poetry class at the South Side Community Center taught by Inez Stark Boulton, who was on the staff of *Poetry*. Richard Wright brought her to the notice of his publishers, Harper & Brothers, in a letter to his editor: "She catches the pathos of petty destinies, the whimper of the wounded, and the tiny incidents that plague the lives of the desperately poor." In 1945 Harper published her first book, *A Street in Bronzeville*, to good reviews, and Brooks found herself named one of the Ten Women of the Year by *Mademoiselle*. Thereafter: eight books, a great many college and university appointments to teach writing, membership in the National Institute of Arts and Letters and its Award in Literature (1946), some fifty honorary degrees, and the poet laureateship of Illinois, succeeding Carl Sandburg. Brooks has read all around the country, including several times at

Harvard, where she was first introduced by Elizabeth Bishop. She lives still in her old neighborhood on the South Side, with an open-door policy to her neighbors.

☼

Brooks opened the season with her poetry reading in an overflowing Coolidge Auditorium on Monday, September 30. Throughout most of her year (she wanted a year's appointment only), reluctant to fly, she rode the Capitol Limited to Washington on Sunday nights, back to Chicago on Wednesdays. (A supplement for transportation was added to her stipend.) Brooks was one of the most accessible of the Consultants, in particular for young people. She replied warmly and constructively to every letter and accepted virtually every request to read and talk in the Washington area. (Requests from places well beyond D.C. she referred to her lecture bureau back home.)

To a young man in Georgia: "About getting your poems published. . . . 1) First, be sure the poems are as well-written as you can manage. 2) Second, try making a list of your favorite publishers and magazines—and go right down the list until *some*one accepts them. 3) Consider publishing a little book, your *self,* then devise interesting ways to distribute it (bookstores, barber shops, supermarkets, drugstores, poetry readings at which you may sell books). 4) Form a little publishing cooperative among people who write poetry—publish each other's work in neat, inexpensive books. Best wishes to you."

To a young woman who sent some poems and wrote, "I'm taking the liberty of asking you to play Mr. Johnson to me": "Thank you for your funny note . . . but—the conditions are hardly similar! I was a sixteen-year-old (yes, I was once sixteen)—and James Weldon Johnson was this gr-r-eat, accomplished poet-supreme. Whereas, you and I are *colleagues!* Your poetry is exciting—it is nimble and *ready.* I *could* say to you what I say to my*self:* revise revise revise."

To an official of the Voice of America, who invited her to speak in its Forum Series (which "brings well-known public figures to our writers, editors, broadcasters, and correspondents"): "I look forward to meeting you. . . .[A question period] will be a fine bow-ribbon to my 'presentation'; *and* I am glad to have a microphone! (Right in the center of the podium, please—unless it's one of those wear-it outfits. Incidentally, I'll be standing.) See you!" (In her talk, Brooks read a new poem, "The Near-Johannesburg Boy," commenting on events in South Africa.)

To a young woman: "You 'wish to write a book.' It 'would start off in the cradle of civilization.' It 'will cover a time period from the early days of Egypt to the present day.' . . . You ask me: '*So* far, what's your honest opinion, Ms. Brooks?' (This after announcing: 'I sincerely hope and dream that it could be a best seller, even a major motion picture.') My honest opinion is that it is a lot of fun to 'hope and dream.' My honest opinion is that hoping and dreaming, more often than not, lead to Slumber. My honest opinion is that you must sit down and write your own *book!* Wishing is not enough."

To a man in a Southern prison (serving time for dealing in marijuana after losing his business, "and as an inmate my dormant talent as a poet have manifest itself to me"): "Another poet, who had your problems, but who came out to teach at universities and to publish books and to lecture, is Etheridge Knight. I met him almost twenty years ago in Indiana State Prison, where he had invited me to speak to the inmates. . . . You *wanted* me to give you an honest opinion. First, let me tell you the *good* things: You have a way of being *direct* that is most appealing. Second, the warmth of your humanity pervades the poetry. Third, in some of the lines there is a Biblical radiance showing through the simplicity of language . . . let's talk about clichés. You know of course, what *they* are . . . [and she gave a list, pulled out of his poetry]. Comb through your verses for unwanted intrusions such as *those*. . . . When you're ready for publishing, make a list of companies that you feel are reliable and honest. Then get a pack of envelopes. . . ."

To a teacher of inmates at the Maryland House of Correction, in Jessup, who had discussed Brooks's poem "We Real Cool" with a class comprised mostly of inner-city black men ("I have never seen them 'go after' a poem in such a manner") and hoped Brooks would come and talk to them: "I'd love to come. I have a packed calendar, but your request is so important, I really want to honor it. . . . We'll somehow arrange a visit!" As she did. (Brooks also talked and read her poetry at the Lorton Prison in Virginia and, in Washington, the Comprehensive Alcohol and Drug Abuse Center and the Seniors' Wellness Center.)

⁂

Brooks's version of the brown bag lunchtime readings took an original turn. She managed three of these. She described the procedure in a memorandum to Broderick: "Two or more poets come [to read] at 12:00 noon. . . . The Poetry-Room-capacity audience talks to the poets, responding to what has been heard, asking questions, making lively comments. Then about twenty of us go to lunch. The first time we went to the Monocle, the second time to Toscanini's. [Brooks picked up the entire tab.] We all enjoyed the communion. The audience, in part happily sprawled on the floor, was richly attentive. At the restaurant last Wednesday We Poets and Poetry Acclaimers were like a bunch of happy youngsters. I pay each reading poet $200. It is understood . . . when any funds leave my hands, that the Library of Congress is *not* involved. In no way is the $200 considered 'an honorarium.' I merely wanted to help out a little with traveling expenses, or, in the case of a Washington-based poet, loss of time from work. It has been my pleasure to do this. I do it all the time. It's like breathing." (When Brooks went to the local Public Radio station WETA to read, she was met at the door by the D.C. poet Henry Taylor, 1985 Pulitzer Prize winner, with a framed certificate signed by Brooks denoting that, twenty years before, she had awarded him a prize of twenty-five dollars as the best poet in her class at Indiana University. Out of her own pocket.)

At the first lunchtime reading, the poets were Michael Weaver, from Brown University, and Grace Cavalieri, of Washington radio. At the second, six poets came: Sam Allen, Hannah Kahn (up from Miami), Dolores Kendrick, Meredith Skeath, Iona Harris, and Mani Philip. The third event featured fourteen poets, opening with Marcus Shaw (aged nine, of Washington) and Lucy Venable (aged seventeen, of South Carolina), and going on with with Margaret Walker, Ethelbert Miller, May Miller, Julia Fields, Ed Cox, Houston Baker, Loi Derricotte, Angela Peckenpaugh, Meredith Skeath, Josephine Jacobsen, Kenneth McClane, and Jane Lunin Perel. Brooks then staged—on April 23, Shakespeare's birthday—a mini-festival, as she called it, with *twenty-nine* poets reading: "locals and poets who had come from many parts of the country, honorariumless and paying their own expenses absolutely."

The Poetry Room hummed with poetry from one until six, as the poets came and went. (All these readings were recorded for the archive. And Brooks left behind a list of a dozen other poets whom she recommended be recorded.)

On the Whittall series, the performers whom Brooks suggested and introduced were Michael Anania and Mari Evans; Angela Jackson and Mark Perlberg; Haki Madhubuti and Sonia Sanchez; Donald Hall and Etheridge Knight; Michael Benedikt and John Tagliabue; Dudley Randall (who was unable to come) and D. H. Melhem; An Evening of Chicano Poetry (Lorna Dee Cervantes, Sandra Cisneros, Alberto Rios, and Luis Omar Salinas); and—the final Whittall event, copiously attended, in April—James Baldwin, reading from his prose. (The previous fall, Brooks had introduced Baldwin at a public ceremony in Chicago, on the day Mayor Washington had declared James Baldwin Day.)

The replete Whittall program included a great deal more that Brooks, in her capacity, introduced. The readers included Keri Hulme and Les A. Murray; Doris Grumbach; Garrison Keillor (tickets for this event were altogether given out weeks before); the Nobel laureate and novelist William Golding; the winners of the PEN Syndicated Fiction Project award—Joyce Carol Oates, Patricia McDonald, and W. D. Wetherell; a celebration, on October 22, of the seventy-fifth anniversary of the Poetry Society of America, with readings by Barbara Guest, Michael S. Harper, David Ignatow, Galway Kinnell, Grace Schulman, and Louis Simpson; Yevgeny Yevtushenko reading his poems, with translations by Albert Todd; and the Ghanaian poet and ambassador to Brazil, Kofi Awoonor, in national costume, reading his poems (and, on this occasion—January 20, 1986—Brooks, in the course of her introduction, read a poem of her own in honor of Martin Luther King, Jr.).

And the Whittall bounty also included, on October 8, a symposium in observance of the 150th anniversary of the publication of Alexis de Tocqueville's *Democracy in America*. The program, sponsored jointly by La Société Toqueville/The Tocqueville Society, included lectures in a closed session by two French savants, François Furet and François Bourricaud, and, at a public convocation in the Coolidge Auditorium, a lecture by the American sociologist Theodore Caplow, introduced by

Daniel Boorstin, and commented upon by Jacques Barzun. On October 29 there was a centennial observance, "Ezra Pound—Thoughts from St. Elizabeths," a monologue performed by the Welsh actor Ray Handy, who had appeared in the Coolidge Auditorium on three previous occasions; on November 5, another one-man show, the British actor Alec McCowen's "Kipling"; on November 18, a program of music and poetry, featuring John Hollander and the composer Hugo Weisgall, sponsored jointly by the two Whittall funds; and the actors Shanks and Woolf, back again on March 10 and 11 in two programs of Whittallesque temper—a reading, "Henry James: The Lion of Lamb House," and "The Moated Grange," by Roger Pringle, a dramatic visit in poetry and prose to some English country houses.

As her closing lecture, Brooks took for her title "The Day of the Gwendolyn"—what her daughter had spontaneously called the day the Consultantship began. Only Kunitz, among the Consultants, had made so personal a final address. Brooks gave a spirited, characteristically happy-hearted, often funny retrospective of her year in the Chair of Poetry, and afterward, at the customary reception in the Whittall Pavilion, she sat at a table for nearly two hours, cheerfully greeting hundreds of well-wishers, inscribing copies of her books, and writing many, many autographs on scraps of paper.

❊

On February 26, 1986, the Librarian of Congress announced that he had appointed Robert Penn Warren—in his eightieth year, forty-five years after his term as the third occupant of the Chair of Poetry, fifty years after Archer Huntington's benefaction had made it all possible—as "Poet Laureate Consultant in Poetry" for 1986–87. The change in title, according to the announcement, "is expected to increase the visibility of the prestigious poetry position." And Daniel Boorstin had the following to say: "Robert Penn Warren is a characteristically American man of letters in the range and versatility of his writings and in his feelings for the promise and the frustration of American life. He has high attainments in poetry, fiction, criticism, and social commentary. He has been a serious though not a solemn surveyor of our America. His materials have included the comic, the violent, and the tawdry as well as the grand and the heroic. He has depicted and dramatized the problems of good and evil and the historic divisions within American society. His works in prose and poetry have been widely read, enjoyed, and reread in the five decades of his fruitful career. If there is any person today whose work unites our America in its splendid variety, that person is Robert Penn Warren. With his advice and guidance we look forward to a great year." The Kentuckian had, indeed, lived more than half his life in the North: at the University of Minnesota through the 1940s (except for his first Consultant year in Washington's regional ambivalence), Yale from 1950 to 1973, and thereafter emeritus, settled in the Connecticut countryside or at a rural retreat on the side of Mount Snow in Vermont. (All this immersion in absolute Yankeedom—plus sojourns in California and Oxford—had in no wise adulterated Warren's vernacular discourse.)

Senator Spark M. Matsunaga of Hawaii, Democrat, was responsible for the creation of the Laureateship. He was born on the island of Kauai in an impoverished Japanese immigrant family and worked as a laborer through high school and after. He went through the University of Hawaii and taught school until World War II. While serving in Western Europe with Hawaii's famous 100th Infantry Battalion and the 442nd "Go for Broke" Regimental Combat Team, he was twice wounded and decorated for bravery. After the war he worked in the federal civil service, then studied law at Harvard; J.D., 1951. In 1954 Matsunaga was elected to the Hawaii Territorial House of Representatives, and in 1962 to the United States House of Representatives, where he served for fourteen years. In 1963 he first introduced legislation, unsuccessfully, to establish the office of Poet Laureate of the United States and continued to reintroduce it in every succeeding Congress. He was elected to the Senate in 1976, reelected in 1982. According to a spokesman, Senator Matsunaga is "known nationally as a strong proponent of renewable energy development, Soviet-American cooperation in space exploration, and the establishment of a U.S. Institute of Peace. . . . A book which he wrote about the House Rules Committee [of which he was a member], entitled *Rulemakers of the House,* is now required reading in political science courses in thirty-seven colleges and universities across the United States." Of the Senator's partiality for and composition of poetry not a great deal is known. A pocket calendar for 1986 that the Senator issued privately during the holiday season is the only documentation available. The Capitol, photographed in a snowy setting, with red poinsettias in the foreground, makes the cover, and there is a prefatory note in the Senator's hand, stating in part: ". . . to celebrate the success of my 22-year effort in Congress to establish the office of U.S. Poet Laureate, I am citing herein a few of my own verses, which I hope you will find quotable," and closing with a greeting in Hawaiian. A brief verse, of a gnomic and inspirational character, accompanies the page for each month—for example:

> In fending Life's soul-trying blows,
> Let Patience be your winning ploy.

> As small as it may seem,
> A good deed is always
> worth the doing.

On the last page, two longer poems are quoted, one of which is entitled "Deja Vu":

> I've been here before, I say—
> That house, that wall, that brook
> I've seen them all before;
> Yet I've never been this way
> Nor read in any book
> Of what I see, I'm sure.
> What strange things
> Our minds must know;
> We know not yet our minds.

To continue, however, with the evolution of the Laureateship: in January 1985, while legislation was under consideration to reauthorize the National Foundation on the Arts and Humanities Act (the basis of the NEA and NEH), Matsunaga offered his bill, S.213, as an amendment. The Poet Laureate, S.213 provided, would be appointed by the Presi-

dent of the United States in consultation with the National Council on
the Arts, "from among poets whose work reflects the qualities and at-
tributes associated with the historical heritage, present achievements,
and future potential of the United States. The Poet Laureate would per-
form duties assigned by the President and continue his or her own cre-
ative endeavors." The bill would leave it to the President to set the
Laureate's compensation, "not to exceed sixty per cent of the salary of
a Federal district court judge." During consideration of his amendment
by the Senate Committee on Labor and Human Resources, of which
Matsunaga is a member, the Library of Congress's Consultantship in
Poetry came to the Committee's (and the Senator's) attention. At the
request of the Librarian of Congress, S.213 was revised so that the Poet
Laureate would be appointed by *him* and would bear the title "Poet
Laureate Consultant in Poetry." The committee went a step further and
authorized the Chairperson of the NEA to sponsor an annual program
at which the Poet Laureate Consultant in Poetry "would present a major
work or the work of other distinguished poets," and for that purpose
also authorized an appropriation to the NEA of $10,000 for each of the
fiscal years 1987 to 1990. On October 3, the Senate unanimously ap-
proved the legislation; the House gave the final approval on December
3; the President signed into law—as Public Law 99-194—the entire
Act, including the Matsunaga amendment, on December 20. The
amendment's provisions are these:

    (a) Recognition of the Consultant in Poetry.—The Congress
recognizes that the Consultant in Poetry to the Library of Con-
gress has for some time occupied a position of prominence in the
life of the Nation, has spoken effectively for literary causes, and
has occasionally performed duties and functions sometimes asso-
ciated with the position of poet laureate in other nations and soci-
eties. Individuals are appointed to the position of Consultant in
Poetry by the Librarian of Congress for one- and two-year terms
solely on the basis of literary merit, and are compensated from
endowment funds administered by the Library of Congress Trust
Fund Board. The Congress further recognizes this position is
equivalent to that of Poet Laureate of the United States.

[427]

(b) Poet Laureate Consultant in Poetry Established.—(1)
There is established in the Library of Congress the position of
Poet Laureate Consultant in Poetry. The Poet Laureate Consultant
in Poetry shall be appointed by the Librarian of Congress pur-
suant to the same procedures of appointment as established on
the date of enactment of this section for the Consultant in Poetry
to the Library of Congress.

(2) Each department and office of the Federal Government is
encouraged to make use of the services of the Poet Laureate Con-
sultant in Poetry for ceremonial and other occasions of celebra-
tion under such procedures as the Librarian of Congress shall
approve designed to assure that participation under this paragraph
does not impair the continuation of the work of the individual
chosen to fill the position of Poet Laureate Consultant in Poetry.

The remainder of the text provides for the sponsorship of a program by
the NEA's Chairperson and authorizes the $10,000 appropriation.

Upon the announcement of Warren's appointment, Senator Matsu-
naga made a public statement: "I am overwhelmingly pleased. . . . I
believe it befitting that Mr. Warren, a poet who served as the Library of
Congress Consultant in Poetry from 1944–45, has been singled out as
the choice for the first U.S. Poet Laureate. I have always viewed Mr.
Warren as an individual who carefully weaves history and culture
through his writings." And, he went on, "Upgrading the Library of
Congress' program and elevating the poetry consultant to the position
of United States Poet Laureate will add greater visibility and prestige
to the art of poetry. Talented young American poets are now provided
with an incentive to aspire for the highest position in their art, just as
the young politically inclined aspire to the office of the President of the
United States."

※

The creation—or intrusion—of the Poet Laureateship was viewed with
a degree of alarm by some of the former Consultants in Poetry. To one
of them, Broderick wrote:

[428]

Red Warren's schedule will be very much like that of Robert Frost, who made exactly four trips to Washington during his year as Consultant. There has been no specified pattern to be followed. The Library has made various kinds of adjustments to accommodate particular Consultants. . . .

As for the invitations—and their name is Legion—the Laureate Consultant does not have to accept *any* of them. Mr. Warren has already declined several, and we have declined others in his name. Having said that, I must say that the laureateship is a new ball game—in scale, if nothing else. Frost's appearance at the Kennedy inauguration manifestly secured a hearing for American poetry in ways not institutionalized earlier. I would be very surprised if the Laureate Consultant were not asked to take part in future inaugurals or lesser state occasions. Is that bad? He or she need not accept, but will it be so bad a thing to be asked?

. . . [The law] spells out possibilities but does not impose obligations on the poet. Some poets may actually *want* to do those things. I can think of one or two who would. Can't you?

And, as Gwendolyn Brooks observed, in her final lecture as Consultant (pre-Laureate): "Those who are concerned about the words 'poet laureate' being added to the title of the Consultantship need not be. The Administration of the Library of Congress in the past has shown great intelligence in selecting sane, talented, and discriminating people for this post—after all, it selected me, didn't it?—and it will continue to do so. It will not select people who will consent to write celebrations for sanitary installations. There is nothing to fear."

The Laureateship inspired at least two poetic efforts by anonymous editorial writers. One in *The Economist* of London, noting the range of American society that will face a Laureate, betrays the influence of another poet in the English language, Longfellow:

> Sing for white men, sing for black ones,
> Sing for redneck, sing for laid-back,
> Sing in English, Spanish, Yiddish,
> One voice only? Land of Frost, of

e. e. cummings, E. A. Poe, O
Land of Cronkite, Land of Carson,
Gertrude Stein and Hammer-ditto,
Dorothy Parker, Dolly Parton,
Land of Lowell, of Howl, of Whitman!

The other, from the *New York Times,* is addressed "To America's First Poet Laureate":

Robert Penn Warren has said he won't commemorate "the
    death of someone's kitten."
So we can forget about that.
Neither does he choose to compose paeans to "the greater
    glory of Ronald and Nancy Reagan."
So that's out too.
Nor will he celebrate "the throne."
We haven't got one.
Of what, then, will Mr. Warren sing?
If he sings.
(He doesn't have to.)

Well, we've got baseball kings, movie queens, assorted teen
    princesses, and Prince.
That's royalty.
We've got monorails and high-rises and cloverleafs and malls
    that'd knock the socks off Dryden
And Cibber.
We've got Oscars and Tonys and Grammys.
They're something.
We've got Superbowls.
They're something else.
So there's stuff.

Robert Penn Warren says that "maybe you save the best
    poems for last."
Maybe so.

He says, "I hope I have."
Yes sir!

✳

One may regard with a certain irony the transformation of the Chair of Poetry into the Laureateship at the very turning point of its fiftieth anniversary. As we have noted, some veteran Consultants—and, it would seem, some members of the community of poets around the country— view the Laureateship as a misfortune. At a luncheon in the Whittall Pavilion to honor Gwendolyn Brooks at the end of her year as the last pre-laureate Consultant, two former Consultants among the guests, Whittemore and Hecht, who had settled in Washington, gave voice to their concern over the new lineaments of the Chair. Both felt that the function and the public image of the Consultant would change in ways that could only be regretted. During the summer, the doyen of the veteran Consultants, Stanley Kunitz, told a visitor that he was disappointed that American poets didn't arise en masse before the Senate Committee on Labor and Human Resources, to defend the integrity of the Chair and to protest such an intrusion into the Library of Congress's province. To some critics, the danger lay in the authorization of funds with which the NEA may sponsor some nature of public program by the Poet Laureate Consultant. Such funding by a federal agency, it was feared, would deprive the Chair and the Whittall series of an advantageous status transcending the bureaucracy—a status supported only by the benefactions of the private donors and presumably not answerable to government.

One can understand that, for those attuned to the word, *laureate* should resound with connotations not quite to their liking. Throughout most of its existence the Consultantship has been a busy, day-to-day affair, embracing a routine of readings, lectures, letter-writing, and encounters with Library officials, visitors, schoolchildren, and other poets, all in the service of the original Huntington/Putnam intention: to encourage interest in poetry and other literature. There is no obligation to write poetry. *Laureate,* on the other hand, smacks of the ceremonial and honorific, the official and formal, of poetry in the service of the State, and, most alarming of all, the production on demand of a swath of verse, possibly bad. The very desire for a laureateship might be thought to imply unfortunate assumptions about poetry: that it should be used as a vehicle for patriotic sentiment and celebration by a high-class booster for the American spirit; that we are one people with one voice, and the Laureate a skillful craftsman of the product of that voice; that the art of poetry needs such an emphasis.

There was a different sort of criticism, too: that the appointment of a new Poet Laureate every year or two would devalue or even debauch the "honor" of a post so-called, which some people seem to feel is ennobled by its British ancestry. In any event, if the appointment in Washington were to take on the presumed nobility of the Poet Laureate-ship of the United Kingdom (*pace* Shadwell and some of his successors) it properly should be for life. And where would that lead us?

Assuming that Public Law 99-194 carries on, in another fifty years there will have been two or three dozen American poets who've worn the *laurus Matsunaginensis* besides carrying the time-hallowed distinction of having occupied the Chair of Poetry; the double honorific will grace any curriculum vitae. The terms of the appointment will, we're assured, be the same, and the old question will ring out still: What in the world does the Poet Laureate Consultant in Poetry do?

The Library of Congress, whose relationship to poetry up to 1937 had been primarily custodial, became over the next half century a principal vehicle of the poetic tradition, which is transmitted to the American public in a flood or a trickle depending on who is in the Chair. The founders—Huntington, Putnam, MacLeish, Whittall—would surely be gratified if they were to watch the story unfolding. The laurel is not likely to clutter the further progress of that story. It may even be seen as a bright plume on the catbird seat.

Appendix I

STATEMENT OF THE COMMITTEE OF THE
FELLOWS OF THE LIBRARY OF CONGRESS IN
AMERICAN LETTERS[1]

The Honorable Jacob K. Javits, of New York, demands an investigation
into the circumstances of the award of the Bollingen Prize in Poetry for
1948 to Ezra Pound's *Pisan Cantos* and into the implications or ques-
tions raised by the attack upon the award in the *Saturday Review of
Literature* and consequent controversy in literary circles.

Mr. Javits further states that all the material on this controversy has
been inserted by the Honorable James T. Patterson, of Connecticut, into
the Appendix to the *Congressional Record* for July 19, 1949. The in-
serted material consists of two articles by a poet, Mr. Robert Hillyer; a
letter, in reply partly to these, from the Librarian of Congress; and an
editorial in reply to the letter, signed with the initials of Harrison Smith,
president, and Norman Cousins, vice-president of the Saturday Review
Associates, publishers of the *Saturday Review of Literature,* of which
Mr. Cousins is also editor, and in which the material appeared.

Reprinted from The Case Against the Saturday Review of Literature (Chicago: Modern
Poetry Association, 1949). Bracketed passages in the text are as in the original.

[433]

It should be pointed out that this was not all the material then available on the literary controversy. Other literary periodicals had published comment and discussion on the award. This was, moreover, not all the material published up to that time in the *Saturday Review* itself. Besides considerable correspondence, there had appeared in the *Saturday Review* for June 11 an editorial, with which the Librarian's reply is also concerned, and which gave unqualified editorial backing to the validity of Mr. Hillyer's "charges." There had also appeared in the same issue [July 2] with the Librarian's letter, two editorial notes. One of these was in correction and clarification of an impression likely to be raised by, and the other in retraction of, a statement developed in Mr. Hillyer's articles. At the time of Mr. Javits' remarks, the editors had had, for over two weeks, a statement endorsed by the jurors, which was published in the *Saturday Review* for July 30, and was accompanied by another retraction of a very important implication of Mr. Hillyer's articles. [Mr. Javits inserted these two documents into the Appendix to the *Congressional Record* for August 2, 1949, p. A5205.] It should further be pointed out that the title given by Mr. Javits to the prize is not its correct published title, which is simply The Bollingen Prize in Poetry. The title, Bollingen-Library of Congress award, used by Mr. Javits, is apparently quoted from the *Saturday Review,* and is employed by Mr. Hillyer and the editors. Whether or not deliberately, in conjunction with other statements and arrangements of material in their editorials and articles, it tends to create a false impression of the jurors' intentions as to the award. Finally, it should be pointed out that Miss Mary McGrory states in the Sunday *Star* (Washington) for July 31 that Mr. Javits was put in touch with the situation through a letter from Mr. Cousins.

Although Mr. Javits does not assert that any members of the Fellows in American Letters are fascists, it is apparent from his remarks, especially in the first sentence, and from the fourth paragraph of his accompanying letter to the Honorable Mary T. Norton, that he does entertain apprehensions of fascist infiltration, through their agency, into the Library of Congress (*Congressional Record,* July 21, 1949, p. 10123.) The sequence of facts to which attention has just been called strongly suggests that these apprehensions have been raised in his mind, and may well be raised in the minds of others, by the Hillyer articles and the *Saturday Review* editorial. How has this been accomplished?

The Librarian of Congress, in his letter[2] published in the *Saturday Review* for July 2, and received by the editors some ten days previously, stated that the authors of the editorials and articles were under a public duty to produce evidence, beyond mere supposition, to support the damaging insinuation that the Fellows had abused for "evil ends" the authority entrusted to them. No evidence has been produced by them since that time to establish that there were fascist influences at work among the Fellows, nor can such evidence be produced by anyone. It has already been said that retractions or implied retractions have been made by the *Saturday Review* of matters bearing importantly on these insinuations. Yet since Mr. Javits and others may have been misled, there may be a public duty on the part of the Fellows to examine and expose the means of insinuation. These are chiefly three and their validity will be examined in turn.

I. *Attempt to Link the Bollingen Foundation with Jung's Alleged Nazism.*

That the Bollingen Foundation, named for the place of residence of Carl Jung, was, by virtue of its donor's and his deceased wife's sympathy with or interest in Jung's contributions to psychiatry, and of Jung's alleged adherence at some time to Nazi ideas, tainted with fascist leanings, and had influenced the award, or the composition of the jury. The editorial clarification already referred to (*Saturday Review of Literature,* July 2 p. 23) is as follows:

> Since the publication of "Treason's Strange Fruit," by Robert Hillyer (*SRL* June 11) the editors have received a request for correction and clarification from the Bollingen Foundation:
> "Readers of Mr. Hillyer's articles might come away with the impression that the Foundation was responsible, in part at least, for the selection of Ezra Pound's 'The Pisan Cantos' as winner of the Bollingen-Library of Congress Award in poetry. While Bol-

[435]

lingen Foundation spokesmen acknowledge that no such specific statement is made by Mr. Hillyer, it is important that no doubt be left in the minds of *SRL* readers concerning the fact that the relationship between the Bollingen Foundation and the Bollingen-Library of Congress poetry awards was confined to the original endowment for the prize, which, through courtesy, bears the name of the Foundation. But the Foundation was in no way responsible for the choice of the Fellows in American Letters of the Library of Congress who make the awards, or for the awards themselves. With the donation of the funds, the Foundation's connection with the matter ended. The Foundation did not know that Pound was being considered for the prize until the jury announced its choice. The Foundation had neither the right of selection nor of veto."

The Saturday Review accepts the foregoing as a correct and complete statement of the facts.

In the Fellows' statement, the Librarian's letter, and the editorial comment on the Fellows' statement, the point is reinforced. It is, then, clearly published and admitted as proven that the Bollingen Foundation is free of responsibility for the award made, or for the composition of the Fellows. It should then as clearly be admitted as proven that the space devoted by Mr. Hillyer to linking the Bollingen Foundation with Jung's alleged Nazism is altogther irrelevant to the formation of any conception whatsoever as to the Fellows' views.

[Mr. Javits has read a draft of the foregoing statement and has asked that it may be made clear that in demanding an inquiry he did not refer to the origin of the word *Bollingen,* the association of Carl Jung with the controversy, or the possible influence of Mr. T. S. Eliot on the other jurors. He has never questioned the right of the Fellows to make the award, but only the organization of the Fellows. L. H. EVANS.]

Insinuations in Mr. Hillyer's articles, however, are of so pervasive a nature that they must be combatted quickly here and there as one might a grass fire on a gusty day. The Fellows are frequently referred to by him as the "Bollingen group" and it may be supposed that the Fellows sought money from the Foundation for the prize, or that the Foundation was willing to grant it, through mutual fascist sympathies. But for this to be true there would have had to be knowledge available to either party of such leanings. It should be sufficient here to call attention to the failure on the part of the *Saturday Review* to produce any evidence of this, and to Mr. Hillyer's statement that there is no implication that Mr. Paul Mellon (President of the Foundation) had any knowledge of Jung's alleged connection with Nazism. The account of the establishment of the prize, on record at the library, shows that the Fellows and the Library sought funds from the Foundation because it had already signified its interest in poetry through a gift of funds for a series of poetry record albums.

Again, and as part of this stage in his process of insinuation, Mr. Hillyer attempts to link in a somewhat vaguer nexus of Jungian-fascistic sympathies the Foundation, the Pantheon Press, and the "new aestheticism," a term used by him for a literary school supposed to include an unspecified number of the jurors, as well as an unspecified number of other unnamed writers supposed to share their literary tastes and tendencies. A retraction as to the Pantheon Press appeared in the *Saturday Review* of July 2, page 23, and ran as follows:

> Also in connection with Mr. Hillyer's article, we received a friendly visit from Kyrill Schabert and Kurt Wolff, the executive officers of Pantheon Books, Inc., who took exception to Mr. Hillyer's statement: "Through the generosity of Paul Mellon, the Bollingen Foundation supports the Pantheon Press, a publishing house which issues many outpourings of the new aestheticism, the literary cult to which T. S. Eliot and Ezra Pound are gods."
>
> We learned that Pantheon Books, Inc., is in no manner supported or controlled by Bollingen Foundation. Pantheon Books is an independent corporation and is not subsidized by the Bollingen Foundation. It does, however, manufacture, distribute, and announce in its catalogs the Bollingen Series, published for the Bollingen Foundation, Inc., which is supported by Paul Mellon. Any inference that the Bollingen Series was in any other way

related to Pantheon Books, Inc., is incorrect. A careful examina-
tion of the list of books published by Pantheon reveals no work
of the nature suggested in Mr. Hillyer's article. Fairness dictates
a retraction, which the editors and Mr. Hillyer are glad to make.

THE EDITORS

II. *Eliot's Alleged Fascism and His Supposed Influence on the Jury.*

The second means by which implication of possible Fascist direction
of the award is made is through the twofold assertion that Mr. T. S.
Eliot is a disciple of Jung and that he undoubtedly "wielded great influ-
ence" in the award. The first statement is so phrased that it may be
taken by persons uninformed in the matter as an accepted fact. As to
this we have Mr. Eliot's word that so far from being a disciple of Jung,
he has, he believes, never read a word of this writer, and knows his
work only by rumor and report. The notion may have arisen through
the fact that Miss Elizabeth Drew, in *T. S. Eliot, the Design of His
Poetry,* makes use of Jungian concepts and treatments of symbols in her
interpretation of Mr. Eliot's poems; somewhat similar use of these con-
cepts had been made by a writer in *Publications of the Modern Lan-
guage Association.* But this can scarcely make Mr. Eliot himself a
Jungian. A study of Blake's thought has been made which carries this
application much further, and Mr. Hillyer, we suppose, would not call
Blake a disciple of Jung. It means no more than that these critics, and
possibly others, have found Jung's terms or concepts useful for their
own purposes of analysis of the poetic texts. An anonymous writer, in
a review of Miss Drew's book in *The New Yorker,* complained of this
very introduction of Jung as irrelevant to a discussion of Eliot.

The second assertion, as to Mr. Eliot's influence over the jury in the
matter of the award, is a speculation on Mr. Hillyer's part, of which the
steps are not given. In the *Saturday Review* for July 30 (p. 22) is pub-
lished a declaration by Mr. Paul Green, a dissenting juror, which says
in part, "Literary judgments and preferences, like other matters of the
mind, should be free. They certainly were in this matter." There also
appears on the same page a statement signed by all other living mem-

bers of the jury which says in part: ". . . the decision of the Jury for the Bollingen Prize was arrived at wholly by democratic procedure." This is followed by an editorial reply which says in part: "We accept without further question their assurance that the decision of the Bollingen jury was 'arrived at wholly by democratic procedure.'"

If more specific comment is needed on this particular assertion the following facts are offered: There is on record at the Library a statement concurred in by other members of the jury that Mr. Eliot neither initiated the award to Pound nor in any way attempted to influence other members to vote for it. There are on record at the Library nine letters from the Fellows, addressed to the secretary, offering nominations for the prize at her request, and mailed from widely scattered addresses. From these the original list of fifteen titles to be considered was drawn up. Mr. Eliot, like some other members, turned in no nominations, and six jurors (one orally) nominated, with the other titles, the work of Pound.

It is unnecessary to deal further here with the means by which Mr. Hillyer saw fit to build up the impression of a dictatorial will at work among the jury, and the presumption that its influence was un-American, fascistic, or proto-fascistic. Two statements, however, must be dealt with, for they bear on the question raised of the representative character of the Fellows as a whole, and the patriotism of those whose allegiance is to the United States.

The first is that "half the committee were disciples of Pound and Eliot and sympathetic to a group which has a genuine power complex." (*Saturday Review.* June 18, p. 38.) This is in part simply rhetorical reinforcement for the impression required by Mr. Hillyer, and cannot be answered since there is no way of knowing to what group he alludes. If to a "group" of Mr. Pound and Mr. Eliot, it is known that except for certain areas of literary sympathy, their views are very divergent. (This is pointed out even by Mr. Hillyer.) If to the group neither named nor numbered, and called by Mr. Hillyer "the new critics," "neo-esthetes," "poetry's new priesthood," etc., it would be even more variegated and include perhaps all those who have found anything to praise in poets Mr. Hillyer does not approve.

That half the group—that is, seven jurors—are *disciples* of Pound and Eliot could not possibly be sustained by examination of their work or of general critical estimates of it. No one juror has been generally described hitherto as a disciple of either, although influences have been remarked in a number of instances. Indeed, to say of this or any group of writers comparable in size, age distribution, and reputation that no such influences, direct or indirect, could be found in their work would be difficult and would amount to saying that they were indifferent to the literary development of their time.

The second statement as to the pernicious example of Mr. Eliot for the jurors is couched in an indirect fashion but can be simply and directly answered. It is to the effect that Mr. Hillyer has no doubt that members of the committee would think our ancestors made a grave mistake in throwing off British sovereignty. Excluding Mr. Eliot, who is a British subject, there is no shred of evidence in any writing or known act of any member of the jury to support this. None of the American-born members can have been called expatriates at any period, although several of them spent a year or more abroad, by the terms of a Guggenheim Fellowship or a Rhodes Scholarship. Mr. Auden, it is true, is an expatriate, but only because he has chosen to become an American citizen.

III. *The Award Itself as an Alleged Fascist Action.*

The third means by which the implication is made of fascist direction of the award is through interpretation of the award itself. This will doubtless seem to many the most reasonable part of Mr. Hillyer's argument. Similar inferences had been drawn by others before the discovery of the Bollingen "plot" in the *Saturday Review,* and it brings up the important question of the ideological approach to poetry and to literature in general. This is, perhaps, the immediately crucial question, and to it the Librarian has provided a reply.[3]

Mr. Hillyer disposes of this third stage by triple action. First, the prize was adjudged in defiance of all critical standards to be a work so "disordered as to make the award seem like a hoax." Hence, the judgment must have been made out of secret sympathy with, or directed by an intention to belaud and advance, fascist and anti-semitic tendencies of the work. Second, the aura of the Bollingen-Eliot "plot" (discussed under steps I and II) is employed to suggest more forcibly that the Fellows had such sympathy; third, the statement of the jury is interpreted by him as saying that nothing matters but the mode of expression. The jury have given, he says, the award on these "neo-aesthetic" grounds and this shows them to be in a state to be moved by "groping fascism," "a guided will" toward a new authoritarianism. In short, they are convicted both of having acted out of sympathy for the content and in total disregard of it. Or perhaps it would describe Mr. Hillyer's logic better to say that he hoped if he failed to convict them plausibly on the first count, to do so on the second.

This Siamese charge is indeed a monstrous one. Besides offending the sentiments of the jurors, it challenges the principle which they felt important enough to stand by in the difficult matter of their recommendation, and it attempts to discredit a large body of writing by other than critical means. It must be fully met.

First, is there evidence that the award defied *all* critical standards? The *Pisan Cantos* was reviewed very favorably indeed in the following periodicals: The New York *Times*, The New York *Herald-Tribune Books*, *The Nation*, *The New Republic*, *Hudson Review*, *The Kenyon Review*, *Sewanee Review*, and elsewhere. These are some citations from these reviews:

> "The best passages in the *Cantos*, which move between verse as speed and verse as song, are supreme."

> "The whole design is gradually becoming plain . . . *many passages of surpassing beauty.*"

> "Of the language one can remark only the perfection . . . The superb 83rd Canto."

> "The Pisan Cantos are beautifully written; the diction firm, sound and elegant; the music and the image adding up to the dance."

"The clown, the great poet, the pure fool, Parzifal, Propertius, and Poor Tom are all here in the new Cantos . . . the Pound of the Pisan Cantos still has the old magnificence."

"At their least valuation I submit that these Cantos in which light and air—and song—move so freely are more exhilarating poetic sketch books—'notes from the upper air'—than can be found elsewhere in our literature."

It is submitted that acknowledgments of this order of poetic distinction were not so widely made, by so many reviewers, for other eligible books. At the conclusion of a less favorable review of the *Cantos,* but one which treated them as a work of distinction, Robert Gorham Davis, in the *Partisan Review,* attributes to the *Pisan Cantos* "a new humanity, tenderness, maturity with no loss of lyric beauty or wit." In an article published after the award in the same periodical, but written earlier, John Berryman speaks of "the marvelous pages of the *Pisan Cantos.*" In the *Saturday Review of Literature,* at the height of the controversy, Mr. William Rose Benét, poetry editor, confessed that he had found in the volume a very fine song, a long passage of "extraordinarily fine and sensitive poetry," moving passages, another long passage of whose conception he says: "The stature of that moment needs no elaboration of my own," and other epigrammatic or descriptive lines which he thinks "will remain."

Secondly, is any suspicion of fascistic or anti-semitic leanings properly to be attached to the jurors through Mr. Hillyer's treatment of the lines which he says the majority of the jurors "not only tolerated but applauded"? Mr. Hillyer after interpreting the lines castigates them as "ruthless mockery of the Christian war dead." Set aside the question of whether this is a proper construction of the lines. Set aside the fact, pointed out by a writer in *Partisan Review,* which had first singled out these lines, that they are virtually the only lines in the poem on which such construction could be put. Is it at all a legitimate extension of the meaning of the award, would it be, of any award, that it amounts to agreement and applause for every sentiment and opinion expressed in the chosen work?

We submit that Mr. Hillyer's treatment of these lines is calculated to inflame the minds of those insufficiently acquainted with the work judged or the works and opinions of the judges, along lines already prepared for by means now admitted to be essentially false. We submit that the charge he makes is indescribably offensive to persons who through their personal and social sympathies were equally involved with others in the anxieties and griefs of the late war.

Or, apart from this peculiarly objectionable paragraph, is the suspicion of anti-semitism, or of fascistic tendencies, to be laid upon the jurors simply because they have pronounced the *Pisan Cantos* to be the best book, poetically, among those eligible for the prize? By Mr. Hillyer's interpretation of the statement accompanying the award, this imputation cannot logically be laid to them. But the affirmative jurors have no wish to equivocate because Mr. Hillyer may have done so in order to avoid libel. An assertion is now made on their behalf, which at the time they felt it unnecessary to make, except as it was to be understood from their joint statement. No sympathy for fascism, no condoning of anti-semitism exists among them. To assume that they may or must have such sympathies is to deny them the capacity to perceive literary distinction in a work, parts of which express and spring from attitudes and opinions that they do not share.

It should have been understood by the editors of the *Saturday Review*, before these attacks were published, that the affirmative jurors did not at least necessarily share these opinions. Two had published comments in the *Partisan Review* (of which one was in part quoted, and distorted, in the *Saturday Review*), specifically dissociating themselves from anti-semitism. One, Mr. W. H. Auden, has given a good deal of expression in his writings to condemnation of fascism, and sympathy for its victims, and is the husband of Erika Mann, an exile from Nazism. The other, Mr. Allen Tate, had from time to time expressed opinions on political and social matters (of which he has now provided a summary)[4] which, whether or not they are majority American opinion, are certainly not fascistic. Miss Louise Bogan, who had reviewed the *Pisan Cantos* in a laudatory manner some months before the award, and so might be presumed to be an affirmative juror, in this, and even more strongly in a review of earlier cantos, had expressed her disapprobation of what she felt to be Pound's attitudes in these respects. So had nearly all the writers of the favorable reviews cited, thus establishing that the incredible or suspect objectivity toward the poetry of the *Pisan Cantos* could be found outside the "Bollingen group." Mr. Eliot, who through his published admiration for Pound's work might be presumed to have been an affirmative juror, and was to say the least assumed to be one, was also known to have served the British government during the late war, and had expressed anti-totalitarian views in his writings.[5]

※

Mr. Hillyer and the editors of the *Saturday Review* indicated that they did not care to believe that the jurors felt they were acting with critical objectivity in making the award. The statement which the jurors offered as to this point[6] was approved editorially in the New York *Herald-Tribune,* the Baltimore *Sun,* and some other papers. Because it has been pretty generally misunderstood, it should be restated in context.

In discussion of the terms of the award as agreed upon with the Foundation, it had been established by the Fellows that the award was to be made for a book published during 1948, and on the book's literary merits. The responsibility assumed by the jurors, then, was to vote, each one, for the book he thought best as poetry. Their statement asserted this. The ballots taken established that to the great majority of the jurors, the *Pisan Cantos* seemed the best book. The letter recommending the award to the Librarian, and from which the published statement was quoted, stated this. The Library did not announce the ballot count, but this is not customary with other prize juries. There was no intention of making the vote appear unanimous, as has been suggested in a *Saturday Review* editorial. It was known that Mr. Karl Shapiro intended to publish his dissent, which had been circulated to the jurors before the final ballot. He did so, simultaneously with the announcement of the prize, and Mr. Green, or any other juror, could have done so, if he had seen fit. It was thought that attention should be called to the fact that the jury were not recommending the award to the *Pisan Cantos* in disregard of its author's indictment for treason, or what was objectionable to them or others in its subject matter. Their statement asserted this; and finally it asserted the principle which in their view overrode the difficulties and dangers of the award. This was, that literary criteria were the only criteria relevant to their task.

From this arises the important question in the controversy over the award. Is a work necessarily condemned *in toto* by having a certain content, or because its author holds certain beliefs or has committed certain acts? The *Saturday Review* editorial denies the Librarian's impression that its editors would apply a political test to poetry, but they do so inconsistently. They say that poetry need not pass a political test, but that, in this case, values expressed in or behind the work necessarily make it ineligible. To argue how this is or is not so with any particular work is much too complex to have been attempted in a joint general statement made for the jury. From the choice, it is evident that the overwhelming majority of the jurors, who have no sympathy with the attitudes objected to by most Americans in Mr. Pound, did not find the *Pisan Cantos* so invalidated. The controversy over the award seems to make this a test case on the point.

It has already been pointed out that Mr. Hillyer's argument is circular and that a certain interpretation of the statement accompanying the announcement of the award is used to support the accusation that the jurors are dominantly sterile aesthetes. This is the third point to be taken up in the question of whether the award judges the jurors. Do they believe, as the *Saturday Review* would like to prove, that the value of a work has nothing to do with its subject matter, and that form and content are unrelated? Any examination of the critical writings of those of the jurors who have published criticism would show that this is not so. To go no further than the immediate problem, in the *Partisan Review* discussions, available to and cited by the *Saturday Review,* Mr. Auden begins his statement by saying: "I fully share Mr. Barrett's concern over the excessive preoccupation of contemporary criticism with form and its neglect of content." Mr. Tate, in the following issue (June) writes: "I have little sympathy with the view that holds that Pound's irresponsible opinions merely lie alongside the poetry, which thus remains uncontaminated by them." After expounding his view of what constitutes coherent form and its relation to a mature and coherent view of life, he then goes on to explain what he, as an individual critic, considers to be the chief poetic superiority of the *Pisan Cantos.*

This charge of irresponsible aestheticism was levelled against a great many critics, among them several of the jurors, by Marxist-dominated criticism in the thirties. Now, by an odd turn of Fate, this charge is being made, not by Communists, but by the *Saturday Review of Literature*. Some correspondents in the *Saturday Review* have expressed fears that a similar authoritarianism is suggested in the *Saturday Review*'s attack: that of standard-brand positive Americanism as a test for literary worth.

✳

When Mr. Hillyer is not attacking the Bollingen award, he attacks the personality and career of Mr. Eliot. Both attacks are a continuation of his long-standing warfare with a large part of contemporary writing. The account of Mr. Hillyer in *Twentieth Century Authors* says: "As he indicates, he feels consciously out of tune with his time." Many poets do, as well as other persons. It is important at this point to take up particular misrepresentations of the jurors as a coterie or pressure group; for these may have a bearing on the second main question raised by Mr. Javits as to whether they "are properly representative of the American people."

In his attack upon the "priesthood," Mr. Hillyer names no names, other than those of Pound and Eliot, "their gods." He does not define their tenets, or indicate their number; "*their* power is enormous," he writes, "especially in the colleges and even the preparatory schools. A large proportion of funds from the great charitable foundations is earmarked for *their* use." Even more significantly, he says that the magazine, *Poetry,* must be falling into *their* hands because its editor also thought the *Pisan Cantos* "incontrovertibly the best book" eligible for the Bollingen Prize. Further, the *Saturday Review*'s first editorial (June 11) states: "The 'new criticism' of course has leaped to the defense of Pound and his book." By such distortion of fact, of course, any non-jurors who uphold the award, and in Mr. Hillyer's view apparently any who praise or have praised the writings of what he considers the dominant group of jurors—similarly never fully named—can be included in the "priesthood." Likewise, the tactics already examined, through which the affirmative jurors are brought under suspicion of anti-semitism, Nazism, etc., may scare off other writers who might be inclined to speak out in support, for fear they too will become fascists overnight.

Mr. Hillyer speaks of *their* pervasive influence, and of *their* subsidized quarterlies. But everyone knows that literary and scholarly journals cannot be supported without subsidies. He talks of "hypnosis," of pressure groups, and of the authoritarian nature of *their* criticism, which merely pretends to polite disagreement. He refers however to *A Glossary of the New Criticism* (edited by William Elton), which was first published in *Poetry* magazine. Nothing is clearer from an examination of this glossary than that there are very large areas of divergence among the "new critics" and the "priesthood," if these are *"they."* Mr. Ransom's book (John Crowe Ransom: *The New Criticism;* Norfolk, Conn., 1941), which first used the term, also set forth opposing positions among the critics there discussed, and assessed their different contributions to an "ideal" criticism. Mr. Hillyer says that the new critics subtly undermine the influence of our great poets, such as Robinson and Frost. But Yvor Winters, one of the new critics, has published a study of Robinson, giving him very high praise. (Yvor Winters: *Edwin Arlington Robinson;* Norfolk, Conn., 1946). Allen Tate, in an essay written many years ago, and reprinted in *On the Limits of Poetry* (New York, 1948), treats of him as a very distinguished poet indeed. As for Robert Frost, he has been given a foremost place in American poetry by, to mention no other, two of the younger "new" critics and poets, Randall Jarrell and Robert Lowell. Certainly no new critic has sought to undermine the reputation of any poet by such means as those employed in the *Saturday Review* articles against some of the Fellows and the unspecified body of the "neo-aesthetes" and the "new priesthood."

More particularly it is suggested that the Fellows themselves may be a pressure group which has used the "prestige of the Government for advancing its own idiom." This is put forth in a *Saturday Review* editorial, July 30, and perhaps there is an implicit abandonment of the other charges. In any event, the suggestion had been made and prepared for throughout the *Saturday Review's* campaign.

Let us examine the probability of this suggestion. Are the Fellows a single school? We maintain that any fair-minded person with a knowledge of, or after examination of, their work and comment upon it would find that they are no more a school, except by being roughly contemporaneous—and they represent several literary age-groups—than they are all idols and exponents of the new criticism. They do seem to have been in substantial agreement on the award, but that this was not brought about by pressure has now been editorially admitted by the *Saturday Review.* If there had been a desire on their part to advance the "idiom" represented by Mr. Pound, would it not have been wiser of them to choose a book in the modern manner which would advance it with less fuss? And as to their using the prestige of the government to advance their idiom, the very manner of the press announcement objected to by the *Saturday Review* belies this. The jury was fully named, and their relationship to the Library stated. It is interesting that the early comment on the award in the press put the responsibility of the choice squarely on the Fellows.

The preliminary announcement of the award, made almost a year earlier, had also carried the names of the jurors, except for one added later, and had set forth the terms of the prize, and the relation of the Fellows to the Library. It is in the pages of the *Saturday Review,* as has been pointed out, that the prize has become the Bollingen-Library of Congress award, and the responsibility of the Library emphasized. The Librarian has made a statement of his position in the matter which has been generally approved, and the *Saturday Review* has replied to him with a curious inconsistency. It says he should have permitted freedom of opinion to the jury, and announced the recommended award, but that he cannot escape responsibility for it. The implication is of course clear: either he is responsible in having been hoodwinked into appointing a clique as Fellows, or he is now required to fire some or all of them because the award has been made. Extension of this by analogy with academic freedom should show that it would really deny freedom of opinion.

✳

Whether the Fellows are as representative a group as could be desired, or as could be brought together for the purpose served by the Fellows, is another question. Mr. Hillyer in his article leaped from his account of the inception of the Fellows to the award, as if to make it had been their sole object. But the Fellows had been serving the Library for four years before the prize was thought of, at no compensation except the travel and per diem expenses for their annual meetings. They had, among other things, consulted with the Library's staff on acquisition of American literary materials, materials proper for preservation in the Rare Book Room, bibliographies in American literature, and had acted as an advisory committee to the Consultant in Poetry (an endowed chair) in such matters as bibliographies, cooperation with the *United States Quarterly Book List,* the formation of an Archive of contemporary poets' recordings, and the issuance of phonograph-record albums. (The list incidentally of their recommendations for the record archive is a catholic one, and the first invitations to record were sent to sixty-odd poets, such as might be included in standard anthologies.) Mr. Hillyer says that the group was established by Allen Tate. This is not true. Mr. Tate as consultant in 1943–44 naturally had no authority to establish an advisory committee for the Library. His suggestion in the matter was passed on by the Library authorities and grew out of a request from the then Librarian, Mr. MacLeish, that he consult someone on the procuring of funds for record albums. During this consultation (with the late James Boyd) the idea developed that a committee might be formed to interest itself in the development and use of the Library's materials in American literature. The Librarian has pointed out that Mr. Hillyer was informed, though he says he was not,[7] as to who appoints the Fellows. They are referred to in the *Saturday Review* as a secret, almost a private, organization. This is altogether untrue. Press releases as well as the Library's Annual Reports have announced the organization of the group, new appointments and resignations, and their annual meetings. These meetings have always been attended in part by officers of the Library, and throughout by the consultant in poetry, who is for the year a member of the Library's staff and responsible to the Library administration. Minutes of all meetings are kept and are in the Librarian's file.

But given that the Fellows are not a private club of Mr. Tate's, are they in their present constitution properly representative? A number of them have first served as consultants in poetry and were chosen for their qualifications for this post, and for their willingness to serve during the year in question. The poets outnumber the prose writers, but several are equally known as prose writers; the principal concern of the group has been with the Library's poetry collections and the consultant's work. As to their being representative, as having been recognized as competent by other professionals in the field, the following facts are offered:

Members of the group are teaching or have taught at colleges and universities of nationwide distribution, including Columbia, Minnesota, University of North Carolina, Harvard, Princeton, Stanford, New York University, Rutgers, Bryn Mawr, Swarthmore, Michigan, University of the South, Southwestern, Chicago, University of Virginia, Bennington (Vt.), University of Washington, Smith, State University of Louisiana, and others.

The list of colleges and universities which have engaged each member for lectures or readings would be too long to quote. Among special chairs and lectureships held by members have been the Avery Hopwood Lectureship at Michigan, several visiting lectureships at the University of Chicago, the Boylston Professorship at Harvard, a membership at the Institute of Advanced Study, a resident fellowship in creative writing at Princeton, and a visiting lectureship at the University of Iowa.

Their books have been published by a great number of American publishers, including Knopf, Houghton Mifflin, Macmillan, Harper, Scribner, Boni and Liveright, Random House, Duell, Sloane, and Pearce, Henry Holt, McBride, Doubleday, Harcourt Brace, Reynal and Hitchcock, Putnam, John Day, Oxford Press (American branch), and the university presses of Columbia, Harvard, Princeton, Chicago, and North Carolina.

Members of the jury have been contributors to the following American periodicals: *Century, Harper's Magazine, Scribner's American Scholar, Saturday Review of Literature, New York Times Book Review* and *Magazine, Atlantic Monthly, Living Age, The New Yorker* (including their poetry reviewer for twenty years), *English Journal, Yale*

Review, Writer, Good Housekeeping, Nation, New Republic, Poetry, Virginia Quarterly Review, American Literature, Southern Review, New England Quarterly, Commonweal, Christian Century, Literary Digest, Commentary, Sewanee Review, Kenyon Review; and others. They number editors, contributing editors, or consulting editors, now or formerly, for some of these and other literary magazines, and for several publishers.

Six members (almost half) of the jury have received Pulitzer Prizes, five have been awarded one or more prizes by *Poetry,* nine have held Guggenheim Fellowships for writing, of which several were renewed, four have received awards from the National Institute of Arts and Letters, three the Shelley Memorial Award from the Poetry Society of America, one has received the Dial Prize for distinguished service to American letters, one was the recipient, last year, of the Harriet Monroe-University of Chicago Award; and among other prizes and honors for members of the jury have been the Academy of Arts and Letters gold medal for poetry, the Society of Libraries' medal, the Book-of-the-Month Club award. This is to omit the foreign honors, including the award of the Order of Merit and, in 1948, of the Nobel Prize in Literature to T. S. Eliot, the juror against whom the Hillyer articles were particularly directed. Mr. Eliot has received honorary degrees from four American, five British, and one French university, and was described last November by Denis Saurat, the French critic, as "undoubtedly the world's most famous poet." The two new Fellows appointed this year, since the award, add another Pulitzer Prize winner, another Dial Prize winner, and swell all these lists either by additions or frequencies.

Among the learned societies to which members of the jury belong, and of which they are or have been officers, are: Society for American Studies (Pres.), Books Across the Sea (Pres.), Modern Language Association (several group chairmanships), Society of American Historians, Southern Historical Association, National Institute of Arts and Letters.

It would seem that the recognition of competence in literary production, scholarship, and judgment among the members of this group is too widespread—on the part of educators, publishers, editors, and professional colleagues—for them to be described as a small partisan group. Since the controversy began the publisher of the *Saturday Review* has written to one of them that he had no wish to attack their reputations and had the greatest respect for them all (*sic!*). Their work has over the course of years been treated with respect in its pages; and only a short time before the award was announced its reviewer wrote of one member of the jury: "Allen Tate is at his best as a critic of poetry." During the controversy, a preface by another juror was commended by the reviewer for its wit and instruction; this juror is Mr. W. H. Auden, whose aesthetic was then being editorially derided, and his preface includes the very unauthoritarian pronouncement that poetry flourishes when opposing schools are determined and evenly matched, and when one succeeds in suppressing its rivals, "invariably declines."

If the jurors are representative in the usual sense of being a group of recognized professionals, differing among themselves in the character of their work, as much as in eminence, should it still be said that in the matter of the award they acted improperly with respect to the American people? The *Saturday Review* editors appear to agree that political tenets should not be made a test of literary worth. The objection they make in their editorial of July 30 would seem to be that they and others cannot concur on aesthetic grounds. But what would be representative of the wish of the American people in a matter of this kind? The American people are assumed to wish for a free and full development of their cultural life, as well as of their economic life. It would not be to the interest of such development if members of a professional advisory committee were to falsify their opinions in order to escape censure, or to make a more popular choice. It would seem to be representative of the wish of the American people that its professional workers express their opinions honestly, and so put their experience and understanding for what they may be worth at the general service.

The Committee for the Fellows:
LEONIE ADAMS, Chairman
LOUISE BOGAN
KARL SHAPIRO
WILLARD THORP

[452]

APPENDIX I

I have no clear idea of the meaning of Fascism when the word is applied to conditions in the United States. At intervals since 1933 I have been accused of "Fascism" by persons who were either Communists or affected by Marxist ideas. In the literary world such charges have little real political significance; they were used against anti-Communist writers as demogogic weapons. The Marxist policy has held Fascism to be a "reactionary" movement, or a return to "tradition." I see it in very different terms. As I understand its European significance, Fascism is a revolutionary movement which prospers only if traditional institutions, social, political, and religious, which have been created with great labor for the protection of the individual, can be so completely dissolved that the individual has no life apart from the State.

Thus Fascism is in its extreme form not only revolutionary but nihilistic; and it differs from Communist totalitarianism in that Communism rationalizes its destruction of the individual with a specious philosophy of the common good. Both, as I see them, represent nihilism and the ultimate tyranny.

I am opposed to all forms of totalitarianism. I am not and have never been a political writer; but in so far as my interests as a literary critic have made it necessary for me to examine the social implications of literature, I have written essays which set forth the desirability, as the best basis for democratic independence, of what has been called the "distributist" or agrarian society. This theory of democracy holds that the strongest bulwark against tyrannies of all kinds, Fascist, Communist, or even plutocratic, is the ownership of productive land or the small factory, usually of family size. The group of writers with whom I was associated in these theories wished to formulate a characteristically American social philosophy, and we were consciously leaning upon the agrarian doctrines of Thomas Jefferson in constructing our theories. We felt that in the United States the choice between Communism and Fascism was an unreal one; we sought an American solution which would circumvent both.

My writings along these lines are publicly available in magazines and books, and are open to inspection.

[453]

In the early 1930's Mr. Seward Collins founded *The American Review* to give expression to the American group with which I was associated and to a similar group in England the most prominent member of which was the late G. K. Chesterton. About 1937 Mr. Collins publicly expressed Fascist sympathies. I declined henceforth to contribute to his magazine; other writers did likewise. About a year later *The American Review* suspended publication for lack of suitable contributors.

I have voted in only one Presidential election, that of 1940. I voted for Franklin D. Roosevelt. If I may be allowed the sarcasm, I may say that although it was said that Communists voted for Mr. Roosevelt, I never heard of a Fascist who did so.

ANNEX II. *Statement of Procedure of the Jury for the Bollingen Award, by Léonie Adams, Secretary to the Fellows in American Letters.*

Before the general meeting of the Fellows to discuss the award and other business, nominations were requested by the Fellows' secretary for the Bollingen prize. Nine letters of nomination were received which named, in all, fifteen books of verse, in addition to a few struck off by her as ineligible. One Fellow made a nomination orally to the secretary. These preliminary nominations, mailed from scattered addresses, foreshadowed the final vote, both as to first and second place choices.

It was apparent from the nomination letters that clarification was needed of the terms of the award, since a book by one of the Fellows had been nominated, and some jurors had offered alternative choices, for a book by a young poet, and for a whole career. The terms were discussed at the meeting, accordingly, first with respect to what the Fellows thought desirable, and then with reference to the correspondence and agreement between the Library and the Bollingen Foundation. It was established that by the agreed terms the prize was to be awarded on the relative poetic merits of a book of poems published by an American, not a member of the jury, during 1948.

This annual meeting was scheduled for November 18 and 19 and was the only general meeting possible before the date set for the award. It appeared that procedure must be devised for consideration of books published before January 1, but subsequently to the meeting. On the agenda, sent out to the Fellows before the meeting, it was pointed out that a committee had been proposed to take care of the procedure of the vote. This was the first item on the agenda, and at the opening meeting, a resolution to form the committee was unanimously passed, and two members to serve with the Consultant were elected by ballot. The committee was established as having no authority, but empowered to express the views of the group on the recommendation to the Librarian, and to receive through its chairman later nominations, revisions of vote, votes from absent members (who would be informed of proceedings through the minutes), and to provide for a letter ballot of ratification, or a new ballot if desirable or necessary. A substantial quorum was present at the meeting—twelve out of fourteen members—and the Fellows proposed that the ballot there taken might stand except in the event of a later nomination, or a recommendation from the committee that a new ballot was required for any reason. After the ballot on the second morning, it was also delegated to the committee to receive and report on special problems, such as an accompanying statement arising from an indicated award to Ezra Pound.

Copies of the nomination list had been presented to the members at the opening meeting, and the list was read aloud by the Chairman, and further nominations asked. On the following morning the list was reduced by nominations from the floor to four to be considered on the ballot. One member said he had not read all the volumes, and an offer was made to provide copies from the Library for members who could not easily obtain them for reading or for further reading. At this second day's meeting a ballot was taken on the four books then in nomination, which resulted in eight first places for Pound's *Pisan Cantos,* two first places for another book, and two abstentions. The four titles were read by the chairman in the order placed, and some discussion took place of difficulties of the award.

The Librarian was presented with the minutes, and the chairman reported to him the ballot (then unchanged) and the jury's views as to an accompanying statement and the final ballot. Shortly after, one revision of ballot and one new ballot were received. There were no further nominations.

The committee (Mr. Shapiro, Mr. Lowell, Miss Adams) met on February 1 to discuss the accompanying statement, a report to the jury and the final ballot. It was decided that this last would be recommended in order to procure the votes of all members after their further consideration, and to preserve the secrecy of the ballot with respect to revised and uncast votes.

A full report was sent out to each juror, enclosing a ballot to be marked 1, 2, 3, 4 and an inner unaddressed envelope in which to return it, incorporating the statement to be used in the event of a final recommendation of an award to Ezra Pound, and reporting the vote as it then stood, and a statement of Mr. Shapiro's reasons for revising his vote.

As a result of the letter ballot, 10 first places were given to Ezra Pound, (in addition, Theodore Spencer, who had died a few weeks previously, had made known his preference for the *Pisan Cantos* at the time of the annual meeting) and two first places to the volume which also received nine second places. No ballot had been returned from Mr. Green's address at the time it was necessary to make the count, and a wire had been sent him. The press release was already being sent out by the Library when a wire was received from him announcing his abstention from the ballot.

ANNEX III. *Letter from the Librarian of Congress to the Editor of the* Saturday Review.

Dear Mr. Cousins:

I am writing you[8] in regard to the article by Mr. Robert Hillyer and the editorial by yourself and Mr. Smith in the June 11 number of the *Saturday Review of Literature*. I hope that you will publish this letter in the earliest possible forthcoming issue of the *Saturday Review of Literature*.

Mr. Hillyer said early in his article that he was unable to discover who appoints the Fellows in American Letters. Mr. Verner W. Clapp of the Library of Congress wrote Mr. Hillyer on April 22: "The Fellows are appointed by the Librarian of Congress."

The Fellows in American Letters were first appointed in 1944 by my predecessor, Archibald MacLeish, to perform assignments of importance to the Library of Congress, and in his opinion and in the opinion of the distinguished workers in the field of American letters who could devote the necessary time to such onerous tasks, useful to scholarship and the advancement of literature. They accepted the tasks of advising the Library concerning the strengthening of its collections and the promotion of bibliographical and publication projects in American literary material. They also advised the Librarian on the choice of the annual incumbent of the Chair of Poetry in English. After almost four years of successful endeavor the Fellows, in addition to their other work, which now included assisting in carrying forward a project to issue albums of contemporary poetry read by the poets themselves, hit upon the idea (in January 1948) of an award for the outstanding publication each year in American poetry. After I approved the proposal an approach was made to secure the funds, with the success which has been noted.

The implications in Mr. Hillyer's article that the Bollingen Foundation had a part in the award to Ezra Pound, or in some way influenced it, are particularly annoying to the Library of Congress, and if in your editorial column you intended to vouch for the validity of such implications, I am sure you were not acquainted with the facts.

So far as my own knowledge and belief go, neither the Bollingen Foundation nor any of its Trustees, officers, or representatives had the slightest connection with the choice of the *Pisan Cantos* for the award. When, at the request of myself and the Library's Fellows, the Foundation agreed to make a grant to the Library, its purpose was to enable that agency of the Federal Government to grant a prize in recognition of outstanding achievement in American poetry. My idea in requesting the grant, and the sole purpose of the Foundation's Trustees in approving it, was to encourage serious endeavors in this field of American letters.

It was the Foundation's definite understanding from the beginning that the award would be solely that of the Library of Congress, made on the basis of the choice of a panel made up of the Library's Fellows in American Letters. It should also be emphasized that the Foundation had no connection with the selection of these Fellows nor any of their activities. They were appointed by the Librarian of Congress, and their selection is the responsibility of that officer of the Federal Government. So far as concerns T. S. Eliot, he had not served as a member of the panel at any meeting when the gift to the Library from the Foundation was made. He was appointed by me on my own responsibility, without any consultation with, or the knowledge of, the Foundation. In short, from the beginning every step was taken to insure that the prize, when awarded, would in fact be that of the Library of Congress, made on its responsibility, uninfluenced in any way by the Foundation. While the prize bears the name of the Foundation, this was a courtesy which the Library of Congress wished to extend in appreciation of the donor's generosity.

It is extremely unfortunate from the viewpoint of future aid to the cultural activities of the Library of Congress that a public benefactor, such as Bollingen Foundation, seeking only to promote the welfare of the Library by a generous gift, should be subjected, because of the Library's application of that gift, to the unfavorable reflections appearing in Mr. Hillyer's article, which are apparently vouched for in your publication's editorial accompanying the article. Furthermore, you will understand that this is highly embarrassing to me and to the Library.

That Mr. Paul Mellon has through some diabolical and perverted motivation tried to influence the decision of the Fellows, is an insinuation which I believe has no foundation whatever. I doubt seriously that Mr. Mellon knows personally a single member of the group of Fellows. All the public can see how generously he has given to worthy causes, without going beyond the press headlines of the past week. Why cannot the traducing of persons of high personal character and integrity be reserved for officers of Government, who must by virtue of the nature of the democratic process put up with it anyhow?

The attack on the legality and the propriety of appointing persons to the staff of the Library of Congress for the purposes served by the Fellows in American Letters ignores the clear statutory authorizations under which the Library of Congress operates (U. S. Code, Title II),

and constitutes a challenge to a broad program of the Library for pro-
moting the arts in America. Under the auspices of the Coolidge Foun-
dation, the Library has for decades commissioned the writing of music,
has awarded medals for outstanding accomplishments in musicianship,
and has provided concerts of high quality.

Surely, it is no service to American culture to make an ill-founded
attack upon the effort made by this great institution to enrich the life of
the people by such means. With the specific approval of Congress also,
the Library prepares a publication known as *The United States Quar-
terly Book List*. This book list has as its purpose the review under the
editorship of a regular Government employee of selected books which
make a contribution to knowledge. The operation involves the editing
by Government employees of evaluations of books made by the indi-
vidual scholarly reviewers who contribute their services for this pur-
pose. The editor has authority to rewrite reviews and to change the
evaluations made of the books reviewed. The signatures of the review-
ers do not appear.

The Congress has also during the past decade or more authorized a
large appropriation to the Library of Congress, currently in the amount
of approximately one million dollars, for the provision of books for the
adult blind readers of the United States. The selection of books to be
put in this program is entrusted entirely to the Librarian of Congress
and his staff. The operation involves the choice of a few books from
the multitude from which the choice is made for the instructional and
recreational reading of blind persons. The responsibility is a heavy one,
and it amounts in effect to calling some books bad and other books
good.

I should like to observe that the question of propriety in a project of
the type I have been discussing is intimately related to the governmental
arrangements for making the scholarly or artistic decisions involved. It
would obviously be improper and an abuse of authority for decisions to
be made as to what is truthful, or what is beautiful, or what is good as
the arbitrary acts of an individual not especially qualified to make them.
By this I mean, for instance, that I as the head of the Library of Con-
gress would be acting arbitrarily were I to pass judgment on what is
good music, assuming that I am not an expert in the field, or selecting

books for the *Quarterly Book List* in fields where I do not have expert capacity, or in picking a book of poetry for an award when I am not a qualified critic of poetry. The only way to insure that choices of this kind are legitimate and acceptable when made by a governmental institution is to conduct affairs in such a way that persons who make the aesthetic or the scholarly judgments are persons chosen for their competence in such work and divorced from general responsibilities for the management of the institution itself. This principle I have striven to observe, and I have, I believe, observed it in the present case.

The Fellows in American Letters are in all cases, I believe, persons of attainment and a high sense of responsibility for promoting and strengthening what is good in American culture. No such serious charge as yours, as far as I know, has hitherto been made against them of being politically motivated members of a clique or a school or a particular aesthetic group, or of being under the domination of any individual. Now that your charge has been made I shall, of course, inquire into the situation with a view to the possibility if it should prove desirable of strengthening the representative character of the group. The insinuation which has been made is very damaging to the Fellows and to the Library of Congress, since it amounts to a charge that the Fellows have not acted, as they were charged to act, as public servants, but rather that they have abused the authority entrusted to them for evil ends. I think evidence should be produced, rather than pure supposition, to sustain such an insinuation. You and Mr. Hillyer are under a public duty to produce the evidence.

I personally regard the choice of the *Pisan Cantos* for the Bollingen prize as an unfortunate choice. I do not feel called upon to go into all of my reasons for feeling this. I think it is sufficient to say that from my poetically ignorant point of view, Mr. Pound's book is hardly poetry at all. I believe now, as I believed at the time of announcing the award, that I would be engaging in an improper interference with free scholarship if I were to substitute my own decision in this matter for the decision of the Fellows. I think that for me to interfere with the work of scholars would be far worse than to award the prize for a book which did not deserve it. After all, a cure is available in scholarly terms for scholarly errors, but I know of no cure for the bureaucratic error of overriding scholarly judgment in cases of this kind. I feel that I would have been striking a blow against the cause of liberty by overriding scholarly judgment, and I do not feel that the blow for unrighteousness, which the award may represent, is nearly as grave.

You and Mr. Hillyer have treated Mr. Pound as though he had been proved guilty of treason. To me, this is not the case. To me also it is irrelevant to the making of the award, since we did not say in the condition of the award that a person had to be one who had not been convicted by courts or found guilty by the public of some crime or other. I should also like to observe that Mr. Pound is a citizen no matter whether it may be desirable in the judgment to be such. The matter of citizenship is one of law and not one of politics or poetry.

The Fellows in American Letters do not have to be citizens. Therefore, the criticism of Mr. Eliot's membership of the group on this ground is irrelevant. Persons are chosen for outstanding accomplishment in the field of American letters, either as creative writers or as scholars in the field. Mr. Eliot meets this test, and I have no intention of asking him to resign. Indeed, I should be very sorry if such a distinguished writer were to cease to be a member of the group.

As to whether a person who is insane can write distinguished poetry, I would prefer to leave that to the literati to wrangle over, rather than try to make a decision myself.

I am deeply disturbed by one point of view which you and Mr. Hillyer seem to share, and that is that poetic quality must somehow pass a political test. In my many years of study and teaching in the field of political science, I came to regard a political test for art and poetry as a sign of a dictatorial, illiberal, undemocratic approach to matters of the mind. The alternative attitude is not necessarily the separation of art from life, or of form from substance. I think you really ought to admit that the principal charge you wish to bring against Mr. Pound's poetry is not that it is form divorced from substance or art divorced from life, but that it is a kind of substance and preaches a view of life which you do not like. I do not like them either. But the question of whether Pound's poetry is art, whether it is *good* poetry, is a different question. As to that question, my answer is also negative, but as I have said already, I do not feel that it would be proper for me to override the judgment of persons in whose competence I have confidence, and who were charged with responsibility to make the judgment.

Sincerely yours,

Luther H. Evans
Librarian of Congress

Mr. Norman Cousins
Editor
The Saturday Review of Literature
25 West 45th Street
New York 19, New York

ANNEX IV. *The Announcement of the Award: Library of Congress Press Release No. 542, February 20, 1949.*

THE *PISAN CANTOS* WINS FOR EZRA POUND
FIRST AWARD OF BOLLINGEN PRIZE IN POETRY

The first annual award of the Bollingen Prize in Poetry has been made to Ezra Pound for his book the *Pisan Cantos*, it was announced today at the Library of Congress.

The Bollingen Prize in Poetry, established a year ago, was made possible by a gift of money from the Bollingen Foundation, and is to be awarded annually on the basis of a recommendation by a jury of selection consisting of the Fellows in American Letters of the Library of Congress. This is an honorary and advisory group appointed by the Librarian of Congress and consists of the following well-known writers: Conrad Aiken, W. H. Auden, Louise Bogan, Katherine Garrison Chapin, T. S. Eliot, Paul Green, Robert Lowell, Katherine Anne Porter, Karl Shapiro, Allen Tate, Willard Thorp and Robert Penn Warren, as well as Léonie Adams, the Library's Consultant in Poetry in English for the present year. Theodore Spencer (deceased January 18, 1949) was a member of the group at the time that the selection was made for the 1948 award of the Bollingen Prize; Archibald MacLeish and William Carlos Williams have become members since the selection was made.

The prize is awarded to the author of the book of verse which, in the opinion of the jury of selection, represents the highest achievement of American poetry in the year for which the award is made. The jury may, however, decline to make a selection for any given year if in its judgment no poetry worthy of the prize was published during that year. The amount of the prize is one thousand dollars.

In recommending that the award be made to Mr. Pound the jury has stated that:

> "The Fellows are aware that objections may be made to awarding a prize to a man situated as is Mr. Pound. In their view, however, the possibility of such objection did not alter the responsibility assumed by the Jury of Selection. This was to make a choice for the award among the eligible books, provided any one merited such recognition, according to the stated terms of the Bollingen Prize. To permit other considerations than that of poetic achievement to sway the decision would destroy the significance of the award and would in principle deny the validity of that objective perception of value on which any civilized society must rest."

Notes

1. A copy of the mimeographed version of this "Statement" was sent in due course to the *Saturday Review of Literature*.

2. This letter is reprinted here [as Annex III].

3. See [Annex III].

4. See [Annex I].

5. "In a period of debility like our own, few men have the energy to follow the middle way in government; for lazy or tired minds there is only extremity or apathy: dictatorship or communism, with enthusiasm or indifference." T. S. Eliot, *Essays Ancient and Modern*, p. 33.

6. The Announcement of the Prize is reproduced [as Annex IV].

7. Mr. Hillyer has since written that he had this information in time to use it, but "carelessly" failed to do so. Letter to the *Saturday Review of Literature*, August 13, p. 24.

8. This letter was published in the *Saturday Review of Literature*, July 2, 1949.

Appendix II

WHAT DOES THE CONSULTANT IN
POETRY DO?

The Consultant in Poetry is a very busy man, chiefly because he spends so much time talking with people who want to know what the Consultant in Poetry does. This brief note, written in such moments as the Consultant can snatch away from his many duties and activities, is intended to answer the question once and for all and so set the mind of the Public again at rest, the normal condition from which it appears to have been somewhat disturbed.

The Consultant in Poetry sits in the right eye of the Library of Congress, in a luxuriously appointed office. His feet sink deep into the white llama-skin rug (gift of the Tashi Lama). His desk is a priceless heirloom, presented to Samuel Taylor Coleridge by a nephew of Kubla Khan. All the books in the room are bound in pure gold; at sunset the place blazes intolerably. The Consultant is protected against quotidian intrusion by a staff of learned and beautiful women, graciously supplied by the taxpayers of America. For moments of more profound meditation, he mounts the spiral stair to the genuine ivory tower constructed by the design left by Saarinen.

From this sanctuary the Consultant directs the destinies of American poetry. This aspect of his work is perhaps best summed up in the lines of the American poetess Emma Woodbine Weed, Consultant in 1929 (Jan.–Oct.):

> Send me thy works, ye poor in spirit!
> Dost thou believe thy triolets neglected?
> Mayhap I shall lift thee up.
> Hast'ou been by publisher rejected?
> The presses roar! Thy babes shall sup!

(The last line has sometimes been felt to be obscure.)

In sharp contrast to the meditative calm of the Consultant's eyrie is the Outer Office, where the phones are constantly in action as the cool, efficient staff handles up to three million inquiries a day, such as: Who is the heroine of Jane Eyre? What is an I am? How would you estimate the influence of Candide on Gulliver's Travels? Is Modern Poetry obscure? What rimes with "orange"? (answer: General *Goeringe,* who dug the Panama Canal. But very advanced thinkers would also admit "syringe.")

The Office of the Consultant is typical of American industry also in that the real work is done elsewhere. Let us accompany, in imagination, the Consultant on his daily tour of inspection. He presses a button; one wall of the office slides smoothly back, disclosing an elevator (when it is not on another floor, that is; Consultants have in the past sometimes been lost this way). We enter, and descend through the stacks, down level after level of what Matthew Arnold called "the army of unorderable lore," and, below the deepest cellar, hidden from public view, its mere existence unsuspected by any save the President and a few trusted aides, is the production line, a long corridor of cubicles lit by weak but naked electric bulbs, in each cubicle a desk, a typewriter, and a poet. The poets would stand to attention to greet their chief, but their feet have been stapled to the floor.

The present Consultant, a grey, cheerful gnome of a man, capable of surprising dignity in view of the fact that he is less than four feet tall, confesses shyly the process of automation in his department is lagging behind schedule. "I'd hoped to have these bums out of here last April," he tells you, with a wave at the poets. "Then we'd have the place air-conditioned. But meanwhile"—he shrugs resignedly—"we make do, we make do."

We stroll down the long line of hunched backs, as the poets bend to their work. The Consultant fingers thoughtfully the tiny silver-mounted whip which is the standard of his Office; its use nowadays, he explains, is purely symbolic. Once in a while our little procession stops, and the Consultant leans over a poet to rip a sheet out of the typewriter for inspection.

"Damn decent adjectives, Pilcherd," he may say with an encouraging smile, "I especially like 'roseate' for its vividness." We walk on, pic-turing vividly those roses, chomping—on what?

Sometimes he may find a fault, and gently admonish or rebuke one of the poets. "This won't do, Magruder, it simply won't do"—tearing the page across and dropping it on the floor—"to say 'your ears, the handles to that vase, your face.' Remember," he adds sternly, "iambic pentameter is out, but out. We are doing Alexandrines this month." Then, as a tear rolls down Magruder's cheek and drops into the type-writer, the Consultant relents. "It's easily repaired, lad," he says in a kindly tone. "Here, I've a notion—why not 'loving-cup' instead of 'vase'?"

"Thank you, sir," says Magruder.

"Just a suggestion," says the Consultant, "but it preserves the meta-phor, doesn't it?"

As we move out of earshot he explains that Magruder has only re-cently been moved up to doing entire lines. "He's a very sensitive boy, Magruder, and it would be in the nature of a personal disgrace for him to be dropped back to the Pure Images Division, say, or the Bureau of Prosody—that's where they program the meters, you know; all the people you see in this corridor are just filling in the words."

At the end of the corridor, we reach the climax of our tour.

"We haven't had the computer for very long," the Consultant ex-plains, patting its console affectionately, "but we're already finding it extremely valuable. You see, we not only produce the stuff, we also have to evaluate it, mark it, Great, Fine, Interesting, or whatever, before sending it to the stacks to be filed for eternity. So we've programmed this machine to do Literary Criticism, and in the past six months I don't know how many semiskilled operators it has helped us to replace. Right now it's testing some work done by the companion model, which we're programming to write the poems now being done by . . ." He turns and looks thoughtfully back at the long line of poets. "But that one is still in the experimental stage, so we check its results out on Felicra here." He smiles. "That's our pet name for this computer. Her real name is Federal Literary Critic, Mark A. Here for example is a poem just sent in by Poco (Poetry Composer, Original) the other machine out at our lab in Magnolia Falls, Maryland."

We are not allowed to see the poem itself, which is still marked Secret. But the Consultant lets us look on, fascinated, while he feeds the poem into the critical computer. There is no visible sign of activity beyond the flash of a light and a brief, almost instantaneous, electrical hum; the critical process is over. At the other end of the computer the page is automatically crumpled and shredded and falls into a waste basket, while before our eyes a tape slides smoothly through a teleprinter forming the criticism itself. It reads: *You are using a Nineteenth Century Computer.*

"Well," says the Consultant ruefully, yet with a boyish grin, "I guess you can't win 'em all."

And, by another elevator now, we ascend through the marble floor of the Library of Congress, say our thank-yous and bid farewell to the Consultant in Poetry, who returns to his many duties.

Emerging into the sunlit world above ground, we pause for a moment to reflect gratefully on the experience we have just been privileged to have, and to think, that, whatever one may say of the rest of the government, at least American Culture, Literature Section, Subsection Poetry, is in good hands.

Howard Nemerov
October 3, 1963

Sources and Acknowledgments

IN GENERAL

The principal source of this chronicle was the rich store of documenta-
tion in the archives of the Library of Congress, variously disposed in
its Manuscript Division, Central Services Division, and Poetry Office.
There are files for each Consultant's tenure, containing (copiously, after
the 1952–56 hiatus) correspondence, internal memoranda, press clip-
pings, etc.; files of the papers of the successive Librarians and other
Library officials; and special files for the Pound and Williams episodes
and the poetry festivals. All that documentation was searched out, in-
spected, and then summarized in an invaluable guiding memorandum,
by Marlene Morrisey, in anticipation of the preparation of a historical
account. (This was a last assignment for Mrs. Morrisey, a longtime
Library official, before her retirement in 1983. Later she supplied rec-
ollections in a personal letter.) The Library's publications were essential
sources, in particular the annual reports of the Librarian of Congress
from the Putnam Librarianship onward (and including particularly, in
the 1946 report, David C. Mearns's 200-page historical chapter, "The

Story Up to Now"); *For Congress and the Nation: A Chronological History* . . . (1979), by John Y. Cole (who was notably helpful in personal discussions also); *Librarians of Congress 1802–1974* (1977); *Literary Recordings: A Checklist of the Archive of Recorded Poetry and Literature* . . . (rev. ed., 1981), compiled by Jennifer Whittington (Rutland); *Sixty American Poets 1896–1944: A Preliminary Check List* (1945), selected, with preface and critical notes, by Allen Tate (rev. ed., 1954, prepared by Kenton Kilmer); *Ten First Street, Southeast: Congress Builds a Library, 1886–1897* (1980), by Helen-Anne Hilker; *The Library of Congress Information Bulletin* and other house organs; and The *Quarterly Journal of the Library of Congress,* vols. 1–40, 1943–1983. I must mention the convenience of having at hand the Library's numerous publications of lectures by Consultants in Poetry and by speakers on the programs arranged under the Gertrude Clarke Whittall Poetry and Literature Fund, in brochure form or collected in the volume *Literary Lectures* (1973); and the (unpublished) reports of the Consultant in Poetry and the Poetry Office to the chief of the supervising division, from the late 1950s onward. In general, the foregoing Library of Congress documentation has not been cited in the compilation that follows, except occasionally for clarification.

I have had conversations with all the Consultants who are living and with the widows of Randall Jarrell and Robert Hayden. All of them have been forthcoming in our talks and in correspondence.

In the Library of Congress community, I am most beholden to an official retired from the staff whose importance in the story of the Chair made his cooperation indispensable: Roy P. Basler, who in the friendliest way has given me a great deal of his time for conversations, in person (at Fenwick Island, Delaware, and Gainesville, Florida), and on the telephone, and has sent me written comments on the work as it took shape. His memories of the poetry programs during the years he managed them are phenomenally vivid, unvarnished, and diverting; they supplement the important information in his collection of essays, *The Muse and the Librarian* (Westport, Conn.: Greenwood Press, 1974)— in particular the long essay of the same title, which anticipates the present work up to the early 1970s, and the essays on his friends Frost and Sandburg. Basler gave me permission to quote, and even allowed me to cannibalize, some entire passages. His successor as director of the poetry programs, John C. Broderick, who as the Assistant Librarian for Research Services conceived the idea of this chronicle and supervised its preparation, was in turn an essential source of information about the later years of the story and especially about the labyrinthine ways of the Library bureaucracy and economy. He has been a tactful, considerate, patient, and humorous guide.

Three shorter accounts of the Consultantship were variously suggestive: "Poets in Washington: The Consultants in Poetry to the Library of Congress," by Mary C. Lethbridge, in *Records of the Columbia Historical Society of Washington, D.C.,* 1969–70; "Dateline—Washington," by Dale Nelson, in *Wilson Library Bulletin,* January and February 1981; and a chapter on "The Poetry Consultant," in *The Library of Congress* (Boulder: Westview Press, 1982), by Charles A. Goodrum and Helen W. Dalrymple.

The two present members of the Poetry Office staff, Nancy Galbraith and Jennifer Rutland, were unfailingly helpful in locating source material, explaining, identifying, remembering, interpreting, warning, photocopying, and a dozen other ways. The staff of the Manuscript Division gave consistent support: the personnel of the Reading Room, scene of the major part of my research, were interested, cooperative, resourceful, and friendly; the chief of the division, James H. Hutson, was a source of information on the Council of Scholars and did me a particular kindness; R. S. Wilkinson guided me to files and background information I might otherwise have missed; Mary Vass, who had worked with Basler and Broderick, was similarly obliging with files in her care. I must also mention Katrina Adams and other members of the Central Services Division staff, who helped me with administrative files in their office; Edward d'Alessandro, of the office of the Assistant Librarian for Research Services, who supplied basic information on the history of the funds that support the literary programs; and Emma Vaughan, special assistant to John Broderick, with whom it was always a pleasure to work.

Two other veterans of the Library staff helped me with their unique recollections: Kenton Kilmer, who was an assistant to the first Consultant in Poetry, Joseph Auslander; and Edward N. Waters, who during his years as assistant chief and chief of the Music Division had a close friendship with Gertrude Whittall (besides writing the informative chapter on the Putnam librarianship in the above-mentioned volume *Librarians of Congress*). Both gentlemen granted me interviews and answered many questions.

In Princeton, Willard Thorp was notably helpful with memories, advice, encouragement, and candid reactions to the work as it developed. Theodore Weiss was forthcoming with suggestions and information. Prof. Janet Martin advised on a Latin phrase.

The staff of the Academy of American Poets, in New York—in particular the Academy's president, Marie Bullock, and its director, Henri Cole—were helpful with research in its archives on the span of the Consultantship, especially the Auslander phase. Mrs. Bullock granted an interview of exceptional relevance. The Allen Tate papers in the Firestone Library at Princeton University were an important source, and I am indebted to Anne Van Arsdale of the curatorial staff for her courteous help.

My editor, James Hardin, who at the beginning was on the staff of the Publishing Office and then, not inappropriately, was shifted to the Manuscript Division, has been a constructive and incredibly encouraging and cheerful guide. For his tough editorial discipline and his tactful and apropos suggestions I'm gratefully in his debt.

PROLOGUE

Extracts of the Consultants' discussion on March 6, 1978, are from an audio tape in the Motion Picture, Broadcasting, and Recorded Sound Division.

PART ONE

The history of the Library of Congress and details of Herbert Putnam's career are from general sources cited above. On Putnam also: his papers, in the Manuscript Division; article in *National Cyclopaedia of*

American Biography, 1962 (particularly on his appearance); remarks by David C. Mearns in an interview, 1956, quoted by John Cole in the *LCPA Newsletter*, February 1971. His correspondence with A. M. Huntington from the Putnam papers.

Huntington: A. Hyatt Mayor's introduction to *A Century of American Sculpture: Treasures from Brookgreen Gardens* (New York: Abbeville Press, 1980): quotations (by permission of the publisher) and information. Data on Collis P. Huntington from biographical sketch with his papers, Manuscript Division. Interview in New York with Mrs. A. Hyatt Mayor and Brantz Mayor (who also loaned photographs). Other biographical data from Beatrice Gilman Proske, *Archer Milton Huntington* (New York: Hispanic Society of America, 1963), and an interview with Mrs. Proske; *National Cyclopaedia of American Biography*, 1962; and Parke Rouse, Jr., "Mysterious Arabella Huntington," in his *The Good Old Days in . . . Newport News* (Richmond: Dietz Press, 1986). Huntington's poem "With What Soft Tread" quoted from an "In Memoriam" by A. R. Nykl (Bethel, Conn.: privately published, 1956). AMH's appearance: descriptions by John Kirtland Wright, in the Proske monograph, and by David Rubio, in *The Hispanic Room in the Library of Congress* (LC brochure, 1984). Story of chauffeur: from José García-Mazás, quoting Anne M. Perkins, AMH's secretary, in a letter, 1957. AMH and the American Academy of Arts and Sciences: the Proske monograph and Huntington papers in the Academy library, made available through the kindness of the librarians, Nancy Johnson and Casindania P. Eaton. The poem "Genius: To the American Academy" from the same source. AMH on women employees: Perkins letter, cited above. AMH and the Hispanic Society of America: the Proske monograph; an interview with Mary Bass Newlin; correspondence and an interview with the director, Theodore S. Beardsley, Jr.; obituary articles by Henry Grattan Doyle, *Modern Language Journal*, 11:1 (February 1956), and in a memorial monograph of the Pan American Union, 1957; LC Archives. Architecture of Audubon Terrace: N. White and E. Willensky, *AIA Guide to New York City*, rev. ed. (1978), and P. Goldberger, *The City Observed: New York* (1979). AMH and Newport News: Parke Rouse, Jr., "Huntington, in poetic company . . . ," *Daily Press* (Newport News), January 12, 1986, p. 13. Gilpin: Martha A.

Sandweiss, *Laura Gilpin: An Enduring Grace* (Fort Worth: Amon L. Carter Museum, 1986), p. 43.

Elizabeth Sprague Coolidge: *Dictionary of American Biography.* A program of the first concert, February 1924, in the Putnam papers.

Whittall gift of instruments: H. B. Wilkins, *The Stradivari Quintet of Stringed Instruments in the Library of Congress* (LC brochure, 1937).

Huntington: The poems "Come to the silver gardens" and "I saw her walk," quoted in the Proske monograph. Interview with Gurdon L. Tarbox, Jr., director of Brookgreen Gardens. Hispanic Room and Division: LC brochure; information from Mary Kahler.

Henry Kirke Porter: *Biographical Dictionary of the U. S. Congress. Who Was Who in America.*

Auslander: Correspondence with AMH from the Huntington Papers in the George Arents Research Library, Syracuse University. Interview with Marie Bullock; his correspondence with her, in the archives of the Academy of American Poets. *Who's Who in America, 1938.* Louise Bogan's digs at Auslander: *What the Woman Lived: Selected Letters* . . . , ed. Ruth Limmer (New York: Harcourt Brace Jovanovich, 1973; copyright © by Ruth Limmer, Trustee, Estate of Louise Bogan). MacLeish's remark to Pound: *Letters* . . . , ed. R. H. Winnick (New York: Houghton Mifflin, 1983), p. 187. Copyright © 1983 by the Estate of Archibald MacLeish and by R. H. Winnick. Untermeyer, *Modern American Poetry,* 5th rev. ed. (New York: Harcourt, Brace, 1936). Interview with Kenton Kilmer, Vienna, Virginia. Sprague collection of Whitman: information from Library of the University of Pennsylvania.

Pound in Washington: Noel Stock, *The Life of Ezra Pound* (New York: Pantheon Books, 1970). Basler, *The Muse and the Librarian,* pp. 17–18. W. C. Williams on Pound: *The Selected Letters* . . ., ed. J. C. Thirlwall (New York: McDowell, Oblensky, 1957), no. 125. Pound's letter to MacLeish, July 19, 1939, from Rapallo, and Putnam's letter to Pound about his visit, both in LC Archives.

Housman mss.: David A. Randall, *Dukedom Large Enough* (New York: Random House, 1969).

MacLeish's appointment as Librarian: *Letters,* ed. Winnick, pp. 299–303. Auden's immigration: Humphrey Carpenter, *W. H. Auden:*

A Biography (Boston: Houghton Mifflin, 1981), pp. 254, 280–81; MacLeish Papers, letter to Auden, Oct. 19, 1939. Letter to Sandburg: *Letters,* ed. Winnick, pp. 303–6. Alexis Leger (St.-John Perse): biographical details from William McGuire, *Bollingen: An Adventure in Collecting the Past* (Princeton: Princeton University Press, 1982), based on information from Dorothy Leger, A. J. Knodel, Bollingen Foundation Papers (in the Manuscript Division); letter to Tate, January 1, 1927, Tate Papers, Firestone Library, Princeton University.

Robinson Jeffers's reading and talk: *Washington Post,* February 21 and March 1, 1941.

Kenn collection in Hawaii: Information from Elizabeth Tatar, Ethnomusicologist, Bishop Museum, Honolulu.

PART TWO

TATE: MacLeish's letters to Tate, 1926 and 1927: *Letters,* ed. Winnick, pp. 181, 198. The other letters referred to in the first paragraph are chiefly in the Tate Papers, Firestone Library, Princeton University. To MacLeish, May 10, 1933, and November 29, 1939. The house in Anacostia and the Cheneys: information from Anne Waldron (biographer of Caroline Gordon) and Meredith's letter to Tate, October 31, 1978, in the Tate Papers. Joseph Frank's information about the Confederate flags came in conversation. Tate's remark twenty-five years later about the *Check Lists:* "Mere Literature and the Lost Traveller," lecture at Peabody College, Nashville, July 17, 1969, in *Poetry,* November 1979, p. 93. John Peale Bishop's appointment: Tate, *Memoirs and Opinions 1926–1974* (Chicago: Swallow Press, 1975), p. 74.

Meredith and Yale Series: AM to Meredith, November 23, 1943, in *Letters,* ed. Winnick, p. 321. Rukeyser and Tate support: Tate to Meredith, September 8, 1943, in Tate Papers, Princeton. Information also from Willard Thorp.

Pound: AM to Hemingway, July 27, 1943, in *Letters,* ed. Winnick, pp. 315–16. Hemingway's reply, August 10, 1943, in *Ernest Hemingway: Selected Letters,* ed. Carlos Baker (New York: Scribner, 1981). The AM/Tate exchange following, August 20, 21, in MacLeish Papers,

Manuscript Division. AM to Bundy, September 10, 1943, in *Letters,* pp. 317–18.

Senate Foreign Relations Committee: Tate to AM, December 6, 1944, in Tate Papers, Princeton. Recollection several years later: *The Dialogues of Archibald MacLeish and Mark Van Doren,* ed. Warren V. Bush (New York: E. P. Dutton, 1964), p. 34. Poem, "A Poet Speaks . . .": in *Washington and the Poet,* ed. Francis Coleman Rosenberger (Charlottesville: University Press of Virginia, 1977; copyright © 1943, 1971, 1976 by Archibald MacLeish).

Summing up of AM: biographical memoir by John C. Broderick, American Philosophical Society, *Yearbook,* 1982.

WARREN: RPW on Henry Miller: interview, West Wardsboro, Vermont. Tate to Eliot, December 18, 1945; carbon copy in LC archives.

BOGAN: to Humphries, July 8, 1938: in *Selected Letters,* ed. Limmer. "MacSlush" and other details from Elizabeth Frank, *Louise Bogan: A Portrait* (New York: Knopf, 1985). Review of *America Was Promises:* quoted by Frank from *The New Yorker,* December 16, 1939. LB to Zabel, July 6, and to Tate, July 9, 1945: in *Selected Letters,* ed. Limmer. Selden Rodman's apartment: LB to Maxwell, October 8, 1945, ibid. Katie Louchheim, and quotation: Frank, pp. 338–39 (KL in *American Pen,* Spring 1975).

Mellon to Cairns, January 21, 1946: Bollingen Foundation papers, LC.

Untermeyer on Pound and Guest: Henry Seidel Canby, in *Saturday Review of Literature,* December 15, 1945.

LB's voice: William Jay Smith, *Louise Bogan: A Woman's Words* (LC lecture, May 4, 1970; brochure, 1971).

Maugham at LC: Ted Morgan, *Maugham: A Biography* (New York: Simon and Schuster, 1980), pp. 498–99.

LB/Tate letters, June-August, 1946: Tate Papers, Princeton. LB to Maxwell, June 26, 1946, and to Zabel, October 24, 1948: *Selected Letters,* ed. Limmer.

Eliot to Tate, July 10, 1946: Tate Papers, Princeton.

SHAPIRO: Tate, "Letter to a Poet," *Common Sense,* February 1943, quoted in Joseph Reino, *Karl Shapiro* (Boston: Twayne, 1981), p. 23. Evalyn Shapiro on Bogan review and other details: interview, Washington. KS in Connecticut: interview with him, New York. KS/Tate letters, July 8, October 2 and 9, 1946: Tate Papers, Princeton. Shapiro's third-person recollections: unpublished draft made available to the writer; later published, with revisions, as "The Golden Albatross," *American Scholar,* Winter 1985/86. Quoted with KS's permission. KS's reading matter at LC: interview; on St.-John Perse, unpublished draft and interview.

Eliot reading, May 23, 1947: Peter Ackroyd, *T. S. Eliot: A Life* (New York: Simon and Schuster, 1984), p. 285.

LOWELL in 1947: Ian Hamilton, *Robert Lowell: A Biography* (New York: Random House, 1982), p. 124. Telegram to Tate, June 4, 1947; remarks about Spivacke and about Cosmos Club, November 4, 1947: Tate Papers, Princeton. Visitors to Pound: E. F. Torrey, *The Roots of Treason: Ezra Pound and the Secret of St. Elizabeths* (New York: McGraw-Hill, 1984), pp. 219, 237; Hamilton, p. 130; Dickey's remark: interview. Austine Cassini column: about October 26, 1947, probably from Washington *Times-Herald* (unidentified, in LC archives). Lowell in Greensboro: Hamilton, p. 131.

Tate to Eliot, about recordings: December 2, 1947, in Tate Papers, Princeton. Other correspondence on this subject in LC archives.

Bollingen Prize: Bollingen Foundation archives, LC. Much of the information as presented in McGuire, *Bollingen: An Adventure . . . ,* pp. 208–18.

Lowell to Tate from Yaddo: undated letter, dated December 1948 by Tate; Tate Papers, Princeton. Lowell's review of *Paterson II: The Nation,* June 19, 1948. Bogan's review of *Pisan Cantos: The New Yorker,* October 30, 1948.

ADAMS (and the Bollingen Prize): Article on Ledoux Collection of E. A. Robinson: LC *Quarterly Journal* 7:1 (November 1949). Interview, New Milford, Connecticut.

Eliot in Princeton: Ackroyd, pp. 287–89. At the LC: Bogan to Zabel, on Eliot: November 28, 1948, in *Selected Letters,* ed. Limmer; Warren on Eliot and Williams: interview.

Shapiro "wrestling with his soul," to Tate, January 27, 1949; Tate to Shapiro, "I fear it is very difficult . . ." April 22, 1949: Tate Papers, Princeton.

Biddle memoir: *In Brief Authority* (Garden City: Doubleday, 1962).

Frost memorandum to Morrison: Lawrance Thompson and R. H. Winnick, *Robert Frost: The Later Years (1938–1963)* (New York: Holt, Rinehart, Winston, 1976), p. 175 (dated c. February 22, 1949).

Cairns's journal: in Cairns Papers, Manuscript Division. Pound's response to *Washington Post* questions: February 21, 1949. Tate to Mrs. Pound: April 26, 1949, in Tate Papers, Princeton. (Winchell quotation untraceable.) Soviet Overseas Service: Text of monitored broadcast in Evans's papers, LC.

Shapiro on Parelhoff: interview.

MacLeish to Harrison Smith: May 27, 1949, in *Letters,* ed. Winnick. MacLeish to Tate, on Evans's manners: September 13, 1949, in Tate Papers, Princeton.

Bogan to Shawn, on Hillyer's book: September 27, 1949, in *Selected Letters,* ed. Limmer.

MacLeish/Tate exchange, on Bollingen Prize at Yale: February 15 and 17, 1950; in Tate Papers, Princeton. Cowley to Tate, October 21, 1949: copy in Bollingen Foundation archives, LC.

BISHOP: "Visits to St. Elizabeths" (1950), in *The Complete Poems* (New York: Farrar, Straus and Giroux, 1983; copyright © 1983 by Alice Helen Methfessel).

W. C. Williams to Tate, on Eliot: July 2 and August 11, 1949; Tate Papers, Princeton. Eliot's cruise to Cape Town: Ackroyd, p. 298. John Berryman and Bollingen Prize statement: Eileen Simpson, *Poets in Their Youth* (New York: Vintage, 1982), p. 197.

Bollingen Foundation officer: Ernest Brooks, Jr., file memorandum in Bollingen Foundation archives, LC.

PART THREE

AIKEN: "Well, yes and no . . .": interview by John K. Hutchens, "One Thing and Another," *Saturday Review,* December 20, 1969. Friendship with Eliot: Ackroyd, p. 43. On *The Cocktail Party:* to Tate, April 4, 1950, in Tate Papers, Princeton. "the Tate-to-Blackmur . . . roundelay": to Malcolm Cowley, February 17, 1941, in *Selected Letters . . . ,* ed. Joseph Killorin (New Haven: Yale University Press, 1978; copyright © 1978 by Mary Hoover Aiken and Joseph Killorin). "with the understanding . . ." and "Of course the statement . . .": to Tate, April 4, 1950, in Tate Papers, Princeton. "it is a sort of . . .": to Tate, April 20, 1950, ibid. To his daughter, Joan Aiken, October 4, 1950: *Selected Letters,* ed. Killorin. On luncheon with Laughton and quotations following: to Edward Burra, March 9, 1951, ibid. "restoring a shade . . ." and quotation following: to Tate, November 18, 1950, in Tate Papers, Princeton.

Basler, on Whittall's literary taste: *The Muse . . . ,* p. 30 (later in a memorial lecture, May 3, 1976). Basler's account of the "Lancelot" embroglio has also been useful. Marlene Morrisey's recollections: letter to the writer, January 29, 1985.

Bogan to Zabel, on resigning as a Fellow: December 30, 1951, in *Selected Letters,* ed. Limmer.

Basler, "As a tryout . . .": interview, Fenwick Island, Delaware.

WILLIAMS: Whittemore's biography: *William Carlos Williams: Poet from Jersey* (Boston: Houghton Mifflin, 1975; copyright © 1975 by Reed Whittemore), p. 302.

Williams to Tate, "It will be quite impossible . . .": October 21, 1948; "Taken all together . . .": October 28, 1948; Tate Papers, Princeton. To Lowell, March 11, 1952: *Selected Letters,* ed. J. C. Thirlwall (1957). Whittemore, "Williams arranged . . .": p. 308; "he had what Flossie . . ." pp. 308–9. Fulton Lewis, Jr., column: New York *Journal-American,* November 21, 1952. Cummins attack: Whittemore, p. 309. Basler, "the loyalty processes . . .": *The Muse . . . ,* p. 20. McGrory, including Cleanth Brooks's statement, in *Washington Sunday Star,* September 26, 1954. "Evans agreed to be less . . .": Whittemore, pp. 312–13.

Huntington on communism: to Marie Bullock, December 5, 1950, in the files of the Academy of American Poets.

Washington Post editorial on WCW: October 12, 1954. MacLeish's "confidential" letter of October 21 to Mumford (LC Archives) is on letterhead of the Master's Lodgings, Eliot House, Cambridge. MacLeish, "McCarthy has already . . .": to Paul H. Buck, January 1, 1953, in *Letters*, ed. Winnick. WCW in *New York Post*, October 13, 1954.

MacLeish to Mumford, "benefit of the presence . . .": September 2, 1955, quoted in Basler, *The Muse* . . . , pp. 37–40. On Mrs. Whittall, ibid., p. 30.

Eliot to Tate, on Pound's broadcasts: March 10, 1955, in Tate Papers, Princeton.

Huntington's bequests: *New York Herald-Tribune*, December 12 and 22, 1955; *New York Times*, December 12, 1955. His relations with Auslander in the 1950s: letters in the Huntington Papers, George Arents Research Library, Syracuse University. Auslander and the Academy of American Poets: letters in the Academy's files; and Brookgreen Gardens: information from Robin R. Salmon, Archivist, Brookgreen Gardens.

PART FOUR

JARRELL's life and work: *Randall Jarrell's Letters*, ed. Mary Jarrell (Boston: Houghton Mifflin, 1985); interview with Mary Jarrell, Greensboro, North Carolina.

Warren at Vanderbilt: *Letters*, p. 1. Lowell at Kenyon: p. 10. Berryman on RJ as reviewer: in *Randall Jarrell 1914–1965*, ed. Lowell, Peter Taylor, and R. P. Warren (New York: Farrar, Straus and Giroux, 1967), pp. 15–16. RJ's review of MacLeish: *Letters*, p. 222. Bollingen Prize: p. 220. RJ's visit to Pound: p. 191. "The Other Frost": p. 182. Benfey: "Poet in the Sun Belt" (review of *Letters*), *New York Review of Books*, May 9, 1985, p. 30. RJ on Bishop: *Letters*, p. 420. On the Consultantship, 1952: pp. 337–38. Ruckus at Woman's College:

Greensboro *Record,* March 29, 1956. Rumor that RJ was a Communist: interview with Basler; *Letters,* pp. 408–9. Corso, Rexroth, and Ginsberg: ibid., pp. 417–18. Basler's summary: *The Muse . . . ,* pp. 41–42.

Pound's court hearing and release: C. David Heymann, *Ezra Pound: The Last Rower* (New York: Viking (Seaver), 1976), pp. 238–57. Thompson on MacLeish's and Arnold's role: *Selected Letters of Robert Frost,* ed. Lawrance Thompson (New York: Holt, Rinehart, Winston, 1964), pp. 563, 575–77 (editorial comment). Seiber report, etc.: Basler, *The Muse . . . ,* p. 18. Pound's visit to WCW: Whittemore, p. 346.

Second Bollingen grant for recordings: Bollingen Foundation archives, Manuscript Division.

Jarrell to Jean Stafford: April 1958, in *Letters,* ed. M. Jarrell, p. 430. Nabokov papers: personal communication from VN. Outcome of Princeton poetry series: letter from Robert Brown, Princeton University Press.

Marianne Moore's Bollingen fellowship: Bollingen archives.

FROST: Basler's essay on Frost: originally in *Voyages,* 2:4 (spring 1969), here consulted in *The Muse . . . ,* pp. 58–67. Johns Hopkins Poetry Festival: Bollingen archives. "The poets were not enthralled . . .": *New York Times,* November 16, 1958. Trilling episode: Thompson, comment in *Letters of Frost,* and letter of June 18, 1959, pp. 582–83. Kennedy letter: quoted by Basler, *The Muse . . . ,* p. 65. Frost's remarks on May 21, 1959: recorded stenographically during his talk and quoted in his annual report, assembled by the Poetry Office (LC archives).

EBERHART: 1956 invitation to the Chair: Joel Roache, *Richard Eberhart: The Progress of an American Poet* (New York: Oxford, 1971), p. 212; and interview, Gainesville, Florida (for other details, too). On beatnik poetry: St. Louis *Post-Dispatch,* September 12, 1959. And Lowell and Auden: Roache, pp. 102–6; Hamilton, *Lowell,* pp. 22–24, 59; Carpenter, *Auden,* pp. 254, 264–65. At Cambridge: Roache, pp. 54, 57. Visits of Sholokhov and Soviet poets: ibid., pp. 214–16. Visits of Oriental royalty: ibid., p. 214; RE's recollections sent to Daniel Boorstin, April 1986. Latin American ode: Roache, p. 214. Changing the tire: interview.

Lucille Lortel: list of her productions at the LC 1960–85 from her office, courtesy of Sandra Starr.

Sandburg and Frost: Basler, *The Muse* . . . , pp. 70–72. Frost on May 4 and 5, 1960: ibid., pp. 67–68.

Kennedy inauguration: RE's letter to Eric Bentley, quoted in Roache, pp. 216–17. RE's later recollection is in the letter to Boorstin, April 1986. Tom Wolfe's article: *Washington Post,* May 21, 1961.

Kenny's account of inaugural ceremony: *Boston Sunday Globe,* January 22, 1962, as reprinted in *Interviews with Robert Frost,* ed. Edward Connery Lathem (New York: Holt, Rinehart and Winston, 1966), pp. 251–52. Pritchard's comment: in his *Frost: A Literary Life Reconsidered* (New York: Oxford, 1984), pp. 254–55. Basler, "he no longer . . .": *The Muse* . . . , p. 75. Wolfe on "coffee hour": *Washington Post,* May 2, 1961.

UNTERMEYER: Wolfe on his appointment: *Washington Post Times-Herald,* August 14, 1961. LU, "I was meant to act . . .": his *Bygones: The Recollections* . . . (New York: Harcourt Brace & World, 1965), p. 215. McGrory on LU's talk to WNPC: *Washington Evening Star,* December 15, 1961. *Post'*s reporter: William McPherson, same date.

LU and Senghor: *Bygones,* p. 219. In India: pp. 221–28; Indian journalist's comment: p. 227; debriefing, p. 228. Press conference upon reappointment: David Breasted, in *Washington Post,* April 11, 1962.

National Poetry Festival: in Basler's thoughts: *The Muse* . . . , p. 46. Many details from Bollingen Foundation archives, Manuscript Division (including Mathews's memorandum about Pound and St.-John Perse). Blue leatherette briefcases: *Newsweek,* November 5, 1962. Auslander in Miami: letters to Marie Bullock, in Academy of American Poets files. *National Poetry Festival . . . Proceedings* (Library of Congress, 1964) is the source for numerous quotations and details. Mary Jarrell on the participants: *Letters,* p. 458. Shapiro on Jarrell: memorial lecture, October 17, 1966, in LC brochure, p. 2. Reactions to the Missile Crisis: interview with Basler; Mary Jarrell, in *Letters,* pp. 459–60. Official spokesman at White House: quoted in Betty Beale's column

"Exclusively Yours," *Washington Sunday Star,* November 4, 1962. Basler on Frost: *The Muse* . . . , p. 76. Bogan's observations: to Ruth Limmer, October 26, 1962, in *Selected Letters.* LU summing up: *Bygones,* p. 220.

Frost on the Bollingen Prize: Thompson and Winnick, p. 338. Untermeyer's visit to him in hospital: *Bygones,* p. 221. Last reading, on December 2: Pritchard, p. 260. "Away!," as quoted by Pritchard, from *Robert Frost: Poetry and Prose,* ed. E. C. Lathem and L. Thompson (copyright © 1972 by Holt, Rinehart and Winston).

Lowell on Williams: "William Carlos Williams," *The Hudson Review,* XIV (Winter 1961–62), p. 534.

PART FIVE

NEMEROV: Phil Casey's article: *Washington Post,* April 17, 1962. HN on Hillyer: *Venture* (University of Delaware), May 1962. At Hamilton College: information from Willard Thorp. *Kenyon Review* recommendations: HN to Tate, January 2, 1958, in Tate Papers, Princeton. Work with Dorothy Goldberg and Voice of America: interview, St. Louis. "The Great Society, Mark X": *The Collected Poems* . . . (Chicago: University of Chicago Press, 1977; originally in *The Blue Swallows,* © 1967 by Howard Nemerov), pp. 382–83.

Auslander's Robert Frost award: *Miami Herald,* January 25, 1964; Poetry Society of America, *Bulletin,* February 1964 (courtesy of Matthew H. Fink, assistant director); letters from Stanley Burnshaw, Edward Connery Lathem, and Frances A. Keegan (with information from Alfred C. Edwards and his secretary Cele Daly).

WHITTEMORE: Pound's visit in 1939: RW, "On Editing *Furioso,*" *TriQuarterly* 43 (fall 1978, on the little magazine in America), pp. 102–3, and interview, Washington. "we discovered that nobody . . .": "A Brief History of a Little Magazine," *The Boy from Iowa* (New York: Macmillan, 1962), p. 106. Ellen Key Blunt's article: *Washington Post,* November 9, 1964. On Eliot's death: *New Republic,* January 16, 1965, p. 28. On Johnson's inauguration (and other details): interview. "Washington Interregnum": copyright © 1977 Reed Whittemore and quoted by his permission. *The Little Magazine and Contemporary Literature* (New York: Modern Language Association of America, 1966). Geoffrey Wolff's article: *Washington Post,* April 3, 1965. Basler's comment: *The Muse* . . . , p. 47. "New York crowd," etc.: interview. White House Festival of the Arts: Hamilton, *Lowell,* pp. 320–24.

Basler, on Mrs. Whittall's death: memorial address at LC, May 3, 1976.

Auslander's death: *New York Times* and *Washington Post,* June 24, 1965. Telephone interview and correspondence with Mrs. Arthur Morris, Auslander's daughter. For information about Auslander in Miami: letters and help from Isabel Mathews, Hannah Kahn, Alice Boyd Proudfoot, Adelaide Sanchez and George Beebe (both retired from the *Miami Herald*), Nixon Smiley, and Richard C. Waller; and reports in the *Miami Herald.*

SPENDER: interview, Durham, North Carolina. "Sometimes on these flying visits . . .": *The Thirties and After* . . . (New York: Random House, 1978), p. 179. On Jarrell's death: ibid., p. 177; Mary Jarrell, in *Letters,* pp. 519–20, and interview. Ralph de Toledano's remarks: in *Human Events,* October 9, 1965. Basler on Tolson: *The Muse* . . . , pp. 154, 151. SS on Dickey: *The Thirties* . . . , p. 187 (identification by permission of SS). "Spender/Splendor": personal observation at Duke University.

DICKEY: interview, Columbia, South Carolina. First press conference: *New York Times,* September 10, 1966. On New Zealand visit: *Auckland Herald,* March 11, 1968. Australian visit: *Poetry Australia* 21 (April 1968).

SMITH: interview, New York (including Helen Handley, who had been on the Poetry Office staff during Smith's term); memoir, *Army Brat* (Penguin, 1982; orig., 1980). Bogan's comments: *Selected Letters,* ed. Limmer, May 10 and November 21, 1969. Her "Come, drunks

. . .": "Several Voices Out of a Cloud," *The Blue Estuaries* (New York: Farrar, Straus and Giroux, 1968; copyright © 1968 by Louise Bogan).

STAFFORD: interview, Lake Oswego, Oregon. His early life: "A Statement on Life and Writings," in *Writing the Australian Crawl* (Ann Arbor: University of Michigan Press, 1978); Meryle Secrest's article, *Washington Post,* November 15, 1970; and Kansas newspaper stories. MacNap article: dateline Portland, Oregon, in the *Washington Star,* May 3, 1970. Advice to young poets: *Family Weekly,* December 20, 1970. Roethke Memorial Prize: letter from Patricia Shek, Roethke Memorial Foundation, Saginaw, Michigan. WS on contemporary poets: "Dreams to Have: An Interview . . ." (1972), in *Writing the Australian Crawl,* pp. 85, 88, 99.

PART SIX

JACOBSEN: interviews, Baltimore. Early life: John Dorsey, *Baltimore Sun,* May 30, 1971. First poetry reading: Dorsey, *Baltimore Sun,* October 17, 1971; William Holland, *Washington Star,* October 5, 1971.

Memorial service for Marianne Moore: information from Patricia Willis, curator of Moore papers, Rosenbach Museum, Philadelphia. "Quiet Requiem" for Pound: information from Henri Cole, director, Academy of American Poets. Pound memorial in Washington: *Washington Post,* April 4, 1973. Pound at Moore memorial in Venice: Heymann, p. 313.

Conference on Teaching Creative Writing: *Teaching Creative Writing,* LC brochure, 1974; Momaday's comments: from a column in a Sante Fe newspaper, quoted in JJ's annual report. JJ, "It's a dangerous situation . . .": interview. "When the five prominent poets": in *The Shade-Seller* (Garden City: Doubleday, 1974; copyright © 1974 by Josephine Jacobsen).

HOFFMAN: interview, Philadelphia. Aiken to high school student: To David Crumm, July 30, 1973, in *Letters,* ed. Killorin. Houses associated with Aiken: information from the Georgia Historical Society, Savannah. Snyder's appearance and Ginsberg visit: interview.

Frost centenary celebration: information from Jean Erdman. Copernicus Society of America: interview; information from the Society and the Academy of American Poets. Authors Guild: interview.

KUNITZ: interview, New York. Biographical details also from interview by Stephen Gayle, *New York Post*, May 3, 1974. Tom Wolfe's comment: *Washington Post*, April 22, 1960. Hanley's comment: UPI dispatch, October 13, 1974, in several papers. *From Feathers to Iron*, LC brochure, 1976.

Conference on . . . Poetry and Fiction: Susan Wagner, "Can Poetry and Serious Fiction Survive?" in *Publishers' Weekly*, November 10, 1975, pp. 28–29; Doris Grumbach in *New York Times Book Review*, October 1975; *The Publication of Poetry and Fiction: A Conference*, Library of Congress, 1977; information (also on Michener/Piszek gift) from Daniel Halpern, Ecco Press, and Eric Nelson, Copernicus Society. SK in Africa: interview.

MacLeish celebration: Broderick, memoir in American Philosophical Society, *Yearbook* (1982); information from Samuel Hazo; A. M. Burnham, *The International Poetry Forum of Pittsburgh 1966–1986* (n.d.). Kernan's comment: *Washington Post*, March 30, 1976.

Roethke prize, 1976: Patricia Shek, Roethke Memorial Foundation.

SK, "distractions of the job": interview. "The Lincoln Relics": in *The Poems of Stanley Kunitz 1928–1978* (Boston: Atlantic Monthly Press/ Little, Brown, 1979; copyright © 1979 by Stanley Kunitz).

HAYDEN: interview with Erma Hayden, Ypsilanti; John Hatcher, *From the Auroral Darkness: The Life and Poetry of Robert Hayden* (Oxford, England: George Ronald, 1984); *World Authors 1970–75* (H. W. Wilson Co., 1980). Dakar prize: Hatcher, p. 40. Evalyn Shapiro's visual aid: interview with her.

Dickey's inaugural poem: Donna Landry, *Washington Post*, January 19, 1977. Lowell's death: Hamilton, p. 473.

Article on RH in *Ebony*: January 1978, by Harriet Jackson Scarupa.

MEREDITH: At Princeton: interviews with Willard Thorp. Tate on class poem: to Meredith, June 26, 1940, in Tate Papers, Princeton. *Contemporary Poets*, p. 475. Tom Wolfe's comments: *Washington Post*, October 20, 1959. Meredith to Tate: October 31, 1978, in Tate Papers.

MacLeish celebration: information from Samuel Hazo.

Hayden at White House "Salute": Broderick, "Robert Hayden in Washington," *Obsidian: Black Literature in Review*, spring 1982. RH's death: Hatcher, pp. 48–49.

Meredith, "On Jenkins' Hill": from *The Cheer* (New York: Knopf, 1980), copyright © 1980 by William Meredith, reprinted in *Quarterly Journal of the Library of Congress* 38 (spring 1981), p. 58.

PART SEVEN

KUMIN: interview, Warner, New Hampshire. *World Authors 1970–75* (H. W. Wilson Co., 1980). Council of Scholars: information from James Hutson and J. C. Broderick. Kernan on Adrienne Rich: *Washington Post*, April 8, 1981. "Washington is not alien territory": *New York Times*, May 8, 1982, "Washington Talk."

Conference on Science and Literature: Broderick's comments in *Science and Literature: A Conference* (Library of Congress, 1985), preface.

HECHT: interviews, Washington and Chevy Chase. His interviews with Gardner McFall, *Washington Review*, December 1982–January 1983; Grace Schulman, *American Arts*, May 1983; and Paul Desruisseaux, *Chronicle of Higher Education*, May 9, 1984. Leithauser essay: "Poetry for a Dark Age," *New York Review of Books*, February 13, 1986.

AH on MacLeish: interview. AM on Pound and Bollingen Prize: his *Poetry and Opinion* (Urbana: University of Illinois Press, 1950); "The Venetian Grave," *Saturday Review*, February 9, 1974, reprinted in *Riders on the Earth* (Boston: Houghton Mifflin, 1978). Letters from Shapiro and Warren, conversation with Thorp. Torrey, *The Roots of Treason*

(1984). Broderick, memoir in American Philosophical Society, *Yearbook*, 1982.

AH, *Robert Lowell*, LC brochure, 1983; *Jiggery-Pokery: A Compendium of Double Dactyls* (New York: Atheneum, 1984; 2nd ed.).

Whittemore, *William Carlos Williams: The Happy Genius of the Household*, LC brochure, 1984.

George Orwell and Nineteen Eighty-Four: The Man and the Book, LC brochure, 1985.

AH, "only disappointment during his term": Desruisseaux interview.

Academy of American Poets programs: Academy publications. Chip Brown on the readings: *Washington Post*, November 16, 1983.

AH, *The Pathetic Fallacy*, LC brochure, 1985.

FITZGERALD: memoir by Penelope Laurans Fitzgerald, read at requiem mass, January 19, 1985. On Pound: Heymann, *Ezra Pound* . . . , pp. 55, 85, 250, and letters in the Tate Papers, Princeton (RF sent copies to AT). *Enlarging the Change* (Boston: Northeastern University Press, 1985). Hollander's comment: *Poetry Pilot* (Academy of American Poets), March 1985.

WHITTEMORE: interview, Washington. *Poets and Anthologists*, LC brochure, 1986.

Fitzgerald: requiem mass, program; letter from Penelope Fitzgerald and her comments on the occasion.

MacLeish to President Nixon: *Letters*, ed. Winnick, June 26, 1969.

BROOKS: interview, Washington. Meeting with Frost, 1962: interview. At Howard University, and her literary influences: Jacqueline Trescott, in the *Washington Evening Star*, April 17, 1973. "a lady Paul Laurence Dunbar": Dorothy Gilliam in the *Washington Post*, November 13, 1976. Boorstin's comment: Diana West in the *Washington Times*, September 3, 1985.

WARREN (Poet Laureate): information from Senator Matsunaga and his office. Text of the amendments to the law regarding the Laureateship: from a Congressional document. "Sing for white men . . .": *New*

York Times, February 27, 1986, quoting *Economist* of recent date. "To America's First Poet Laureate": ibid., February 28, 1986.

✷

Acknowledgment is gratefully made for permission to quote from writings by or pertaining to the following writers:

Aiken: *Selected Letters of Conrad Aiken,* ed. Joseph Killorin (copyright © 1978 by Mary Hoover Aiken and Joseph I. Killorin), by permission of Yale University Press. Letters in the Allen Tate Papers, by permission of Princeton University Library, Mrs. Conrad Aiken, and Joseph Killorin.

Auslander: Letters in the Archer Milton Huntington Collection, George Arents Research Library for Special Collections at Syracuse University, by permission of Mrs. Arthur Morris.

Basler: Roy P. Basler, *The Muse and the Librarian* (Contributions in American Studies, No. 10, Greenwood Press; copyright © 1974 by Roy P. Basler), by permission of Roy P. Basler.

Bishop: The poem "Visits to St. Elizabeths" from *The Complete Poems 1927–1979* (copyright © 1957 by Elizabeth Bishop; copyright © 1983 by Alice Helen Methfessel), reprinted by permission of Farrar, Straus and Giroux, Inc.

Bogan: The poem "Several Voices Out of a Cloud" from *The Blue Estuaries* (copyright © 1968 by Louise Bogan) reprinted by permission of Farrar, Straus and Giroux, Inc. *What the Woman Lived; Selected Letters of Louise Bogan, 1920–1970,* ed. Ruth Limmer (Harcourt Brace Jovanovich, Inc.; copyright © 1973 by Ruth Limmer, Trustee, Estate of Louise Bogan), by permission of Ruth Limmer. Letters in the Allen Tate Papers, by permission of Ruth Limmer and Princeton University Library.

Eberhart: Joel Roache, *Richard Eberhart: The Progress of an American Poet* (copyright © 1971 by Joel Roache), by permission of Oxford University Press, New York.

Eliot: T. S. Eliot's letters in the Allen Tate Papers, by permission of the copyright owner, Valerie Eliot, and Princeton University Library.

Fitzgerald: A letter of Robert Fitzgerald, 1928, quoted in the pro-

Index

INDEX

INDEX

INDEX

INDEX

INDEX